National Security Decisions

The Participants Speak

Edited by

Robert L. Pfaltzgraff, Jr.
The Fletcher School of Law and Diplomacy,
Tufts University

Jacquelyn K. Davis
Institute for Foreign Policy Analysis, Inc.,
Cambridge, Massachusetts

Lexington Books
D.C. Heath and Company/Lexington, Massachusetts/Toronto

Library of Congress Cataloging-in-Publication Data

National security decisions : the participants speak / edited by
  Robert L. Pfaltzgraff, Jr., Jacquelyn K. Davis.
    p.   cm.
  ISBN 0-669-24488-0 (alk. paper).—ISBN 0-669-24494-5 (pbk. :
alk. paper)
    1. United States—National security—Decision making. 2. United
States—Foreign relations—1945-   . I. Pfaltzgraff, Robert L.
II. Davis, Jacquelyn K.
UA23.N2485   1990
353.0089—dc20   90-32416
                              CIP

Published simultaneously in Canada
Printed in the United States of America
Casebound International Standard Book Number: 0-669-24488-0
Paperbound International Standard Book Number: 0-669-24494-5
Library of Congress Catalog Card Number: 90-32416

The paper used in this publication meets the minimum requirements of
American National Standard for Information Sciences—Permanence of
Paper for Printed Library Materials, ANSI Z39.48-1984. ∞™

The first and last numbers below indicate year and number of printing.

90 91 92 10 9 8 7 6 5 4 3 2 1

Contents

Preface

This volume is an outgrowth of the Oral History Project that was developed over a six-year period by the International Security Studies Program of the Fletcher School of Law and Diplomacy, Tufts University. Oral history interviews were conducted by the editors of this book and by Professors Igor Lukes, Uri Ra'anan, and Richard H. Shultz, Jr., with the assistance of a team of outstanding graduate students, ably directed by Dr. Steven Adragna. A large number of interviews were conducted with émigrés from the Soviet Union and other Communist countries and with former members of the Western policy community, drawn from the United States and Western Europe. The extensive documentary materials that resulted from the Oral History Project are now on deposit at the Fletcher School, which has copyright to the transcripts, and are now available to the scholarly community.

The Oral History Project was made possible by two three-year grants from the J. Howard Pew Foundation Trust to the International Security Studies Program. It was possible to set forth in this book only a small portion of the material accumulated in the course of the project. Therefore the editors faced difficult choices in selecting those sections of interviews to be included. This volume is confined to those interviews that had U.S. or NATO-European issues as their focal point. A companion volume that draws upon the Soviet and East European interviews by Uri Ra'anan and Igor Lukes is another result of this project.

This work is the product of the labor of many persons. Special thanks are given to several graduate students at the Fletcher School who assisted in the preparation of this book: Randall Bentley, Ted Gistaro, and Hilary Scott. David Lutkins of the Institute for Foreign Policy Analysis assisted in the laborious tasks associated with the final compilation of materials for publication. Several drafts of the manuscript as it neared completion were typed by Marjorie Duggan of the Institute. Earlier versions of materials for this work had the secretarial assistance of Roberta Breen and Freda Kilgallen.

Introduction

Many direct participants in the great events of statecraft publish memoirs or keep diaries that form part of the record available to the historian, political scientist, or other observer having an interest in the process and substance of foreign policy. Such accounts, necessarily drawn from the particular experience and vantage point of one who was present in a role of greater or lesser importance, are of immense value to a contemporary generation and to those that follow. In their own right or as part of a broader stream of evidence, the recorded perspectives of those who were present at such times afford insights that cannot be gleaned from documents or data about the phenomena under investigation. Yet a large number of those who have played roles of major importance in the development of foreign policy do not publish systematic accounts in the form of memoirs or diaries—or if they do, space limitations preclude the recording in fullest detail of the events or process in which they took part.

Oral history furnishes a means of narrowing, if not eliminating, such gaps. Most former policymakers appear to be prepared to record their recollections as part of an oral history exercise and, as a result, to contribute to an archive that can become available for scholarly use. Ideally, such accounts, used by those engaged in research on a specific episode of, say, U.S. foreign policy in the two generations after World War II, can yield information, and nuances, that will corroborate or modify findings from other sources. Alternatively, oral history can be published on its own, as in the case of this book, for the perspectives it provides on the variety of phenomena that fell under the purview of those interviewed. For example, the scholar studying, say, the decision of General Charles de Gaulle to remove France from NATO's (North Atlantic Treaty Organization) integrated command structure, or the person seeking to gain insights into the national security decision-making process of various American presidents from Eisenhower to Reagan—all addressed in this book— can read oral history in conjunction with other works or as an exercise in itself. Although the memories of oral history interviewees, like those of others, are fallible, they nevertheless provide unique perspectives and information.

Such is the utility of this work, drawn as it is from the extensive archives generated by the Fletcher School of Law and Diplomacy, Tufts University, Oral History Project. This book is published in order to make available reflections from the large number of persons interviewed as part of the project. Taken together, their professional careers in the policy communities of the United States and several West European countries encompassed nearly all of the major events of the two generations that followed World War II. Far more extensive materials are contained in the full interviews themselves. Hence the purpose of this book is to furnish excerpts organized around such principal themes as the national security decision-making process, issues of defense and foreign policy, transatlantic relations and the Atlantic Alliance, and crisis management. By the very nature of the persons interviewed—participants in the policy process—the materials presented contain individual opinions that are often freely and fully expressed. Hence oral history in general, and in particular the excerpts contained in a work such as this, must be read with this inevitable circumstance and condition in mind. This should be seen as a strength of oral history so long as it is recognized as a likely characteristic.

To understand the assumptions—correct or faulty—as well as the expectations—attainable or excessively ambitious—which guided the thought patterns of those who play a part in momentous events is to gain access to vitally important data. Oral history then is a statement of perspective and opinion: the perspectives of one participant should be weighed and checked to the extent possible against those of others who took part, and the opinion of one participant about his or her role should also be measured to the greatest degree possible in relation to that of others who can shed light on the subject matter of interest. Although this book provides sometimes diverse and divergent perspectives on a particular topic, its objective is not to survey in any exhaustive fashion the views of all or even a large number of those who took part. Of necessity, therefore, its treatment of any of the issues addressed is incomplete. The accounts contained in the pages that follow can best be read for the insights provided by the various interviewees into the events in which they participated. They should also be considered within the context of the times in which the events took place. In a rapidly unfolding international environment, the conditions surrounding and giving rise to many of the events described in the following pages have undergone major transformation. Nevertheless, insights provided by participants are of enduring value, just as the history of the period that has led to the momentous events of 1989 and beyond will be of continuing importance. The entire oral history interview can be consulted by those seeking to delve more extensively into these and other policy episodes of which those interviewed were a part.

Last but not least, we have been content, given the nature of this book as a direct output of the Oral History Project, to provide excerpts that, in some cases, are extensive in order to let the participants speak for themselves. We have endeavored to keep the interpretive materials provided by the editors to a minimum—to whatever was deemed necessary for purposes of offering background or for enhancing the organizational unity within and among each of the chapters. A concluding chapter has been prepared by the editors as a synthesizing device designed both to summarize much of what is contained in the book and to highlight for the reader excerpts drawn from the oral history interviews themselves.

Part I
Framework for National Security Decision Making of the United States

National security decisions for any given country are made within the context of an organizational structure and process. But which element—the decision makers, the structure, or the process—exerts the greatest influence upon decision making? This question and others are addressed in part I as the framework for national security decision making of the United States and are described by notable participants from the past four decades. Chapter 1 examines the National Security Council (NSC), created in 1947 better to coordinate advice to the president; it focuses particularly on how individual U.S. presidents used the organization to aid their decision making. Since the NSC itself was created to facilitate intragovernmental coordination, especially between the Department of Defense and the State Department, the role and impact of these two executive branch departments are addressed in chapters 2 and 3, respectively. The problems inherent in sharply distinguishing military policy from foreign policy are evidenced in participants' comments in these chapters, as well as in the general trend of increasing influence for the Department of Defense and relatively declining influence for the State Department in U.S. national security decision making. In chapter 4, the context of U.S. national security decision making is broadened from one country to the current sixteen nations of the North Atlantic Treaty Organization, created in 1949. Yet the dominant position of the United States within this alliance as the most formidable military member is substantially offset by the political and consensual organization of NATO. The resultant hybrid decision making, at times determined solely by the United States while at other times determined by multilateral processes, is addressed here. Finally, chapter 5 includes observations about the United Nations and its relationship to issues of U.S. national security policy.

1

The National Security Council

Although it is necessary to set forth the formal structure within which national security decisions are made, such an exercise in itself is inadequate to an understanding of how specific decisions are taken. Each president, together with the personnel who act on his behalf, possesses his own style of operations. Indeed, the institutions that exist for decision making may be more or less effectively or extensively used by successive administrations. This chapter contains insights drawn from interviews with persons who occupied positions enabling them to participate directly in, and to observe, the national decision-making process. According to Adm. Thomas Moorer,

> The way decisions are made depends on whose ego is being bruised, what ambitions they have, and so on; generally speaking, the idea that you can draw a wiring diagram and put all these people in a little box is a fallacy.

Former secretary of state Dean Rusk observed,

> When people take high office in our government, they do not come in with a clean slate. They have a firm mind-set.

Each president uses the National Security Council in a way that fits his decision-making style. The Eisenhower administration was the first to attempt to develop a National Security Council staff structure within the White House. The approach taken by President Eisenhower to national security decision making is described by Gen. Andrew Goodpaster, who was defense liaison officer and staff secretary to the president:

> Eisenhower himself attended all the NSC meetings, or essentially all. He had the papers in advance, and he would enter into the discussion. He did not necessarily take the leading role in the discussion but would intervene whenever there was something he wanted to bring out. The president felt that that was vitally important—that he should not just be briefed, but should participate in the substantive deliberation prior to making his

decisions. He wanted to go through this process, and crystalize the issues, the way he did in his "summation," in order to lay down a clear line of policy for everybody at the same time that would guide his administration in the same terms.

Adm. Thomas Moorer had an excellent vantage point from which to observe President Johnson's use of the NSC structure in his capacity as chief of naval operations from 1967 to 1970:

> Mr. Johnson used a "Tuesday lunch." Sometimes he would invite the JCS [Joint Chiefs of Staff] chairman, sometimes he wouldn't. So, when you put into the law that the chairman of JCS would be a member of the NSC it is ineffective because if the president doesn't want him there he won't have NSC meetings, he'll have a "Tuesday lunch" and only invite those he chooses. You can't force the president to operate his staff, except his own way. So, they're all whistling Dixie. To find out about pending decisions we had to wait for the "Tuesday lunch." [President Johnson] took the decision and then they had the NSC meeting—because he had already had his meeting.

General Goodpaster, who became deputy commander of U.S. Forces-Vietnam in 1968, made the following observation on President Nixon's NSC:

> When Mr. Nixon became president, I came back from Vietnam at his request to work for about four or five weeks with Henry Kissinger in designing the security affairs structure that he would use. It was very similar to that which existed in the Eisenhower time, except that he added a refinement—which I think was a good one—that the Planning Board process would aim to postulate options or alternatives rather than coming down on a single recommendation where there was full agreement, or just a statement on a set of differing views where there was not full agreement. I think Mr. Nixon found the development of options valuable. I believe that went back to his own experience, and to his desire to have the issues opened up a little more fully in that way.

Lawrence Eagleburger was Henry Kissinger's special assistant in the early years under President Nixon. He further described how Kissinger went about setting up Nixon's NSC:

> Henry Kissinger had in the back of his mind, clearly at that stage, the informal advice that we had received from a group of people he knew in the early stages of setting up the NSC system. It was very clear that Richard Nixon wanted foreign policy run from the White House. He wanted to have direct personal involvement in it, and, frankly, he did not have a great deal of confidence in Secretary of State Rogers's ability to

manage foreign policy issues anyway. Indeed, I think he put Rogers there because he wanted foreign policy to be run somewhere else. It clearly also suited Kissinger's temperament and essentially his views on the management of foreign relations. His view then—and to a degree still, but less so, I think—was clearly that the State Department had too many constituencies, was too infected by clientitis, was too diffuse, and, with the exception of some people, by and large not capable of strategic thinking about major foreign policy questions. It was clearly his view that once policies were established and articulated, it was extremely difficult to count on the Department of State (or the other agencies within the government that had anything to do with foreign affairs, Defense and so forth) to carry those policies out with precision and clarity. Even with fundamental acceptance of many of the objectives, you had to have the policy formulation process located in close proximity to the president and under the direct control of the national security adviser. You also had to have a reasonably competent body of people to make sure that instructions were, in fact, carried out once they were issued. The philosophical basis of all of this is a belief that the major policy issues—particularly if you are entering a period of time when you want to make some very fundamental changes in direction from what foreign policy has been—have to be addressed in an organizational structure near the president, and have to be highly centralized, both in terms of the formulation of the policy and in terms of the implementation of policy.

In 1970 Admiral Moorer became a statutory member of the NSC when President Nixon appointed him chairman of the JCS:

When I was told I was going to be chairman, I informed Mr. Nixon that I wanted to attend the NSC meetings and to be a member of subcommittees that were making military decisions if I was going to be expected to go to Congress and defend them. I didn't like the idea of defending operations when I wasn't part of the plan. He said, "fine," so, the whole time I was there I always attended NSC meetings.

When Nixon came in, since he had already been vice president under Eisenhower, he took his cues from Eisenhower and made continuous use of the NSC and the supporting agencies like the WASAG [Washington Special Action Group], the under secretaries' group, and always the CIA [Central Intelligence Agency] and JCS. I went to all these meetings. The name of the committee was indicated by the subject. In other words, the under secretaries' job was to make sure decisions were being carried out, and the WASAG's idea was to come up with options and proposals to help the president handle crises. And then, generally speaking, that went into the NSC, and then the president finally made his decision. He would not always make a decision immediately, but often he would get up and leave. Later that day there would be a PDM [Presidential Decision Memorandum], and it would say this: "The president has decided that . . . " That was that. Nixon had the NSC meeting and then he took the decision.

Retired Air Force Lt. Gen. Brent Scowcroft served as military assistant to the president (1972–73), deputy assistant to the president for national security affairs (1973–75), national security adviser from 1975 to 1977, and again in the Bush administration. He notes how the NSC operated in the last days of the Nixon administration and during the Ford administration:

Actually [Watergate] affected it very little. The whole NSC system of foreign and national security policy was fairly well insulated from the political impact of the Watergate crisis. Vice President Ford was briefed on a regular, usually a once-weekly, basis either by Henry Kissinger or myself, and we would generally, each week, run over with him the major foreign policy issues that were current and what had happened to them over the week. As a result, he was really quite familiar and quite comfortable with the ongoing operations when he took over as president. It was not a traumatic shift for him to move in.

I think the best way to describe the structure of the NSC system in the Ford administration is to say that it was a fairly direct continuation of that of the Nixon administration. Indeed there were few organizational changes, and at the outset of the Ford administration, of course, Henry Kissinger was still wearing two hats, secretary of state and national security adviser. The structural changes really followed the intelligence investigations of 1975. In 1976, there were some modest organizational changes but not significant ones. Basically, the interagency structure of the NSC system was broken down into a number of subcabinet committees. By and large they had the same membership, but they had different titles, depending on the subject to be taken up. Each of these committees was supported by experts from various groups, like the Special Review Group, which dealt with diplomatic/foreign policy issues; the Washington Special Actions Group, which dealt with crisis management; the Forty Committee, which dealt with intelligence and covert actions; the Intelligence Committee, which dealt with intelligence procedural matters. That was basically the structure.

According to General Scowcroft, however, there were important differences in approach to national security decision making between the Nixon and Ford administrations:

The operation varied slightly from that of the former administration to accommodate the personality of the new president. In the latter days of the Nixon administration the activity of the NSC changed somewhat from the earlier years, when it was very active in terms of the number of NSC meetings. Once the basic policy decisions had been made for different geographical and functional areas, the incidence of meetings declined. President Nixon didn't like meetings in the first place. He would much prefer to take the documentation up to his study in the residence, review it, then ask any questions he might have. He made his decisions based on written input more than discussions from a meeting. In his administration, the number of meetings actually declined quite sharply. President Ford was quite the opposite. He was a fairly voracious reader, but he liked to come to his decisions as a result of the give and take of debate among his principal advisers, so we returned to a much more active NSC meeting schedule. It was the way he liked to make his decisions, and I guess inevitably, as a result, the quality of the papers declined somewhat. There was not a regularly scheduled NSC meeting on the agenda. Meetings were scheduled according to the occurrence of issues which needed resolution at that level; it is not possible to say how often it met.

Donald Rumsfeld served as President Ford's chief of staff and later as the secretary of defense. He suggested that Kissinger's dominant role as national security adviser, while leading to dramatic results, perverted the purpose of the system:

In his Department of State he reported through the National Security Council, so he reported to himself [as long as he also held the title of national security adviser]. If you think of the participants in the national security process—State, Defense, CIA, ACDA [Arms Control and Disarmament Agency,] and so forth—the others reported to the NSC just like State, but they ended up reporting in to one of the principals who, in his other hat, was one of the principal actors. So you had an unevenness in the system. You had a conscious decision by President Nixon, in the first place, and then President Ford, to continue it. And if that is how they wanted it, that is how they had it; they knew what that was and they lived with it—but that is a lot of control.

David Newsom served as under secretary of state for political affairs from 1978 to 1980. He observed the strains that developed within the Carter administration between the Department of State and the national security adviser:

Structurally you had the two interdepartmental groups. One was called the Policy Review Committee [PRC], which was chaired by the secretary of state, and one was called the Special Coordinating Committee [SCC], which was supposed to be a crisis management committee that was headed by the NSC adviser. I came into the administration from the Philippines in April of 1978, a little more than a year after the administration had come into office. By that time my impression is that Zbigniew Brzezinski [President Carter's national security adviser] had been able to gain greater control of the policy machinery by emphasizing the crisis aspect of events and therefore putting them into the SCC rather than into the PRC. He who seizes control of crises seizes control of policy.

Jimmy Carter never wanted to make a clear decision on any given issue or permanently favor the NSC adviser over the secretary of state. My impression is that every administration, whether Republican or Democratic, is basically a coalition of tendencies, and presidents put their team together with representation from a spectrum of opinion and ideology in which center segments of the two parties to some degree overlap.

Ronald Reagan came to the White House committed to a decentralization of the foreign policy process within the relevant cabinet departments and related agencies. His first national security adviser, Richard Allen, encouraged the NSC as a coordinating mechanism, drawing not only on its own core staff, but also on advice, insights, and ideas from outside experts:

It had been my intention to create a larger body of people with access to the National Security Council and with NSC staff access to them. What I had considered doing was to set up a group of fifty to sixty people, all of them cleared, some of them former military men, others former diplomats, and academicians, who would not or could not come into the government, give them the clearances that they needed to do their job, and give them office space. The purpose of giving people access but not having them inside the compound was because there was not any space, and their presence would be threatening to the younger staff members that you have on the NSC.

It seems to me that every NSC staff comes in and they have to reinvent the wheel. They have to set their own system going. You have a bunch of Middle East, African, Asian, European, arms control, and intelligence specialists. All of the sum of postwar history is available to them through people who are still living. It struck me that this enormous amount of gray-haired wisdom—diplomats, military officers—that was available went unused. To have a network of people that were compatible with people who had the same outlook as the president and who were knowledgeable by virtue of study, experience, and contacts throughout the world would have been an invaluable asset.

So I was going to call these people counselors to the NSC, and set it up along these lines. They would be paid, but only a pittance. They would not be encouraged to spend much time because they too have egos and if we did not hold their hands they would become reluctant and say, "Well, you did not take my advice, and all you have got over there is a bunch of young driveling fellows who do not know what is going on." Therefore, the management of that would have been a difficult intellectual task, but it was my idea to try to figure out how we could continue the advisory system drawn from a broad policy community that we used in order to win the presidency, at least in the issues side of the presidency in foreign policy.

Martin Anderson [member of President Reagan's Foreign Intelligence Board, 1982–85, and Economic Policy Advisory Board, 1982–85] did the same in domestic policy. I could never get time to focus on it, although I had the intention of doing it in the second year. It was too late at that point. This would have also been a very good idea because therein would have resided an instantaneous crisis management group—people who served fifteen, twenty, thirty-five years ago, could be flown in at a moment's notice. Why should we let some thirty-five-year-old with a Ph.D. decide that he knows what is going to go down in the Gulf of X, because he cannot possibly know. He should have other people to whom he can turn.

Mr. Allen reflected on the qualities that, in his view, are important for the success of a national security adviser:

What kind of person ought to be selected to be national security adviser? Should he be a brilliant strategist, a thinker or academician, or should he be someone who has a practical bent? I think it does not matter too much, but the question of his receptivity to the ideas of others does. Not in the case of Henry Kissinger, who simply adopted everyone else's product as his own and created a legend in his own time. He used it to build himself up in the end. However deservedly brilliant Henry Kissinger is, this device of constant exposure to the media was well known. Then, of course, he managed to keep the rest of his staff, other than me, in total isolation, including even from buying a hamburger from the White House mess, although he told them he was always for them. It seems to me that Henry Kissinger's ability to take ideas from others and to restate and reformulate them and put them into a policy context is something that is highly desirable. Yet a person who sits in that seat has to do it with only the interests of the president at heart. Maybe the best way to do it would be to take away the social invitations from such a person so he would not become enamored of his own importance.

In the past we have had such people who have adopted the low profile. In the case of Brent Scowcroft, of course, that was enforced by Henry Kissinger, and it also matched Brent's low-key character. Bill Clark was a low-key person. Of course, John Poindexter was, but I believe that was of necessity. Colin Powell fits this category. Certainly McFarlane was not because McFarlane somehow got the idea that he was being shortchanged as the history of national security advisers was being written, and he thought of himself as an innovative theorist. You do not have to have a grand design for the world. You just have to understand how the world works, how the United States can best defend it, and how you advance U.S. interests.

David Newsom argued that the NSC has changed substantially over the last thirty years in its structure and in the role it plays in the national security decision-making process:

My own view, which is different from a number of my State Department colleagues, is that the role of the NSC in the conduct and the making of policy was inevitable, certainly after the late 1950s, when the U.S. responsibilities around the world began to embrace not just diplomatic tasks but strategic military and economic considerations as well. Thus, it was also inevitable that a point would be reached in which a secretary of state, unless given a very special mandate—of the kind that presidents are reluctant to give—would no longer be able to summon the secretaries of defense and treasury, or the head of CIA to his office, because they would say, "We are working for the president, not for you."

According to Ambassador Newsom, the change in the role of the national security adviser from coordinator to policy figure in his own right had important implications for the decision-making structure and process:

That worked when the individual in that spot saw himself as a coordinator to draw these various bureaucratic elements together to synthesize the differences in recommendations and present a fair and clear pattern of alternatives to the president. Difficulties arose when the NSC adviser began also to become a diplomatic and a public figure. To some extent that was inevitable also as it became clear both to the diplomatic corps and to the press that decisions were being made in the West Wing [of the White House] and not the State Department. Of course some NSC advisers were not averse to stimulating that concept. As a result you had a shift of power and inevitably a competitive atmosphere between two elements of the bureaucracy. That atmosphere has a tendency to filter down to where various people at the staff level personally felt the need to follow and defend the boss. They were also conscious of the fact that, if they move away from the boss's position, it would not be long before that deviation was reported back.

Robert McFarlane, drawing on his years of experience in the Reagan administration's National Security Council (ultimately as national security adviser himself), addressed the evolution of the NSC by describing dual functions in U.S. foreign policy making:

I think you must parse the conduct of foreign policy into planning and operations, and recognize that management of the planning function must then repose at the White House level because of the interdepartmental nature of that process. Now management of the planning process doesn't involve any visibility or public role necessarily at all; it is management. It is making the trains run on time. It is doing essentially three things. It is tasking the community in writing in the name of the president, saying the president wants you, secretary of state, defense, treasury, Congress, JCS, CIA, everybody else, to sit down around a table for the next six weeks and examine U.S. policy toward Libya. Second, the following questions must be examined, and third, answers and options of various costs politically and financially proposed. Then report by X [time] so that you get people together, bring out the knowledge available, come back with a paper and that somebody who simply may not go along with consensus can't paralyze it—that the system knows the issue and they see the president is going to decide it. If you don't want to be party to it, okay, but you can't paralyze the system by that.

The only way you can is because people are [given this task]—the secretary of state and defense and everybody on the mailing list of this thing—and know that the person in charge, the national security adviser, is right next door to the president [and has authority from the president], and that they cannot simply obstruct by not playing. Now that isn't to say that the national security adviser should do anything else or that he is disproportionately influential or the dominant figure in the administration. Indeed, the secretary of state must be, I think, [and must be seen to be] the dominant foreign policy figure in the administration. Ultimately, that is true because of the nature of the implementation of policy: it is by State Department employees, and unless they are party to and acknowledged to be the stewards of the policy, it will not be faithfully carried out. It is a matter of self interest—if the president identifies the secretary of state and his department as the stewards of foreign policy. Publicly—talk shows, newspapers, congressional hearings—every dimension of foreign policy from diplomacy to press ought to repose with the Department of State, but planning should be managed at the White House. Operations should be carried out at the State Department.

Another element involved is oversight—just watching that the president's policy is faithfully carried out. After the [NSC] planning, the tasking is done and the analysis comes back and the decision is made, the decision is written down and published for the community [in writing] that the president has decided U.S. policy toward Libya will consist of the following nineteen elements. The NSC sends out [this decision] and then watches the cable traffic, and—just by listening to what is going on in the community—can tell whether State is saying, "Yes, that is the policy and the embassies are doing it." If they don't, the president could then send out another message that says, "You, State, aren't doing this right, and please retract the last cable you sent out, and [do] whatever it takes to get it back on the rails." I don't think there really is much disagreement on that among people who have tried it both ways. It is arguable that it is more an academic exercise than a reality. If you ask Brzezinski, Kissinger, Scowcroft, myself, I don't know anybody who doesn't believe that the NSC system ought to be an invisible manager and that the State Department should be the visible, protagonist [and] advocate.

Mr. Eagleburger also offered several caveats and expressed some reservations about placing the NSC at the core of policy formation and decision-making processes:

My very deep conviction is that there is no natural place for the policy formation process. It really does depend on judgment on the part of the president of what he wants. If the president wants it there, that is where it is going to be. Now, having said that, if I were writing a public administration textbook and were trying to describe an ideal and could create my own precedent, I would say no, that is not where it belongs, and I think that is what Henry Kissinger would now say. I feel very strongly that in the absence of a president who is himself particularly adept at foreign policy and a national security adviser who is equally adept (forget for the moment whether you agree with the policies they design or not) it cannot possibly work. Even if you have those two conditions met, it seems to me that over time it tends to corrupt the process because there is no small institution, no matter how capable the people are, which can manage the range of activities involved.

Under any circumstances, in my judgment, the minimum the president has a right to demand of an NSC staff and the NSC adviser (and that is where I would put my ideal if I could create one) is a staff that assures the president gets a comprehensive picture of alternatives, of options, in as sterile a way as possible. I do not myself believe the NSC adviser can be an eunuch and not have views on the subject. And indeed those views ought to be articulated. But in the process of laying out alternatives for the president, he has to pull himself away from that process as far as he can until it comes to his making a recommendation to the president. But the president needs to know what his secretary of state has recommended, what his secretary of defense believes, and indeed what his national security adviser believes, but with the alternatives laid out and the potential consequences explored.

Mr. Rumsfeld discussed the important role that the National Security Council must play in the foreign policy formation process:

> Given the nature of our world, there are very few issues that are single department or single agency issues. For example, the matter of selling grain to Poland is simultaneously a matter of interest for the Departments of Agriculture, Treasury, State, and Labor, and for congressional relations, the general counsel, and probably several other departments and agencies. So it is not possible to turn government over to the cabinet and expect it to work. Coordination is needed. That is a responsibility of the White House. It falls essentially on the NSC to serve as the coordinator for the principal participants in the national security and foreign policy decision-making process, namely, State, Defense, CIA, ACDA, the Chiefs. But it also involves the analysis of foreign or defense policy with considerations relating to economic policy and even domestic policy.

Finally, Mr. Eagleburger suggested that the national security adviser, as part of the important function of making available all major policy options to the president, should perform the role of devil's advocate. Such a contribution, he holds, is necessary if only to strengthen the president in presenting and defending, ex post facto, the choice that he has made from the available options.

But there is the devil's advocacy function, even with regard to proposals made by a national security adviser. That is what the president seldom gets, particularly if he is not knowledgeable in foreign affairs. It is what is most needed, and I do not think you have to go very far in history to establish an example of what happens when the naysayer is not given his chance; Iran-contra is a clear example—it would not have happened with a more competent NSC staff. I accept that fact. It is not likely to have happened because a competent, reasonably intelligent national security adviser would have been able to describe fairly quickly what the offside was and not push it with the president. But my point is nevertheless that in the formulation of policy it is essential that the president get a broad picture of the various land mines that may be around.

There is one element in this that is particularly important which is, no matter how good you are, the hermetically sealed environment of the White House can, over time, not only corrupt judgment [but also] can mean that you are not getting the sorts of inputs that a broader-based institution will get. One of the prices you pay for a more broadly based decision-making apparatus is that it does not move as fast, and it often tends to obfuscate issues. It is there, I think, that the national security adviser is absolutely critical. He has got to be able to identify those issues and make sure they are not obfuscated. He has got to go back if necessary five times to his secretary of state and say, "You know, this is not yet ready for the president, because you have not answered the following ten questions." Again, devil's advocacy is not the only element that the NSC should play, but it is absolutely critical and essential.

2
The Department of Defense

T he Office of the Secretary of Defense, created by the National Security Act of 1947, vests control of the U.S. defense establishment in civilian hands. The president of the United States and the secretary of defense compose the National Command Authority. This chapter contains reflections on the role of the secretary of defense, the role of intelligence in defense policy formulation, and the role and organization of the Joint Chiefs of Staff. Robert McNamara was secretary of defense for seven years; his performance was analyzed by Adm. Thomas Moorer, who was chief of naval operations at the time:

I think McNamara did far more damage than any secretary we ever had, and I would even include [Louis A.] Johnson, who was secretary in Truman's administration. McNamara was packed full of intellectual arrogance. He came in having been originally concerned with cost-effectiveness and therefore, he pulled everything up into his own office and brought in several new people. These new people wanted to decide how to do this and do that. We had what we called issue papers—these things would come in like snowflakes. McNamara prided himself on making all the decisions. The way he made decisions was that the staff put everything in ABC order—these are the issues and these are the decisions; which one do you want? McNamara would check these things with a pencil and that was his decision. That was the way he made decisions. The problem was there was an option that never got on the paper, which was the right way of doing it. And he was into detail. I just thought he did a tremendous amount of damage. He saw to it that no decisions were made in the field, and he did more than anyone to build a mind-set into military people not to exercise initiative. What he did was go to all the services and pull their technical people into the office of the secretary of defense, which just ballooned. He was the same way about operations.

Admiral Moorer gave the following example regarding McNamara:

He would tell us how many bombs to put on each plane, what camera to use, all in the greatest detail. For example, [in Vietnam] they started out with a political tit-for-tat. When we had a hotel blown up in Pleiku that killed seven Americans, the idea was to bomb the North Vietnamese barracks. When we had Tonkin Gulf, we were ordered to bomb their oil supply. It had to be related to what they had done. Now, the best way to attack targets was with napalm. I made up the targets. Initially, McNamara never would accept napalm. Finally, I got a message stating that I was authorized to use napalm. So the next day they gave me the target—the Ho Chi Minh Bridge—which was made of iron and steel. So I sent in the target list without napalm. I soon got a telephone call from MacDonald [William MacDonald, special assistant in the office of the secretary of defense, 1962–68], who suggested I use napalm or have the authority withdrawn. So I sent out two airplanes with napalm; it only blackened up the bridge a bit. They were so into detail; McNamara and McNaughton [John McNaughton, assistant secretary of defense, international security affairs, 1964–68] would go to Vietnam and write up the trip report before they even got there. Robert McNamara was strange, really strange.

From his own experience in the Ford administration, Donald Rumsfeld set forth perspectives:

As secretary of defense, I felt then (and today) that the principal responsibility of the president and the secretary of defense is to assure that there is an appropriate national consensus on defense investment. None of our other goals as a society are possible without peace and freedom. Peace and freedom are purchased by defense investment, among other things. The president presides over the decisions made by his predecessors, in terms of U.S. military capabilities, and any decision he makes will not benefit him but his successors. I attempted to convince President Ford that we simply had to increase defense investment and he stepped up to the fight and did it, saying, "No new domestic spending programs." He vetoed seventy-six bills, I think, in two and a half years. He said we were going to increase the defense budget, which was not a very popular thing to do at the time.

The effectiveness of a secretary of defense, in Rumsfeld's view, depends crucially on managerial skills:

You decide what is important and work on those things yourself. You delegate the other things to people less important and you pick good people to manage them and you work the dickens out of them. You decide how you want to measure progress; what you measure gets better, there is no question.

The greatest obstacle to change within the Pentagon, Donald Rumsfeld suggested, was the legacy of the Vietnam War, which had a profound effect on the ability of members of the defense establishment to think and act creatively.

> The Pentagon is filled with people who are still suffering from the trauma of Vietnam, where they saw their institution damaged, after which their funds were denied and their capabilities eroded. They consider other things as their first priority. It is filled with people who recognize the fact that you do not do something well unless you practice it, get good at it, train for it, and deploy for it. They also had a bad experience in the aborted Iranian hostage rescue of 1980, so it is going to take time. And even today, they are a long way from there; it is going to take much better management than it is getting.

The role of intelligence in the formation of policy is critical. Gen. John Vessey pointed out the difficulties of getting good intelligence to the necessary decision-makers:

> Intelligence is a matter of priorities and efforts; you cannot look at the whole world with the same degree of intensity all the time. I talked about warning and the use of intelligence and the importance of time—that is, stressing the fact that warning time lost is time that can never be recovered—and the importance of the integration of intelligence with the whole deterrent philosophy and in the day-to-day of intelligence to make deterrence effective.
>
> That would help them set their priorities a little better, rather than running out and saying, "Tell me everything I want to know." It was important that we were understood, that we were looking at what our potential enemies might be able to do ten years from now, five years from now, and right down to two hours from now. We had to look at the entire picture all the time and we had to understand that we were looking at only fragments of the picture at any time. An integration of that picture— something that we thought pertained to ten years from now—might be related to something that somebody on an outpost saw that would be related to two hours from now. We had to have a system that integrated that, because what we thought might be the ten-year-from-now picture might in fact be part of a nearer time frame.

As an example of the need to understand properly intelligence that is collected, General Vessey discussed a large analytical project he had initiated as commander of United Nations forces in Korea (1976–79):

> We collected a tremendous amount of intelligence about the North Koreans, but it just lacked the analytical focus it should have had. So this

group went through stuff that had been collected—photographs, SIGINT [signal intelligence], and human intelligence—and did a good job of collating and correlating it and coming up with the revised intelligence estimate. So the analytical effort went on, and we worked to try to get the intelligence agencies of both countries working together as well as to go back through the history. The history of that study is a good case study of intelligence fusion and its importance. You could see where NSA [National Security Agency], DIA [Defense Intelligence Agency], and CIA had gone their separate ways, and the national intelligence estimates had fallen somewhere in the middle of all that. In fact, it was negotiation and not analysis that was getting us to the estimate. By starting with a clean sheet of paper and saying let's go back through the intelligence again, we could find the clear picture of the North Korean military buildup.

We could find it in references in the SIGINT to construction programs, and then by looking at the photos you could find the construction. It was a tremendously laborious effort in going through agent reports again, but it is a magnificent piece of work and a magnificent piece of fusion. They came up with a good estimate. I think what has happened in intelligence with Korea since that time is a good case study in how to use intelligence both for national policy and for military planning and decision making.

Gen. Brent Scowcroft, President Ford's national security adviser, pointed to a similar project that he organized to review Soviet strategic nuclear programs:

My notion of the development of the A-Team/B-Team concept came out of the president's Foreign Intelligence Advisory Board, which wanted to look closely at the Soviet order of battle. As I recall, they seemed to have detected a fairly consistent pattern of underestimating events. In other words, comparing the estimate with subsequent events, there seemed to be a pattern there of underestimation, and they developed the hypothesis that it was perhaps because of the estimators themselves and their particular individual qualities and so on. Or perhaps the framework that one employs in estimating year after year had a built-in bias toward demonstrating the wisdom of their previous estimates—in other words, to see whether or not there were some threats which could be uncovered as introducing bias into the estimates. I think it was a very interesting sort of a notion.

The A-Team/B-Team idea was to set up a panel and counterpanel predominantly composed of what you might call skeptics of the U.S.-Soviet relationship—in other words, people tending to be hard-line—and to see, given the same body of data to evaluate, how an evaluation by a group like this might differ from that of the professional community. That was the theory behind it. George Bush was director of Central Intelligence [DCI] and reacted with some enthusiasm to this notion, as I recall. My recollection is that he basically selected the members of B-Team. The NSC staff was not involved in the selection of the B-Team. It was an eminent group of individuals.

I think what happened to the exercise is that it got caught up in politics—national politics and Republican politics—in that some members of the B-Team decided that this was a national issue, and rather than continue in the discreet vein that we had proposed, decided to go public. This counterteam notion was a very valuable one, but I think the idea has suffered badly as a result of the experience of the B-Team. As far as I know, it demonstrated the kinds of inadvertent biases that can be introduced into intelligence [estimates] by the nature of the process. Such a thing is worthy of investigation. I think that this is a model that possibly might be applied to other national security issues. Whether this is precisely the model to be used is another question, but I think that we ought to be continually questioning and evaluating the process as we go through it in order to make sure that in fact we are getting the best results that we can get. This was an attempt to do that. Despite the B-Team problem, I do not think it was inevitable that it had to go the way it did.

The role and organization of the JCS has evolved over time. Gen. Andrew Goodpaster had the opportunity not only to observe the relationship between President Eisenhower and the Joint Chiefs of Staff, but also subsequently to serve as assistant to the chairman of the Joint Chiefs of Staff:

President Eisenhower wanted the Joint Chiefs of Staff to function as a corporate body—conducting planning, looking at our problems, and making recommendations from the standpoint of national security. He kept trying to draw them into that role, and kept trying to put more and more emphasis on their corporate function. In a way, that went back to his own experience, first when he was chief of staff of the Army, and then when President Truman called him down from Columbia University to serve as a kind of acting chairman of the Joint Chiefs to put together the first consolidated military budget. Eisenhower also had a strong conviction on the need to have coordinated operations arising out of his experience, particularly in North Africa, but also in the many operations in Europe. He looked to the chiefs to try to do that within the overall policy that was laid down, and wanted to hear their views and receive their contribution to the formulation of overall policy.

General Goodpaster continued;

He then wanted that structure to take the guidance he gave them and solve their problems, and not to keep bringing back their problems to him. I say that because that was an element of frustration to him—that they wouldn't take this responsibility and shape up their actions within the guidance that he had given. He would have them over, work his way through the issues, and lay out the guidance that he expected them to follow. The strongest constraint that he put on them was a fiscal constraint.

Adm. Thomas Moorer, chairman of the Joint Chiefs of Staff from 1970 to 1974, notes how the JCS operated under President Nixon:

> Kissinger would come in and say this is the issue and these are the options, and there are those in favor of this option and those in favor of that option. When that was finished the president would turn to the secretaries of defense and state and then to me. I would say, "Mr. President, the JCS position is such and such, but it is my duty to advise you that the chief of staff of the Army does not agree with us. His position is so and so because . . ." Immediately after the meeting I'd get all the chiefs on a conference call and tell them what happened. That's the way you do it. Each chief can make a dissent and if necessary see the president. So can the chairman. I think the important issues of disagreement were always presented. I'm proud of the fact that I have letters from Wedemeyer [Albert Wedemeyer was deputy commander-in-chief under Louis Mountbatten during World War II] and the older Army officers, and they all used the same two words: *eminently fair*. If you don't want opposition, limit your question to a single person. That would be unhealthy. He could be wrong.

Gen. John Vessey, chairman of the Joint Chiefs of Staff from 1982 to 1985, points to the role that he saw himself playing in the decision-making process:

> The chairman was a servant of three bodies; the first body was the National Command Authority: the president and the secretary of defense He was a servant of the body of which he was a member, the Joint Chiefs of Staff. Then he was a servant of that other, more loosely tied body, the commanders-in-chief of the United Commands. He had to represent in each of those bodies the views of the others.

Vessey also noted,

> Agreement among the JCS in advice [to the president] was very useful and desirable, but it would be surprising if the JCS always agreed. In the JCS there was a total of 150 years of military experience, and it came from different backgrounds, from different parts of the military establishment, and it was unlikely that we would always agree. I intended to carry out my duties as diligently as I could—that is, to take their advice to the president and the secretary of defense and to explain differences that existed.

General Goodpaster suggested that there were problems in the JCS structure. The Eisenhower administration, in the Defense Reorganization Act of

1958, took steps to improve the JCS structure. General Goodpaster described the problems that President Eisenhower sought to address in his JCS reform:

> The chiefs were not giving primacy to their corporate function, they were pursuing service interests. He flared out one time and used the term *parochial* in talking about this constant interservice rivalry or struggle. As he saw it, each service was attempting to promote its weapons systems, and to create public concern, which would just do the opposite of what he wanted. He didn't think this was necessary or desirable in the national interest, but thought it was being done for parochial purposes. Finally, he concluded that an initiative to try to strengthen and unify the joint elements would be worth the effort. He met a lot of resistance, some of it passive, much of it active, up in Congress, even over in the Defense Department. But he became determined that some change was needed. Had he felt it was feasible, I think he would have gone to a single chief of staff. At the time, however, that was clearly well beyond what could be obtained. He did, however, stress the corporate identity of the chiefs. He provided that in each service there would be a vice chief, who would have coextensive authority with the chief, and who could deal with problems within the service, while the chiefs would give primacy to their joint role. At the same time he felt that there were restrictions in the National Security Act of 1947 and in the Reorganization Act of 1953 on the authority of the secretary of defense, and he wanted to clear those up. Those were the two principal things that he did.

At the operational level, General Goodpaster noted the career of President Eisenhower:

> He felt that it was desirable to make clear that the forces in the field should be commanded as integrated forces, and that was his reason for setting up the unified and specified commands. They would have an operational role, and he wanted to withdraw the service headquarters in Washington from that operational role. The Washington level would be exercised by the chiefs in their joint capacity but not in their service capacity. I think that those conditions were the main elements that entered into it. His proposals met with great resistance up on the Hill. Bryce Harlow, in particular, and Fred Seaton had major responsibilities in finally working it through. In the Defense Department there was a constant tendency to try to water it down and weaken it, so Eisenhower himself had to continue to hold a firm position on it.

Gen. John Vessey served as chairman of the Joint Chiefs of Staff between 1982 and 1985, after having held the post of vice chief of staff of the U.S. Army. During his tenure, numerous important changes were initiated. The culmination of discussion in the early 1980s about the JCS structure and its operation was the Defense Reorganization Act of 1986. General Vessey described the problems that he encountered as chairman:

> There are layers of competing staff that dilute the advice and create delay and duplication and confusion. The lines of responsibility for advice are not as clear as they could be. Multiple assistant secretaries and defense agencies provide advice. We said very frankly that the JCS had not been carrying out its statutory responsibilities as well or as completely as it could or should.
>
> We pointed out that the JCS and the Joint Staff, which were to be the secretary of defense's principal military advisers, were the smallest staff that he had. We also pointed out to him that the law says he shall have no other military staff other than the JCS. We pointed out to him that there are more military officers on his civilian staff than the law permits him to have on his military staff. We said that somewhere in there there's a turkey. We pointed out to him that these military officers up here work for assistant secretaries and so forth, and what happens here is that your military advice goes to your civilian staff.

The issue of JCS reform was widely discussed in the Congress, in the Reagan White House, and in the Pentagon. General Vessey led the JCS effort to study and recommend changes in the JCS structure.

> The fundamental thing (as we examined laws, duties, regulations, and past organizations) that became clear to us was that the fundamental problem was making the secretary of defense the best secretary we could make him. When you looked at what the law said, the secretary's duties were extraordinarily burdensome, a job with extraordinary responsibilities and with extraordinary authority, far different from other cabinet secretaries.

Vessey also outlined how the reform proposals were to be judged:

> The chiefs proposed these four criteria: Would the change improve the nation's ability to wage war? Would it assure that the president and secretary of defense would receive better and more timely advice than they had under the present system? Would it ensure that the requirements of the CINCs [commanders-in-chief] of the Unified and Specified Commands would be met better than they were now being met? Would it improve the ability of the United States to allocate its resources more wisely and efficiently? We proposed these four criteria for examining the proposals for change.
>
> Secretary [Caspar W.] Weinberger said, "Okay, I agree with you and with this letter, except that I want to add one other criterion, and that is, would the suggested changes be consistent with civilian control of the United States military?" We agreed that that would be a good criterion to add.

General Vessey opposed the idea of making the chairman the sole military adviser to the president:

> I think it is a mistake to make the chairman the principal military adviser. If you have a chairman they trust, and he carries out his duties, he is going to tell them what the other chiefs believe and he also has an extraordinary opportunity to give his own advice. There is nothing that precludes him from giving his own advice. So the issue is not as important as it appears to be, but changing it the other way may weaken the defense establishment.

Admiral Moorer shared General Vessey's view:

> The danger is to say that the chairman of the Joint Chiefs is the sole adviser to the president; then you are in trouble. I do not object to the JCS chairman being one of them, but he should not be the sole adviser. That could be dangerous. We realized then that here the secretary wears three hats. He is a cabinet officer, like the other cabinet officers, but he is also the chief executive officer of the biggest corporation in the United States. You have seen these headlines and articles recently about how the Pentagon spends more than General Motors and General Electric and so on and so forth—it is true. He is responsible to the president, the Congress, and the American people for doing that efficiently. But more importantly, he is the president's agent for commanding the Armed Forces of the United States.
>
> It is that last job that drives the others; if you did not have to do that, you would not be the CEO of an outfit with a $300 billion budget. We suddenly realized that here is the key to the problem: How do you make the secretary more effective? The JCS, as a body, has the duty to make him effective as the president's agent in commanding the Armed Forces of the United States. So we said, let us go back now with this newfound wisdom (which should have been self-evident to us at the very beginning, but was not and is not yet to many people who are examining the business of defense organization and the JCS) and examine the problem again, and say, "How do we look at all of these issues again?"

General Vessey presented the JCS corporate view of reform:

> We told the secretary of defense what the purpose was: to provide the best possible military advice to the president, the secretary of defense, and the National Security Council, and to clarify the roles of the JCS in the context of the entire Defense Department in helping the president and the secretary carry out their national security responsibilities, thus, trying to raise it right from the very beginning into this larger context.
>
> We proposed very carefully worded language for the change, because we recognized that you did not want a uniformed commander-in-chief or

a vice commander-in-chief for the president. We wanted to maintain civilian control and we wanted it to be clear that the president was the commander-in-chief and not give anybody the idea that we were proposing an opportunity for a man on a white horse in uniform. We proposed very carefully structured words to make it clear that they were subordinate to the president: "The chain of command runs from the secretary of defense through the chairman of the Joint Chiefs of Staff to the Unified and Specified Commands. Orders to such commands shall be from the president and secretary of defense through the CJCS, by authority and direction of the secretary of defense." This made it clear that the chairman was not acting in his own right as subcommander.

3
The State Department

This chapter offers perspectives on the State Department's role in making foreign policy; advances in communications technology and their impact on decision making; general changes in the State Department and the Foreign Service since World War II; the divide between where foreign policy is formulated and where it is implemented; the changing role of the ambassador; and finally the authority and effectiveness of ambassadors. Dean Rusk served as secretary of state from 1961 to 1969. Here he addressed the extent to which an administration can generate strategic policy:

> Dean Acheson once said, "You can only think in action when you think about foreign policy." He was opposed to the notion that you can ponder your navel and come up with great foreign policy. There is something to that, but there are occasions when a searching review of ongoing policy comes about. Every important problem has locked up in it dozens of secondary and tertiary questions. These are changing day by day. Generalizations do not help. All sorts of questions must be taken into account. The complexity of that process is enormous. We have in the Department of State a section dedicated to reading everything they could get their hands on that was put out by academics and to call important material to the attention of policymakers. Rarely do you come across a book or an article applicable to your immediate problems because of time and other factors. That material does not point to a decision. But I think that it is appropriate that the department have such a group. Every policy officer must also be a planning officer. He must always be thinking about the long run and the general aspects of the policy that he is considering. Planning cannot be the monopoly of the [policy] planning staff. Planning people are often called upon to help with immediate problems.

Flexibility, Mr. Rusk maintained, is a key ingredient of policy-making.

> One must always be willing to re-think patterns of policy. I established the Open Forum for young Foreign Service officers to stand aside and challenge traditional assumptions and raise new ideas. The world changes. For

example, the impression in the 1950s was that neutrality and nonalignment were immoral. President Kennedy thought that any country that was secure and cooperative was in the interest of the United States [even if they were neutral or nonaligned]. The distinction between neutrals and allies had become greatly exaggerated. We thus made a special effort to improve our relations with the nonaligned leaders: Tito, Nehru, Nasser, Nkrumah, Sukarno. We did not always succeed because some of those people turned out to be rascals; but we made the effort. We worked out a multimillion-dollar, three-year program to feed Egyptians, but Nasser told the people to throw the aid into the Red Sea—and the Congress did just that.

The former secretary of state also stressed that while technology and other factors influence decision making, it is still the president who most affects the basic contour of U.S. foreign policy:

President Kennedy was very conscious of the fact that he was the first president to have been born in this century. He looked on himself as a new generation, and he wanted to ask fresh questions about ongoing lines of policy to see if they were adequate to the new world he felt was coming into existence. If you think about the presidents we have had since World War II, the differences between each of them are extraordinary. Each of them is going to want to handle his office in a manner with which he is comfortable. President Eisenhower wanted a system of committees. President Kennedy swept it away. It was a more streamlined, ad-hoc kind of organization. During Eisenhower's administration, a manual was prepared on American national security policy. When President Kennedy came in, the policy planning staff tried to get him to keep it. He would not approve it because he felt that these generalizations did little to help you solve the problems you run into on Monday morning.

Mr. Rusk outlined the State Department's decision-making process during his tenure:

The secretary of state usually will have a meeting every morning with his senior staff. We would take up a lot of these questions about the status of certain decisions at these meetings. Each morning I would get forty-five to fifty of the more important outgoing cables that had gone out the day before. It gave me a chance to keep my eye on things. The process of monitoring is not institutionalized in terms of a staff of permanent functionaries to monitor; but it does occur on a regular basis.

John P. Roche, who served as special adviser to President Johnson on foreign and domestic affairs from 1966 to 1968, recalled President Johnson's personal political style, particularly surrounding the conflict in Vietnam:

The intriguing thing was coping with a nonideological president. Here is where I was involved very deeply at the observer level—not ever at the participant level—in this looney negotiation series. In his memoirs, Johnson lists every one of the negotiations to try to find out what the North Vietnamese wanted—there were seventeen, I think [see *The Vantage Point: Perspectives of the Presidency* (New York: Holt, Rinehart and Winston, 1971)]. In February 1967, Ho Chi Minh released an appendix to the president's memoirs, *The Vantage Point* [see Ho Chi Minh, *Réponse du président Ho Chi Minh au président L.B. Johnson* (Hanoi: Editions en Langues Étrangeres, 1967)]. Ho Chi Minh's reply was February 15; Johnson's letter was February 8; the release of the letters occurred while we were on the plane. Johnson said, "Why would he do that?" I sat down and tried to explain that Ho Chi Minh was not a Mayor Daley who was waiting to be bought. Johnson did not have an ideological bone in his body, and he was convinced that everybody had a button. So, if you are dealing with Ho Chi Minh, find that button—it was sort of like Roosevelt's attitude toward Stalin. In fact, it is an interesting parallel because Roosevelt was Johnson's idol. Roosevelt viewed Stalin as being a Mayor Hague with an overactive police force. They did not understand this sort of ideological content at all. Johnson kept saying, "What does he want?"—as if three post offices, a new municipal sewer system, or something like that would do it.

John Roche described his attempt to clarify the Vietnam situation for President Johnson:

I wrote a memo, in which I said [Ho Chi Minh] wants to win. Like an old Leninist, he is willing to negotiate whether you are bombing or not. Now I happened to disapprove of Rolling Thunder right from the beginning— that is, the strategic bombing of North Vietnam. Bombing is only useful when it is essentially mobile artillery. It was very misleading; they would come back and report that they had taken out the biggest machine shop in Haiphong, and it was probably about the size of my garage. Johnson said, "Well, we give him a bombing pause and nothing happens." I said, "He wants to win. If he thought it would be useful to his cause he would negotiate with you with bombs coming down his chimney." As indeed did happen later on, when Nixon dropped them, really quite literally, the precision bombs practically did go down the chimney. "He is waiting to throw in negotiations, negotiations as a weapons system. He is waiting to utilize it at the most vulnerable time in American politics, namely, just before the election of 1968." I laid out the rationale for this in some detail. He could not figure out what made this guy tick because he came from a world where people like this just were not around. It clouded his whole perception of the war and of Ho Chi Minh and the Lao Dong and all these various and sundry sidebars that went along with it. He threw it off because in his whole political career he had never run into anybody, any people, who worked in this kind of mind-set.

Tapley Bennett, former ambassador to the Dominican Republic, who also served as U.S. representative to the United Nations (1971–76), and subsequently as U.S. ambassador to NATO (1977–83), also commented on President Johnson's style of decision making:

> Johnson was always very emphatic, but he did agonize over decisions. He was a warm, emotional man, and he cared deeply about people and what happened to them. He always wanted to have a range of options to choose from. He would poll every man in the room: "What do you think, what do you think, what do you think." I had quite a few phone calls from President Johnson during the Dominican crisis in 1965; he was in effect the Dominican desk officer there for several days. We were sitting in my office one of those evenings in Santo Domingo when the phone rang—it was the president. We were faced with some decision and there were, I think, nine of us in the room, including [McGeorge] Bundy, [Cyrus] Vance, and [undersecretary of state Thomas] Mann. He polled each of us over an inadequate international telephone.

Dean Rusk noted that increasingly sophisticated communications technology is changing the dynamics of today's foreign policy decision making:

> Among other things, the communications explosion causes a ripple effect; all the State Department's geographic bureaus get involved in most major policy decisions. Sometimes they are in competition with one another for influence. The most senior officers seek to define the national interest in terms of their geographic bureau. During the decolonization process, the European section was not responsive to the African and Asian sections. That has to be reconciled, sometimes by the president. The danger is fumbling and bumbling. Foolish men allowed the assassination of an archduke to move step by step into World War I. We have to be very careful so that events do not take control—to keep them insulated so they can be controlled.

Another communications advance of the modern world, air travel, directly affects the way U.S. foreign policy is made. Beyond this, the burgeoning size of the U.S. government complicates both policy formulation and implementation. Ambasssador Tapley Bennett explained:

> With jet aircraft, and the government having a large fleet, there is today much too much of Washington sending out special missions. I am saying this as a general proposition. The delegations from Washington we used to have at NATO were never less than thirteen to fifteen people when a maximum of three would have been sufficient for most of those meetings.

But that is the way the Washington bureaucracy has grown; you must have a representative from the Pentagon, from State, from Treasury—you need to have this or that, always separate, and sometimes several from the same agency all watching one another. Washington wastes a lot of money sending out special missions. If Washington does not like the job the ambassador's doing, it should remove him and get another. Otherwise, leave him to do the job he was sent to do. Special missions should be employed only in very special situations.

Especially since World War II, the U.S. diplomatic establishment, and in particular the Foreign Service, has undergone a transformation of major importance. Changes in the size of U.S. embassies around the world, reflecting the numerous bureaucratic elements that are part of the diplomatic process, together with the enhanced ability for rapid movement and for instantaneous communication, have altered the scope of American diplomacy. Such changes affect—directly or indirectly—the structure and process of U.S. foreign and defense policy-making. According to Ambassador Tapley Bennett,

The changes in the State Department and in the Foreign Service have been in line with the transformation of our country—the enormous growth and expansion and the diverse interests of the United States which have developed in the decades since World War II. The State Department was relatively small; it still has the smallest budget of any cabinet department. When we entered World War II, there were less than one thousand officers in our worldwide service. It was too cliquish, obviously, and too confined in its reach. The salaries were practically nothing; when I went to work for the government in 1940 my salary was $1,620 per year. In 1941 I entered the Foreign Service at $2,500 a year, which was considered a generous entering salary. After all, ambassadors to major capitals got only $17,500 a year in those days.

During the war the State Department played a distinctly subordinate role. The State Department became active on the economic front, and that was largely due to trying to deny the Axis powers raw materials—there was the preemptive buying of minerals in Spain and other places. For the first time we began an information program. Nelson Rockefeller started that through his committees in Latin America and his making of that film, *Brazil*. They were small things, but indicative of big changes under way. The information program is now a major activity. Then just after the war with the devastation of Europe there came the Marshall Plan and then the beginnings of the aid programs in underdeveloped countries.

The United Nations was formed in 1945. That was a new development. I was in the delegation to San Francisco as a very junior member. In fact, by that time I was a corporal in the army, and I was borrowed back by the Department of State to go to San Francisco to work on Nelson Rockefeller's staff on the Latin American end of the United Nations. All of these new activities led to an enormous expansion in the State Department year by year.

David Newsom, who has had, like Ambassador Bennett, over thirty years experience as a Foreign Service officer, noted a similar shift:

The Foreign Service of the United States before World War II had 750 officers and was very much European- or Western world–centered in the traditional mold of European diplomacy and law. The Foreign Service after World War II was in many ways quite different; and it was a difference that not all old-timers fully welcomed. It was different because first there was, as far as the United States was concerned, a genuine expansion of overseas responsibilities and activity also. An embassy was no longer just a small group of more or less collegial colleagues concentrating on the traditional aspects of negotiation, protection, welfare. Suddenly you had information programs, cultural exchange programs, economic aid, and military aid. Gradually you had a greater emphasis on the commercial promotion aspect as export trade became more important. Inevitably, therefore, also an expansion of the intelligence function took place. An ambassador became much more a manager as well as a representative.

The second great change is that our diplomatic representatives and responsibilities moved into the Third World. The world was to many of the old-timers of the service a colonial world in which the authority was not indigenous, but British or French or Portuguese. Even those parts of the world that were not strictly speaking colonial (the mandates and Arab states of the Near East) were terra incognita to a lot of the old Foreign Service. I remember when I was in London taking a dispatch on the situation in Saudi Arabia to one of the old-timers of the service. He said to me, "Does anybody really give a damn what happens in Saudi Arabia?" This was in 1961; now we do.

Although policy formulation takes place in Washington, D.C., its actual implementation usually falls to an ambassador and his staff in the host country. Ambassador Bennett described the problems often faced by such a U.S. representative:

When you are the ambassador out in the field, you get a lot of things in writing and you get a lot of background papers. What you miss, being 3,500 miles away, is what happens in the corridors between the meetings and who influences whom that you do not have so much feel for unless you are back in Washington. In Brussels we were kept quite well informed step by step, but I would not feel involved or conversant with how a given step was arrived at. Obviously, there were meetings day after day between State and Defense; and the NSC gets into all this—that is a very intrusive force in American policy-making. Possibly it should be, but it certainly complicates the issue from time to time.

Dean Rusk reflected on his relationships as secretary of state with U.S. diplomatic establishments abroad:

I believe that the Foreign Service of the United States is second to none and it is the most professional in the world, but we do not insulate our officers from the political process as do the British. Their civil service supports one political party at a time. Under our constitution it is our civil service's duty to take direction from the people put there. That is not always understood.

The conduct of our foreign policy is a mass business. Three thousand cables a day go out of the State Department. The secretary might see six or seven of them before they go out, the president maybe one or two. The rest go out on the basis of responsibility delegated to hundreds of officers throughout the department. Otherwise it could never get its work done. In eight years, out of 2,100,000 cables that went out with my name on them only four or five had to be pulled back and rewritten because the person who had written them had missed the point of policy to be followed. This is an extraordinary level of performance. The officers respond to the direction they receive. I have never seen any examples of officers revolting against the policies of their superiors.

David Newsom served as ambassador to Libya, Indonesia, and the Philippines. He discussed the changing role played by the ambassador:

You mentioned the change in the role of the ambassador because of more rapid communication networks. Certainly in major posts more available communications facilities have changed the role, to some extent, because heads of state and foreign ministers now can communicate directly. The other thing that technological advances have done is to increase, to an almost irresistible degree, the temptation of Washington agencies to do their own negotiating through delegations sent abroad and not through the ambassador. I remember being in Japan a few years ago when U.S. Ambassador Mike Mansfield was complaining that the embassy in Japan had become little more than a support group for delegations from Washington.

Another thing that more rapid travel did was to elevate major negotiations to the level of the foreign minister or secretary of state. I suppose this really began during World War II and immediately afterwards with the foreign ministers' conferences on postwar problems. It meant that once you have established negotiations at that level the expectation of other countries is that your secretary of state will ultimately be drawn into the negotiations and perhaps visit. If he does not, at least some countries draw the conclusion that suddenly you are giving less priority to them or taking an issue less seriously. The other thing that has increased with travel is the growth of multilateral organizations which annually or sometimes more often hold ministerial-level conferences. Again, if the American secretary of state does not attend the NATO ministerial conference or, when it existed, the Baghdad Pact meeting or now the ASEAN meeting with the foreign ministers of the major trading partners, the United States is perceived as moving away from serious support. So the burden on the secretary has increased enormously.

Tapley Bennett addressed the issue of ambassadorial authority.

Actually, the authority of the ambassador is much better established now than it used to be. In the late forties and fifties, ambassadors had a terrible time because you had all these bloated establishments abroad—too many people from the military, from the aid program, from different activities that had grown up during the war. The ambassador had nominal authority, but it was not real, and you had all these different voices reporting to Washington.

That all finally began to be attacked in the Eisenhower administration. I believe he was the first president to write a letter to each ambassador saying, "You are my representative and you speak for the country." The country team, a regular group composed of heads of major sections of the embassy and representatives of each U.S. government agency in the country and presided over by the ambassador, was formed around that time, and has proven to be an effective means of coordinating U.S. activities in a country. The ambassador's authority as the principal U.S. representative has been upheld, I believe, by every subsequent president. I know there was a letter from Kennedy, although I myself did not become an ambassador until Johnson's day. From the five presidents I served as ambassador, I have a letter from each one of them.

At one time in Paris we had six or seven ambassadors, each with different responsibilities. In my time in Brussels we had three: the ambassador to the Belgian government, the ambassador to the European Community, and to NATO. That takes a certain amount of footwork. People have to agree to get along, you know, and you can get personality clashes if you are not careful.

Ambassador Newsom also pointed to changes in Washington that have affected conduct of U.S. diplomacy:

In Washington you had the growth of the foreign affairs bureaucracy with a number of new players. You had the rise of a structure within the White House, the NSC staff, as well as the other agencies. There developed a role for the Defense Department, particularly with the creation of the International Security Affairs structure in the Defense Department in the 1960s. So the whole task of representing the United States and managing that representation both in Washington and overseas is totally different.

With the growth of the U.S. foreign relations bureaucracy, numerous agencies in the field were represented by those whose future depended not so much on the evaluation of the ambassador but the evaluation of an agency in Washington. The ambassador no longer became a commanding officer, he became a mediator among representatives of conflicting agencies. He might have a letter from the president of the United States stating that he is in charge, but it was my experience that if you tried to act on that basis you were in trouble. However, if you recognized that you were presiding over an amalgam of separate bureaucratic entities and knew what they are supposed to do, you might be able to guide them into some kind of cohesive or coherent approach to the country.

The individual makes a lot of difference. The best ambassadors were those who understood Washington as well as they understood the country in which they were working. That was not a lesson all American ambassadors learned. Where they understood Washington well and acted on the basis of that knowledge, both in their reporting and in their recommendations, they did well. They did not necessarily tailor a recommendation to fit the political climate, but they were not totally without awareness of that climate when making recommendations in reporting. Llewelyn Thompson [U.S. ambassador to the Soviet Union in the Kennedy administration], for example, was an influential player in the Washington scene as he was in Moscow. This is also true of Raymond Hare in the Middle East during the Nasser period.

Tapley Bennett offered a somewhat different perspective:

I think it is largely a matter of personality. The ambassador now has all the authority that he needs under existing regulations and under the president's specific letter of authority. Quite aside from all that, it is the fact that he is the president's representative. Military officers are accustomed to a chain of command; they are accustomed to taking orders as well as giving orders. I never had any problems, and I suppose that was one reason I was chosen to go to NATO. I was known as a person who got along well with the military. There has to be mutual respect on both sides. Each has to respect the other's responsibilities, the other's role. There was never any question at NATO or elsewhere that on political matters the final decision was mine. I have always had four-star generals and admirals, just as much as anybody else, say, "If that's the way you want it, we will do it that way." Now, if it is a regional military headquarters, the ambassador does not have that authority. There, if differences exist, they have to be submitted to Washington, and I have had that occasionally.

Ambassador Bennett also pointed to the following example:

In the Dominican Republic case, the only difference I recall with General Palmer, who was there heading the military forces, was not really a serious one. It was related to the movement of our troops. We discussed what time of day would cause the least disruption to normal civilian life. I opted for the afternoon siesta period when I thought all the Dominicans would be in bed. Palmer thought it was better to go just at midnight. We were to move by a certain date, but we could not move before that midnight. He wanted to go right after midnight and I wanted to do it in the daytime. We put that to Washington, and the decision backed him, and he was right. We moved at one o'clock or three o'clock in the morning, and it was absolutely flawless. The streets were silent, and it went without a hitch. That was not a different policy; it was just a difference of timing.

4
The North Atlantic Treaty Organization

NATO, like all other organizations, has an internal dynamic that affects the alliance's decision-making process. Here, the structural dynamics of NATO are addressed, as are the roles of the NATO secretary-general, the supreme allied commander, Europe (SACEUR), and the Nuclear Planning Group (NPG). Ambassador W. Tapley Bennett, U.S. ambassador to NATO from 1977 to 1983 offered his observations on NATO's structural dynamics:

> NATO is more or less permanently in crisis, and that is not an unhealthy thing. It is very natural when you have a grouping of, now, sixteen nations, fifteen during most of my time there (Spain came in while I was there). All of them are vigorous powers and the bulk of them large powers in the old-fashioned sense of the Concert of Europe, now much diminished in their outreach. One thing that distressed me during my time at NATO was to observe how parochial most of the Europeans have become, including their governments, in looking at world problems, and how they have shrunk back into the attitudes of middle-sized or even small powers. The British still have something of a worldview, and they still turn out awfully good people who look at things in the large. The French have their interests around the world, but by and large they concentrate now on Europe and on trade and things of that sort. And in security, while they talk about it a lot, they all know that they are ultimately dependent on us for their security. That is not a very healthy relationship, particularly when it involves proud nations with a great background of having run the world in the nineteenth century.
>
> So you have got that kind of built-in tension in the relationship. It impressed me how proprietary the Europeans feel about the United States. They reserve the right to criticize everything we do, to tell us how we could have done it better. I took occasion more than once to remind my colleagues there that they had not done very well at avoiding war when it was just Europe managing it, and that now, since they have the United States in their security complex, Western Europe has enjoyed the longest reign of continent-wide peace. It is a tremendous achievement. It is

unique in history. But if you look at it day-to-day, there is always something wrong, plenty of reasons for vigorous countries, democratically organized, to have differing views; and that is healthy. But the pundits and the academicians are always finding NATO in disarray and in imminent danger of collapse. We made a study while I was at NATO and we found that since 1949 NATO has been pronounced by these people to be in disarray on an average of every fourteen months. Yet we have survived. We jump every hurdle, somehow we get past each crisis. If you read Kissinger's memoirs of the late sixties and early seventies (you could write them today), you would not know you were talking about a different period [see Henry A. Kissinger, *White House Years* (Boston: Little, Brown, 1979); *Years of Upheaval* (Boston: Little, Brown, 1982)]. This has always been part of the vitality of NATO, they are always arguing about something.

Now there will always be pulls and tugs. The history of NATO is that America takes positions and Europe complains, but then gradually falls into line on the decision—and sometimes we make wrong decisions. The Europeans down through the years have been subject to too many urgent American initiatives put forward with all the push and shove that energetic Americans summon in the more sedate European atmosphere. We sometimes tire of our initiatives after two or three years and you do not hear them anymore. The Europeans are quite ready to keep book on you and tell you, "Oh, we've heard all this before; two years ago you wanted us to do something quite different."

Joseph Luns was Dutch foreign minister between 1956 and 1971 and secretary-general of NATO from 1971 to 1983. He offered his insights into the structure of the Atlantic Alliance:

You have in NATO one very big country, the superpower America, and about three or four important countries. I would name the Federal Republic of Germany; Great Britain; perhaps in some way, but not in a military way, Canada, which has a rather weak military establishment; and Italy. Then there are a few countries like Spain, Turkey, and the Netherlands, which are in a middle category, and then you have very small countries: Norway, Denmark, Luxembourg, Portugal, and Greece. Germany is the most important member after the United States since it is very dangerously situated strategically.

Luns discussed the role played by the secretary-general of NATO in the formulation of an alliance consensus and the decision-making process:

Especially as contrary to the Warsaw Pact, the Americans have no hegemony in NATO. Everything must be done by unanimity, by consent, and that was not very easy. We had a lot of talking to do to try to find a formula which would be acceptable to all.

Thus, the secretary-general is boss of the whole organization, for thousands of people everywhere. He decides on the agenda every week. He makes the agenda. He has the right of initiative, and the right to get in touch with heads of state and heads of government. All that together makes quite some influence. For instance, I took the initiative of sending a memorandum pointing out that it was necessary to give military assistance to Turkey, Greece, and Portugal. Portugal profits very little from NATO, but Greece and Turkey have received very massive aid. As secretary-general I had a certain influence, but you must not show it too much. It was from time to time even necessary to decide in confidence with the principal countries, especially the United States, as to how to deal with the Soviet Union. I would say to the secretary of state, "How do you think we should play this thing? How will I introduce it?" I was far more in contact with America than the Allies knew, and I thought that was very necessary.

Luns also discussed his relationship with SACEUR (supreme allied commander in Europe):

It is axiomatic that there should be a good relationship between the secretary-general, SACEUR, and the chairman of the Military Committee. I must say that with Gen. Bernard Rogers [SACEUR from 1979 to 1987] it was particularly good—we often met. Mostly he came to Brussels, but from time to time I insisted on going to SHAPE [Supreme Headquarters, Allied Powers Europe] to meet him.

Ambassador Bennett commented on the relationship between SACEUR and the civilian structure of NATO:

I believe there is a weekly meeting with the secretary-general, and then SACEUR comes back and forth whenever necessary. The members of the NATO Council see each other quite often, and SACEUR has a very active entertainment program. He goes down the list and has every NATO ambassador to dinner on a regular basis. Then General Rogers developed the practice of having the council go up to his headquarters for a formal briefing—I believe that is still on an annual basis—but he has the whole group come up together for a full day. All the permanent representatives would go to his briefing room and get a full briefing, followed by lunch and then more briefing. These would be updates of the Soviet threat as well as NATO improvement programs.

In a typical week, between SHAPE and the U.S. mission there would be back and forth traffic every day and certainly at all levels of the mission. The U.S. mission at NATO has more Defense Department officers, both military and civilian, than civilians from the State Department. Those people are in touch throughout the day, every day, at their levels with SHAPE officers. I was fortunate in having very close and very happy relations with both SACEURs, Alexander Haig [SACEUR from 1974 to 1979] and Rogers. During my time at NATO we would see each other at dinners, or if he needed to come to my office when he came to Brussels, he would do so. The supreme commander comes to Brussels from his headquarters forty miles away to report to the secretary-general quite often. I did not drive up to SACEUR's office very often, but if it was necessary, I did. We were about forty miles apart, and he has a helicopter to get back and forth.

Reflecting on his experience as U.S. permanent representative to NATO, Ambassador Bennett expressed opposition to an idea put forward by Henry Kissinger that the post of supreme allied commander, Europe (SACEUR), which has always been held by an American, should instead be given to a ranking military person from one of the NATO-European countries.

There was a proposal put forward, some time ago, by Henry Kissinger to the effect that it might be symbolically and psychologically beneficial to have a European SACEUR and an American secretary-general. That is an absolutely frivolous proposal. I can not imagine why Kissinger would say such a thing as that except to be provocative. For one thing it is impossible. Since we are the principal nuclear power, you could not have a European commander who would command the nuclear force; our laws would prevent that. Personally, I think that it is much better to have the political side under the European than under the American; we would be that overlord from overseas. It is much better to have a European secretary-general, and he should be, except in rare cases, from one of the smaller countries. Carrington [Lord Carrington, British Secretary of State for Defense (1970–74), foreign affairs (1979–82), and NATO secretary-general (1984–88)] was an exception and he did an excellent job. He had the panache and the élan that you need for that sort of thing. While I was very strongly attached to Tindemanns [Leo Tindemanns, Belgian prime minister (1974–78) and foreign minister (1981–89)], an excellent alliance man, he would not have given the post the drama that Carrington was able to bring to it.

When the issue of control and targeting of nuclear weapons arose as an alliance concern in the 1960s, NATO created the Nuclear Planning Group (NPG), including the United States, the United Kingdom, the Federal Republic of Germany, and Italy as permanent members, together with several term members. As Britain's minister of defense between 1976 and 1979, Fredrick W. Mulley had an excellent position as his country's representative for participating in the work of the NPG. As a member of Parliament with a strong interest in defense issues, and as minister of aviation in the late 1960s, Mr. Mulley (later Lord Mulley) observed and took part in the formation and evolution of the NPG.

The whole question of Europe and nuclear weapons was [in the 1960s] very much an issue. A lot of our European Continental allies were concerned that they were dependent on American nuclear cover. It all developed of course when the Soviet Union demonstrated that they had the capacity to hit the United States. European countries were a bit afraid they might get involved through some hasty decision by the U.S. president, and there was a strong feeling that they ought to participate in the decision and one way that was suggested was a multilateral force. The actual nuclear warheads, just like the warheads on the short-range systems, were going to be under American custody, but the submarines would be manned by a mixed European crew. We never thought that was a very good idea, or in fact that it would have worked, or met the genuine concern of participation that the Europeans wanted to have.

I had just written a book [*The Politics of Western Defense* (New York: Praeger, 1962)] in which I had set out what I thought was necessary, and I was able, in fact, to see that achieved, namely the setting up of the Nuclear Planning Group, in which all the European members of NATO participated. Initially, for some years it used to be that all the bigger countries were members, and the smaller countries rotated their membership. They all go to these meetings, except France, of course, which does not participate in any of the defense activities of the alliance. I think that Greece used to be in the odd position of coming to the nuclear ones but not to the others; but now I think they do not come to either. But that apart, we got the [NPG] system, and I actually worked out the agenda with Robert McNamara's international adviser, John McNaughton. He came over and spent a couple of days, and we worked out the agenda for the first meeting of the Nuclear Planning Group. I stressed that the important thing was to put all their nuclear cards on the table at the first meeting, to list all the places that they had weapons in Europe. If you do that, everything being told to the Europeans, you will have no more trouble. We did not have any more trouble; it worked and is still working today.

It is a far better system than the MLF [multilateral force], which I am afraid we had to kill. The problem was that it was nurtured by certain American academics in the defense field and some U.S. congressmen. What interested me very much was the provision for an MLF nuclear contribution that was included in U.S. forward planning. We studied this particularly since Denis Healey as secretary of state for defense [1964–1970] wanted to introduce here forward-planning procedures and cost-control mechanisms similar to those pioneered in the United States by Robert McNamara; but after the Nuclear Planning Group was established, European concern gradually disappeared and this argument just went away. But I did argue in my book the reasons I thought this was the way to do it. People did not physically want to hold things, but they wanted to feel that their input would be in that famous black box along with everyone else's input.

Mr. Mulley outlined how the NPG functioned:

As far as I know, it still follows the same pattern as in my time. It has quite an agreeable method of working: one meeting a year is held in the NATO headquarters, and the other meeting is held at the invitation of one of the member countries. They do that in the way of providing a suitable and secure environment for the meeting. Often we went not to the capital but somewhere else. For example, after my time, they had the U.K. meeting in Edinburgh. It is generally a relaxed occasion; the actual meeting really depends entirely on the United States—which also provides the agenda.

The success of the meetings depends on a report by the U.S. secretary of defense on the developments in the nuclear field. Occasionally there cropped up a special issue as well, like the so-called neutron bomb issue. In that case, it was put down as a separate agenda issue. The U.S. secretary of defense provided the documentation and explained how he saw things in the balance between the Soviet Union and the United States. The United States provides the agenda because they are in the negotiating chair with the Soviet Union on arms control. Only the United States is in control of the nuclear arms of the alliance. The French do not participate. [The British] could provide a situation report [to the United States], and the minister of defense now I suppose gives a report on progress being made to bring the British Trident along, or on the length of time Polaris may last, but there is not very much interest in our nuclear weapons.

5
The United Nations

As a founding member of the United Nations, the United States has played a role of major importance in the international organization, although American influence has declined as UN membership has increased over the years. In this chapter, perspectives are offered on the UN Security Council decision-making process, the UN Command in the Republic of Korea, and UN involvement in the Congo (now Zaire) crisis. Ambassador Tapley Bennett served with the U.S. delegation to the United Nations between 1971 and 1976. He described the decision-making process within the United Nations and, in particular, the Security Council:

> The Security Council was the principal body of the UN. You have to abide by their decisions. You had five great-power vetos. The idea was that these nations had the primary responsibility for keeping the peace. These veto powers have been used often over the years. The council has been expanded from eleven to fifteen and has, thus, lost some intimacy. A great deal of the process involves consultation, taking days or weeks. The final voting meeting comes after these talks. The actual meeting is often a mere formality, as people give set speeches and drama is rare. The presidency of the Security Council rotates month by month and is not that critical. The president often conducts informal consultations but generally is impartial.

Ambassador Bennett discussed the consultative process between the administration in Washington and the U.S. representative to the United Nations:

> The Bureau of International Organization Affairs in the State Department is in touch with us constantly. The representative has offices in the State Department. The UN representative is a cabinet member, unofficially but in practice. He was in the Nixon administration also; Henry Cabot Lodge in the Eisenhower administration also took orders from the president and not from the State Department. We had many experts come to the U.S. mission to the United Nations from the Department of State. There was constant interplay with the White House.

Ambassador Bennett also noted that while structure was important, the personality and the decision-making style of key policymakers are of major influence:

> We had Kissinger as secretary of state and Moynihan [Daniel Patrick Moynihan, ambassador to India (1973–74), permanent representative to the UN (1975–76) and U.S. senator (1977–)] as UN representative during my tenure, and they clashed. It was interesting. They each had respect for each other; Kissinger felt that Moynihan was his equal intellectually and politically. Kissinger wanted to be number one. I recall once that I had to make a decision on a vote and I could not reach him. He got angry but I was able to explain to him the situation.
>
> Moynihan, of course, was a controversial representative. He came to the UN during a period when we were on the receiving end of all the attacks and criticisms by the Third World and the Soviet Union. We were taking it. Moynihan was combative. He defended U.S. interests and U.S. motives. Then he conceived the idea of withholding money from countries who did not vote with us. This was difficult to do. He said things that needed to be said and certainly raised U.S. morale. However, he carried it too far and it became counterproductive. He came to the UN at the right time and left at the right time. He mirrored the feelings of many Americans who were tired of being kicked around.

Ambassador Bennett set forth his perspectives on the relationship between the United States and the Soviet Union as reflected in the United Nations:

> In the 1970s we were on the defensive on a lot of issues—the Soviets always wanted to shape a resolution to make us veto it, in order to embarrass us. Yet on some things we and the Soviets saw eye to eye. These included nuclear nonproliferation and the UN budget. Soviet diplomats in the UN were not at all international servants. Arkady Shevchenko [senior counselor, Soviet permanent mission to the UN 1963–70], who subsequently defected to the United States in 1979, estimated in his book [*Breaking with Moscow* (New York: Knopf, 1985)] that the number of Soviet intelligence operatives numbered in the hundreds. It is probably true, although I cannot say for sure.
>
> Andrei Gromyko [1909–1989; Soviet foreign minister, 1957–85] was a figure at the UN who was tremendously able, very dour, and had a phenomenal memory. We saw a lot of him at the UN. He might have even been difficult for the Soviets. He was very anti-Chinese, and did not respect them at all.

The locus of power most often lies with the permanent members of the Security Council; Ambassador Bennett discussed the role of its other members:

> Some nonpermanent members [of the Security Council] had great influence—Australia, for example. Also, Secretary of State Dulles wanted to

break deadlocks with votes in the General Assembly; in those days, that helped us. Therefore, U.S. efforts at coalition building were in the General Assembly, as opposed to the Security Council. The big debate was whether the Security Council should be enlarged. Maybe India, Brazil, or Japan should be members. Japan's status was talked about a lot. No resolution was brought into the open. But Japan had a lot of terms on the Security Council as a nonpermanent member; there was never any objection to the Japanese reelection. I suppose the rest of the Asians felt that Japan should be represented, as should India.

One of the international crises of the Nixon administration was the war between India and Pakistan in 1971, which led to the secession of the eastern portion of Pakistan and the formation of Bangladesh as a new state. Ambassador Bennett described the Nixon administration's experience with the United Nations at this time:

> In contrast to other cases when we could stop a war from breaking out, here we were not successful. India blatantly overrode. India is great on self-righteousness. They played a delaying game and went right ahead with their plans. The process has grown quite large. There is a lot of hypocrisy in the UN. They only consider Israel or South Africa "dangers" to the world. So many countries make speeches regarding these issues that the process becomes remarkably cumbersome.

Echoing such criticisms of the United Nations, Joseph Luns, who served as permanent delegate of the Netherlands to the United Nations between 1949 and 1952, set forth his views on the organization and its inherent limitations:

> In 1949 I read a newspaper headline saying that "yesterday the problems of Palestine were solved by the adoption by the Security Council of resolution such and such." I thought such an assessment might be somewhat optimistic, but the United Nations was a strange place. De Gaulle termed it the "so-called" United Nations. In the late 1940s you had the rather old and sort of pompous U.S. representative, Warren Austin, the senator; I still hear him saying, "I would like to urge upon the Jews and the Arabs to try to solve their difficult problems in a real Christian spirit." The Jews and the Arabs!
>
> The United Nations is an organization we should keep, but it has very little power. Once it made an important decision because the Russians made the mistake of boycotting the Security Council at the time of the Korean conflict.

As commander of UN Forces in Korea from 1976 to 1979, Gen. John Vessey described the structure of the United Nations Command:

There were two elements of the UN Command, and that was the 600,000-man armed forces of South Korea, the 42,000 Americans, and a platoon of British, Filipinos, Thais, and so on. There had been very little integration of Koreans with Americans. There were a few liaison officers and the UN Command, U.S. Forces Korea, Eighth Army—all one head-quarters and one staff. There were a few additions, the UN liaison officers of countries that were still involved, and a few Koreans. When I had my first meeting of the UN Command staff, there were probably three Koreans in the room. I asked the Americans, how many of you can ask your way to the men's room in Korean and to raise their hands if they could. There were three, and that was a sorry condition for an alliance operation where most of the alliance forces were from the other country. The Koreans had been trying to work for some time for more integration. Gen. Richard Stil-well [commander-in-chief, UN Forces, Korea, 1973–76] had worked for more integration, but there was much opposition on the American side.

On the subject of command structure, General Vessey stated:

In name, the commander, UN Forces Korea, really did not have opera-tional control of any of his U.S. forces. But in fact he did; U.S. forces were going to do what he wanted done; that was not as big a problem as the lack of integration. I told [the Koreans] that I would work toward an integrated command. Clearly, there needed to be some sort of integration. Then we got agreement from Washington to go ahead and work toward integration after the withdrawal announcement because, I think, the people in Wash-ington looked at it as sort of a sop to the Koreans to assuage their injured feelings. So we worked toward it, and in the fall of 1978 we actually orga-nized the activation ceremony of combined forces, and that has moved along reasonably well. A lot of good work had been done beforehand to lay the groundwork, like designing HANGUL—English teletype systems and so forth. But we got some impetus going in 1976–77.

I asked that a special language program be set up at the U.S. Armed Forces Language Institute, as well as study materials for us in-country, and we got Americans into the Korean Command and General Staff College and into the Korean military schools. They were some hardy pioneers, but it was amazing that we had not done it in all those years. But it was sort of that syndrome—that we were going to get out of there soon and that we do not belong there. The funny thing is that we got support for these pro-grams for all of the wrong reasons, those associated with withdrawal, but it worked out very well.

General Vessey had the task of managing yet another complex alliance relation-ship, in this case with the armed forces of the Republic of Korea.

It is a narrow beam to walk—that is, to maintain credibility on both sides when there are controversial issues between the United States and some of its allies. You see it in the NATO command from time to time, and you see it here. It calls for some understanding on the part of the political leadership in this country regarding the sort of box the commander is in. I just wanted to call attention to that problem because it is one that gave me a lot of sleepless nights making sure that I stayed on the beam so that I did not lose my credibility with the Korean government and people—that is a tough thing to do. One of the things that an American commander of allied forces has to remember is that he is in fact an American and that it is the security interests of the United States that he has to pay attention to.

Among the international issues in which the United Nations played a crucially important, and yet controversial, role was the Congo (now Zaire) crisis, which erupted shortly after the Belgian colony was granted independence in 1960. As U.S. ambassador to the Congo between 1962 and 1964, Edmund A. Gullion observed and participated in the decision-making process. He commented on the role played by the United Nations:

> The United Nations had an enormous stake in the Congo question. The entire United Nations Charter was questioned during the affair. If you look at the charter, it envisages a strong and active role for the UN. It is not simply the town meeting of the world. There is a strong element of sanctions and force as well. Once the UN embarked on what was an enforcement action, it would have been a severe moment if it had been defeated. The United States was one of the founding fathers of the UN. In the early 1960s it was viewed in the United States as a prime instrument for peace. So its failure would have been a blow to the organization and also to U.S. interests. The United States had given preference to the United Nations on the Congo question from a very early date. When Prime Minister [Patrice] Lumumba came to New York, he was told by Secretary of State [Christian] Herter to try the United Nations. After UN Secretary-General [Dag] Hammarskjöld's successful role in the Suez crisis, it was felt that the powers inherent in the position of the secretary-general could be used for a resolution of the conflict. At first the Soviet Union went along with it, but later its position changed.

Ambassador Gullion recounted the problems confronting the United States when he arrived in the Congo in 1961 and the efforts of the United Nations and its secretary-general, Dag Hammarskjöld.

> When I arrived in the Congo it was a very stormy time indeed between Operations Marthor [Hindu for *smash*] and Rumpunch. The consulate in Elisabethville was surrounded by Katanga leader [Moise] Tshombe's forces. Communications were very difficult during the first week. I had seen [Swedish diplomat Carl] Linner, who was then the head of United Nations operations [in the Congo]. He hinted at something when we talked,

but I had to go back to him to find out what it was. Linner then told me that an operation was planned to clean up some of the loose ends hanging over from Rumpunch. The idea was to expel the mercenaries who supported Tshombe's secession. United Nations forces had rounded up mercenaries and expelled some of them during Rumpunch, the first operation of that kind. Then the Belgians had interceded and offered to take care of the rest of it. However, they did not move out the rest of them, so Marthor was supposed to be extended.

United Nations Secretary-General Hammarskjöld had proceeded on his way to the Congo, still in a hopeful spirit. I am inclined to believe that he did not know that the Marthor operation was still in progress or the severity of it until he had his stopover in Accra [Ghana]. I would speculate that he expected a limited police action following the first operation. He was astounded when he got to Accra and discovered the scope of the fighting then in progress. I based that on the talk I had with him when he came to Leopoldville [later Kinshasa]. At first he refused to see me, because he was under great pressure from the British, from Minister of State for Colonial Affairs [George] Lansdowne, to end fighting in Katanga [province] and to prevent further operations. He thought that that was what I was going to say too. I had no such idea in mind, although the policy of our government, as I understood it, was to try to avoid excessive use of force. I had not gone to see him to ask for restraint. I talked to him, and he said he would go to talk to Tshombe at Ndola. His main concern at the time was the attitude of the Leopoldville government, which finally gave him clearance to meet Tshombe.

Hammarskjöld then proceeded there, using Swedish transport planes and pilots of private contractors. He flew to the meeting with Tshombe. The United Nations people on the spot, [Tunisian diplomat Mahmoud] Khiary, [Irishman Conor Cruise] O'Brien, and [Ghanian diplomat Robert] Gardiner, did not want him to do this. They thought it was really inappropriate and could enhance the status of Tshombe. The next day I had a telephone call from Linner, asking for help. He said that the secretary-general's plane had disappeared. It was difficult to find it because he filed—on purpose—a false flight plan. In any case, the route was very roundabout. The reason for this was just that Tshombe had obtained a single, armed, fighter-trainer jet aircraft, probably through the French Secret Service. At the time there were no other fighters, and Tshombe had dominated the air. I was very concerned when I heard the news from Linner, for humanitarian and other reasons. Should Hammarskjöld have died, this would open a constitutional crisis in the United Nations about his successor. The Soviet Union, having distrusted Hammarskjöld all along, had proposed the idea of a troika of general secretaries which would have paralyzed UN action —so the situation was urgent. I used a code in my emergency transmission to Washington that gave absolute priority to my message. All other traffic was driven off the air. Worldwide communications had actually stopped due to the priorities of that message.

We did our utmost to help in the search, although it was general United States policy not to be directly involved. But we sent down some of our attaché people—with blue [UN] berets—to find out what had happened. Their version was that Hammarskjöld's pilots had flown way over their maximum hours and were all tired. It was also said that the controllers at Ndola tower had gone off the job, because the plane had not arrived. In any case, our air attaché's view was that the pilots, not having gotten a clear vector into the airport, flew according to certain preestablished flight patterns in their approach to the airport but somehow got it wrong. It was a pilot error.

Hammarskjöld had brought with him some United Nations security guards who carried sidearms. Apparently some ammunition had gone off, which led to the theory of assassination; I do not believe that theory to be valid. In my view it was an accident. One of the curious things about it was that Hammarskjöld had strong premonitions about his flight. He was something of a mystic in that respect. He had spoken of the flight and he had a book on his bedside table in which he had underscored some passages in a manner that indicated a sense of fatality. His death led to an upsurge in United Nations activities. Equipment was more readily available. Up to that point there had been no United Nations fighter planes. After the accident, fighter planes were supplied by the Swedes and Ethiopians. Other materials also were more readily available.

Ambassador Gullion discussed perspectives that came to the fore in Washington in the immediate aftermath of the death of Secretary-General Hammarskjöld, together with the dangers and opportunities confronting U.S. policy and the United Nations operations in the Congo:

In the final analysis the ending of hostilities came about primarily by direct United Nations intervention. The fighting came to an end because the objectives of the United Nations had been obtained in that round. I was not particularly interested in ending the fighting. This was the point of contention between me and the government. There was always the hope, urged by most people in Washington, that we should try to get some type of coalition government together. It was only after some experience with Tshombe that I realized that this was not going to be possible unless there could be an element of compulsion. When the showdown came in the last round, people in Washington backed away from the use of force again. I objected to that.

The views in Washington generally were obscured by a misunderstanding as to the degree of violence that occurred. Washington looked on the matter as if we were dealing with a conventional war in Europe. It viewed it as if we were marching twenty thousand United Nations troops against a large number of Katanganese, or it was felt that the United Nations would not be capable of doing the job. In any case, heavy civilian losses were expected. This, of course, was all nonsense. I quickly learned that enormous gains could be made with only small investments in force. A small, disciplined unit can do enormous things in such circumstances. The opposition is largely untrained and has a short span of attention. I never anticipated any trouble at all if it would come to a final showdown. This was part of my disagreement with [Under Secretary of State for Political Affairs (1961–63)] George McGhee and Douglas MacArthur, and intermittently even Kennedy, who feared bloodshed.

There was an enormously effective Belgian propaganda organization headed by a Belgian, Michael Struelens, in the United States. He was able to paint a picture in the United States of atrocities committed by UN forces and vast bloodshed. There was also a great fear that there would be property damage to the mines. McGhee even came out to put handcuffs on me in respect to the use of force just before the final round. Personally we were friends, but I felt that he would undermine my approach to policy. In discussion with Gardiner, McGhee actually said that the United States would not support the UN forces if it really came to a showdown; this was intolerable to me.

My approach was in line with the U Thant plan. The plan was quite stiff. It provided for gradual sanctions to be applied against secessionist Katanga at specified points in time. The Swedes had proven that limited force could be employed without causing incidental damage. After Hammarskjöld's death they had sent a fighter unit. That unit took out the two Katangan planes in a very limited and precise surgical strike, showing that limited action indeed was possible. The U.S. population does not think of the United Nations as an organization that actually takes guns in its hands and really fights, in spite of the fact that UN units have been used for peacekeeping purposes many times. The United Nations is endowed with an enforcement capability, and there were enabling resolutions to that effect.

My general views about the United Nations started out rather naive. I had had an interest in the UN peace enforcement provisions from early on, and I studied the charter, which impressed me as a strong document at the time. I say naive because I had assumed that states had abandoned national sovereignty for the sake of collective security and a truly international body run by international civil servants. I soon found out that the United Nations is composed of individual states, and an opportunity presented itself to use it for our own purposes. UN policies coincided with ours, which was a united Congo. That corresponded to both a liberal and a conservative view at the time. The liberals wanted to encourage decolonization, and the conservatives wanted to prevent the former colonies from breaking up because a predatory power would pick up the pieces. To us, the idea to use the UN system as long as our interests paralleled seemed obvious. As long as this was the case we could use the United Nations without launching a great-power confrontation. When Lumumba visited the United States in 1960 and asked Secretary of State Herter for strong U.S. bilateral assistance to him, Herter referred him to the United Nations. Lumumba at first had high praise for this idea.

The United Nations could, in general, be persuaded to act in concert with the United States. In many ways the United Nations would not have been able to fulfill its mandate without our assistance, specifically in Kitona and during the last round of the conflict. Most of our efforts involved the United Nations. My own mission was rather small. There were limited things we could do on the spot. When the Soviets sent a medical mission to go up to Stanleyville, I concluded that the Soviets really were trying to bolster [Antoine] Gizenga through foreign representation. I persuaded local UN representatives to join me in frustrating that endeavor. The Soviets were delayed and the UN authorities kept them busy until they left without having achieved their purpose.

Ambassador Gullion briefly summarized lessons derived from his experience in respect to UN peacekeeping:

The biggest and most unfortunate lesson is that it can never be repeated. The circumstances were unique. Of course there was a crisis for the United Nations also, the financial crisis, the discussion about the replacement of the single secretary-general by a "troika." For the most part, we were able to see to it that the United Nations and the United States were marching toward similar goals. We were able to exert considerable influence. However, this will hardly be possible in the future. The UN forces, of course, were not always effective. Such was to be expected from a multinational enterprise without central staff, but the United States indeed appeared in good light because we supported the United Nations so strongly and successfully.

Part II
The Dynamics of American Domestic Politics upon National Security Decision Making

National security decisions are not made in a vacuum; factors both internal and external to a nation shape those decisions. Part II stresses the internal factors affecting decision making for the United States by probing executive-congressional relations, bureaucratic interaction dynamics, public opinion, and the media. Chapter 6 surveys the efforts of the executive branch to assert authority in national security policy over the legislative branch, while the latter tries to do the same. Thus, participants consider such issues as consultation, bipartisanship, oversight, and the extent of constitutional authority. In chapter 7, the attention shifts to bureaucratic interaction in Washington, D.C., or, more specifically, to the interplay of people in complex bureaucratic organizations where titles and positions are coveted. This chapter touches upon a variety of topics, including dealing with the Vietnam War, coping with bureaucracy, and making the transition from one president to the next—all viewed in relation to national security decision making. Last, chapter 8 delves into the interaction of public opinion and the media with decision making; here, participants speak about, among other things, the impact of the electoral process upon decisions and the media's broad influence upon foreign and domestic policy.

6
Executive-Congressional Relations

The relationship between the executive and Congress, based on the separation of powers and on checks and balances as set forth in the Constitution, has often been a source of frustration to both branches of government. It has led to confusion and bewilderment both at home and abroad. This chapter presents the perspectives of six decision-makers, all of whom served in the executive branch. Their observations, sometimes critical of Congress, provide insights into the process of relations between two of the three branches of government of the United States, and particularly cover executive branch consultation with Congress, bipartisanship in foreign policy, congressional oversight of the executive branch, the War Powers Act, the Clark Amendment, human rights and defense policies, congressional travel abroad, and special commissions. These observations furnish a necessary setting and context for the decisions and issues discussed in later chapters of this book. Gen. Andrew Goodpaster described the executive-congressional relationship as it evolved in the Eisenhower administration:

[Eisenhower] wanted to work with the Congress and did. It was very clear that he would never have something develop, as was charged to President Truman, that committed the United States without consultation with the Congress on action such as might involve a foreign commitment of force. The first thing he would want to do was to get congressional leaders to the White House. Here, oftentimes, you would see an interesting reversal. Where previously it had been their complaint that they had not been consulted, they would now be telling him, "Well, Mr. President, we look to you to make these decisions." On occasion, one had a very strong sense that they were quite anxious to get out the door. He would tell them that, no, this was a responsibility we would have to share—that it is a duty of the president, but that you must be part of this as well. I do not recall any occasion on which there was a charge of a failure of consultation on his part. He was, in fact, very determined to keep it always the other way.

General Goodpaster pointed out, however, that consultation did not always mean agreement:

> In a couple of areas [Eisenhower] was dissatisfied with the action of the Congress, and this was not necessarily the opposition party. On trade issues he had a very tough time, and that was especially so in his first administration—the first couple of years—when Congress was led by his own party. He felt that they had been in opposition so long that that was the only role they knew in respect to the president on issues of trade and the like. They had a very strong sense of the prerogatives of the Congress in controlling policy on trade, while the president, of course, felt this was a very important area of foreign policy as well.
>
> Another area in which it was difficult for him to get what he felt was needed was in the foreign assistance programs, particularly economic and technological assistance. That is one of the things he worked at the hardest. He felt that some of that opposition was really quite small-minded and simply unwilling to look to the larger issues that were involved. These, to him, were instruments by which the United States could build relationships that would be healthy and constructive with these emerging countries. Another area that he was keenly interested in was the U.S. Information Service—public diplomacy. Again, he felt that Congress was too niggardly in this and that as a result we were failing to put the positive part of our story across. Those were some of the main elements in his relations with the Congress.

General Goodpaster also noted that, for President Eisenhower, the military budget was an issue of particular contention with the Congress:

> There also came this business of the Congress and various congressional leaders pressing for military programs beyond what he thought was necessary. Initially, during the first Congress of his administration, there was challenge within his own party that the military budget was too high, and there was a lot of attack on that issue, but he felt that $35 billion was a good figure and held to it. But later the pressures came from the other side and generally from the other party. He liked to consult with such people as Sen. Arthur Vandenberg and Sen. Walter George. He spent a lot of time talking with them on foreign policy issues, often with John Foster Dulles also participating.

During the 1958 U.S. intervention in Lebanon, David Newsom was directed to conduct daily briefings for the Senate Foreign Relations Committee and the House Foreign Affairs Committee to keep them abreast of developments.

> Bill Macomber and I were the briefers for both of these sessions and that was a fascinating experience because you saw the difference in perspective

on foreign affairs between the House and the Senate. The House was concerned about domestic reaction and casualties, while the Senate took a broader view, except for [Sen. James William] Fulbright, who was angry with Dulles. I will always remember one episode in which either Bill or I had said something, and Fulbright said, "Well, all right, you have told us what you are doing. Now tell me this, what is Mr. Dulles's policy on this, if Mr. Dulles has a policy." Hubert Humphrey, whom I always found very fair and intelligent in a small executive meeting but uncontrollable when he got onto his political stage, spoke up and said, "Senator, this is not a hearing, this is a briefing, and I think we should let Mr. Macomber continue." At which point Fulbright got up and left, spoke to reporters outside, and said he would not be part of a star chamber procedure. Other than that, it was handled very well.

Robert McFarlane also highlighted the issue of executive branch consultations with Congress. The specific incident related concerns the Reagan administration's decision to intervene in Grenada in October 1983 and its efforts to involve Congress in this process.

We called together the [congressional] leadership for early evening about seven o'clock or eight o'clock that night, Monday night, and we only brought five people, three from the House—Tip O'Neill, and the majority leader, [James] Wright, and the minority leader, [Robert] Michel—and two from the Senate—Sen. [Robert] Byrd, the minority leader of the Senate at the time, and majority leader Howard Baker. It was interesting; not one of them supported [the decision to intervene in Grenada]. Howard Baker said, "I think you should do it." That is fair, he did support it, but he said, "You are just going to take a lot of heat here."

I stress that because it shows, I think, how secondary the notion of national perspective is among congressmen. They are so much more—understandably, I guess—responsive to their districts, to the pulse of people in the mainstream, and to their own sense of vulnerability to violence or criticism to violence, the loss of American lives and so forth. I do not think it was partisanship. I think it was just the nature of the political animal, that members of Congress are much more attuned to what they see as a sentiment of their people who vote for them, and much less to any concept of the national interest. It is not that they are unpatriotic, it is just that they do not have the scope to adopt a national perspective on national interests. I generalize, as if that is true with all of them, but it certainly was true that night.

The speaker of the House was violently opposed to this. Tip O'Neill said, "This is a nutty idea. You are going to get Americans killed down there. There is no real risk. This does not threaten American interests. This is crazy. We do not know what is going on. Do you really believe that there is a Cuban threat to that island? I don't believe it." He was very, very vocal—bitter in his opposition to it. Jim Wright [was] less vehement, saying, "No, I do not think you'd better do this, Mr. President. This is really one of those times you ought to pass, wait for it to get close to home.'' Bob Michel, who is the ultimate equivocator, will always tell you, ''Well, on the one hand it would be the right thing to do, on the other hand it would be risky. Therefore, I am not so sure I know.'' Senator Byrd was not superficial. He said, ''I understand what you are saying, but it does not seem to me as clear as you make it out to be, Mr. President, that we really have this kind of East-West threat at hand. I think you are overdrawing things here. I do not think you really ought to do it. The evidence is not persuasive to me that we have a problem here. The American vulnerability seems to be grossly inflated.'' Baker said, ''I think it is the right thing to do, Mr. President, but you are really going to take gas on this, there is not anybody going to support you on it, on the Hill. This is just going to be very, very unpopular because it is going to cost lives. It is not clear that it is all that important, and this notion that there is a Soviet menace on this little island in the Caribbean is just not credible.''

I make the point as a comment on the nature of the animal, but also as an object lesson in consultation, and the relationship between the two bodies in forging foreign policy. Consultation is or should not be a matter of rhetorical purpose; it should be to inform decision making, and it does, and it did in that case. It informed the president of the United States that Congress's sense of a national interest was quite different from his, but I think the reality of that very different perspective on the national interest is an untenable situation for a country which is a global superpower.

Dean Rusk, who served as secretary of state in the Kennedy and Johnson administrations, addressed the question of bipartisanship as a necessary basis for an effective foreign policy:

Bipartisanship is very important in the conduct of our foreign relations. We need to strive for a national party that will have broad support. Beyond that, the two parties do not have any distinct differences in their view of foreign policy. One thinks about the working relationship between President Truman and Republican senator Arthur Vandenberg, chairman of the Senate Foreign Relations Committee in the Eightieth Congress, or between Kennedy and Johnson and Senator Dirksen. It strengthens our relations with other countries to have our foreign policy on as broad a bipartisan basis as possible.

To that end, I spent a great deal of time with the Congress. I met with them very often. The problem is that the pressures of time upon senators and congressman are so great that it is difficult to get their time to sit down and discuss foreign policy at length. The separation of powers is central to our system of government, but the late Chief Justice Earl Warren said that if each branch of the federal government were to pursue its powers to the end of the trail the system would freeze up like an engine without oil. Cooperation is essential if we are to avoid the impasses which are principal threats in our system, but it can not always be obtained.

The Atlantic Alliance, Ambassador Tapley Bennett suggested, represents one key issue area in which the goal of bipartisanship, as well as executive-congressional cooperation, has usually been achieved.

NATO has been a largely bipartisan issue in the Congress, including the bipartisan feeling that the Europeans are not doing enough. I think this is sometimes exaggerated; after all, the Europeans do furnish the bulk of the forces and the people on the spot. I think that the Germans, with the offset program, pay their way. But there is a feeling in the Congress that Europeans need to do more. The truth is we all need to do more, and Europeans do give the impression of dragging their feet.

In General Goodpaster's view, Congress has moved into areas that appear to lie at the edge of, or even beyond, its prerogative:

In recent years the oversight function of the Congress has almost run wild—the growth in staff—and when these people learn that they have to earn their brownie points from their superiors, they do it by tinkering with something. They are constantly intruding into the executive branch under the cover of the oversight function of Congress. Sometimes that can be wasteful and troublesome. Every member of Congress tends to think of himself as a secretary of state. Congress is so powerful in the foreign policy field that it can usually find ways to give expression to its interests. Sometimes you get members such as Senators Vandenberg or Dirksen who understand that the powers were given to the Congress as a corporate body and not individually. They must make adjustments in their individual views to come to a congressional point of view. But sometimes some of them overlook that. But a great deal of foreign policy is determined by law. The first sentence of Article Two of the United States Constitution, which many people ignore, states that executive power shall be vested in the president—period. It is only the president who is elected by the people to execute the laws.

Ambassador Bennett also pointed to the growth in the numbers of congressional staff as a major source of the ability that Congress has acquired to influence U.S. foreign policy:

The enormous growth in staff structure on Capitol Hill has resulted in a staff of 20,000 people taking care of 535 members of Congress; it has grown out of all proportion. That many people make many problems among themselves. I believe that Congress would be more efficiently served with several thousand fewer people, but this country goes in for bigness, and our whole bureaucracy has expanded the same way. Secretary Shultz said, "Two assistant secretaries that I have to have close by are, first, the assistant secretary for public affairs who handles the press, and, second, the assistant secretary for congressional relations, because that is where I can get into trouble.''

In 1973 the Congress enacted the War Powers Act. Here, Gen. Brent Scowcroft, former military assistant to President Nixon and assistant for national security affairs in the Ford administration, described some of its effect:

> The War Powers Act was in train for several years, although it had gone through different kinds of approaches. One of the unfortunate aspects of the War Powers concept was that among the congressional leadership there were a lot of liberal Republicans, including Sen. Jacob Javits and Sen. John Sherman Cooper. This made it very, very difficult to try to deal with. I think in the larger sense that what we were seeing was one of the greater swings of the pendulum in the nation's history of executive-congressional relationships on foreign policy. Under the impetus both of Vietnam, especially the increasing congressional unease about Vietnam, and the weakness of the president as a result of the brewing Watergate problem, the War Powers Act became a reality. We tried to deal with our congressional friends on it before the president, of course, vetoed it. However, events were in full swing and its passage was preordained. It was one of the opening steps in a fairly constant series of attacks on presidential prerogatives on foreign policy, followed by increasing restrictions in Vietnam—a couple had preceded it—in foreign aid, in foreign military sales, and so on. The subsequent Greek-Turkish-Cyprus case and Angola exemplified instances where the presidency lost some of its strength and the Congress moved in to take it over. I think that since World War II—or since the outset of World War II—that Congress had seen a series of dynamic, activist presidents who took over more and more authority. The War Powers Act was a congressional reassertion of its role.

General Scowcroft suggested that the War Powers Act has had serious consequences for the United States in the conduct of foreign policy:

> I think one of the unfortunate things in looking at this in historical terms is that this period coincided in the Congress with a collapse of congressional discipline, if you will, and a fundamental change in the makeup of the Congress. As a result, the possibility of a reasonable and cooperative relationship with the Congress decreased at the very time that it became more important. This also coincided with the rise in the power of congressional staffs and the decline in the power of the committee chairmen. Together, these factors have contributed to making things particularly difficult in the area of foreign policy formulation and legislation.

Similarly, Richard Allen, who served as President Reagan's first national security adviser, offered a harsh assessment of the role that the Congress has taken upon itself in the field of foreign affairs:

> After the Clark Amendment [which cut off U.S. aid to the National Union for the Total Liberation of Angola, or UNITA, forces in Angola], the Congress had become so used to usurping foreign policy functions, even micromanagement functions, that it was very difficult to reverse. I think Reagan reversed it, to some extent. The early years of the Reagan administration demonstrated that it could be reversed with a working majority in one House and a relatively clear vision on the part of the president; but Vietnam redefined the balance. I suppose that this power will ebb and flow, but I do not see much ebbing of it now. The micromanagement, the invasion of what was traditionally thought to be the prerogative of the executive branch, will last until laws are passed that will change the situation. This is a deeply disturbing fact of life. While the executive can and does arrogate many powers to himself in the field of foreign and national security policy, he is going to have to rely on at least the cooperation and tolerance of the Congress for much of what he wants to do. Look at the reporting requirements on covert actions and look at the further damage that has been done by the lunacy of the Iran-contra scandal. In the next ten years I would not look for a reversal of that.

Ambassador David Newsom, under secretary of state for political affairs under President Carter, offered yet another perspective on the role of Congress in the foreign policy process:

> The human rights policy of the Carter administration was not just based on the inclination of Jimmy Carter. It was based on the eleven or so bits of legislation that had been enacted by the Congress which required attention to human rights circumstances in economic aid, foreign military sales, and export credits. Warren Christopher [deputy secretary of state, 1977–81], who takes the law very seriously, felt that whatever the inclinations of the administration were, the laws on the books had to be taken seriously and administered faithfully.
>
> This approach was reinforced by the transfer of a number of the staff people who had worked on this legislation in the House to the staff of the Human Rights Bureau in the State Department. So within the department a strong advocacy group existed. Some of this group clearly had an agenda of their own which was to get rid of the Shah of Iran, to get rid of [Philippine president Ferdinand] Marcos, and to get rid of [Nicaraguan president Anastasio] Somoza. They sought to block every transaction that, in their view, would seem to strengthen these rulers. Argentina, of course, was another area of contention. People in the geographic bureaus were reluc-

tant to raise the issues to the Christopher Committee; they tried to work them out at the lower levels at the department. The result was that when I came into the State Department I think there were some fifty unresolved disputes between the Human Rights Bureau and the geographic bureaus which I had to work with Warren Christopher. All of these did not get resolved, but one of these was the question of riot control equipment for Iran, which, in the middle of 1978, was a very lively issue within the department. I emerged as a kind of symbol of the division within the Carter administration over whether the shah was worth saving or not. A smaller group of three officers went out to Iran in the summer of 1978 not long after I came back. They returned with a very gloomy picture of what was happening in Iran and the feeling that we should not be encouraging the shah to crack down on his population. You can imagine that that was not a message that was well received. So you had this current of concern about what was happening, in part based on intelligence and in part based on the general sentiment about the shah, among this human rights group that had come from the Hill.

Drawing especially upon his experience as chairman of the Joint Chiefs of Staff, Gen. John Vessey described what he regarded as one of the deficiencies of the decision-making process for defense policy: the inability within the present system to assess the results of policies pursued and choices made.

The biggest single weakness in our overall system is that we spend 90 percent of the time on the front end of the process—that is, deciding what to build or what forces to have, or what budget to have. But we spend very little on reviewing, what did we get for what we decided to do? How far along did we get? As a result, we are always disconnected. We think this year's budget is going to get us this far, but the Congress makes sure that it will not get us that far. Then human inefficiency reduces it a little farther. So we are laying out the next years and the following years from starting points that we are never going to reach. Thus there is not sufficient feedback in examination of "where did we get?" In some cases we produced far more than we expected. In some cases we produced less.

This is one of the problems where lack of progress still looms in the minds of many congressional people and the public as a big issue. Actually, far more has been done than has been recognized, even though we are not inhibited by lack of room for more improvement. The Packard Commission [that is, the President's Blue Ribbon Commission on Defense Management, chaired by David Packard] rightly recognized that it is in procurement, the clarification of requirements, and in the overall relationship between the executive and legislative branch where real progress needs to be made. The number of committees and subcommittees of the Congress that examine the defense budget has grown astronomically. The number of congressmen who examine the defense budget has grown, even though the defense budget as a percent of the federal budget and as a percent of GNP has not grown. The defense budget remains the largest part of the federal budget that the Congress feels free to dabble with, and therefore it gets an awful lot of attention. Clarification of responsibilities in the Congress, laying out and agreeing with the executive branch on where we want to go, is sorely required.

We need to have common language for the defense program and the defense budget. If we had one set of language right from the very beginning—do away with the line-item appropriations that the Congress has, and have the Congress and the Defense Department agree on a mission-basis budget—we would save an incredible number of staff officer hours, and we could probably organize another division, or air wing, or something, with the staff officers saved.

Also concerning defense policy formulation and Congress, Sen. Sam Nunn has striven to achieve a more equitable formula for transatlantic burden sharing. In 1984 he introduced legislation the effect of which would have been to reduce U.S. ground force levels in the central European region unless the NATO-European allies increased the levels of their military stockpiles. The reasoning was that if Allied armies could fight for only several days because of ammunition and other shortages, U.S. forces would be unable by themselves to sustain a defense against Warsaw Pact forces. The result was a decision by the NATO-European allies to add to their stockpiles in order to enhance NATO sustainability. Ambassador Bennett commented on these developments:

Nunn's initiative was different from [Ambassador and former senator Mike] Mansfield's some years before, in that Senator Nunn said from the beginning he meant to strengthen NATO, not to harm it. He was trying to prevent NATO from going in a direction he thought was wrong, because the backlash to that would result in really damaging things being done to NATO. However, his proposal to withdraw American forces on a graduated scale from Europe was wrong in the sense of the effect it would have on our relations with proud nations. We told him so, and he said from the beginning, "I do not intend to win this; I have raised it but I do not mean it to pass."

Once you got into the give and take of the legislative process, in my opinion, Sam Nunn wanted to win. We in the administration waged a first-rate battle on it, including calls to individual senators from the president. It got up to that level as an issue. Sam Nunn said to me afterwards, in a laughing way, "I told you I did not want to win; you did not have to steamroll me with fourteen votes"—which is what our margin was in the Senate vote; those fourteen votes were not achieved without a lot of effort. However, he did not make the same proposal the next year. Indeed his subsequent initiative, setting aside $100 or $200 million—I believe it shrank to about 93 million in the actual process—for joint NATO projects is one of the most constructive things done in years. I found when I later visited NATO that they were busy at work on six alliance initiatives that the Nunn money will go to support, so there is general action on that and even some enthusiasm for it. Senator Nunn is doing exactly what he said he wanted to do: strengthening NATO with a certain amount of stick along with the candy. I am all in favor of that.

Despite the tensions and inconsistencies, however, Ambassador Tapley Bennett, who served as assistant secretary of state for congressional relations between 1983 and 1985, contends that while the administration might not always see eye to eye with the Congress, the relationship is more often than not a symbiotic one. Here he addresses the issue of congressional travel abroad:

> At NATO we had a lot of visitors from the Congress, both senators and representatives. Once, the Senate majority leader, Howard Baker, came with a group, and we all went together to Germany to visit a Pershing missile site. They wanted to see things on the ground; I happen to agree with that and I have always been in favor of congressional travel. It can make a lot of headaches for the person on the spot or the mission on the spot— because they can be very demanding and their staff members can be even more demanding—but travel enlarges congressional understanding of these very delicate and complicated issues. I think the pluses vastly outweigh the minuses for members of Congress going abroad. Members of Congress not only visit NATO headquarters frequently, but they are also active at Atlantic Treaty Association meetings and in the North Atlantic Assembly [NAA], which is made up of parliamentarians from NATO countries.
>
> Nobody, including our NATO-European allies, fully understands the role of Congress in American foreign policy. Various presidents have had trouble assimilating the Congress into their calculations. Certainly the Europeans do not understand it as well as they should, although I would say they probably understand our congressional scene as well as any foreigners do because they study it intensively and their ambassadors in Washington certainly cultivate individual members of the Congress, as they should.

Finally, R. James Woolsey (under secretary of the Navy, 1977–79, and delegate-at-large to the Soviet Arms Talks, 1983–86) discusses the role of special commissions or committees established by the executive branch, with particular emphasis on their possibility for use in a "matchmaking role" with Congress. He specifically refers to the Scowcroft Commission, which was set up early in the Reagan administration to examine U.S. nuclear force modernization issues:

The executive branch might pull [special commissions chartered to produce reports] together because the White House does not want to do some work itself and cannot seem to get a recommendation it likes out of a cabinet department (which is what I think Secretary of Defense Weinberger felt was going on with both the Scowcroft and Packard Commissions). So the cabinet department that is chiefly concerned tends to be resistant to them. Sometimes [special commissions] may be pulled together to give a genuinely objective outside scientific opinion on a subject that crosses jurisdictional lines and over which cabinet departments may even disagree or just have not been able to get organized. Sometimes [special commissions] may be pulled together because the talent of government people is insufficient due to the difficulty of getting good people into the government. [Finally,] sometimes [these commissions] are pulled together to serve a "matchmaking" function, to broker deals between different parts of the government.

I do not know why the Scowcroft Commission came about; it was Robert McFarlane's original idea and I do not know how McFarlane pictured those reasons he had in mind when he put it together. What ultimately happened was that we essentially brokered a deal between the Democrats in the House—or at least enough of them—and the Department of Defense to get the country back into the business of modernizing its ICBM force. The Scowcroft Commission, more than Packard, was involved in operations and analysis, but it was also coming up with solutions which we felt we had to take the initial steps to implement or nothing much would happen. That was essentially this matchmaking role, going back and forth between the boy's family and the girl's to arrange a marriage. We did a lot of brokering.

Part of the down side may be that [special commissions] come out with recommendations that are impractical because they are put together by people who do not have to implement them. Part of the danger is that they will not take account of all the things a government has to take account of, such as cost. If you select the personnel well, then those are probably the only two *major* risks. I think the advantages are just like those of a matchmaker who has to deal with a situation in which the girl's family wants to marry off its oldest daughter and the boy's family wants to marry off the number-two and ugliest son; who will come up with a marriage in which the oldest son marries the number-two daughter? It is not exactly the marriage that either family had in mind, but at least it is a marriage. In a similar fashion, on the Scowcroft Commission, we came up with a solution which neither the Democrats in the House nor the Department of Defense would have regarded as their first choice and neither knew it, but we came out with what was probably the second choice of both of them (their first choices were completely incompatible with one another). Sometimes you can get something put together with this brokering function that you cannot otherwise.

You must be pretty brave or pretty senior to go to Congress and start playing with wildly different ideas. Congress has a little more flexibility, but the executive branch has difficulty exploring new possibilities with the Congress that depart from current policy. A senior official who has the president's confidence can tell the president he is going to the chairman of the House Armed Services Committee to discuss such and such. Then he can ask, "Mr. President, what do you think?" The president might say, "Well, okay, but just don't get us committed."

7
Bureaucratic Interaction
in Washington, D.C.

very president comes to office with not only a policy agenda but also a decision-making style. Although each must work within an established constitutional framework and within the organizational and bureaucratic structures in existence, the opportunity exists for the president to use and to shape such entities in support of the administration's priorities. How the policy machinery will be employed depends to some extent on those whom the president selects as his key advisers and on their ability to work with the president, with the Congress, with each other, and with those below them. In this chapter, key figures from several administrations offer perspectives on dealing with the Vietnam War, Henry Kissinger's approach to the bureaucracy, transitions from one presidency to the next, the "lunch of principals" bureaucratic phenomenon, Reagan's national security decision-making structure, and intrigue in the Reagan administration, with emphasis on the problem of "interposition." On the management of the Vietnam War, Adm. Thomas Moorer discussed the widening divergence between the executive and the Congress:

> Nixon asked me how long it would take to make plans to mine Haiphong Harbor. I said, "Zero time." "Will you assure me it will not leak?" Nixon asked next. I assured him it wouldn't, and it did not leak. That decision was made by the president due to the fact that the North Vietnamese had violated all of their agreements and had no intention of stopping the war. Another decision made upon the same lines was the Christmas bombings in 1972. That was made in a very small group. Again, things are different when you do not have public support for managing a crisis. As you recall, there were constant demonstrations. The country was in a state of near anarchy. It got to the point when certain things expected to cause tremendous press reaction would be scheduled a day after *Time* magazine went to press. It was really a wild time. I remember very clearly decisions which were not made by formal means. I think that was a different kind of environment we were operating in; there were different congressional and public attitudes. When we first started, Congress said, "Get in and win." When they saw we were not going to apply much force they

said, "Win or get out." The next phase was "get out," which they enfe
by cutting off the money. In the process we sacrificed the South Vietna
to the Communists.

Henry Kissinger enjoyed both with President Nixon and President I
a professional relationship that is perhaps unique in the annals of Ame
statecraft. Yet the decision-making styles, as well as the substantive b
ground in foreign policy, of Nixon and Ford stood in sharp contrast to
other. Nixon brought to the White House an exceptional level of knowledge
experience in the field of foreign affairs; Ford has neither. Brent Scowc
from his vantage point first as deputy and then as the national security adv
both observed and contributed to the formulation and conception of for
policy in the Nixon and Ford administrations.

I think Henry Kissinger's greatest strength lies in the fact that he has a
strategic mind. There are not many like him in the country, with the ability to see events and patterns not as disparate events but in a comprehensive whole, and to plan their reaction to individual events in relation
to their contribution to where you wish to end up a year, two years, three
years down the line. I think this is a very unusual ability, and Henry
Kissinger has it. However, in order to develop that kind of a strategy, he
did turn to what, by and large, you might call a secretive method of operation; he did not try to clarify for other people all the threads of his strategy. Consequently, he aroused some antipathy toward himself.

His relationship with Nixon was a complex one. He and the president
had the same kind of personality and tended to work together effectively.
President Nixon also knew pretty much where he wanted to go; Kissinger
knew exactly how to get there. Nixon knew what he wanted, but not
exactly how to get it. Kissinger put the fire in the engine, if you will, to
move Nixon's thoughts. Nixon sought out a few alternatives to test ideas
with, but they were all very individual, very personal initiatives. The two
of them made quite a team, and had a relationship whereby each one
respected the other's intellectual ability greatly, but it was always a difficult relationship and I was frequently in the middle.

When Ford came in, the process changed not in appearance but in
substance significantly. Ford is a very different type of personality. First
of all, he had little background in foreign policy. He had some in national
security policy—he had been on the Armed Services Committee of the
House, and the Appropriations Committee—so he knew the budget aspect
of foreign and national security policy. He was very much a man of the
Congress with a very short-range outlook and looked at most difficult
issues to see where there are the elements of compromise—the typical sort
of legislative approach that you would expect from a House minority
leader. Unlike Nixon, he was a novice in dealing with Henry Kissinger in
an intellectual sense. He did not disagree; he just did not know fundamentally enough to deal with Kissinger intellectually, as Nixon had. But he

also liked to make decisions in a more open debating forum and had a wide circle of friends whom he consulted on various issues. He tended to use me not as a foil to Henry Kissinger but as a constraining influence on some of Henry's flamboyance and rhetorical excesses. He relied frequently on me to tell him where Henry was really going.

ımenting on the "dual hat" position in which Henry Kissinger retained the tion of national security adviser for several months after becoming secretary tate, Scowcroft contended,

The two-hat situation was never a reality in practice because what in fact happened was that gradually I took over more and more of the NSC operation, and Henry tended to concentrate on the State Department. As one of the obvious contrivances, Henry still chaired the subcommittee meetings as the national security adviser. He got his preparation and briefing for the NSC meetings from the NSC rather than from the State Department, although obviously he gave them from the State Department institutional view in the meeting. He did not do that after the first three or four times; it was awkward.

After Kissinger lost his second hat, he developed a confidence in me and with Ford. There was a lot of pressure again from the political types to respond to the Reagan charge that Kissinger was the president for foreign policy and to demonstrate that President Ford did not rely exclusively on Henry Kissinger, which was true. Thus, there was a lot of pressure to put me on the Sunday talk shows. I told the president that I would do whatever he wanted, but I thought it would be counterproductive. To Ford's great credit (politically it would have been very advantageous for him to have me play a more visible role), he continued to leave Kissinger unrivaled in the public eye, and he did that at some political cost to himself.

Ambassador David Newsom held numerous official appointments in the . Foreign Service; in his three decades of service he observed a total of eight ınistrations come and go.

My recollection of the transition from Johnson to Nixon was that it was a very professional transition. There was a recognition that the people in the Johnson administration had things to pass on to the new administration regarding both people and issues. There was a considerable exchange and briefing of operational people as one moved out and the other moved in, in part because I think there were still people of the immediate postwar generation who moved in and out of the administrations and who spoke to one another and who had been in government before and had experienced moving back into government. Then there was a respect for the professionalism of the career people in government, as well as a recognition of the complexity of the problems that the United States faces. The first real change in the transitional relationships occurred during the Ford-Carter period during which the Carter people, many of whom were new to government and were, in their own way, ideological, did not want to hear much from the Ford people about what went on. They had their own ideas.

Newsom recounts a similar phenomenon between the Carter and Reagan administrations:

When I would talk to people in the new Reagan administration about the transition, saying, "Well, why don't you do it this way," they answered that "this is not the way the Carter people handled us when he first came to office." What appeared to be the case was the previous transition from Republican to Democrat affected the subsequent one of Democrat to Republican. Also affecting the Carter-Reagan situation was the fact that in the Reagan group a substantial number of people who, both on political grounds, because they felt Carter had made a mess of things, and ideological grounds, wanted to have no identification with anything that Carter did. The Reagan people went so far as to refuse the opportunity to be briefed on what the Carter administration had done.

According to Ambassador Newsom, positions taken by presidential candidates during their campaign do not necessarily provide an adequate basis for policy once they are in office. Moreover, decisions taken even during the transitional period after the election but before the inauguration of the new president may come later to be rejected and even reversed.

Some members of the Reagan team also did some overseas traveling, conveying messages about what the Reagan administration was going to be doing in southern Africa and Latin America. As events turned out, that first transition team group represented the Reagan campaign positions but not necessarily the positions of the new administration in office. As a result, I would strongly suggest to any new administration that the president appoint his principal cabinet officers, particularly in the foreign affairs field, the day after the election, or as soon thereafter as possible so that you don't have a period in which there are people speaking for a future administration who have never conferred with the future secretary of state or the future secretary of defense. In traveling, fanning out around the world, the Reagan people gave an impression of what the new administration was going to do in certain areas. In some cases these positions came back to haunt the new administration. It was not until about the nineteenth of December that Haig was appointed, after which he threw out the whole transition team. Another factor affecting the transition was the mistrust by the Reagan people of the personnel who had worked for Carter, including the professional and career Foreign Service officers.

This had a devastating effect on the transition process. About two weeks before the Reagan administration came in, a directive went out from Richard Allen's office that no presidential appointee of the Carter administration was to be at his or her desk on the twentieth of January. Now in the State Department, unlike most of the other executive departments, there are a lot of professionals who are presidential appointees at the assistant secretary and under secretary level. I went to Al Haig and told him that you could not operate the State Department if you remove all of the professionals from the positions that they now hold. So he took the list of everybody who was in the department at that time in a presidentially appointed position and sent it to Dick Allen. It came back with three names deleted and all the rest were permitted to stay. They were: Bill Bowdler, the assistant secretary for Inter-American Affairs; Jim Cheek, one of his principal deputies; and Peter Tarnoff, the executive secretary of the department, who was a professional, but was part of the unpleasant transition in 1976.

Only after a new administration actually establishes itself in office does it become apparent which of its members will emerge as influential decision makers. Differing capabilities, personalities, and styles—not to mention bureaucratic structure—shape relationships between the president and his key advisers. Ambassador Newsom explains:

Zbigniew Brzezinski [national security adviser, 1977–81] was a natural NSC adviser; he not only had his own personal predilections regarding how policy should be made, particularly where it related to the Soviet Union, but he also was conscious of protecting the president's domestic flank. To some extent he was correct in that because one of Carter's great weaknesses in the American political scene was the impression he gave that he did not fully understand the Russians. Brzezinski was conscious of that and therefore emphasized his views in this area. Brzezinski was in a primary position both because of the absences of the secretary of state (on Capitol Hill and abroad) and because of the NSC machinery, which allowed him to seize a large part of the action.

David Aaron [Brzezinski's deputy at the NSC], Frank Carlucci [deputy director, CIA, 1978–81], Bob Komer [Adviser to the secretary of defense for NATO affairs, 1977–79] in the Defense Department, and I worked closely together on a number of matters. One bureaucratic phenomenon is the "lunch of principals" where three or four principals get together for lunch, sometimes without note takers and without papers. This used to happen every Tuesday or Thursday involving Harold Brown [secretary of defense, 1977–81], Zbig Brzezinski, and Cyrus Vance [secretary of state, 1977–80], during which time they sorted out problems and prepared for the Friday breakfast with the president. It was sometimes necessary for Carlucci, Aaron, Komer, and me to get together to negotiate out what the three at lunch had really said to one another because they occasionally reported back somewhat different versions of the conversation. So there was a very good working relationship at our level and in certain other geographic areas, although not in all. In Soviet and Eastern European affairs, Marshall Shulman inside the State Department and Brzezinski and people around Brzezinski dealing with Europe in the NSC had quite different ideas. There was a very good relationship on Middle Eastern affairs. The relationship was less good in Latin American affairs. This reflected the ideological differences between Brzezinski and Vance on how to deal with Central America. So the relationship was mixed but not totally adversarial.

Recalling the first weeks of the Reagan administration, Ambassador Newsom gives his perspective on Alexander Haig's first National Security Decision Directive, or NSDD-1:

> There was the famous memorandum by Haig concerning the duties of the secretary of state; Haig drafted, or had drafted, a memo which was to be a presidential directive. The president presumably would issue it after the inauguration. Its thrust was to bypass the NSC in policymaking through the creation of two interagency groups. One was to deal with national security policy, chaired by the deputy secretary of defense, and the other was to deal with foreign policy, chaired by the deputy secretary of state. There were several defects in this which we pointed out to Haig at the time. The first related to the lack of a mechanism to decide what was a national security problem and what was a foreign affairs problem. For example, was the NATO INF [intermediate-range nuclear forces] issue a different national security problem or a foreign affairs problem? With two different individuals like Frank Carlucci, then deputy secretary of defense, and William Clark, then deputy secretary of state, the struggle over who gets that particular responsibility would be a very uneven one. With these personalities the role of the State Department in the conduct of foreign affairs was not likely to prevail. Secondly, there was no provision in the memorandum for crisis management. This issue came up later when [then] Vice President Bush put in his bid for responsibility for crisis management. The third problem was the memorandum itself; you do not seize power in the bureaucracy by using pieces of paper—you issue the pieces of paper after you have seized power. I was surprised Haig did not recognize that. My conjecture is that all of Haig's principal nonmilitary experience in the bureaucracy had been in the White House. He had been in a position where if you got the president to sign a piece of paper it had the force of a writ throughout the bureaucracy. He did not see the difference between his generating a memo as a cabinet officer outside the White House and someone who can generate a piece of paper under the umbrella of the presidency. There is a big difference; I do not think he saw how much of a transition he made away from the White House. The chief of staff to the president could use this device, but the secretary of state could not.

Richard Allen, national security adviser to President Reagan in the first year of his administration, summarized the National Security Decision Directive (NSDD) debate within the White House staff:

Just like any agreement that is signed, it will only be as good as the intent behind it. NSDD-1 would not have been workable. NSDD-1 was almost 100 percent the work of Haig and the State Department in its original draft. I let him do this because I knew what was in his mind and I knew it would not fly. In the spirit of the new collegiality, I thought the best solution was to let some of my colleagues have some exposure to what was on Al Haig's mind. Al and I had talked during the transition, and he had showed me various drafts but never left with me his ideas on NSDD-1. Now recall that Al believes himself to have been given the charter for everything outside of the three-mile limit. This was his understanding; this was the understanding that he asserts in his book [*Caveat: Realism, Reagan and Foreign Policy* (New York: Macmillan, 1984)]. In point of fact, he campaigned actively for the job of secretary of state with that idea in mind. He thought that to make it all fit together he would have to have his version of how things were to be organized. Well, they would have worked only his way, and they would have worked to the detriment of any president. So, recognizing how far apart he was from the real world, I decided that the best thing to do would be to call together Jim Baker [chief of staff, 1981–85] and Ed Meese [counselor for the president, 1981–85; attorney general, 1985–88]. They had been named members of the NSC— why, I am not entirely certain. I was not terribly opposed to it, though, because I did not think that either had much to give substantively, but on the other hand Ed Meese did have great powers of summation and analysis. This is something of great value to a president. Baker would probably have some spin, looking at foreign policy or national security issues, that while nonsubstantive might either make it a heftier initiative or stop us from a mistake. There is never anything wrong with roundtabling an idea. So my view was to bring them into the office immediately following the inauguration. We went into the White House to have some pictures taken in the Oval Office with the president. This was Meese, Baker, [Deputy Chief of Staff Michael] Deaver, [Press Secretary James] Brady, and I. Then I said to Baker and Meese that we had to get together, so we went out into the front room, which had been the office of the national security adviser but which Meese had taken over, and we sat around a round table that was there.

Secretary Haig then came in and presented his draft of NSDD-1. I had copies made, and he thought we were going to get this thing signed off. Well, immediately his motives were suspect. Why should this have to be signed off by chief assistants to the president just hours after the inauguration when it easily could have been taken up the next morning if it were so important, or the next afternoon? In other words, what was so important about it? So both Meese and Deaver became highly suspicious of the motives, and I just sat there waiting for someone to speak. They then read it through and Baker said, "Why, this is preposterous. This would give you charge of virtually everything in the government." Al said, "That is the understanding we had, the president and I." I said, "No, that's not the understanding," and Meese said, "No, that's not the understanding at all." Haig then became very agitated and said, "Well, this is the only way it can work," and Meese, Baker, and I said, "That's not so either because there are lots of ways to make things work in the government, and we know a little bit about it too." [Haig] said, "I know exactly how it is supposed to be structured and this is the way that will bring about the finest results." We simply said, "This is not the time to go into it. We will look at it and get back to you shortly."

Well "shortly," as it turned out, was a whole year. That was due to Ed Meese's never being able to find time, and it was not important to me because all that was important was that the paper flow went the way that I wanted it to. It did not matter who was in charge of *x* or *y* or *z*. What was important was that we got going. We had deliberately decided that foreign policy decisions would be deemphasized publicly and carried on privately. Soon we learned, however, with a secretary of state whose orientation is essentially a public one, private execution [of policy] becomes difficult.

Mr. Allen went on to express his regret in the delay over a response to NSDD-1:

So it is lamentable that NSDD-1 in some version was never signed off as it should have been, in some form, in the first weeks of the administration. That would have been an orderly progression for it. Had Al been sensible instead of trying to lunge for the full dollop of authority that he felt he needed to be secretary of state on the afternoon of the inauguration, had he been more judicious or circumspect in his planning, he would have called an NSC meeting or sought an early meeting with the president and with others of us who were concerned present; and provided us with a paper of it in advance and let us have a chance to study it in its full detail, discuss it internally, and then come to a conclusion obviously after adjusting the paper. This demand that was presented by Al in the name of his new-found authority as the "vicar of foreign policy" was the first in a series of events that eventually led to enormous distrust of him and consequently to his downfall as secretary of state.

President Reagan came to office with a series of goals for domestic, foreign, and defense policy. In the actual detailed implementation of policy, Mr. Reagan relied heavily on his subordinates. Richard Allen observed,

[James] Baker brought no immediate strengths to the NSC process other than those that I have described. I cannot think of any instances in which he intervened to try to sway policy in one direction or another, because he was essentially value-free in this regard. He is not a man motivated by strong policy considerations, but more so by considerations of political success—and there is nothing wrong with that. That perspective can be a worthy one in the national security process. You do not have to have a license to practice foreign policy, nor do you have to have an accumulation of degrees to be able to come to some decisions about it, because if you took a look at our presidents over a long period of time you would see that they were not very well qualified, but after all they are the chief arbiters of what policy is going to be.

Recalling Edwin Meese when he served as counselor (a special adviser to President Reagan), Allen said:

Meese on the other hand . . . possessed two things: one, a wonderful insight on how Ronald Reagan arrives at a decision and how he wants to exploit the process of collegiality in trying to get the best ultimate result put up to him for decision; and two, his powers of summation. Meese could listen to the drivel of an argument for an hour and neatly summarize it in terms Ronald Reagan liked to hear, and Meese never failed to take that initiative. I did it myself on many occasions, but since my job in the NSC was to run the meeting as the honest arbiter or broker, I limited myself to doing that. The summations that I would make would generally be those at the beginning of the meeting, summarizing the arguments of various cabinet members and then writing this up. Whether it was in accord with Meese's summation or not was not particularly important. But these gifts Meese had were brought to bear in that process, and therefore he was an asset to the national security process.

Nevertheless, recounts Mr. Allen, the organizational structure within the White House established early in the Reagan administration was detrimental to the effective operation of the national security adviser.

The imposition of Meese between myself and Martin Anderson [assistant to the president for policy development, 1981–82] and the president was a terrible mistake; and it was something that we did not expect when we accepted the appointment in our respective capacities of national security adviser and domestic policy adviser. It happened between the time of our appointment and the beginning of the administration. Our view was that we had Ed Meese on our side. We had, after all, worked with Ed Meese, not for him, for years, and both Marty and I enjoyed a rapport and an informal one with Ronald Reagan that was highly successful for our purposes, including the capability of calling him at any time, directly; we went through no channels. When I was asked and accepted to serve in the administration, I assumed it was going to be just the same, but then you see this curious system of having Baker, with his deputy Deaver, and Meese all involved in things—[this] was what complicated the entire process. It was very interesting how it happened.

We considered Meese an enormous blocking back who would clear any pathway to the president for us so that we might get our job done. Meese, on the other hand, decided that he was going to become czar of policy, all policy—domestic, foreign, space, and everything else—because he believed that was the role that best suited him as counselor to the president. What happened was that he was simply inundated in paper and bureaucracy; he had no idea really of how Washington works. He was from California, and even though California is a very big state and Ed Meese is a very able guy, not even Ed Meese, based on his California experience and his own natural ability, could cope with this. So he made the mistake of blocking access to the president. Now this does not mean that I did not have independent access to the president, because I did, whenever I wanted it. The problem was Meese always wanted to be there. He had an insatiable desire to be there and when he was there, Baker had to be there, and then even Deaver would come into some of the sessions. This meant you already had five people involved, and thus the ordinary national security briefings that ought to be conducted by the national security adviser for the president (and at maximum the vice president, when he wanted to sit in) soon grew in size.

This transformed the very nature of the morning briefings, and diminished the value to the president:

The process of briefings in the morning even became group therapy sessions in the following way. Meese would want to come in and listen to the briefing. That would bring Baker, and then Deaver would come in so he would not miss anything, and then the vice president, and the vice president's chief of staff, Adm. Dan Murphy, wanted to be in the briefings. Then after that, Secretary of State Haig wanted to be in the briefings, and he tried to use the briefings to hang around after they were over to have a word with the president on the side to try to move something through. Meese did not want that to happen. No one wanted that to happen. The president was very uncomfortable when Haig would try to do this. Pretty soon, [CIA Director] Bill Casey wanted to come in and pretty soon the secretary of defense [Caspar Weinberger], so what you had was a cast of thousands coming in to what essentially should have been a briefing for the president himself. Haig became so insistent that when he was not around he would send Bill Clark [deputy assistant secretary of state, 1980–81]. Clark had an easy working relationship with the president but did not contribute very much. What then transpired was that in order to get rid of this, in order to get [Haig] out of the briefing, we would simply announce that they were no longer being conducted at 9:15; but they were conducted—they were just taken off the schedule.

This caused confusion both inside and outside the administration, as Allen relates:

Zbigniew Brzezinsky has written that the briefings to the president mid-year [1981] became paper briefings and not person-to-person briefings. This is simply not so. Zbigniew and others at the time fell under the impression that the briefings had been canceled. They had not; we just tried to get a better handle on it. However, it was cumbersome and in terms of the procedural aspects of the NSC—that is, getting things onto the national security agenda—it was a nightmare. As a result of this, our friends in the State Department began to talk about the inefficiency of the National Security Council staff. The NSC itself was by no means inefficient. At one point we had as many as eighteen to twenty issues awaiting consideration. They simply languished in the "Meesecase"; by this I mean a briefcase without a bottom. So Ed's horrible inefficiency led to this situation. The National Security Council meetings, once held, were very efficient. We dispatched a number of issues with considerable speed, and we were able to get through the agenda. But this bureaucratic impediment, these hurdles that were put in place primarily due to the insatiable curiosity of Baker and Deaver, and their unwillingness to be left out, on one hand, and Ed Meese's insistence that he was going to be the policy czar, on the other hand, led to a good bit of paralysis. All of that was not bad given the fact that we had decided not to emphasize foreign policy, but still the decisions would have to be made and they were not made in a timely way. Eventually we got the backlog under control.

Some aspects of the organizational problems of the Reagan administration in its early stages can be attributed to the interposition of the so-called troika, Baker, Meese, and Deaver, which turned out to be a worthless troika; it did not run well and it did not run fast. However, on the domestic side, I must say they achieved some considerable success. The other reason was Al Haig's unbelievable suspicion about the motives of others. The man was engagingly charming and in many ways was an enormous asset and very bright. He simply could not stand it and believed that rumors were being spread to the press. Actually, since he was an inveterate leaker and was well accomplished in the use of the press against internal adversaries, he attributed it first to us.

It is very important to keep in mind that Jim Baker did not agree with the interposition of Ed Meese between me and the president. He told me so on a number of occasions. So Baker was very realistic in this regard. I did not go and complain to Baker because, after all, he was not a particular ally of mine, although I fully accepted Jim Baker; he is a very likable, engaging, and highly talented individual, but he saw the problem and brought it up on more than one occasion. He said, "I am trying to get this impediment removed so that you can get on with your work with the president, because that is what I believe you ought to be doing and I do not need to be in there (in these meetings)." But as long as Meese was going to be in there, that was going to be the case. In the end, while this sounds like carping, I believe that Meese's decision to interpose himself both domestically and in the national security realm, to make himself a czar of policy, was a horrible mistake and did not serve Ronald Reagan well.

8
Public Opinion and the Media

Especially since the Vietnam War, public opinion has played an increasing role in the U.S. foreign policy process. Successive administrations have sought both to build and sustain support for their initiatives and to respond to public sentiment. In articulating the impact of public opinion—and, relatedly, of the media—upon the foreign policy-making process, this chapter delves into, among other things, the relationship of presidential administrations with the media; the impact of upcoming elections, of Watergate, and of domestic political competitors upon foreign policy; the catalyst the media may be for high-level personnel changes; and, finally, the broad influence the fourth estate may have upon foreign and domestic policy. Gen. Andrew Goodpaster, then defense liaison officer and staff secretary, contends that President Eisenhower viewed the electronic media as an important instrument of communication to be used in support of U.S. interests:

> He was keenly interested in what has come to be called image projection, or telling the American story around the world. He was never satisfied there—and was often somewhat frustrated, I think.

In his own way, General Goodpaster explains, President Eisenhower also used the press to convey his intentions on the use of nuclear weapons in the Formosa Straits crisis. As General Goodpaster saw it,

> The president reserved to himself any decision about their use, and there remained an ambiguity about their use, which was just the way he wanted it, I believe. For example, when the press tried to squeeze out of him, under the Formosa Resolution, just what would be considered an attack on [the islands of] Quemoy and Matsu that constituted an attack on the Pescadores and Formosa, he simply would not be drawn out. That is the first time he said "I know what I'll do, I'll confuse them," through the so-called garbled syntax or something like that, in my opinion," and [the press] won't understand what I'm telling them [but the Chinese will]."

General Goodpaster describes the media problems confronting the Eisenhower administration at the time of the U-2 incident, in which the Soviets shot down an American reconnaissance aircraft over the Soviet Union in May 1960:

> Our first information was that it was overdue and assumed to be down. We had a set cover story that was to be used. Indeed, we went forward to use that cover story. Then a day or so later, while just by chance we were at a meeting at one of the protected sites, we got word of Khrushchev's announcement that this plane had been shot down. We got back to Washington, and of course the press was in a great state of excitement, putting great pressure on our public information people to provide information about this. After some difference of views, we at the White House staff went in to the president. We had a recommendation from our public information office that the press secretary be authorized to announce a statement would be made by NASA [National Aeronautics and Space Administration], which was the channel through which the cover story had been promulgated. The president made his decision, authorizing the press secretary to say this, from the White House. Then everybody, the press included, went over to NASA, which was totally unprepared for this, and it was apparently quite a tumultuous operation. But, in any case, we got beyond that, and Khrushchev sprang his trap, saying that they had the pilot, that it was not what had been announced, that it was not a high-altitude research plane that had strayed off course, but something quite different. Then we went through the well-known sequence of things. There, my idea was to try to give some degree of satisfaction to the Russians, to see if they would then cut the thing off, and resolve the thing that way, but they kept pushing, pushing. Finally, we worked up a statement that was put out by the State Department, hoping that would be enough to meet the problem. Khrushchev was really projecting this attack at Eisenhower. Eisenhower would have a choice—either to say he did not know about it, in which case it would be very damaging to his leadership position, or that he did know about it. Khrushchev seemed to be trying to draw him into saying that he did not know about it, but the fact was that he did know about it and that made that alternative unavailable. We all came to the view that the moment the president himself said something it had to be true. Of course, that was Eisenhower's view as well. Subordinates could do other things, but the president himself had a position such that, if he made a public statement, it had to be true. So he worked out a short statement that he then used at his press conference.

Although the role of domestic factors in the foreign policy process increased enormously during and in the years following the Vietnam War, they were apparent, although to a lesser extent, in the early 1960s. Ambassador Edmund Gullion discussed the domestic aspects of U.S. policy in the Congo that he, as ambassador stationed in Leopoldville (later Kinshasa), the capital of the Congo, now Zaire, had to address.

Outside the government, there were various lines of opposition. The Belgian propagandists made optimum use of stories about the Congo which they exaggerated or fabricated. They played on the sentiments of domestic institutions like the churches. I tried to counter this policy. I remember once sending down a United States military mission and the press to see that destruction was very limited in the military operations.

Besides those who opposed our policy for humanitarian reasons, there were the staunch anti-Communists. Tshombe skillfully exploited their fear of Communism. People like Herbert Hoover and Sen. [Christopher] Dodd were drawn to this. Dodd was against everything we did. I always wanted to face him in one of the congressional hearings I attended, but he never was present when I appeared before his committee. Finally, there were those who saw our policy as an unnecessary strain on the alliance. Those people included [Dean] Acheson, my old boss. They saw our policy as a dispersion of effort in our containment policy. This was a serious point of contention.

In our efforts to address all of these concerns we were at a disadvantage because lines of communication were very thin. At times we communicated over short-wave amateur radio, although this was not in line with proper procedure. At times even Kennedy would call up. He did that maybe four or five times. Later we had to switch to the military radio. At times even that did not work, due to atmospheric conditions. None of these communications were secure at all, but things moved fast and we had to cope with what we had.

According to Adm. Thomas Moorer, who was then chief of naval operations, the Johnson administration was especially concerned with public opinion at the time of the 1968 presidential election. Admiral Moorer remembered that

at one lunch during the Nixon/Humphrey campaign, Johnson gathered us hurriedly together and announced a halt in the bombing and even recalled General Abrams and General Westmoreland from Vietnam and then he outlined the conditions. Of course, the North Vietnamese violated all of the conditions. It was political and you could see that something was up because Humphrey was not present. He wasn't there. It was all done solely to help him out. Nixon did not do anything as blatantly political as that. Johnson wanted to give the public the impression that the war was winding down a week before that magic [election] day in November [1968]. I'll never forget George Christian, his public affairs officer, whom he turned to and asked, "What will the public say when we stop this bombing?" Christian said, "They're going to say you stopped the bombing because of the election," which is true.

Later, as chairman of the Joint Chiefs of Staff under President Nixon, Admiral Moorer observed the effects of the Watergate crisis on Nixon's ability to manage foreign policy. Watergate—a domestic problem—weighed heavily on

Nixon's mind and consumed increasing amounts of his time in the months before his resignation in August 1974.

> My impression was that he was heavily preoccupied by Watergate, but that nevertheless he was always on top of foreign policy. Once we had a meeting with several subjects on the agenda. We could tell he was totally preoccupied with domestic subjects, but the minute you got into a foreign policy item he would get right into it. I may be wrong, but I could see the expression in his face change depending on what the subject was. The idea that he was not running foreign policy is incorrect; to the very end he was in charge. There was no question about it.

Regarding the increasing isolation of President Nixon in the final months before his resignation, Gen. Brent Scowcroft, who was then deputy national security adviser, commented,

> Henry's role in Watergate was not prominent. The president sometimes talked to him about Watergate issues as did other people. Henry Kissinger's increasing preoccupation was the fact of the preoccupation of the president on perceptions around the world of his position. There was a question in a lot of countries as to what was going to happen in the United States and as to the degree on which they could count on the United States to perform. This is true, interestingly enough, more on the part of our friends and allies than on our enemies. It took the Soviets a long time to come to the conclusion that they needed to trim their sails and hedge against the possibility that Nixon would not survive.
>
> President Nixon was preoccupied and tended inevitably to look somewhat more at foreign policy as a vehicle to rescue his tenuous political situation, although I will say to his credit that he never let domestic politics color his foreign policy decisions. The president did not play as prominent a role in national security policy; however, Henry Kissinger was never a free agent in that sense of the word. The president always retained his commanding heights.
>
> The Soviets for a long time assumed that Nixon would survive and did not fully understand the impact of the Watergate crisis on his presidency. I think they still do not understand. Indeed, few outside the United States really understand what happened and why it happened. It is fairly incomprehensible, even in parliamentary democracies. The Soviets had placed a great investment in the Nixon presidency. They were midcourse in what they hoped would be another series of arms control negotiations, and also in the blossoming of the relationship in the areas in which they were even more interested—that is, trade, and so on. This was coupled with their absolute incomprehension that a sitting president could be brought down by some third-rate break-in of a group of people. I think this led them to discount significantly the events which we here tended to take more seriously.

However, Donald Rumsfeld, who was the U.S. ambassador to NATO at the time and subsequently secretary of defense in the Ford administration, offered another perspective:

If you go from 1969 to 1972, clearly Richard Nixon was the president for foreign policy and national security. As you go into his period of weakness, the Watergate period (1973–74), there is also no question but that Henry Kissinger stepped up and made a great many more decisions that would have been presidential decisions had we had a strong president. It is a question of which period you are talking about.

In 1976 President Ford was attempting to complete negotiations for the SALT (Strategic Arms Limitations Talks) II Treaty with the Soviet Union while also seeking the Republican presidential nomination, for which Ronald Reagan was challenging him in the various Republican party primaries. Brent Scowcroft, Ford's NSC adviser, suggests that the Reagan challenge affected Ford's negotiating positions on SALT II and ultimately his prospects for reelection:

My own judgment is that the impact was fairly disastrous, that it distorted the foreign policy of the Ford administration, hampered the development and execution of policy, and indeed, I would suggest, cost President Ford the election. It was perceived by the political advisers of the president that the principal threat to him, in foreign policy, was from the Right and from Ronald Reagan's fairly wholesale attack on détente, Ford's foreign policy, and, most especially, Henry Kissinger. They believed the way to deal with that attack from the Right was to move to the right—in other words, to meet it on its own ground. It was not that President Ford changed his own notion of policy, changed his own personal views about détente. I feel both in discussing it with him and from what I know of him that that was not the case. It was a reaction and a political tactic to deal with the Reagan challenge. I think it was precisely the wrong way to do it. First of all, President Ford could not take away the Reagan constituency. Instead he should have appealed to moderate Republicans and, indeed, to moderate Democrats in terms of foreign policy. I think that the strategy which was adopted prevented us from getting an arms control agreement, which, at least in talking to some of the people in the Carter camp, was their greatest fear during all of 1976. As a consequence, President Ford went into the campaign without any foreign policy achievements to which he could point. I don't think at that point the mood in the country was the way it was in 1980 and in 1984. Ford did win the contest within the Republican party, albeit by a narrow margin, but unfortunately he tended to continue the campaign tactics of the primary in the election, and tended to run against Jimmy Carter as if [President Carter] were Ronald Reagan. I think the overall impact of the emergence of the Reagan threat had a seriously deleterious effect on the Ford presidency.

As secretary of defense, Donald Rumsfeld observed the implications and effects of the 1976 presidential campaign for U.S. arms control policy:

> The president ended up making [arms control] decisions that were disadvantageous in the context of the campaign and, I believe, for the president. I felt at the time that he made them because he decided that that was the right decision. Indeed, some columnists have made the case that the election was lost because Rumsfeld in the Pentagon would not agree and give Ford a SALT agreement.

The media can highlight differences within an administration about policy issues, which sometimes lead to personnel changes initiated from the highest level. Gen. John Vessey pointed to the divergent perspectives concerning the use of U.S. ground forces in South Korea, in which he as UN commander and his chief of staff, Gen. Jack Singlaub, disagreed with President Carter on the issue of withdrawing such military units:

> There were two sorts of forces that met during President Carter's years. The first was his policy that he had announced during his campaign. None of us in uniform really understood how serious he was about the withdrawal policy. Most of us thought, Well, we'll wait and see, because a lot of people have run for office on one platform and then come into office and accepted the responsibilities and have seen the need for other courses of action.

In early 1977 General Vessey briefed President Carter on the Korean situation

> Mr. Carter told me that he had run on the campaign of pledging a withdrawal of our ground forces from Korea, but the information that I had given had to be weighed before he made the decision.
>
> And then in March, at a press conference—and I'm not sure whether it was a press conference or a press announcement—but anyway, word came out of the White House that we would go ahead and withdraw our forces over a long period of time. And of course that stirred up a lot of hornets, including one from an interview with my good chief of staff, Jack Singlaub. A few weeks after the press conference in Washington, Jack Singlaub's interview hit the front page of the *Washington Post*. Basically, what he had said was the same thing that I had said to a *Washington Post* reporter in December or January, that withdrawing our forces would increase the danger of war. My interview was printed on page B-25, but Jack's interview made the front page. The Singlaub affair and its influence on the administration's Korean policy may be worth examination.

General Vessey continued:

I got a call early in the morning from the vice chief of staff of the army about something else, and he told me that my chief of staff was on the front page of the *Post*. Later on in the day, toward evening, I got a call from George Brown, who was chairman of the Joint Chiefs of Staff. George told me the same thing—that Singlaub was on the front page of the *Post*—and he gave me the outline of what the headlines and the interview had to say. George went on to say that the White House had a full head of steam over the issue. Jack Singlaub had a reputation for sticking his foot in his mouth occasionally, so I told George to try to calm them down, and tell them it was my fault and that I would take the action over here. Well, that was maybe nine o'clock at night our time.

About one o'clock in the morning I got another call from George saying that the White House wanted to call Singlaub back. I told George Brown that that was a very dumb thing to do. I said that I disagreed with the administration's policy but the president knew where I stood on this thing and he promised that he was not going to withdraw the forces until he had talked to me again. I said whatever [President Carter] is going to do, he is going to jeopardize his decision-making flexibility if he calls Singlaub back. Just chew my tail or something like that, fire me, but do not call Singlaub back. George said, "Okay, I understand what you are saying, I agree with you and I'll raise the issue again."

Well, about four o'clock in the morning, the phone rang. It was George Brown again. He said, "Jack, I want you to turn your transmitter off, turn your receiver on, and when I'm done transmitting, you turn your transmitter on and say, 'Yes sir.' " He went on to say that Singlaub was to be on the first aircraft coming back. He was not to talk to any reporters and he was to report to him and then the secretary of defense and they would go see the president. So I said, "Yes, sir."

The comedy got worse when I told Singlaub his instructions. He saluted and went off to go. I had a special adviser at that time, Jim Hausman, who was an old Korean hand who was going home on leave, and he was at the airport waiting to get on the same airplane. There was a young woman talking to Hausman, and Jack Singlaub thought that the woman was Jim's daughter. Well, as it turned out, she was the wife of the reporter to whom he had given the interview in the first place. She worked for CBS. Jack Singlaub thought he was speaking privately, but by the time the airplane had landed, he had not only the *Washington Post* interview but also what had been overheard by the woman from CBS.

General Vessey described the effect of the interview:

The whole incident helped turn up some focus among congressmen who had been sort of ho-hum about the Korea issue. We got kind of a better hearing, at least on Korea, as a result of the Singlaub canning. So I think that the significance of Singlaub was probably greater in the long run than we are likely to credit it. It served as a lightning rod to draw attention to the Carter administration's plans.

Richard Allen, national security adviser from 1981 to 1982, holds that President Reagan sought to mold public opinion rather than simply to reflect its current state.

Now the question you just asked has to do with the prominence of the public relations ear to the ground. Ronald Reagan, as I have known him, has never been a man who was led by public opinion polls but always sought to lead public opinion. Richard Worthlin, who is the president's pollster but has known him for a long time, would be the first to tell you that Ronald Reagan sees accurate poll taking and the pulse of public opinion as a tool to lead rather than an indication that he ought to change policies. I do not believe that you will find an instance where Ronald Reagan has changed a fundamental belief. For instance, the fact that the majority of people oppose aid to the contras only reinforces him in his belief, and you can find countless examples of this in Ronald Reagan.

General Vessey, who became chairman of the Joint Chiefs of Staff under President Reagan, noted the consequences of leaving the press out of the Grenada rescue operation of October 1983.

We told the president that there was not time; that this thing, if it was going to be successful, had to be a secret. And there were already little indications. We knew the Cubans had sent a special colonel down there the day before to try to buck up the defenses. We knew he was there and the last thing we needed was a leak. Now, if I had been smarter and if there had been a little more planning time, we would have picked somebody [in the press] to go and it would have been a good thing to do, because the armed forces of the United States would have gotten a lot of good publicity and the American people would have had a lot more confidence in their armed forces. As it was, the operation and the forces got pretty sour treatment from the press.

The press can also be used to bolster the administration's position through careful prompting or preparation. Robert McFarlane, then national security adviser, detailed his efforts to harness the power of the news media to strengthen President Reagan's popular support before the November 1985 U.S.-Soviet summit meeting.

I was trying to develop a speaking schedule before we went to the [Geneva] summit that would put Reagan's popular support up around 70 percent. Anytime you go into a negotiation with anybody, you want your boss to be sitting there enjoying very high political backing. I thought that it was important for Gorbachev to be looking at somebody across the table who not only felt strongly but could carry his program—who had the strength at home to do what he was saying—not just to deal with some iconoclast who was intent upon SDI, but [that] he had the political roots back home that would carry it. I wanted the American people to understand that here is an agenda; it is the correct agenda and the positions that we are taking on the agenda are good ones, and that our president is correctly leading us in this negotiation and that the allies understand that.

Well, that sounds easy but it is not easy. In a democracy, informing the public is a very hard thing to do. There are a lot of ways you can go about it. You have a lot of instruments at your disposal. Most importantly you have the president. He is a wonderful speaker and able to explain things very well. So, the first instrument that you plan and prepare is the president and speeches, concretely. I thought that between September and November, in that three-month period, we needed to have the president give a speech on each of the four themes: regional disagreements, bilateral relations, human rights, and arms control. So you have to stop and think, where should he give those speeches, when, what audience, to get the most multiplier effect and reach the most people in the United States.

Then, because the president in one speech with twenty minutes each will not reach more than 10 percent of the population, you want to try to magnify that by talking via subordinates—the secretary of state, the secretary of defense, and the national security adviser—and other spokesmen for the president getting other reporters in, meeting with editorial boards so that you get downstream echos of what the president says or commentary on it and it takes a lot of work, especially in dealing with a White House press corps. The White House press corps is a corps of journalists; it is not like the State Department or the Defense Department press corps. In those agencies, while their agendas are quite large and reporters at State must be able to cope with everything from Angola to the Kurile Islands, at least it is foreign and they in the foreign domain are more knowledgeable than, say, the people at Energy. But, with the White House press corps, you have to deal with everything from abortion to election reform to strategic arms talks; you know the consequence is that you really are about a mile wide and a half-inch deep on any issue, and that is unavoidable. It is not a fault. It is the nature of the system and so for those of us in the national security community, your job is to take essentially a well-meaning group of people, an intelligent group of people, and to get them to understand your strategy and what you are trying to do and then for them to say it. Well, they are never going to say it quite the way you would want it said, but that is the cost of doing business. You are going to have this effect and so you just have to try harder, and over and over again, and I think on the whole the White House press corps does a pretty good job.

There is a dramatic difference between press media and electronic media, just in the nature of the media. In electronic media you are never going to get more than about ninety seconds an evening; you may induce the weekend talk shows to devote a program to part of this agenda, but even that is only going to reach one-tenth of 1 percent of the American people. So, print media is a much more productive way to get depth of knowledge to people. There again you are only going to reach about 20 percent of the American people who will read past the headlines to the depth of a foreign article.

But I was spending about a third of my time, on the order of five hours a day (in the fall of 1985) in preparations of the press—background sessions where you are not visible, or at least not very often very visible, but just explaining to a White House press corps, here is the nature of our bilateral agenda, covering everything from the Bering Sea boundary disputes to possibilities for open-heart research to START [Strategic Arms Reduction Talks] and INF and putting it all in a historical context and how does it contrast with détente of the early 1970s and so forth. I don't say that to be kind of puffery so much as to give you a sense that it is not enough to think up good policy; you really do have to promote it, and a third of my time and I think a third of George Shultz's time was taken up in those three months of *promoting* the policy by press here, with the press for the overseas papers, and through the State Department diplomatic channels, and having our ambassadors engage with counterparts in Bonn, London, Paris, Rome, to get the message out into the governments of those host countries and in terms to stimulate those host leaders.

All of this effort is designed to have an effect in the Kremlin to where the other guy gets his morning take from the KGB and it says that allies are supporting Reagan, the American people are supporting Reagan, the U.S. Congress is supporting Reagan, this is terrible. So, the president who worked very hard in this preparatory phase signed on to doing these four speeches, and we wrote them, he gave them, he traveled to the UN. He met visibly with all of the six other leaders of the industrial countries that are part of the economic summit that [Britain's] Thatcher called.

By the time he went to Geneva in November of 1985, Ronald Reagan had built a 71 percent popular approval for his foreign policy, the highest of any postwar president. That is of no importance except [that] when he sat down with Gorbachev in Geneva on November 18, and went through his reasoning for SDI, and Gorbachev came back with all of the predictable criticisms—the quite emotional reasons why not—Reagan came back and went through it all again with a very methodical delivery. Gorbachev said just about two lines: "Well, I disagree with you, I think you are dead wrong, but I will reconsider." I think that was importantly a consequence of Gorbachev seeing that this was a man, Reagan, who had enormous political backing, and who had also had a dimension of planning for the summit that involved excruciating consultations with the allies, but by the time he got to Geneva, the three constituencies that are important in exercising power in negotiation were all very solidly behind him: the allies through briefings, the Congress through briefings, and the American people. It paid off.

According to Gen. Pierre Gallois, professor of strategic studies at the French War College, technology in the open society confers upon the electronic media an unprecedented position of political power and influence.

> For about twenty years a revolution—another revolution—has been taking place which is not a revolution in space, not a revolution of electronics entirely; it is revolution of the media. It is very important. The media are now very powerful. They are between the government and the public opinion. They are another form of government. Although media people have no program and are not elected, they just do what they think is their job. Because of television, because of the capability of one man to reach 20–40 million people each day, society has been progressively changing. This is extraordinary because these people have no official role, but because of what they say on television they are capable of great influence. They are more powerful than legislative power, than executive power, than the judiciary power—more powerful. One man on television may launch a campaign explaining that we should take into account the past of a criminal and he is not to be condemned and so on. When there is a movement of public opinion, the government changes its mind.
>
> You may, with the growth of home personal computers, be in a situation in the future where, for instance, political leaders go on television and they explain their policies, and people respond directly to his speech. On the screen they might say that they have no confidence in what he said. If this leader is the president of the republic, imagine his position, so what is needed to garner their support, their immediate approval, is to be a great demagogue. You cannot have a foreign policy based on emotional, instantaneous movement of public opinion; it is impossible. So, in my opinion, the media have such power that they paralyze completely any foreign policy in a democracy. That to me increases the gap between autocracy and democracy and gives an edge to the autocracies over the democracies—but a very important one.

Ambassador David Newsom noted the change that has taken place in the attitude of the media toward the U.S. government, especially since the 1960s. The result has been the emergence of an adversarial relationship in which differences of objectives have become apparent to what may be an unprecedented extent.

> I think the more dramatic shift, in my mind, is that between my dealings as a State Department officer with the press in the 1960s and dealing with the press in the late 1970s and 1980s when I returned from overseas. I think the real shift in the relationship occurred as a result of three things: Watergate, Vietnam, and television. Before 1965 the relationship between the two professions (Foreign Service and media) obviously had different objectives, but it was not to any degree the adversarial relationship that it later became. In that earlier period you could sit down with a reporter

from the *New York Times* or the *Washington Post* or one of the major news magazines and you could say, "This is what we are thinking about. Obviously we need to do a lot more consulting before we can reach a decision on this, and we will keep in touch with you." The reporter would probably not feel compelled to report the conversation. Today, you would be reluctant even to speculate against that background. The competitiveness and the greater distrust was not only manifested in the reporters that covered the State Department in later years but was also manifested in their editorial management. I have had reporters—good diplomatic reporters— at times say, "I prefer that you not tell me something because I cannot make the editorial decisions as to whether this is to be published or not. My editor will do so, and he may have a different view than me." So it was a very different atmosphere in later years.

Part III
National Security Decision Making within the NATO Context

For over forty years, U.S. national security decision making has been intimately influenced by U.S. participation in the North Atlantic Treaty Organization (NATO). In part III, our insight into national security decisions is substantially broadened from the concerns of the United States alone to the security concerns of the Western European nations composing NATO. Particular emphasis here is placed upon the roles of West Germany, France, and the United States in this alliance. Chapter 9 highlights West Germany's acceptance and participation in NATO and France's decision under Charles de Gaulle to withdraw from NATO's military structure yet remain politically involved. Chapter 10 explores the West German *Ostpolitik*, or policy toward the East. Next, the role of both conventional and nuclear weapons in the defense of Western Europe is surveyed in some detail in chapters 11 and 12. Here decision-making participants from both sides of the Atlantic articulate views on diverse issues such as German rearmament, Franco-German military cooperation, conventional military strategy and force structure, nuclear deterrence and the credibility of U.S. extended deterrence, U.S. strategic nuclear systems and their modernization, and the Strategic Defense Initiative. Importantly, chapter 13 elucidates French decisions for creating their nuclear *force de frappe* and for distinguishing their nuclear strategy from that of NATO. This same chapter briefly touches upon British nuclear forces, the multilateral force idea, and Franco-German nuclear coupling issues. The final chapter in part III, chapter 14, investigates arms control initiatives between NATO and the Warsaw Pact and between the United States and the Soviet Union as they specifically relate to alliance politics within NATO.

9
The Political Dynamics of NATO

I n addition to its status as a military grouping designed to deter a Soviet attack in Europe, the Atlantic Alliance provides for its members a multilateral framework for the respective bilateral relationships of its members with each other. Each has used the alliance within the context of its various national interests and foreign policy goals. The list of NATO political issues illuminated here includes West Germany's position within the alliance, France's withdrawal from NATO's military structure and its consequences, Spain's entrance into NATO, the Greek-Turkish rivalry, NATO defense spending and burden sharing, the neutron bomb imbroglio and double-track decision, the Soviet gas pipeline deal, and the U.S. position within the alliance.

The Atlantic Alliance as well as the European Community are perceived by the Federal Republic of Germany not only as crucially important instruments for security and economic growth, but also as the means by which West Germany could be linked to the Western community of nations, clearly a major goal of its first chancellor, Konrad Adenauer, and his successors. Kai-Uwe von Hassell, from his vantage point as a Christian Democratic Union (CDU) party parliamentarian, and later as minister of defense, describes his perception of the policy process of the Federal Republic of Germany:

> The security debate was already an issue before the first general election in 1949. Before this Adenauer had clearly gotten the approval of the Christian Democrats and its sister party in Bavaria that we should first go westward for our political relationships. But when Parliament came into being in autumn 1949, it always came up again that the Socialists were against ties with the West and with the United States. They were instead in favor of neutralization and going with the East. Adenauer said that it was impossible to have reunification and at the same time have close contact with the Western world which was absolutely necessary because our security could be guaranteed only by means of sufficiently strong Western armies, air forces, and navies. He argued that we would never reach freedom and guaranteed freedom if we joined East Germany in a reunited Germany. This was a problem very often debated in Parliament. The Soviets, for

instance, were in favor of neutralizing the Federal Republic in order to get the chance to reunite with the East, whereas we said that we must have the Federal Republic of Germany in complete freedom guaranteed by the West. Therefore, we must pursue a policy with the West. The Socialists would have neutralized Germany if they had had the chance for reunification. We countered, "No, we will not take that chance. We will also lose our freedom if we join with East Germany, and this will lead to nothing but a Soviet-controlled, united Germany."

Von Hassell underscored Adenauer's view of the importance of the FRG's relationship with the United States:

I would say there was no question of relative importance in having a relationship between the United States and Germany. It is the most vital part of our foreign policy to have this cooperation. Europe, Canada, and the United States must be partners; they must stick together to stop the Russians. In this context of an overall policy, an alliance of the United States, Canada, and Western Europe—and inside Europe, relationships between France and Germany were indeed both vital. But first ranks the relationship with the United States, second the relationship with France.

France has played an important role in the Federal Republic of Germany's foreign policy. Dr. von Hassell explained this role:

Adenauer thought it was necessary for France and Germany to come to a reconciliation—after the Franco-German War [1870–71], World War I [1914–18], and World War II [1939–45]. His view was that we must come to a settlement of the disputes of a hostile history, and we must try to become partners in Europe and might be friends later on. He thought that a prerequisite for halting the Soviet Union was the achievement of a unified Europe. Everything he undertook before he became chancellor and later, when he became chancellor, was directed toward the goal of this partnership between France and Germany. Therefore, his main issue was to achieve this solution and later to push for European unification on this basis of Franco-German reconciliation.

He observed how the FRG's relationship with France fostered the growth of factions within the political parties inside the government coalition of Chancellor Adenauer:

First, the Atlanticists [the West German political faction that saw FRG security tied to the U.S. nuclear deterrent] did not view [French president] de Gaulle as an outmoded nationalist. They believed that France was the most important partner on the Continent but that even so it was unable to ward off the Soviet threat, to deter the Soviet Union. The Atlanticists believed that de Gaulle was heading for superiority, that he was heading for hegemony.

The so-called Gaullists [the West German political faction that sought FRG security through closer military and political ties to France] in my faction—Adenauer or Franz-Josef Strauss [chairman of the West German Christian–Social Union party and prime minister of Bavaria, served as defense minister, 1956–67]—were also of the opinion that we must first have close contact with the United States and then with France, and not with the United States instead of France, or with France instead of the United States. Even the Gaullists said we must have both.

The West German Gaullists were pro-French but not anti-American. They were in favor of very close cooperation with America, but they wanted stronger ties with the French, especially after France left the NATO integrated command.

We had no instrument to deal with these differences. Differences at the time of Adenauer, and later on with Erhard [Ludwig Erhard succeeded Adenauer as federal chancellor, 1963–66], were overcome first within the CDU/CSU [Christian Social Union] in the cabinet. Then, if we were on common lines, we informed, consulted, and spoke to the FDP [Free Democratic party]. We then had to build a compromise for the political parliamentary group. In this parliamentary group we had a lot of responsible people. On one side, for instance, the Gaullists: Dr. Krone [Heinrich Krone was a founding member of the CDU, and a member of the German parliament between 1949 and 1969], and Franz-Josef Strauss [German defense minister, 1956–67]. On the other side, we had Atlanticists: for instance, Dr. Gerhard Schröder [minister of the interior, 1953–61; foreign affairs, 1961–66; and defense, 1966–69], Ludwig Erhard [West German minister of economics, 1949–63, and chancellor, 1963–66], Erich Rende, and me.

Dr. von Hassell pointed out that there were occasionally problems and tensions in the Franco-German relationship:

Take for instance the fourteenth of January, 1963, press conference by de Gaulle vetoing Britain's membership in the Common Market—this was also done before consultations. We were embarrassed. We, the Atlanticists, believed that de Gaulle decided and we more or less had to follow. For example, take the summit conferences between de Gaulle and Adenauer, between his cabinet and our cabinet. I took part in eight of these summit conferences. Now I think there have been some forty. If we made a proposal, de Gaulle would reflect whether to accept it. If de Gaulle made a proposal that we did not follow immediately, then he was annoyed and very displeased.

Then he started saying emphatically that Germany and France could solve all the problems. I was very impressed. The German-Franco Treaty of 22 January 1963 was a tremendous event, but the alliance brought problems. My Dutch colleague in defense, for instance, said that the smaller members of NATO felt uneasy about this new axis. They believed that they would have to follow what we two decided and this would be a very uneasy situation for them. They could not bear this. Later on, when the treaty was put before parliament, a preamble about NATO was inserted. I had tried in the preparatory conferences to bring NATO into the treaty. But it was absolutely impossible to have it inserted. De Gaulle wanted no mention of NATO. I told him that we felt obliged to tell everyone that for us, NATO was also indispensable. This preamble was adopted and eased the situation for other members of NATO. They did not fear that we would go ahead and they would have to follow. So, this would not have spoiled NATO, but it no doubt would have made it more difficult.

Another element of the Federal Republic of Germany's role in NATO has been the defense perspectives of the various political parties. Dr. von Hassell described the threat perceptions among the parties and their opposition to security:

There was complete unanimity in the CDU/CSU regarding the threat. There was a difference only between the coalition parties [CDU/CSU and Liberals] and the Socialists. Some of the Socialists thought that the threat was exaggerated, whereas we took the files and saw exactly what was on the other side, derived from all sources of information, including secret military information. We had a complete picture of the military situation on the other side. Accordingly, we said this is the situation of the threat. The Socialists doubted these figures. They thought we exaggerated in order to get more money for defense. But inside the coalition there was never any dispute about the real strength of the other side.

In our Parliament we had a lot of big debates on defense and security—for example, on nuclear armament. We had a united front of the coalition parties on the one side, and the Socialist opposition on the other side. Up to 1960, the Socialists were strictly against Adenauer's policies. In 1959 they wrote a new Socialist [Social Democratic party, or SPD] program, the Godesberger Program. This scrapped the old policy and went in a new direction, hoping to influence the intellectuals and to gain voters among them and in the middle class: low-ranking civil servants, skilled laborers, not only factory workers, but also people from intellectual life. They succeeded. They got a great many intellectuals, including Protestant clergy and doctors.

On June 30, 1960, the chairman of the SPD political group in Parliament, Herr Wehner [Herbert Wehner was chairman of the SPD between 1958 and 1973] made a sensational speech. He left the past (when the SPD said no to NATO, to the Bundeswehr, to nuclear arms, and so forth), and went forward. He revised Socialist policy. Later on, we had sharp debates on special items of defense. For instance, the [Lockheed F-104] Starfighter [a joint Belgian, Dutch, German, and Italian effort to produce a European version of the American F-104; it was the largest integrated production program ever, producing some one thousand aircraft] crisis was blown up by the SPD; some nuclear components were blown up by the SPD. In general, however, they agreed to be pro-NATO, pro-Western defense, pro–sufficiently strong forces, pro-Bundeswehr, and so on. During the Grand Coalition between 1966 and 1969, there was no sharp debate whatsoever in Parliament because there was only a relatively small opposition. With the exception of some minor debates, the time of the Great Coalition was very fruitful with regard to defense.

In the Godesberger Program of 1959 which I referred to, the SPD changed its entire policy, and a year later Wehner reshaped the attitude as regards defense. This was the valid policy until 1969. Later, during the Socialist-Liberal coalition after 1969, they reduced the importance of their foreign policy vis-à-vis the West, defense, and security, and shifted more to *Ostpolitik*. This received more importance than the policy vis-à-vis the West. But this was not a change in the general line. After 1981 it completely changed. It is wholly different now.

In 1966 President de Gaulle announced that France, while remaining a member of the Atlantic Alliance, would withdraw from the integrated command structure. De Gaulle believed that, by this action, France would gain greater independence and flexibility in its foreign policy. Gen. Pierre Gallois, the French strategic thinker, described what was initially regarded in Europe in the year just after World War II as a hopeless situation. He attributed possession by the United States of a nuclear capability as the principal deterrent to a Soviet military advance to the Atlantic. The function of the Atlantic Alliance in 1949 contributed immeasurably, in General Gallois's view, to the means for deterrence against such Soviet action.

It is important to take into account what was going on in Eastern Europe between 1946 and 1949. The European nations, including France, were in panic. We thought that the Russians might invade all of Western Europe, with what was taking place in Czechoslovakia, Romania and so on. The result of the lack of compliance with Yalta by the Russians was a fear that they would go to the Atlantic shores. The panic in 1947 was so great that some members of the government had aircraft at a military airfield ready to take off. There was unrest in France, with strikes and Communist agitation. We thought that a combination of Soviet military movement to the West, plus the internal unrest, would keep the Russians in complete control of Western Europe. The Polish ambassador told me that in 1944 plans were prepared in Moscow for the Soviets to go to the Atlantic, based upon the speculation that the British and the Americans would demobilize immediately, as [they] did, and that the French were no longer a force in Europe. Germany was destroyed and Italy was nothing. There was no defense. It was only because of [the bombing of] Hiroshima that the plan was changed, because the Russians realized that even a few bombs could change the picture. I do not say that that was deliberate planning which would have been followed, but among many plans, that plan was prepared. We owe to Hiroshima the fact that the Russians definitely changed their plans.

Clearly, the French situation and the European situation were very difficult, unstable, and we welcomed as something very important the Washington Treaty that created the Atlantic Alliance. Already, as you know, the Brussels Treaty [which formed the Western European Union] had been signed in 1948, but we knew that, militarily speaking, the treaty was empty, because it combined no forces. It was full of good intentions, but the units were nonexistent. The treaty was a treaty of intention. Happily, when in 1949 the Washington Treaty was prepared, signed, everything changed among the military. When General Eisenhower installed himself at the headquarters near the Étoile, at the Hotel Astoria, we were all delighted. We thought that once again the situation could be stabilized by the American intervention. Nobody except the Communists forgot the Marshall Plan. The combination of the Marshall Plan plus the existence of a military headquarters with an American general installed in Europe completely changed the morale of the situation. In 1952 I had the privilege of joining NATO as a member of its planning staff. I was very pleased because I had the feeling that I was accepting a good job. I was invited to witness a nuclear explosion in Nevada, and I had the feeling that we were making one force against the Russians and not a mosaic of forces.

Ambassador François de Rose, who held many important diplomatic posts, including that of France's permanent representative to NATO, presented perspectives on the motives that led de Gaulle to withdraw from NATO's military command structure:

The reasons given, which the French tend to forget, were that within the integrated military system, the strategy of the alliance was that of the United States. This created a risk to those involved in that integrated military structure to become involved in conflicts that the United States might be engaged in elsewhere outside of Europe and which would be foreign to our interests or our commitments—there was the Near East, Indochina, and Vietnam, and so on and so forth. But I think personally that there were other reasons, such as for de Gaulle to take the decision—and I knew that has never been written down, so that it is my explanation. I think he wanted to embark on a policy of détente with the Soviet Union. He felt that he could not do it while France was the absolute center of the whole American system in Europe.

There was a story that was told when Khrushchev paid his first visit to Paris. He was reported to have been asked in a press conference how he had spent his nights in Paris. He said, "I couldn't sleep because all the

American warplanes flying over Paris prevented me from sleeping." I don't know if this is true, but I personally believe that de Gaulle, in order to approach the Soviets as a man who wanted to start détente, was infinitely stronger having ousted all the American installations, NATO, and all that. He could come and say, "I am completely independent." I believe that was an extraordinarily strong reason for de Gaulle's decision.

The second reason is related to the crisis in the French Army. You must realize that the defeat of France in 1940 was something absolutely new—not that she was defeated, but in the consequences. It was the first time in the history of Europe that the fate of France, either winner or loser, did not decide the fate of Europe. Through the centuries, our wars against the Spanish, against the Austrians, against the British, against the Germans—what happened to France decided the fate of Europe. For the first time, in 1940, France was defeated; the war went on, and she was eventually liberated by the joint efforts of the British, the Americans, and the Russians. There was a very great danger that the French would consider that their own fate was no longer their own business. De Gaulle emphasized all the time that the defense of France is France's responsibility and that as long as she was in NATO, the French people would have to assume that it was an American responsibility.

General Gallois recounted some of the circumstances that contributed to President de Gaulle's decision to withdraw from the NATO command structure and to exclude NATO facilities from French territory. Almost immediately after his return to power in 1958, de Gaulle confronted the integrated NATO military facilities in France being used by the U.S. military in Lebanon, in which France was not a participant.

In 1958 the Chinese were bombing Quemoy and Matsu, the two Nationalist islands. Mr. Dulles moved the Seventh fleet and some F-104s. At the time there was a report in the press that the aircraft had some atomic bombs in their bays. De Gaulle had a feeling that a serious incident could occur and that the NATO countries should be concerned and involved. That was not Dulles's view; he considered the problem to be an American-Chinese issue. De Gaulle wanted to participate, so he wrote his memorandum to President Eisenhower proposing a joint American, British, and French directorate in the area; you know what the answer was. In the same period in 1958 we had the crisis in Iraq. On July 14, 1958, the king of Iraq was assassinated, and immediately thereafter the British and the Americans sent an expeditionary corps to Lebanon. Aircraft landed at NATO airfields to take on supplies and to refuel. On each NATO airfield we had a French officer representing French sovereignty. This officer had not been informed of the landing. He was awakened by the noise of the aircraft. The next morning the Élysée was informed that during the night American transport aircraft had refueled at French NATO bases. There were probably seven hundred British and American aircraft landing and taking on fuel and ammunition which were then sent to Lebanon. General de Gaulle went nuts.

De Gaulle asked, "Why are they using airfields on my territory for an operation in which I am not involved? Why are they landing in a friendly country, Lebanon, to which I have special links, and I do not know about it? These aircraft overflights must cease, and these airfields must return to purely French control." That was one of the key elements in his decision to leave NATO. It took time to implement because the idea was first to get our nuclear weapons capability, which we did with the planned procurement of the first Mirage aircraft squadron in 1964. The first sixty-four Mirage IVs were in the state of military readiness in 1966, and then we left NATO.

Ambassador de Rose pointed to the policy course that, in his view, would be appropriate from France at the present time:

Now that the Americans are withdrawing some of their nuclear weapons, with talks of withdrawing conventional forces and so on, we really need the Europeans to take a greater share of responsibilities for their own security. I think that France is the only nation that can give the shock, the psychological shock, that would help reassemble the Europeans. To that end, when I say that I am accused of trying to bring France closer into integration, that is completely wrong. We could very well not emphasize integration. There is no need for our forces to be earmarked or assigned to NATO, or for our officers to be in the NATO hierarchy. What we should do is to take part in discussions of questions such as, what is the threat, what strategy can counter that threat, and what are the means to serve that strategy? These decisions are discussed in the DPC [Defense Planning Committee], from which France is absent. They should be discussed in the [North Atlantic] Council, where we are. France would take part in, but not reintegrate within, the military structure, and so on. But take part in those discussions because, if we do not, then we will still have our own strategy and our other allies their own strategy, which will lead to disaster. That is what I maintain.

The French withdrawal decision had wide repercussions. The West German defense minister Kai-Uwe von Hassell recalled his reaction at the time of the announcement of France's decision:

As regards the French, the Atlanticists said that France left NATO without consulting us. In 1966 I was minister of defense. My French colleague, Monsieur Mesmer [Pierre Mesmer was French minister of the Armed Forces, 1960–69], with whom I had very close contact, did not tell me that they were to leave. He said they might leave, but before they would leave they would go into real consultations with us and try to see what the consequences would be.

From our point of view, it was a pity that they left. The reasons lie only with the general, not with his cabinet or with his military people. The general made up his own mind without consulting his good friend Adenauer. He decided without consulting his good friend Kai-Uwe von Hassell. The general decided, and Mesmer had to follow this decision. There was some indication at the beginning of 1966, Mesmer said, that they might consider leaving the organization, but that before they decide they would talk to us and see what could be done. This consultation never happened. We were simply informed; nothing occurred before that.

This created a good variety of difficulties. One was we had our depots in France. They had to be moved. The Americans had many depots in France, and all the lines of communication ran through France. This all had to be moved into Holland, Belgium, and the FRG. This created great difficulty, but it was not a cabinet-level problem. We had to deal with it in the Defense Ministry. Cooperation with France went on but, as I said earlier, was slowed because Erhard was unfamiliar to the French; he was uneasy with them. So, during the coalition with the Liberals under Erhard, it was difficult. In the Grand Coalition [West German coalition government composed of both major parties, the SPD and the CDU/CSU, 1966-69] the cooperation with the French improved; it was because of Kurt Kiesinger, who was chancellor at the time, was on very good terms with the French.

The French always said that they had to be prepared to guarantee security for Europe, even if the Americans leave. I always told my French colleague in public and private that it is not a question of what to do if the Americans leave—our aim must be to do everything so that they do not leave. The anti-American atmosphere created by France was not the best circumstance for the Americans to decide to remain in Europe. Facing such anti-Americanism, the United States might someday decide to go. If the United States pull out, then the French could say that they had always said that the United States would go, but they did a lot to drive the Americans out.

Our whole philosophy since the beginning had been that we must all stick together and that if we do so we could deter the Soviet Union. But if there is a split—which is the Soviet goal—if NATO weakens from a split or lack of commitment, it weakens the alliance's deterrent. The policy must always aim at telling the Soviets that if they attack, they must know beforehand what would happen to them. It must be an incalculable risk; but if the alliance is not united, then the Soviets can balance the pros and cons and decide whether the situation is now positive for them because the alliance is weakened.

Joseph Luns, foreign minister of the Netherlands at the time of the withdrawal announcement, was asked if he thought of trying to talk de Gaulle out of his decision.

No, I did not attempt to dissuade him because it was a sort of decision that could not be altered by intervention by America or Britain or the Netherlands. As a matter of fact, de Gaulle had for a moment the idea of withdrawing from the alliance altogether, but Couve de Murville [Maurice Couve de Murville was French foreign minister, 1959–68, and prime minister, 1968–69] dissuaded him. He said, "But Monsieur le President, why throw away a guarantee for our independence without any reason?"

Luns subsequently was NATO secretary-general, and he here observes the effects of France's withdrawal from the integrated NATO command structure on the operation of the alliance:

> When I became secretary-general, France had already withdrawn from the military integration. That's all they did; for the rest, they remain 100 percent members of the alliance. And, in fact, it works quite well. The French, officially, do not fall under the command structure of NATO, but they conform to what NATO does. For instance, at naval maneuvers you will read that NATO navies will have exercises in the Atlantic Ocean, and at the same time, and in connection with these maneuvers, the French Navy will also exercise. That means that they are taking part. It is the same with army maneuvers. They are members of the Military Committee. They have liaison missions at all big command centers, and in fact it works smoothly. It was of course generally regretted, and we did not know how it would work out, but in fact it has worked out quite well. After de Gaulle left, of course, and the cooperation improved. President [Valéry] Giscard d'Estaing [1974–81] was not very much pro-NATO and was not a friend of the United States, but President François Mitterrand [1981–] is.

Lawrence Eagleburger was the political officer at the U.S. mission to NATO when the United States took steps designed to mitigate and minimize the adverse consequences of France's withdrawal from NATO's command structure and of the removal of NATO facilities from French soil. Subsequently he served on the NSC staff under Henry Kissinger.

> First of all, with regard to relations with NATO-Europe, there was a strong feeling on the part of both Nixon and Kissinger that we had dealt absurdly with de Gaulle from 1964 to 1966, and that France was far more important to a solid U.S. position in Western Europe than the [Johnson] administration had acknowledged, and that that relationship had to be repaired. Second, and this is an important element in the Soviet issue, both Nixon and Kissinger clearly felt that if we were going to deal with the Soviets we had to do it with a substantially repaired NATO relationship. On Nixon's first trip [to NATO-Europe] as president, which I was involved in, it was fundamentally to begin to try to get away from issues like offsets, and troops in Europe, and the very issues that had so much been a part of the problem with Western Europe in the Johnson years. Within that context, there was a major effort, and indeed virtually a Nixon love feast with de Gaulle, to try to begin to shift that relationship around.

Now, in retrospect, it was clear that de Gaulle had his priorities set too, and there was only a certain degree of latitude that he was going to permit; but there is no question that relations with Paris improved.

Ambassador Tapley Bennett, U.S. permanent representative to NATO, from 1977 to 1983, reflected on the contribution that, from his perspective, France made to the Atlantic Alliance, even though the French government no longer participated officially in the NATO command structure:

The French are an intelligent people, very logical, sometimes overlogical. Excessive reliance on Cartesian logic leads them to some strange illogic in the end sometimes, but they are quick, able, difficult people. They are difficult with one another and they are difficult with allies. On the other hand, France puts her money where her mouth is; she has never hesitated to spend the money on defense that she considered necessary, and she has carried her public opinion along with defense spending better than any other country I know, including our own. Whatever the reasons for her nuclear program—and a lot of it, in the beginning, was that old French *grandeur*—it is now a recognized element in the world power structure; and it is a useful one from our point of view. You have to accept that France is going to be France; it is going to be different, but she pays for her views, she does not ask other people to carry her load. France is like a coquettish woman—vain, inordinately sensitive, and insistent on being courted.

The French characteristics made it difficult at times on day-to-day matters. But I, for one, never forget, and I have said it in the NATO Council, that France is our oldest ally. There is an overarching usefulness and necessity for our relationship that overrides day-to-day disputes, and I think most of the French feel that way too. It is interesting to me today that the French people—and all the polls show this—have a much higher opinion of Reagan and of American leadership than do the British. Despite the close cooperation of Mrs. Thatcher, we are very low in British public esteem at this time; it is not just Reagan, although it obviously relates itself to the administration in power at any given time.

The French were always disassociating themselves from this and that decision at NATO. They insist on being "independent" within the alliance. Sometimes they take the position that only France is loyal to the essential principles of NATO, that everyone is out of step but France. At times it can become downright ludicrous.

The French often took the position "Leave us out, we are not involved" on NATO Defense Committee matters. They do not sit on the Defense Committee, but they will stoutly tell you that "France is a member, a leading member of the political side of NATO. We never left the alliance, and we believe in the alliance but on our terms." I think that there has been a gradual evolution of French policy from the complete distancing of the de Gaulle years, down through the seventies, to now. Jacques Chirac [French prime minister, 1986–88] was very much a Gaullist in the years I was at NATO in the late seventies. I remember going to

102 • *National Security Decisions*

Paris—he was even then mayor of Paris—for a meeting of the Atlantic Treaty Association, the first time in years, if ever, it had met in Paris. At that time, Chirac was pretty much a firebrand on French independence. He was having nothing to do with United States leadership in the military field, that kind of thing. You do not hear that today so much. Now that he is prime minister, I think it is already clear that he has modified some of those views. That does not mean they are going to rejoin the integrated military structure of NATO.

After France had withdrawn from NATO's integrated command structure in 1967, it continued to participate in other work of the alliance. Ambassador de Rose described France's relationship with the alliance after 1966:

Oddly enough, I was still so convinced that France was in the alliance that I considered being out of the integrated military structure did not mean we were indifferent to what took place in the military field. Rather the contrary. I did not take part in the Defense Planning Committee [DPC], nor in the Nuclear Planning Group [NPG]. My first American colleague then was Robert Ellsworth, who was U.S. permanent representative to NATO [1969-71]. I called on him, and we got on well. I was myself so convinced of the need to have good relations between France and the alliance that I also called on General Goodpaster, who was SACEUR.

Things were settling down progressively. The 1972 French White Paper on Defense had not yet been published, but we were working on the assumption, alluded to first in the letter that de Gaulle had originally sent to all heads of state, that arrangements would be made for the cooperation of French forces with the alliance forces in case there was a war in Europe. Rather than overplaying attention to that possibility, I thought it would be more productive to proceed on a low-keyed basis. Soon my colleagues in NATO considered that I was really a member of the team all the same. There is the institution of the Tuesday lunch, and of course I took part in this Tuesday lunch. In those lunches, I expressed my views on military matters as if I had been a member of the DPC. And my colleagues, knowing my background and my training in these positions, were very friendly with me. So I happened to be informed of a good deal of what was going on. I think that I knew at least as much as many of my colleagues, and probably a little more in nuclear matters. I never had the feeling that I was excluded from something except for the technical reasons. I had especially close relations with Andre de Stoczke, who was the Belgian representative and dean of the council, and also with Manlio Brosio who was then secretary-general, later succeeded by Joseph Luns.

I considered that my job was to try to be informed of the important things that were going on where France had no seat. Another aspect of my job was to assess areas of potential interest for Paris. In that context I tried, where possible, not to ask for instructions from Paris on tricky matters because I knew that if I did there was a chance I would receive negative answers. But if I acted in a way that I felt was sensible, probably Paris would be grateful rather than being embarrassed, and it worked out all right.

However, de Rose noted some areas of friction:

One difficulty was over the NATO-wide communications system, of which France is a member. It was considered that it could be improved and that it could be developed so that there would be communications not only between the headquarters and the capitals, but also between the political and military headquarters and all the way down to the division levels. It was a coherent system whereby everybody would have the same system of communication. It had been called NICS (NATO Integrated Communications System). So I got my instructions as to the conditions under which France could adhere to the new system. It was a sensible thing to do. I explained to Stoczke and Brosio as far as I could go. Everybody was very keen on having France in the system, because it was a move forward, and the negotiations went all right. Stoczke would negotiate with the council and would then negotiate with me. And eventually I got about 90 percent of what the French government wanted—not 100 percent—just for cosmetics, but we had all that we really wanted [and] I was very pleased. I suddenly got a message that France refused. So I went to Paris and discovered that Michel Debré [French prime minister, 1959–62; minister of finance, 1966–68; foreign affairs, 1968–69; and defense, 1969–73] had found out what had happened. Debré told me, "You have made a wonderful negotiation, you have won everything that we wanted, and I can only congratulate you as a diplomat. It was an outstanding success. Nonetheless, I don't want France to be part of that system." And I discovered that someone in his cabinet had told him that NICS stood for NATO Integrated Communications System. If only it had been NATO Inter-Allied Communications System it might have gone through. I was absolutely furious. Really furious. It is just one of those stupid things.

I think the next incident was France's mistake [regarding] the AWACS [Airborne Warning and Control System]. I personally pressed for France getting into the AWACS. I think they were afraid of the cost, but eventually France had to buy several of these [Boeing E3-A] aircraft after five years, ten years, of waiting, and it is absurd. I mean, when de Gaulle pulled French forces out of the integrated command structure, he was careful to leave France in NADGE. NADGE, the NATO Air Defense Ground Environment, is a system of radar which can detect airplanes when they fly above the horizon. The AWACS is a system which can detect planes 300 kilometers inside enemy territory. If it was necessary for France to be in NADGE, it was necessary for France to participate in AWACS.

The French AWACs will not be tied into NATO. I think the idea is that they will cover a mission to the south, Africa and the Mediterranean, which is understandable. But if it is entirely for overseas service, then all right. If it is for detection of planes in Europe, it is irrational not to be in the NATO system, because that is where the attack would come from, and we should be informed. To be very cynical, I think that we think that if there is a war, our allies will give us the information. We do not pay for the system, but they would have to give us information anyway because the air battle will be so integrated that we will not pay, but we will have the information.

Spain joined the alliance in 1983. Tapley Bennett, U.S. ambassador to NATO at the time, discussed the question of Spanish membership:

I personally always thought that Washington was pushing too far and too fast to bring Spain in. I often made the statement, which some people still recall, that if we found France difficult to deal with, just wait until we get Spain into NATO. There are no more egocentric people than the Spaniards. They are even more egocentric than the French, and in addition they have been isolated for all these years so they do not really understand how multinational organizations, a multilateral system, works. However, we went all out to bring them in. NATO Secretary-General Luns had doubts too about Spain, and they finally did come in, but not without a lot of problems. For one, in Spain—you mentioned the economics of it— the Spanish military thought they were going to be showered with free arms once they joined NATO. That was never going to be the case. The Spanish Army is antiquated in its organization and strategic planning, as well as in its equipment. The Spanish Air Force is not too much better. The navy was the only Spanish service which was in a position to contribute anything to NATO from the beginning, if they had been disposed to do so. However, there was a deep cleavage in Spanish opinion as to whether Spain should join NATO. The conservative, middle-of-the-road government was all for it and did push it through Parliament.

[Thus,] I retain my earlier reservations about the practical benefits of Spanish membership, but obviously, once they were in we had to keep them in and work to make them fully participating members in the future. Part of it is just lack of understanding on the part of the Spanish as to the proper role of an alliance member. It will take time, but with the modernization of their armed forces there should be more broad-minded thinking on the part of the Spanish military.

Bennett described how Spain's entry affected other members of the alliance:

Anyway, they did push it forward and then we got into a lot of problems. The Dutch still had sticky feelings about Spain, and it was not easy to work out the terms of Spain's joining, how it was going to be phased. By that time Andreas Papandreou [chairman of the Greek socialist party and prime minister from 1981 to 1989] had come to power in Greece, and he almost blocked it at the very last minute. There were all sorts of frantic activities; I remember that the British ambassador was the one who organized the joint group of ambassadors from NATO countries to talk with Papandreou and get him to agree. Finally, Spain was voted in. But all the details had been left undone, and when talks began on the military arrangements connected with membership, the Spaniards began to drag their feet.

The Portuguese were never enthusiastic about Spanish membership. Questions arose as to how military commands for the Iberian region were to be organized. The Portuguese were adamant that they were not going to give up their IBERLANT [Iberian/Atlantic] Command, which, in my opinion, is not a very important one. I was in Portugal when it was established and wondered at the time whether we were not just putting on another military layer. However, it is there in Lisbon, and it gives the Portuguese a sense of participation. And they are a charter member of NATO. When you moved into the Mediterranean, then you stepped on Italian toes, so it was not easy to fit Spain in.

But by that time, in my opinion, the Spaniards were looking at the French example of holding aloof from NATO's integrated military structure and thinking, "We can dine à la carte from the NATO menu just as the French do." It seems to me that the Spaniards have decided they are going to act like the French, which makes it not so important in practical terms whether they are members or not.

Joseph Luns, then secretary-general of NATO, also commented on Spanish entry into the alliance:

The campaign on the NATO vote was typical of Spanish politics. The Conservative opposition in Spain was all in favor of NATO but would not vote for it because it was the Socialist prime minister who was proposing it. Ruperez was the Spanish representative to NATO under the Conservatives. He had been a senator; he was a very young man.

As to the plebiscite on NATO in Spain, Felipe Gonzalez [Socialist prime minister since 1982] certainly won a great personal victory, as well as a victory for NATO. It seemed to me that there would have been little practical effect in an affirmative vote; we would not be any better off on the military side. However, if Spain had voted no and withdrew from membership in the alliance, it would have been a great black eye for NATO. So I am glad it came out the way it did, but I do not think it has improved the NATO posture one way or the other.

Farther east, in NATO's southern region, relations between Greece and Turkey are deeply rooted in a history of enmity. As members of NATO they have confronted each other on the issue of Cyprus, partitioned by Turkish forces in 1974, and in other disputes, including access to resources and conflicting claims to the continental shelf and seabed in the Aegean. Ambassador Tapley Bennett reflected on the Greco-Turkish relationship.

The Greek-Turkish rivalry and animosity have been going on for two thousand years. NATO has never been able to heal that relationship, and the situation probably is worse now than it was earlier. In my opinion, the Greeks are more the cause of irritation than the Turks are these days. Every Greek is convinced that Turkey is poised to invade Greece and take them over. I had never seen the slightest evidence of that, nor has, I think, our government ever believed that for a minute.

However, it came close to war in the summer of 1976, and I happened to handle that case in the United Nations Security Council. There were all kinds of frantic discussions back and forth. Secretary Kissinger came up to New York and spent a whole Saturday on the problem. We had the Turkish foreign minister to breakfast, and then we traipsed down the hall in the Waldorf Astoria to the Greeks; we went back and forth all day long and neither would budge. When Kissinger went back to Washington late that afternoon, he said, "This problem is even worse than the Arab-Israeli dispute, because these people really enjoy scratching each other."

The following week Under Secretary Philip Habib came up to New York and repeated the whole exercise. Well, at the end of about six weeks we finally got a resolution in the UN Security Council which composed the matter for a brief time. The two foreign ministers agreed to meet and actually did have one or two meetings, but it never went very far because there was too much suspicion on both sides.

I think the Greeks aggravate it more now than the Turks do, but the Greeks have a constituency in this country and the Turks do not. Now we are tied to this ten-to-seven ratio in aid to Turkey and Greece, which is ridiculous in view of the size of the two countries and their alliance responsibilities, but that is the way it is.

The Turks need so much in the way of defense, and Turkey is a vital anchor for the whole NATO alliance. Gen. Bernard Rogers [supreme allied commander, Europe, 1979–87] tore his hair out over it because every time he got something stitched together on command arrangements for the Aegean area, the Greeks torpedoed it or pulled out on it. And they are simply not responsible for Cyprus. There again, Clerides [Glaukos Clerides represented the Greek Cypriots during the UN-sponsored intercommunal talks, 1975–76] is the best Cypriot I know; he would be willing to make some arrangements with the Turks and had proposed one earlier much better than what they will ever get now. However, even if the Greek Cypriots were disposed to deal, which they aren't, the Greeks would step in and torpedo it as they have done more than once, so it's not a very happy situation.

The Greeks raise all manner of problems now over NATO maneuvers. I think it has been a long time since they have taken part in one. Several times they have promised and then they get up to the eve of the maneuver and they pull out with full drama. It is a bad situation, and the Turks do not always help their own case. The Turks are difficult to deal with on their side.

Secretary-General Luns shared this view:

> I had been given the task of watching over Turkish-Greek relations. But unfortunately, the Greeks, I mean Papandreou, did not accept my interference. I never could go and talk to them. The Turks were ready to accept my mission, but for all sorts of reasons the Greeks stymied it. There were very strong attacks on me in the Greek press.
>
> At one time, I said, "Now you Greeks, you may not like the Turks and it is your right not to, and you have some good reasons not to like them; but to consider that Turkey is planning to attack Greece is rather farfetched. The Turks may be unpleasant, but they are not mad. I assure you, there is not one Turkish general or admiral who thinks of invading Greece." That was what they considered as a pro-Turkish statement.
>
> Now the Greeks—who are very difficult in the alliance—will not quit the alliance because they know that if they were to do so they would be without friends. Secondly, Turkey would become l'enfant chéri of the alliance and certainly the Greeks would miss hundreds of millions of dollars every year in military aid from America. Even so, they are grumbling because they get less than Turkey, but Turkey is far bigger and more important to NATO than is Greece.

In the mid to late 1970s there was growing interest in NATO in defense modernization, not only in the nuclear arena, symbolized by the decision in 1979 to deploy intermediate-range systems—Pershing II ballistic missiles and ground-launched cruise missiles—but also at the conventional level. The most tangible outgrowth of such sentiment was the commitment of NATO members to making real increases in defense spending of 3 percent per year to be allocated to conventional modernization. Joseph Luns, NATO's secretary-general during this period, recalled some of the circumstances surrounding this decision:

> Harold Brown, the U.S. secretary of defense at the time, said to me, "Secretary-General, how much do you think the NATO countries might be willing to add in real terms every year to the defense budget?" I replied that 3 percent might do the trick, and that was adopted, so I invented the 3 percent. There was much debate within the alliance, but it was finally accepted.
>
> Of course, I think that Europe should do something more for defense. However, it is forgotten that we have conscripted armies, which means that in time of war our armed forces will be increased enormously. Take the Netherlands, for example. We have about 125,000 men under arms; it will be about 400,000 in time of war. Beyond that, we Europeans, especially Germany, provide the expenses for the stationing of American troops in Europe: barracks, exercise fields, schools, and so forth. These expenses are not covered in our defense budgets. So, in fact, for Germany it is

reckoned that they spend about 4 percent of their gross national product on defense, which has never been taken into defense expenditure accountings. People often say things without quite knowing what they are talking about. They give the impression that Europe is not doing much in the defense area; we have far more troops than the United States, and we provide half the naval capabilities of the alliance, but when you read American papers, you think that only the United States and the Soviet Union count. But Great Britain has an important navy; France, an important navy; Italy has quite a navy; Germany, Spain, and the Netherlands, likewise. The Netherlands' Navy, although not very large, is very good and very modern. More than 80 percent of the naval craft are new and modern ships.

Nevertheless, Dr. Luns pointed out, the problems associated with NATO modernization are increasing in complexity and magnitude. Other priorities, those of the domestic sector, are gaining in ascendancy.

Our priorities have changed. We give such enormous sums in the social sector that we are simply not able to allocate more for our defenses, although the countries of Europe are far better defended, far stronger forces, than, let us say, in 1940–41. To give you a figure, the Netherlands is spending $54 billion a year in the social sector—which is a lot of money for a country of about 15 million people—and $6.5 billion for defense.

On the whole, because of NATO, we spend more on defense than we would do without NATO. We would have to spend far more without NATO, of course, but we would not. And what is not realized is that one of the great advantages of NATO is that even the smallest country, Luxembourg, knows that what it is doing in the military sense has value. The battalion of Luxembourg, which I have seen in northern Norway, is part of our shield; just imagine, Luxembourg troops fighting in northern Norway! It is the same with the other countries, so there is no place for despair.

Another area of friction between the United States and its European allies is the issue of burden sharing. There are those in the United States who believe that European alliance members should bear a larger part of the cost of NATO defense. The Europeans argue that they already carry a substantial burden as the front-line states of Western security. Kai-Uwe von Hassell pointed to burden sharing as a problem for the alliance in the 1960s when he was West Germany's defense minister:

The interests of the United States were security, freedom, and defense. They were ready to place their forces here to safeguard the freedom of Europe, and they sacrificed by sending their people here to guarantee it. Their second interest was to minimize costs. For the $2 billion it cost to station troops here, they wanted $600 million to flow back to the United States [as an offset]. This was the problem of offset agreements. But how could we make up $600 million with the dollar at 4 marks? At that time, we ordered weapons and paid for the training of our aircraft and missile people in Arizona—all of this to offset the cost of putting U.S. troops in Germany. We had to buy Nike and Hawk air defense systems, as well as aircraft and guided missile destroyers from the United States, instead of getting them produced in our own factories in Germany; we had to buy American. We could not buy French, and we could not build weapons under license. This resulted in criticism.

Many people, including many in the CDU, said this policy was expensive, detrimental to German industry, and bad for European cooperation. Franz-Josef Strauss could not be critical because he had negotiated the offset agreement when he was minister of defense. The problem was either that we assist the Americans in solving their monetary problems, or the Americans will reduce their forces in Europe to cut costs.

Von Hassell discussed the impact of pressures within the United States, and especially in the U.S. Congress, to withdraw American ground forces from NATO-Europe:

In the late 1960s Sen. Mike Mansfield [former U.S. senator from Montana, 1952–76; U.S. ambassador to Japan, 1977–89] began to call for the withdrawal of U.S. troops from West Germany. It created uneasiness. We were very upset that there might be a development in this direction. This was one of the reasons why I tried to do so much for offset agreements. Mansfield argued that it was too expensive to keep troops in Europe and asked what the Europeans were doing for their own security. We tried to do everything to move influential Americans and the U.S. Congress away from this idea. The offset agreements were very helpful in this regard, for they enabled the secretary of defense to go to Capitol Hill and say that the United States was getting its money back.

Another significant problem in NATO relations was the ill-fated U.S. decision during the Carter administration to deploy the neutron bomb. Tapley Bennett was U.S. ambassador to NATO at the time. He described how the issue was addressed by the alliance:

I have heard Harold Brown [then secretary of defense] say that the president had determined that the United States was not going to take all the political heat on this weapon—the Europeans were going to have to join with us and share in this decision. The problem of the enhanced radiation weapon [ERW] was put into the NATO Council so as to have the Europeans share in this decision. The rationale was, if we made it and they were not going to accept it on their soil, then there was no point in it.

Secretary-General Luns warned from the beginning that we were making a mistake in trying to put this through the council and have a council vote of approval. He argued, "America is the nuclear power; you are the people who produce these things; you should go ahead and do what you think is right and is necessary and then the Europeans will accept deployment." Well, Luns's advice was not followed. Whether it would have been different [if his advice had been followed], I do not know, but that was his point of view as a European with very long experience and completely pro-American in his outlook.

We did go to the council with it, and there were problems from the beginning. But we gradually got the balky sheep through the gate, and we were ready to close the gate on that issue the next Monday with a vote. This was Easter week of 1978.

People like Helmut Schmidt [West German federal chancellor, 1974–82] have always been very resentful of the sudden American shift, and with some reason, but let me also say squarely on the record that the Germans were never as brave at the time as they now remember themselves to have been in facing up to this decision and being ready to vote for it. They were going to vote for it, but it was after a great deal of prodding on our part and agonizing on their part and reluctance to come to a decision. However, we had it all set and we were ready for the meeting on Easter Monday. On the weekend—I forget whether it was Saturday or Sunday—I suddenly got instructions from Washington to have the Monday meeting canceled at NATO because "we were too busy with the Middle East." Well, now, that was such a ridiculous reason to ask for a meeting of that importance to be canceled that obviously it was not the real reason, and nobody knows—at least I do not know—what did happen with President Carter on that, whether Brzezinski or someone else got to him. I have heard the story that Andrew Young, then the U.S. representative at the United Nations, went down from New York and met with President Carter on Easter weekend at Sea Island in Georgia. Young, who was opposed to the policy but whose business it was not, went down and worked on the President's "born-again" nature and said that this would be a terrible thing and brought about the reversal. I don't know whether that is actual fact or not, but at any rate Carter did reverse it; and I do not think either Vance's or Brzezinski's memoirs shed much light on what happened in this case.

Bennett pointed out the impact of this shift in U.S. policy:

Our sudden reversal fell like a bombshell in Europe after all our efforts to get approval. We paid for it in the loss of credibility and doubts about our seriousness for several weeks after. It did affect the development of the double-track decision for INF [intermediate-range nuclear force] deployment—fortunately, it did not derail it—but the background was not very good. I thought it was the worst error in the security field, as regards

NATO, of the Carter administration, and we paid for it heavily. It had a lingering afterglow that just would not go away.

Finally, Ambassador Bennett noted how the situation could have been handled differently:

> Had we made the decision and then gone to the Europeans and said, "We have this weapon, now we have got to deploy it," I do not know whether that would have made a difference. It would have been more in line with earlier policies where we had, as the largest nuclear power of the alliance, developed various devices and then said to the Europeans, "Now we find that it is time and it is important that we deploy this particular weapon." It would then, under normal procedure, have gone through the force goals and defense planning cycles. I do not believe the European allies had ever turned us down on a defense measure we thought necessary. Luns may have been right, but I cannot swear to you that he would have been.
>
> It would have been unanimous because we had not at the time evolved to today's practice where you have [NATO] countries taking abstentions and footnotes. By such action the Danes and the Greeks and now the Spaniards show their lack of agreement with a NATO policy decision. This is a bad trend in the alliance, but it has developed. But you had not yet had this situation at that time; I think you would have had a unanimous vote had we gone ahead.

Lord Mulley, who was the British Secretary of Defense from 1976 to 1979, also spoke about the problems caused by the ERW decision:

> [The Europeans in NATO] complain that they are not getting the leadership from the United States, but then when they get such leadership, they say they have not been consulted. It is the eternal problem, but some of Carter's diplomacy was particularly inept. The classic case was the instance of the so-called enhanced radiation neutron bomb. When the issue was raised, the most dramatic press stories went around Europe, and, for example, an emergency session of the Dutch Parliament was called. The Dutch minister was that day attending a meeting of the NATO defense ministers, and he had to leave at once to go back to the emergency debate in The Hague. The odd thing was that we had meetings over a period of time to review possible new weapons. The enhanced radiation warhead was down on the list; it did not cause any concern at all. It was this publicity that came out from the leak in Washington. I gather that the journalist who actually wrote the first piece wrote later that he had obviously exaggerated things, but, of course, this article got no publicity at all. There are people around here who think we can have a bomb on the Houses of Parliament and that you and I would disappear but your tape recording would still be working, recording it all. It really is quite incredible, and the real truth is that if we already had the enhanced radiation

warheads on the artillery in Germany and it was proposed to replace them by what are now current, it would be quite likely a source of a great and correct argument because the ERW are in a military sense more effective as a deterrent to massed Warsaw Pact armor and also their collateral damage is very much less than the ones we have now. This is all part of the new situation, but Carter—having sent people around, and with a lot of trouble [having] squared governments in Europe, even the Dutch, preparing everyone (Schmidt and Callaghan [James Callaghan was British secretary of state for foreign and commonwealth affairs, 1974–76, and labour prime minister, 1976–79] particularly did a lot of work to get all this)—then changed his mind and withdrew the option. That annoyed people.

Beyond the neutron bomb controversy, NATO in the late 1970s was moving toward the double-track decision taken in December 1979 to deploy intermediate-range nuclear systems if the Soviet Union did not dismantle its new generation SS-20 and older systems targeted against NATO-Europe. Ambassador Bennett recalled events leading to the NATO decision:

> The landmark speech by Helmut Schmidt in 1977 set off the events that led eventually to the double-track decision. But I would not have said that [the United States was] not in the front rank of those involved; there was a gradual response and organization. This was a perceived need of Schmidt's; then later, after the Germans began to get nervous about it—and even Schmidt stepped back—we had occasion to remind them more than once, "This all originated with you; you were the first to ask for this." But once it got into the process, I would say that we took active leadership. Certainly there was leadership under both Lawrence Eagleburger [assistant secretary of state for European and Canadian affairs, 1981–82] and Richard Burt [director, Bureau of Politico-Military Affairs, 1981–82, and assistant secretary of state for European and Canadian affairs, 1982–85]— now this is already the Reagan administration—but even before that Les Gelb was very prominent as the head of the Political-Military Affairs Bureau in the State Department during the Carter administration, and David McGiffert [assistant secretary of defense for international security policy in the Carter administration] did the [Department of] Defense side. The NATO Defense Committee depended on a number of uniformed officers who made an expert analysis of what was needed to counter the Soviet SS-20s, how many, and all that. I was not too close to that myself, but I relied on the experts. It was their estimates, more than anybody else's, that governed the decision of 572 as the number of missiles to be deployed for NATO defense.

Ambassador Bennett described the reactions of members of the alliance at the time the double-track decision was made:

> The Germans, of course, were strong on it, provided they were not left isolated as the only Continental power. It was not enough that the British

were going to deploy. There was never any doubt about British participation. The Germans insisted on at least one other Continental power. In the end, that brought in Italy, Belgium, and the Netherlands. The Italians were and have been enormously stalwart on the issue. In some ways they have been, I would say, more consistently solid than the Germans. They have never wavered, despite the fragile balance they have in their political life. The Dutch were always the weakest because they had a real public relations problem at home, a public opinion problem. The Belgians were rather quiet, as is their way.

The day of the decision was an unprecedented event, in that it was a joint meeting of foreign ministers and defense ministers who took that decision in December 1979. There are two important meetings at NATO in December. The defense ministers usually meet a few days before the foreign ministers—all of this in the first half of December. In 1979, with the double-track decision pending, it was arranged that the two meetings would overlap. The last day of the defense ministers' meeting was the first day of the foreign ministers' meeting. The joint meeting went on and on—we did not get out until 8:30 at night, which is unusual for NATO meetings.

At that lengthy joint meeting, the Danes, as so often, were making trouble. The Danes often do not take part in these military actions, but they do not hesitate to throw hookers in to make it difficult. At times you would say to them, "Why don't you just stand back and let the rest of us get on with the work; if you don't want to take part, just stand there out of the way." But no, the Danes would have qualifying language which could make great difficulties. With the Danish wording in the document, you would have lost other members, including the Dutch and the Belgians, and then the Italians would have unraveled. At about five o'clock that afternoon, we were faced with a situation which looked quite dangerous in the sense that, if one thread were pulled, the whole sleeve would unravel. It was [Henri] Simonet, the Belgian foreign minister [1977–80], who came up with the compromise language which everybody could live with. To that extent he saved the situation and made a great contribution to the double-track decision. It turned out later that the Belgians themselves were having trouble living with what he had come up with. But Simonet made a singular contribution, and there was never any doubt of his devotion to the alliance and to doing what was necessary for defense.

Simonet's compromise put it together; once the agreement was reached that evening, no one was more strongly in support of it than the Italians. The British never had any question under the Thatcher government as to where they stood. The Germans were quite strong but with heavy pressures on them. After all, the Germans never forget that they are sitting there on the front line.

One of the greatest clashes between the United States and its allies arose over the Soviet Siberian natural gas pipeline deal. The Carter administration and its NATO European allies had agreed to export technology needed by the

Soviet Union to build a pipeline to export natural gas to Western Europe. The Reagan administration shifted U.S. policy to one of opposition to the pipeline project. The result was dissension between the administration and even its closest NATO European allies. Yet behind the scenes, the Reagan administration's decision regarding the natural gas pipeline was fraught with personality conflicts and assertions of authority at the top of the administration. Robert McFarlane, President Reagan's former NSC adviser (1983–85), added an interesting perspective on the pipeline decision. He related President Reagan's reaction to Secretary of State Haig when Reagan evidently perceived that Secretary Haig was not adequately consulting with the White House on policy issues; the situation came to a head after the June 1982 economic summit meeting in France.

Secretary of State Haig felt that his power was being undercut by the White House staff. He thus began to make statements of policy without prior consultation with the White House. This was especially true during his trip to Europe. This caused a great deal of hostility between Haig and the White House. When Haig returned from this European trip with this hostility—artificially induced between the president and the secretary of state; it was very real though—the next decision that came across [Reagan's] desk was going to be used by the president to assert his authority. It would not have mattered if this involved using nukes in Grenada. I mean the president would have asked one question: "What does the secretary of state want?" And he would have decided the other way. That sounds very trivial and childish, but it was not childish. It was a matter, though, of the president wanting a vehicle for demonstrating his dominance of the process and the next decision happened to be the oil pipeline in Europe. The president said, "What does the secretary of state propose?" [Haig] said, "Don't do it." [Reagan] said, "Let's do it," in just about those terms. It had much less to do with considerations of extraterritoriality and all of these legal considerations. It was an assertion of presidential authority.

Lawrence Eagleburger, who was under secretary of state for policy at the time, offers his perspective on the pipeline problem:

The foreign policy objective of the United States is the maintenance and the improvement of the transatlantic relationship for the strengthening of NATO. Now if that is an objective, which it is, how do you explain pipeline sanctions? You explain them by saying, "Well, I have other things I have to worry about too," and the issue then becomes relations with the Soviet Union and strengthening the Soviet economy, and putting the West Europeans in a condition of greater dependence on the Soviets because they may decide they will not sell you natural gas tomorrow. This all turned out to be wrong, and the Europeans spent a great deal of money on a pipeline that does not mean a thing.

Dr. von Hassell made a similar point:

If eastern [Soviet] gas reaches a percentage of our total gas supply of 30 percent, then we are in their hands. So we approved the pipeline, but only up to a certain percentage of our total use. There is a parallel with Iran. The shah decided to arrange a pipeline from Iran into the Soviet Union and then to Western Europe. I asked him why he did not pipe this gas through Turkey, because piping it through Russia made us vulnerable, but my argument did not carry. We followed the decision of the United States.

Joseph Luns believed that the Europeans, by participating in the pipeline project, were making themselves more vulnerable to Soviet influence.

I doubt whether it was a very wise decision because the Russians can close the tap at any moment. Now a country like the Netherlands has not much to fear from it because we have an enormous reserve of natural gas, and we export to other countries too. But Germany and other countries, would they get it from the Russian pipeline in an emergency? The pipeline is now there. It was rather hotly debated. The United States, I think rightly, was far from enthusiastic.

Ambassador Tapley Bennett argued that the pipeline controversy, strictly speaking, was not a NATO affair.

The gas pipeline was never really a NATO issue, although it has been commonly considered one and the press certainly has treated it as one. That was an issue between the United States and individual countries, and we were very careful to keep it out of the [North Atlantic] Council; we never discussed it in the council. I do not recall the pipeline really ever coming up except maybe on the sidelines. We went individually to the British and to the French. It was a bilateral problem between important NATO allies. I do not recall that we ever took it up. It might have been referred to peripherally, but it was not an issue on the agenda; and we were very careful to keep it out of there because it was very divisive. I think that the Reagan administration came on a little too strong on the pipeline. I do not differ with the analysis or the aims of the policy, but it was divisive with a number of our allies. It is hard to predict those things. You do not know who—ten years from now—is going to be stuck or which side is going to suffer from it.

Finally, Lawrence Eagleburger noted the important role that George Shultz, as secretary of state, played in repairing the damage of the pipeline affair:

In the aftermath of the pipeline sanctions and the effort to put things back in order, George Shultz was superb from an alliance management point of view. I am talking not about the substance of whether you agree or disagree with the pipeline sanctions. The pipeline sanctions, in my judgment, very quickly became unmanageable. By the time George Shultz came in, it was very much an issue of how do we manage this nightmare that we have created? And George Shultz, I will say immodestly, with a lot of help from me, pretty well put that genie back into the bottle for a time, and I think the allies gained a great deal of respect for him in the process because he did it while at the same time managing the White House quite well.

Other factors as well shape the relationship that evolves among NATO members. They include the personalities of heads of government. Brent Scowcroft spoke of the role of an idiosyncratic variable, personality, in relations between the United States in the Nixon-Ford administrations and other NATO members, especially the government of the Federal Republic of Germany and its chancellor, Helmut Schmidt:

> I think that there was a real change in the personal aspect of U.S.-German relations between President Nixon and Chancellor Brandt, and President Ford and Chancellor Schmidt. Nixon really was unable to relate to Willy Brandt, and they had a very cool, formal relationship. Willy Brandt was a kind of an off-in-the-woods specialist as far as Nixon was concerned, and Nixon thought he was wooly-headed and just did not deeply respect him. Ford and Schmidt hit it off beautifully—very different kinds of people. Schmidt is an extremely cerebral person who does not tolerate fools lightly, a very haughty kind of a person. Ford is a down-home Midwesterner, open, warm. The two of them got along just beautifully together, to the point where Schmidt practically campaigned for Ford in the election of 1976. They used to pick up the phone and talk to each other, which is a really very unusual phenomenon. They cooperated closely, somewhat in the financial crisis with Italy, but especially in the British financial crisis. The two of them worked very, very closely to coordinate positions on that. It is a good example of the degree to which things go better when the leaders have this kind of relationship. It was sort of that way with Giscard [Valéry Giscard d'Estaing, French president 1974–81], although not quite so outgoing, but nonetheless warm, and I think that our relations with the French improved dramatically. There were several cases of informal cooperation, which made an enormous difference. Schmidt started out not liking Jimmy Carter because he had thrown his friend, Gerald Ford, out of the White House, and it went downhill from there. Hence, he was disposed to disliking him, and then Carter rubbed him the wrong way and so on. That was a good example of how important personalities are.

General Scowcroft made a similar observation with respect to relations between Presidents Nixon and Ford and British prime ministers Harold Wilson and James Callaghan:

I have a recollection of Nixon with Wilson, and Nixon did not trust him. I do not have any recollection of Ford with Wilson. The recollection I have with Ford was with Callaghan, who started out, of course, as foreign minister in the Wilson cabinet, and then when Wilson resigned he became prime minister. That, again, was a very warm relationship which has continued to this day. They related very, very closely to each other. I guess you would have to say that Ford really had a knack of getting close, especially to our European friends.

However important may be the ability of the heads of government of NATO members to relate effectively to one another, the alliance is ultimately dependent on sustained public support. Dr. von Hassell commented on support for NATO in the Federal Republic of Germany's opposition Social Democratic party (SPD):

> The majority of Socialists favor denuclearization. They follow the extreme Left, although it might be that Dr. Hans-Jochan Vogel [chairman of the West German Social Democratic party since 1986], the president of the party, will get rid of these people. He is more to the center-right. But the spokesman for defense, von Bülow [Andreas von Bülow was parliamentary state secretary of the German Federal ministry of defense, 1976–80], came back from Moscow and suggested that the ministers of defense from the FRG, the GDR, and the Soviet Union should meet to discuss their problems. This is at present premature.

Lord Mulley discussed the defense perspectives in the British Labour party:

> I do not think the unilateralists were a great problem in the 1970s until after the 1979 general election. I was amazed that they were building up a little bit in anticipation of resisting a commitment which they thought—wrongly—that the Labour government was going to make prior to the election to replace or just to renew the Polaris. They began to build up in 1977–78 on that issue, but their main argument, their main objection to defense was the classic one—which makes their present posture so impossible—that too much public money was spent on defense and too little money taken from defense in general for other things—they did not specify in what areas. Labour said defense should be cut and more money should be spent on education or housing or whatever you mention. It was designed to appeal to any particular cause that a particular person may support—education or the health service or housing or old age pensions, or whatever, that is where public money should go, not on defense, they say. In general terms, it was not particularly nuclear related, when the facts were known. Mostly, people were very ignorant about it, but those who bothered to make a little inquiry realized that of course the actual cost of nuclear maintenance in the defense budget was very low. It was only when

as I say, the replacement issue came to the fore that they began to build up to gain support within the party. The significant thing—which I think, perhaps, people do not appreciate—is that the extreme hard Left (the militants) really wanted to use the defense and nuclear issues as a means of getting rid entirely of the leadership.

Joseph Luns commented on Dutch opinion with respect to the Atlantic Alliance:

> The Dutch position vis-à-vis NATO is still very positive. More than 70 percent of the public favors NATO. It had been 80 percent, but it is more than 70 percent now. The left-wing parties and the left-wing press give another impression. The Dutch, including the left-wingers, were very strongly pro-American, but little by little that support has been eroded, partly because of a sense of jealousy and partly because of the impact of subtly promoted Soviet propaganda. There was opposition, but it was academic opposition. What bothers me is the anti-Americanism in left-wing circles in Europe. It is very unjust to put the United States on the same low level as the Soviet Union. First of all, there is a certain jealousy of the power of the United States. A large power is always subject to such jealousy. Then, there is a mistaken belief that America uses Europe only to further American interests, and certainly a mistaken belief that the Cold War and everything else is also partly the fault of the United States— which is not the case. Then, there is the left-wing propaganda written by people who do not like America at all.
>
> They played on the fear of atomic war, and they said ridiculous things like, "The Soviets have promised us that if we do not deploy INF systems, they will not attack the Netherlands with atomic weaponry." This is ridiculous, of course, and naive. The governments were at fault because they did not want to stir up the pot. They ought to have explained more fully the real situation, but they were silent—not so much the Germans, but especially in the Netherlands.

Mr. Luns pointed to what he regarded as the importance of NATO to its members and to the United States:

> The great advantage of NATO for the European members is that even the smallest of them—Luxembourg—knows that what they are doing is of use. [This is so] because can you imagine a country like Denmark if it stood alone? They probably would argue, "What is the use? Why should we maintain anything? We will be overrun in a week or in a day." That mentality has been completely changed because of NATO, and the integrated defense command—in peacetime, integrated defenses—is something completely new in the history of alliances and is remarkable.
>
> As long as the United States maintains 325,000 men [in Europe] and as long as it has a number of short-range atomic weapons, and as long as

you in the United States remain convinced that Europe is essential for the defense of the United States, I am not worried about it. I once testified before the Senate Foreign Relations Committee; Sen. William Fulbright [Democratic senator from Arkansas, 1945–74, and chairman, Senate Foreign Affairs Committee, 1959–74] said, "You Europeans, you are all the same. You come here, you want us to defend you." I replied, "No, Senator, you are completely wrong. If the United States government and Congress and the United States people come to the conclusion that Europe is not essential to the defense of America, my advice to you is to clear out tomorrow rather than after tomorrow because foreign policy is not a question of philanthropy, it is a question of hard interest; but, as long as you consider that Europe's defense is important to the United States, there are some consequences."

10
Relations between Western Europe and the Soviet Union

A lthough the focus of the foreign policy of NATO-European allies, especially in the early years of the alliance, was at the transatlantic level with the United States, the allies nevertheless evolved increasingly important relationships with the Soviet Union. Of special significance is the West German *Ostpolitik*, together with the Eastern Policy of France under President de Gaulle. Kai-Uwe von Hassell, who was minister of defense in the Federal Republic of Germany between 1963 and 1966, describes West German policy toward the Soviet Union during the period of Konrad Adenauer's terms as chancellor:

> When I came up in politics, when I got to know Adenauer, we were of the unanimous opinion that the Soviets were completely different from the West. The common belief was that "Hitler is dead, the Nazis are overcome, now we can go ahead with a peaceful future with Russians being at the same table as democrats and peace-loving people." We warned everyone that this would be a tremendous mistake—I go back thirty years—we must be prepared until they come to new solutions in the Soviet Union, to a new policy. We must be prepared to face the Soviets from the very beginning—with a united Europe, with a worldwide defense organization. We must try to tell America, "If Europe falls and the Soviets are on the Atlantic coast, your freedom is also at stake." Adenauer thought the only nation, the only force, able to stop the Russians from going westward was the United States. Besides the United States, there was not anyone else, really, that could stop them from their aims.
>
> The Soviet Union did not disarm; it reshuffled the whole army, it rearmed, it brought up its conventional forces to top level. In the United Kingdom, the new government of the Labour party withdrew its forces from all around the world. The French had nothing to disarm, they had only a few divisions they brought up in North Africa in the latter part of the World War II. The Americans also disarmed. They scrapped their air force and their planes. Adenauer was of the opinion that we had to convince the Americans not to go on disarming, because their partner in the alliance during World War II—the Soviet Union—was not disarming as they were.

In the early 1950s the Soviet Union attempted to lure the Federal Republic of Germany (FRG) away from the close relationship with the West through hints of the possibility of German reunification in return for Bonn's adoption of a policy of neutrality that would have prevented its membership in NATO and active participation in West European integrative organizations. Ambassador Rolf Pauls was the personal assistant to Walter Hallstein, who served as secretary of state in the Foreign Office from 1951 to 1958. He observed the following:

> We saw some signs as late as 1950–51. Was Stalin holding out the bait of reunification, including an independent Germany, so long as it was [not integrated with] Western Europe? It culminated of course in the so-called Stalin Note in March 1952, just eight weeks before the signing of the treaty for the formation of the European Defense Community [EDC] was to take place. This recollection is very important. There were basically two schools of thought. One said, "We have made use of the negotiations with the West. Now we can have Germany reunited." That was one school, which, of course, could not be expressed. The second said that "all endeavors by the Soviets are (at that time the Austrian Treaty was negotiated but not yet signed) leading towards a decoupling between the FRG and the West. The Soviets will use this bait to postpone negotiations between us and the West, and the interruption of this process will be enough for them." All the problems that exist between the FRG and the West are small compared to the relationship at that time. The slightest blow could have destroyed everything achieved since the Berlin blockade and the creation of the FRG. That would have been enough for the Soviet Union. I think that the operational approach of the Soviets was to interrupt negotiations with the West in order to split the FRG from the West. This has always been an operational goal of the Soviet Union, and one must consider this when viewing the possibilities of the present Soviet proposals. The goals remain the same, but the methods are much more refined.

On the issue of German reunification, Dr. von Hassell discussed what he observed to be the position of Chancellor Adenauer:

> Adenauer knew perfectly well that there would be problems regarding reunification, given the situation in the world vis-à-vis Germany. When I became president of the European Union of Christian Democrats in 1972, I saw very good examples of this. In 1973—nearly forty years after 1936—as president of European Union of Christian Democrats I saw that the Socialist *Ostpolitik* of Chancellor Brandt was hailed in the beginning of the 1970s (he took over in 1969) by all foreigners, including the Christian Democrats. However, in the 1940s and 1950s they saw that if Western Germany could be reunited, there would be together 77 million Germans: 60 million Germans in the West, and 17 million Germans in the German

Democratic Republic [GDR]. At that time, even Christian Democrats outside our country knew that Germany was the strongest European nation with regard to finance, economy, military organization and forces. If these 60 million Germans in the West would be united with the 17 million in the GDR (which ranked, I think, as number twelve and thirteen worldwide in economic production), this would be of paramount danger for the Danes, the Dutch, Belgians, Luxembourgers, the French, and so on. Adenauer knew very well that if we were to be reunited, we would have problems with all our friends and partners in Western Europe and overseas who believed this would be too strong a majority of Germans which might someday dominate Europe. Therefore, he was very reluctant to go ahead with reunification—which was no doubt his aim—but not in 1946, or when he was first elected chancellor in 1949, or in the 1950s and 1960s.

In 1955 Dr. von Hassell accompanied Adenauer on his visit to Moscow, the purpose of which was the establishment of diplomatic relations between the Federal Republic of Germany and the Soviet Union. According to von Hassell, this marked the beginning of *Ostpolitik*. He commented on his first German-Soviet summit:

It was really an event when Adenauer went to see the leaders of the Kremlin in 1955. At the time I was the president of the Bundesrat. There was no doubt that there were two different aims. The Soviets wanted to use the opportunity—his visit—to establish diplomatic relations, and Adenauer wanted German prisoners of war retained mainly in Siberia returned home. The people hoped to achieve this aim and pressured him to do it. He knew what this meant for those retained in concentration camps because he had been imprisoned himself in World War II in a concentration camp, and he could imagine what it was like for a German soldier. Thus, it was also his personal view. There were other issues, but these were the main issues. If the Soviets were ready to release the POWs, he would be ready to establish relations. After ten years of no relations, relations would allow Moscow to enter into this part of the world. For them, it is advantageous to have a diplomatic mission here, an ambassador and his staff. Everything will follow from this—trade and other agreements.

After two or three days there had been no result on the question of the prisoners, then Adenauer ordered his plane to come back from the Lufthansa base at Frankfurt. He got the order sent to Frankfurt over an open telephone, knowing that this order would be intercepted. The Soviets saw that Adenauer would indeed leave without agreement on the establishment of relations, if the prisoners of war were not returned. On the next morning, the Russians decided to say yes. This was the trade-off.

Ambassador Pauls was also at this meeting. He recounted the following:

At a reception at the Bolshoi, Khrushchev made another toast—there was toasting all the time—in which he said, "The key to permanent peace is built on our common ground. We Russians and Germans, let us dig it out and bring peace to the world." Adenauer wasn't so much a poet and responded in a very sober way. [Adenauer discovered] that Khrushchev always invited a toast to drink to "X" but never drank himself. Adenauer said to the KGB officer with the bottle to go fill the general secretary's glass. He did this, and then Adenauer said, "to 'X.' "

Another issue of interest was the POW question. Before going to Moscow we had a discussion about this matter. We prepared for the talks and then finally decided it might not be a good idea to go ahead with that because it might weaken our position. But Adenauer mentioned this to Khrushchev and was treated to an incredible outburst, with the general secretary speaking loudly that there were only criminals in prison and that if it continued to be mentioned, then negotiations would cease. He also told Adenauer that "you need us more than we need you."

And I thought, How do we get out of this? We said a few dignified words covering our departure, and then Adenauer said, "Mr. Secretary, that wasn't very polite." The Soviet side was rather surprised, and we discovered here that we had hit a weak point. If you regard the Soviets as uncultivated, they become vulnerable. Then Khrushchev said, "Mr. Chancellor, I am sorry that you got the impression that I was impolite. I only wanted to make things clear and help our negotiations."

The surprises came after the negotiations at the reception at the Kremlin. We were all seated at the head table, and after a toast to Adenauer, Khrushchev said he would look into the POW issue. If Adenauer had said, "That's fine, now let's have it in black and white," the whole thing would have failed, but Adenauer was trusting by nature and felt that they would follow their word. That was a surprise.

Adenauer remained in power until 1963. Dr. von Hassell offered his assessment of *Ostpolitik* under Adenauer:

Adenauer made several proposals regarding relations between the Federal Republic and the then so-called Soviet Occupied Zone. He knew exactly the situation behind the iron curtain. We had a great many contacts with the people there. We saw what Walter Ulbricht [East German Communist party secretary-general, 1948–71], the strong man there, pursued as his policy. Adenauer was afraid that we would not succeed in having the Soviet Union ever agree to let the GDR get autodetermination, even if we agreed to diplomatic relations. Nevertheless, he made a secret proposal to Ivan Smirnov [then Soviet ambassador to the FRG] to neutralize the GDR, to guarantee that it would be neutral in the future, say, in ten years for a plebiscite for a decision on unification. Adenauer no doubt knew that a period of ten years was far too short. This would have meant that Ulbricht and his party people, his *nomenklatura*, would more or less have to be ready to give up their jobs with all advantages.

Hans Globke [state secretary in the chancellor's office, 1953–63] was also said to have had a plan—the so-called Globke Plan—which was not supported by the people because they knew that the other side was firmly in the hands of the Kremlin—they are not able to do as they wished. They are under Soviet control in all dimensions.

Both plans—one by Adenauer to Smirnov and the other by Globke— were invalid because everyone knew they never would be successful. On the other hand, he tried everything to improve, to ease the situation for our people.

During the 1950s there were a lot of people in refugee organizations who said that Adenauer did not want reunification for a simple reason: he was Catholic and the GDR was a Protestant country. Of the 17 million people in the GDR, 16 million were Protestants, mostly Lutherans, and 1 million were Catholic. Adenauer, being a devout Catholic, could not be interested in an FRG with a very large Protestant majority, with the Catholic minority decreasing to 35 or 30 percent.

My view was to tell the people that even if they were right, they must know that if reunification took place between the FRG and the GDR, the line of freedom would move East to the Oder-Neisse line, and just behind it is a Catholic Poland interested in having a free, united Germany close to its border. A Catholic Poland must be interested in a Catholic/ Protestant free, united Germany close at hand. The influence in Bonn might be in favor of the Catholic much more than if they were far away behind the iron curtain.

An important element of Adenauer's success as chancellor, von Hassell contended, was his ability to build public support for the integration of the Federal Republic of Germany into the West as the necessary basis for any improvement in relations with the East.

Public opinion [in the Federal Republic] did not say, "Now turn East." It said, "You have established excellent contacts and relationships and very strong ties to the West. From this strong Western-oriented position, you are now able to concentrate also on *Ostpolitik.*" Public opinion was going that way. It did not stress abandoning the Western ties to achieve reunification. Everyone who was responsible said it was necessary to maintain relations with the West in order to secure freedom and then to try to see what you can do—offer trade, credits, and materials. It never said abandon the West. This was now in addition to it.

Therefore, *Ostpolitik* would be built on a strong basis in NATO and the Western world. If we are really stable, then we might not be influenced by a visit to the Kremlin, and by being received there with a lot of vodka and caviar. As long as there is instability in the West, you are not allowed to go there. If there is stability, then we can try to shape *Ostpolitik,* and Gerhard Schröder [minister of foreign affairs, 1961–66, and minister of defense, 1966–69] did so.

Dr. von Hassell noted how *Ostpolitik* endured in the years immediately following Adenauer's resignation as chancellor in 1963:

> When Ludwig Erhard succeeded Adenauer, there was no difference. *Ostpolitik* was started by, as I said, Schröder, who was foreign minister for Adenauer in 1963—it began that year. When Erhard took over in October 1963, Schröder went more strongly into *Ostpolitik*, not because Adenauer did not block him, but because it was settled vis-à-vis France, and we could go East with more energy, but not with the energy the Socialists put into it later on.
>
> *Ostpolitik* during Adenauer's time—until he left office in 1963—was not a big issue. It started to be strengthened under Schröder in 1964–66. Gerhard Schröder—not Willy Brandt—built up all the original contacts. He went to Romania, Czechoslovakia, and Hungary with his people and established the first contacts on trade issues—what we call *Handelsvertretungen*. It is a fairy tale if the Socialists say *Ostpolitik* was started when they came into government. It started three years earlier, and the one who started it was Gerhard Schröder.
>
> There was more or less a constant development from Adenauer's time through Schröder and Erhard with the first steps of the *Ostpolitik*. I know those who went to Warsaw and Bucharest for discussions. They were excellent diplomats, and they were very careful. There was no worry that they would go too far; and then the Grand Coalition shifted the intensity toward *Ostpolitik*, but still in a tolerable degree. Later on, when Chancellor Brandt was free to decide his *Ostpolitik*, then *Ostpolitik* was exaggerated and brought us a lot of problems with tremendous debates in Parliament.
>
> As long as Schröder was responsible for foreign affairs and *Ostpolitik*, I was absolutely sure we had the guarantee that he would not enter into a field of uncertainty. He was a clear-cut defender of NATO. There was no question about his solid policy vis-à-vis the West. Therefore, he could carry out *Ostpolitik*. As long as Schröder was in government, responsible for this field of activity, I said, let him do whatever he believes to be suitable.

Between 1966 and 1969, the Federal Republic of Germany was governed by the Grand Coalition, composed of the Christian Democrats and the Social Democratic party, with Kurt Kiesinger as chancellor and Willy Brandt as foreign minister. With the rise in SPD influence resulting from Brandt's accession, the pace of *Ostpolitik* quickened. According to von Hassell,

> *Ostpolitik* was done through the minister of foreign affairs. He was a Socialist and was able to pursue a policy, and if it was not in line with the chancellor, then a compromise would be fashioned between the chancellor and the foreign minister, because he is the minister responsible for *Ostpolitik*.

Von Hassell told how the Christian Democrats attempted to thwart SPD efforts to accelerate *Ostpolitik:*

> During the Grand Coalition, we formed defense policy in the party group, in the leading body of the Christian Democrats over in the Adenauer House. This applied not only to defense, which was easier because the Socialists were on the same path, but also to *Ostpolitik.* We always tried to back Kiesinger as chancellor, and his people—Gutenberg, for instance—and to watch the foreign ministry carefully, so as not to go in a direction where we might get ourselves into danger. Schröder was minister of defense. He could only watch *Ostpolitik,* as I did, in the party group, not in the cabinet. We backed Chancellor Kiesinger and Gutenberg in the party organization, where we regularly met Tuesday night with Kiesinger to plan the Wednesday morning cabinet meeting.
>
> In our constitution, the chancellor has the right to define general policy; we call it *Richtlinienkompetenz* [literally, "guiding principles"]. He has to say that this is the way we go. It is stated in the constitution. We never made use of this. I had the same right as a prime minister in Schleswig-Holstein and never made use of it. I tried to persuade the Liberals in my coalition. If they did not agree to my views, we met separately and tried to find a common solution. This also happened in the Grand Coalition. For instance, the Socialists Brandt and Bahr [Ambassador Egon Bahr was director of the planning staff, Diplomatic Service, 1967–68, ministerial director, 1968–69, and state secretary, in Berlin, 1969–72], in particular, saw that we carefully watched them, so they were more reluctant, more careful.

After the election in 1969 of an SPD government with Willy Brandt as chancellor, the *Ostpolitik* gained further momentum. The CDU, in opposition, was seen by many observers as a restraining influence, warning of potential dangers and pitfalls. According to Gen. Franz-Josef Schulze, members of the military as well feared that *Ostpolitik* might be seen to be incompatible with the procurement of adequate defense capabilities. General Schulze, who commanded forces on the NATO central region, explained this perspective:

> No one can deny today two things: first of all, that the *Ostpolitik* had some results—more visits between the two Germanies and other relief. Secondly, we cannot overlook the fact that the Soviet Union used the period of so-called détente for a buildup of forces without any historical precedent. All those presentations on the threat, on the increasing conventional superiority of the Soviet Union, and the ever more obvious attempt to deprive NATO of defensive options, particularly in the conventional but also in the nuclear field, and the ever increasing danger that the Soviets would be able to start an unreinforced attack, had little resonance. Today it is obvious what the Soviet buildup of forces was aiming at: maintaining

under all circumstances their conventional superiority as a strategic instrument of their foreign policy.

My impression is that most of the military people feared that this kind of policy—the overtures made to the Russians, the Poles, and so on—would very quickly lead to an erosion of the threat perception. "Let us do away with the *Feindbilder*" was the order of the day, as if we had ever educated our soldiers to look at the Soviets as enemies rather than a potential aggressor.

We never had a *Feindbild*, but we have had and have to be aware what the capabilities of the other side are. We have to do a sober assessment of the threat. I still believe we could have made *Ostpolitik* without telling our own population that there is no threat and that there are no risks. It was not only the loss of perception that there is a military threat. It was an atmosphere where people even lost the ability to realize the fundamental differences in the political structure of the societies. You may even go so far as to say that it was here where a development of public opinion towards equidistance started.

Ambassador Pauls made a somewhat similar point:

Ostpolitik was a major focus, and we had to see how far and fast we could go with the alliance. I thought that the philosophy of *Ostpolitik* was justified under the aspect of our foreign policy in line with the American policy. I criticize in retrospect the speed with which we acted and put ourselves under time pressure. This proved to be a mistake. But the results of the policy are not as useful as some say, nor are they as disastrous as others say. After the treaties had been signed they needed to be ratified. Otherwise the West German government would have been inoperable. However, we were in agreement with American policy.

Finally, Richard Allen, himself an astute observer of the West German political scene, offered a perspective on *Ostpolitik:*

To a large extent, *Ostpolitik* has continued even today in the hands of what is thought to be a conservative administration. Maybe it is only relatively more conservative. I have thought of *Ostpolitik* as divisible into three levels. The first is the question of *Ostpolitik* in what concerns inter-German relations—that is, the relation between the Bundesrepublik [West Germany] and the GDR. That is essentially a German question in which we are interested, but in which I do not think we have any long-term interventionary capacity. The Germans, after all, if there is going to be a solution, which I do not foresee, will have to arrive at it themselves and not have it imposed by someone from the outside. The conditions for reaching some sort of modus vivendi may be seen by Gorbachev if he stays around long enough, to be somewhat advantageous, at least in terms of neutralizing Germany, through the process of baiting the West Germans. Nationalism is a very powerful pull, and you almost have to be German to understand the pull and its impact, particularly on this chancellor, Helmut Kohl.

The second level of *Ostpolitik*—and I mean *Ostpolitik* in the 1966–68 period in terms of its formative stages—concerns the relationship of the Federal Republic to the East European states, and in that we have much more than just a passing interest. But there is not much we can do about influencing that situation either. That, after all, began as sort of a form of reparations for the atrocities of World War II and the way this was to be done. *Ostpolitik* was to aid the East European countries economically, and I cannot say that this has been, by any stretch of the imagination, a failure. After all, look at Hungary today and see what distinguishes it from Romania or any of the other East European countries. So there are differences. I think *Ostpolitik* has contributed to this process of differentiation. I do believe that *Ostpolitik* has played a role in the transformation of Eastern Europe, I think for the better.

Then there comes that third level of *Ostpolitik* which pertains to the Soviet Union, and that is very much our business. It is here that we may have dissipated and lost an advantage by virtue of our recent behavior in the negotiation and conclusion of the 1987 INF Treaty and the prospects for concluding a START Treaty. We have now made it impossible for the Germans to argue for a strong and effective defense in Western Europe. That is why some of the ideas that are being circulated around Washington and that will inevitably come up during the debate on INF will, I hope, eventually accumulate some credibility. Namely, that at the very moment that we disarm in certain sectors with the Soviet Union we will be able to start a program of getting better conventionally, including the stationing of huge numbers of conventionally armed cruise missiles in Western Europe. Lots of little weapons, conventionally loaded, with unerring accuracy, makes good sense to me. Unless managed carefully politically, the process of *Ostpolitik* is likely to get out of hand.

11

Conventional Weapons and the Defense of Western Europe

NATO has always had as the basis for deterrence a reliance on escalation, if necessary, to the nuclear level. As early as 1950, however, the alliance began to build a deterrence posture that also included a conventional capability for forward defense. Without the Federal Republic of Germany, NATO lacked both the territory and manpower with which to mount a forward defense. Thus, this chapter begins with an emphasis on German rearmament and various plans put forward to tie the Federal Republic of Germany firmly to other Western Europe powers; the Franco-German Treaty of 1963 and the Franco-German brigade of the late 1980s are also addressed. In addition, a variety of NATO issues related to conventional military strategy and force structure are elucidated. These include the evolution of NATO conventional doctrine, NATO arms procurement and production, demographic trends affecting military manpower, emerging technologies and the European Defense Initiative, French defense strategy, and the U.S. contribution to NATO. Gen. Andrew Goodpaster was an officer at SHAPE in the early 1950s. He stated that the United States saw German rearmament as crucial to the ability of the alliance to deter a Soviet attack. He also outlined steps taken by the United States in an effort to overcome French fears of German rearmament:

> Before Eisenhower was appointed supreme allied commander, Europe [SACEUR], in the fall of 1950, proposals were made to form a collective military force in Europe, and this was being discussed within the NATO structure. General Marshall was secretary of defense of the United States by that time. The United States was insistent that if the force were developed, West Germany should be brought into association with it and rearmed. It was only on the basis of French agreement that that would be done—the French having been in opposition—that the United States agreed to the establishment of the Allied Command and a commander, who turned out to be Eisenhower. When he got there, one of the things he went to work on was to resolve this issue with the French in some practical way. René Pleven [French prime minister, 1950–52, minister of defense, 1952–54, and foreign affairs, 1958] came up with the idea of the

European Defense Community [EDC]. At SHAPE we established a small section of international officers working on that on an international basis. Through the months they tried to work this out, but the support within the French government was very narrow and very uncertain, and even with all of the work going on, it was far from clear that this would be accomplished.

There are some analysts and writers who suggest that the French never expected their plan [the EDC] to succeed, that it was put up as a French proposal which would be inevitably shot down. I think, from what I know of Eisenhower's view, that he thought they were sincere. Further, he thought that they would be able to put it through, although he did not underestimate the difficulties. There was considerable [French] opposition, which soon began to show up openly. The minister of defense was adamantly opposed to it, fighting it all the way. The French military was not in favor of the kind of amalgamation that was proposed here. Eisenhower thus knew there were difficulties, but he continued to work the problem, so to speak. At the same time, he went forward with building the collective NATO force without the Germans. Eisenhower declared himself in favor of European unity, speaking for it very strongly as allied commander, and saying that real defense could only be achieved if they could achieve some degree of unity.

That is about where the matter stood when he left in May of 1952 to come back for his run for the presidency. In the meantime, that work went on and a very elaborate plan had been developed for the achievement of this force, but when it finally came to the point of decision, the French vetoed, and that created something of a crisis. It was resolved by discarding that plan and moving toward German rearmament and entry into NATO—the Federal Republic of Germany entered NATO under special provisions, voluntary on their part, but as part of the package deal. At the outset, the Federal Republic of Germany faced the question of the size and structure of its military units. Of immediate importance were lingering French sensitivities, together with concern in Bonn that rearmament be undertaken in such a fashion that her neighbors would not become fearful of a revival of militarism.

Dr. Kai-Uwe von Hassell discussed the consequences of rearming Germany:

For the first time we had to think about what type of divisions we could have [in the Bundeswehr]. Let me add one point. You know about the Pleven plan. [René Pleven proposed in October 1950 permitting German rearmament in the framework of a highly integrated multinational European Defense Army.] It was quite clear to us that this was impossible. The lowest possible level for integration was the corps, and we developed our plans for German units according to this idea, at the division level, distinct from the political possibility of the Pleven plan coming into effect.

It was in these first plans that we said that the FRG could have only twelve divisions. There were several reasons for this: One was because the allies, especially France, were not willing to allow us more than twelve divisions. This was a snag, and all of the difficulties were with France. It was not the United States, and not even Great Britain, but always France. We used to say that the French were thinking, The new German Army must be smaller than the French one, but bigger than the Russian one! As a condition for its rearmament within NATO, the Federal Republic of Germany agreed to restrictive arrangements, including a prohibition on the manufacture of atomic, biological, and chemical weapons.

When the revised Brussels Treaty was signed in 1954—the Brussels Treaty dated from 1948 [the 1948 treaty formed a common defense system composed of defense ministers of the U.K., Belgium, France, Luxembourg, and the Netherlands], but was revised when we became a member—it was fully understandable that the seven (Germany and the other six) said, "We must control Germany. They are now starting to build up their own forces inside and assigned to NATO. We must ensure that they have no chemical weapons, no biological weapons, and no nuclear weapons. We must guarantee they do not build submarines of large size; production of aircraft must be limited, and so forth." I fully realize that from their point of view, it was necessary to control the Federal Republic after all that happened from 1933 onward and during World War II. Later on, I think everyone among the six of the Brussels Treaty, and the NATO partners, the fourteen others, saw there was no reason for mistrusting Germany. Everyone knows that the FRG does not have nuclear weapons—they have delivery systems but no warheads—everyone knows that they have a controlled shipbuilding program; everyone knows that this new Federal Republic must not be mistrusted.

Dr. von Hassell explains that certain treaty restrictions placed upon the FRG should ultimately—in the spirit of trust West Germany is trying to develop—be removed:

We did [achieve the lifting of certain restrictions] in 1979 or 1980. The first to be scrapped, for instance, regarded shipbuilding. We were not allowed to build ships above 1,500 tons, with the exception of ships for the German Navy. But we, as a shipbuilding nation, had a lot of states around the world interested in having German frigates or German submarines. We, therefore, always had to ask Western European Union headquarters in London if we could be allowed to build the ships and to sell them. Then we encountered the problem that other shipbuilding nations got knowledge of this and tried to [use it to their advantage]. I got the Western European Union to cancel this paragraph, so that we need not ask beforehand if we wished to build six frigates—three for Argentina, then three for us. If we built six, they are cheaper than if we only build three for ourselves. This is a commercial problem for a shipbuilding nation. These old restrictions also were therefore a means to get German competition off the world market for ships. They have scrapped these paragraphs. It is completely different now.

The effect of the North Korean attack on South Korea in 1950 and the conventional response mounted by the United States and its allies, and notably the Republic of Korea, was to focus attention on NATO's conventional military needs. Among the results was the NATO ministerial meeting in 1952 which established the Lisbon Goals, calling for large-scale NATO conventional forces. Although such capabilities were never in fact created, NATO proposed a strategy and a document providing for conventional capabilities. Gen. Pierre Gallois described this process from his perspective as a French representative:

The idea was to prepare a new strategy in light of the failure of the 1952 Lisbon Conference to achieve its intended goal of greatly increased NATO conventional forces. I was working on preparations for the conference where we asked for an enormous amount of money for conventional forces. We told the Americans that they had to pay almost half of the expenditure. The Americans said, "No, no question, we cannot." Gen. Alfred Grünther and Field Marshall Montgomery were given the task of studying a new strategy, taking into account the following elements. The first was that we could not afford in peacetime (so-called peacetime, Cold War time) to maintain conventional forces necessary to contain the Soviet forces. Next, the Soviets were beginning to make atomic weapons of their own. Third, we had only a defensive posture, as far east as possible, to include the Germans, but a defensive posture nonetheless. When you have a defensive posture you possess the terrain. If you possess the terrain you must equip forces for its defense. Our hope was to create a new form of defense with light units having no supplies to bring with them. The supplies would be buried or prepositioned in advance on the territory.

The aircraft were supposed to take off from a portion of the highway, the autobahn, in Germany and never land in the same place to avoid being hit by surprise attack. We went to all member governments to explain to them that strategy. We went to Norway, to Turkey, to Greece, to Britain, we went also to Norfolk to the Atlantic Command, to Naples, and everywhere; we had a DC-4 for our travels. Finally, a document, SHAPE 345, was written and presented to the NATO Council in the autumn of 1956.

It was fantastic because with 200,000 men and some 200 aircraft we could win in three days, instead of the 1.5 million men of the previous plan and some 20,000 aircraft which was proposed at the Lisbon meeting of 1952. So we went to see all these governments and we delivered to them a big document with many blanks where there were references to the numbers of weapons we should use. The documents were complete for the Americans, the British, and the French members; not for the others. Anyway, I had the feeling that many governments took it and put it in a safe without reading it because they were scared of what was inside. The result was that in 1956, when NATO was asked to approve the document, everyone approved it because they were not ready to read it.

Although France had opposed German rearmament in the early 1950s, a decade later, in January 1963, President de Gaulle and Chancellor Adenauer signed the Franco-German Treaty of Reconciliation. The result was an enhancement of political-military cooperation between Paris and Bonn. In the years immediately following the conclusion of the Franco-German Treaty, Kai-Uwe von Hassell was minister of defense of the Federal Republic of Germany. He described the early evolution of the Franco-German relationship that, as he recounts, was emerging even before 1963:

I was in Paris from 18 to 20 October 1962. My partner there was Pierre Mesmer, who was later to become prime minister [1972-74]. This was a form of cooperation between France and Germany mainly for research and development [R&D] for military materiel—for instance, missiles against low-flying aircraft, armored fighting vehicles, and so on. During this meeting we had long talks about German-Franco military cooperation. Both ministers showed their satisfaction about the beginning of the production of the transport airplane [C-160 Transall], which had been under development over several years prior to the agreement. We concluded the main points of the agreement, which would soon be signed on electronics, data systems, and general research and development. They signed an agreement for the joint development of a weapons system to counter low-flying aircraft.

This system seemed to be very simple with regard to repair work and maintenance and seemed cheap because it was not very sophisticated, although [it was] very effective. This system would be produced by a group of electronics companies in Germany and France, with both German and French officials participating as directors. It would be similar to existing antitank missile systems and other jointly developed systems. There would be close cooperation in the field of radar equipment between French and German companies. We both agreed that research and development would be fertile in the future because it is the start of this new era. This was the closest cooperation we could introduce in the field of research and development, but it brought problems.

Dr. von Hassell provided an example of the inherent problems of such cooperation:

My predecessor and his French colleague, Chaban-Delmas [Jacques Chaban-Delmas was president of the French National Assembly between 1958 and 1969, and prime minister between 1969 and 1972], signed an agreement to develop a new tank. The French and Germans would develop three prototypes each. When ready, they would be examined under all environments of war—deserts, mountains, swamps, and so forth. A group of international experts would then carry out exercises and evaluations and choose one proposing this should be produced by both France and

Germany. In 1963 we had three French prototypes called AMX-30 and three German prototypes called Leopard. They were tested under all conditions, and the German Leopard was better by far. I told the French the result, and Mesmer agreed. But he told me in the same instant I could hardly expect a French minister of defense to buy a German tank.

This Franco-German agreement on R&D started with a mistake. They should have inserted a paragraph reading that both armies would introduce the better vehicle jointly. It was wrong to have six national prototypes, three French, three German. They should have had three joint prototypes. If you decide in favor of one, it is always a Franco-German prototype. At the beginning it was positive. They went together, but only halfway. If later we had coproduced the Leopard and introduced them in both armies and perhaps sold them to others, this would really have been an advantage. It would be much cheaper to do research and development once and not twice. We could coproduce with two or three lines of production and could have spare part depots supply both armies. An important part of the agreement was to reduce this duplication, to save money. By the way, the Leopard is an outstanding vehicle—everyone has bought it— but we could not agree with the French.

Dr. von Hassell also pointed out that Franco-German cooperation was always viewed from Bonn's perspective within the broader context of the Atlantic Alliance. A stronger NATO-Europe, of which the Franco-German relationship was the core element, would form a stronger transatlantic posture for the United States. In working as closely as possible with France, Bonn sought to avoid the need to choose between Paris and Washington, for without the United States, in von Hassell's opinion, credible deterrence for Western Europe against Soviet expansionism did not exist.

The newspaper reports on the [1963] agreements were also interesting. A Paris newspaper reported that, according to French military sources, France and the FRG were developing joint plans to fight a war in Europe if the United States would withdraw its troops. French Defense Minister Mesmer, the article stated, denied the story. This story was absolutely wrong. We never discussed plans of what to do if the Americans would leave. Our policy was always to tell the Americans that they must stay or else we will never be able really to deter the Soviet Union. My own view and that of the military was not to see how to deal with fighting a war but to deter the Soviets in order not to have a war. You cannot deter a war when we have a secret plan for dealing with the question of what to do if the Americans leave, because the Soviets know that Europe cannot possibly deter the Soviet Union alone. If deterrence fails because America is out of Europe, then the Soviet Union will be able to probe, just to see what they could achieve, attacking on a small scale, just to see what the reaction might be. Therefore, we avoided everything giving the Soviet Union a hint that there might be plans to defend Europe without the Americans.

We never had to decide between Bonn-Washington *or* Bonn-Paris, but always pursued the policy that we must have the strongest ties with both. Inside the Atlantic Alliance it is necessary for the FRG to have a relationship with France because they are in the rear and we are on the front. We are interested in what is going on in our rear. Will they assist us? Is there collaboration? Inside the alliance a special relationship with France is very important for the FRG—but not instead of the alliance with the United States.

In 1987 France and the Federal Republic of Germany announced the formation of a joint Franco-German brigade. Although such a unit clearly symbolized the crucial importance of defense cooperation between Paris and Bonn, it left unresolved, and even pointed up, continuing problems resulting from the fact that France is not a member of NATO's integrated structure, while West Germany constitutes its most important Continental participant. Ambassador de Rose comments;

I think that the brigade is a symbolic gesture. I wrote an article in *Revue de Défense Nationale* ["Grands problèmes posés par une petite unite," *Revue de Défense Nationale,* 44 (October 1987)]. I call it a small unit that raises big problems. Because Mr. André Giraud has said very rightly that it is a good idea, but we would have to decide what is the defense concept that this unit is going to serve because the French Army is committed to the strategy of national deterrence, and the Bundeswehr is committed to the strategy of flexible response. [Therefore], we always come back to that problem: the lack of coherence between the strategy of France and the strategy of the alliance. I think it did not matter so long as the conventional capabilities were more or less the same. . . . Now that the Americans and the Germans are making an effort to have a longer lasting capacity, it does not matter. Second, if the French Army stays as a general NATO reserve, then it will intervene when the Russians have broken through West Germany and our intervention would be for a very short time with conventional weapons. Whether we would use nuclear weapons after that, well, that is what the doctrine says. I think that now it is becoming more and more important because the idea of flexible response is more difficult to implement. I think that the conventional capacity is becoming more and more important. France should agree with the rest of the allies on what is the likely Soviet strategy. That means a lot of studies which I am not in the position to conduct—it is the business of the ministry of defense and the military to study. The Soviets are pulling out a certain number of weapons. They want to put out of service more nuclear weapons. What is their likely strategy? I think personally that their likely strategy is a crisis strategy. But we should discuss what strategy we should have in order to check the Soviet one. If we do not do that, what do we do?

Dr. von Hassell took a somewhat different position on the issue of the Franco-German brigade:

The cooperation with France is now really excellent. Under Chancellor Kohl and Minister of Defense Manfred Wörner [now the secretary-general of NATO], many ties were strengthened. We have French officers in our Führungsakademie [Officer Training School] at Hamburg, where they are trained for the general staff. We have French officers in considerable numbers in our forces. We have large common exercises. We have all sorts of general staff exercises. The high-ranking officers—colonel and above—of both countries have served in the army of the partner country. Many German officers now speak French, although they all speak English. But this is not anti-American. [Although] in the French Army there was anti-Americanism to a certain extent, now the French understand that the Americans must stay, because without them deterrence would be weakened; their attitude toward America has also changed.

Lord Mulley noted that the United Kingdom has a shortfall in manpower to meet its defense requirements:

By this time, the early 1960s, we were having a manpower problem as a result of the Conservative decision to abolish conscription, the draft, in this country. For a while, recruitment kept up for a year or two, with the people who had been deferred and people who were still doing their tours. That was the other difficulty. NATO allies, many of whom had terms of conscription for eighteen months, now talked of reducing the length of time. With reductions in the tour of duty in other NATO-European countries, it would not have been possible for the United Kingdom to reintroduce conscription unless we chose a longer time period—say, two years. If we wanted certain people to serve in Singapore or Hong Kong, you just could not manage with six months in England and six months out there. We wanted a two-year period and that was unpopular.

So it was not a practical proposition to revert back. At this time, in the 1970s, we had fairly full employment and the army just could not recruit. One of my biggest problems (as minister of defense) was merging regiments because they just could not recruit enough to be at full strength. Later we were already having to take [British] troops out of Germany. We got the number reduced from 64,000, and we were having to borrow a battalion here or a troop of artillery there to cope with crises, for example, the Aden crisis at this time as well. With all these bits and pieces around the world, which at any time might demand troops, we were having to take strength from the British Army of the Rhine, which did not go down very well with the Germans, but apart from that, it really did not make sense for people to leave their tanks behind, any more now than it does to go to Northern Ireland. It seemed to me quite wrong to leave all their tanks or their guns and come and march in the streets of Belfast. They can do that part of the job, but they had to do a bit more. As soon as I left office they returned to doing that. Signals engineers, and so forth, are involved, which is total nonsense when you are training people for specific jobs in Germany.

That was a problem—we just could not cope without manpower and training, and the new generations of equipment. Until then we were basically living on the equipment of World War II. Perhaps having a few replacements here and there, but nothing new came in. And we found that every time we went to buy something new, it cost five times more than the World War II model or the one you had bought in the mid-1950s. If you wanted to go and buy it in 1965, it was probably three to four times more expensive. For extrasophisticated air-land missiles the costs were just phenomenal. So this was the argument that we went on.

Among the problems that began to confront the Federal Republic of Germany in the mid-1980s was its declining birthrate, with adverse implications for the ability of West Germany to maintain its armed forces at their NATO-authorized levels. Dr. von Hassell discussed this issue:

Today Germany is facing a demographic crisis. As of 1989 conscription has been extended from fifteen to eighteen months. [This was later rescinded to remain at fifteen months.] Defense Minister Wörner wanted to increase the armed services as a percentage of the population. He was also trying to introduce service for women. I started in 1964 to consider whether women should be drawn into the service, but only in the special services—in hospitals or as typists, for example. I would need, I calculated, 100,000 unarmed women in a crisis for nursing and in communications centers. This was in 1961, but we could not discuss it at that time. The Nazi era, in which we had the Women's Auxiliary Corps, was so fresh that most—and especially the trade unions—were strictly against it. They strongly opposed the bringing of women into any service. Now this has changed. Now the Defense Ministry has begun to look into the issue. In the end, I believe we will have a great many posts allotted to women. This will happen within the next five years.

Ambassador François de Rose also addressed the problem of the implications of demographic trends for the force levels available to the Federal Republic of Germany in NATO:

The assumption is that the Germans have conventional forces. That certainly will not be an assumption that you can rely on as we near the twenty-first century, given the demographic problems they face and the need to reorganize and rely increasingly on technology to offset manpower shortages that they are facing. I think there is only one answer for that problem. Whether it is a complete answer, I do not know. It is emerging technologies—whether we can do more with less men and more equipment. But that equipment is expensive, although not all that much if you go by the book on improving conventional defense. It says that to attack air bases with combat planes and conventional bombs, you need between thirty and fifty planes costing an average of $20 million. That amounts to something between $600 and $1,000 million. Five missiles, costing less than $10 million could do the same job. Of course, airpower would still be needed for other missions. But the cost-effectiveness of sophisticated armaments often makes them a better bargain.

Dr. von Hassell also spoke of the potentially important role that emerging technologies will play in bolstering NATO conventional defense:

From my point of view, you can increase conventional weapons greatly without high cost. There are a great many new developments in the field of conventional weapons; they are outstanding. There are new sensors. There are new mines, which roll themselves along the battlefield until they find a target. They don't explode unless they find a large military target. These new developments would highly increase conventional capabilities, without spending billions of marks. But at the beginning the ministry was reluctant to go into these new developments. I told people that we could use the space-based developments of SDI [the Strategic Defense Initiative] in application to weapons technologies on the ground. These are two branches of the same instrument. The spinoffs from the space elements of SDI can be used to fight conventional forces on the ground. You cannot attack with it, you can only use it to defend. Sensors and X rays, for example, can be used against conventional weapons. This is not yet common philosophy among our defense people. You call your American program—the vertical program into space—SDI. We call ours EDI [European Defense Initiative] to deal with low-flying and conventional forces, that is to say, in the horizontal area. It is based on the same technologies, but we concentrate on the horizontal rather than the vertical. The name is unimportant; it is the concept we need. The Americans are interested in space, but we are also interested in the battlefield, on the conventional side.

Von Hassell also pointed out some difficulties that must be taken into account:

When SDI and EDI came up, we were preparing for a general election. We were preparing for closer cooperation with the French after the change in government there. (The relationship between Mitterrand and Kohl is better, perhaps, than between Kohl and Chirac.) We could not enter into the EDI debate because of these preparations. I greatly regret that it has not been taken up again, but they are so busy with other problems.

EDI means that if SDI works, and no doubt it will, then the Americans will be out of danger. At this point comes Soviet pressure on Europe. If [the Americans] would develop SDI from the beginning for the conventional threat on earth, they would be able to do it. Why not do it? We do not know what the result will be. We participate only in R&D. Then, if we decide it works adequately, we could scrap forward defense; but until it can be guaranteed that SDI and EDI will work, we cannot scrap flexible response and FOFA [the strategy of follow-on forces attack]. We have to have research; it has applications today. They have built a laser beam on a vehicle the same size as the M-113 [armored personnel carrier] and fired it at an attacking armored car at 1,000 meters and destroyed it. Why not develop this? It is the inflexibility of some in the military.

Dr. von Hassell commented on the benefits of FOFA:

I go very much along the line that has been advocated by Gen. Bernard Rogers as SACEUR. I think what he says—I do not judge because I do not know enough—but I think what he says makes a lot of sense. Let NATO have enough to stop [Warsaw Pact] airplanes. Let us have enough to stop some of their missiles. Let us have enough to stop their Operational Maneuver Groups. That is for the defensive part. In the offensive, let us be capable of follow-on forces attack. We must have a mix of all the weapons needed for flexible response. This includes weapons which could penetrate to a depth of 200–300 kilometers to destroy the assembly area. It is a political argument to say that we must scrap the offensive weapons. We have no offensive weapons, like aircraft carriers. Only America has them; NATO does not. This is only a *Schlagwort*, a headline [catchword or slogan]. I hope that the [political] Left will not try to elaborate on some vague new strategy. Forward defense is the only acceptable strategy for Germany. If there is a penetration, we must try to regain the lost German territory. I do not believe FOFA takes forces away from forward defense. Forces can as well be taken from the rear. This is a technical problem. The whole concept fits together. FOFA and flexible response strengthen the whole.

According to Gen. Graf von Kielmansegg, who served as allied commander of the central region, the use of surprise by an attacker furnishes a basis for a decisively important military advantage. Yet surprise can also be used to good effect by the defender of the NATO central region within the concept of flexible response.

Surprise is not always surprise in attacking. There are four factors. You can be surprised as to time, spot, strength, and in direction. For the defending side, it is much more difficult to use surprise as a means to accomplish our purpose, but it can be done. This is the secret behind mobile defense; you can create surprise only in a mobile defense. In a static defense, you can never do it. In a mobile defense, a counterattack can be surprising in the four ways I have mentioned.

But armored movements are still possible, believe me, in spite of developments in air power. Distances can be covered by night, even in spite of infrared, and you have no other way. If you wish to attack the Russians [while they are engaged] in a big offensive, [by] local counter-attacks, you cannot do it in any manner except than under the protection of armored [forces]. Defense without attack is no defense for success.

General von Kielmansegg also argued that the principal military problem is not posed by strategic surprise (that an attack will take place), but instead by tactical surprise (when and at what point an attack will be mounted):

It has been very important, and this element of surprise is still today of the greatest importance. That is one of the disadvantages we have in our defense today—we cannot surprise. They know all, and they know more or less what we can do. The other side can surprise, not in general, but they can surprise in where they come, how strong they come, and when they come tactically. My thesis has always been that strategic surprise is more or less impossible if our side is vigilant. Tactical surprise is always possible. As commander-in-chief I said the first news that I will get about the [enemy's] crossing of the front I will get from journalists. There can be tactical surprise, and then [the question is] when and where [the hostile forces] have their *Schwerpunkt*, their center of gravity and concentration.

Not one single offensive has been started by the Soviets until they had a superiority of five to one in divisions, and seven to one in tanks, and that is the lowest level they accepted. Even with Berlin in the final days of World War II in Europe, when [Nazi Germany was] down, [the Germans] could never understand why the Soviets did not attack for two months. (I was on the western front at this time, having been released from prison, and the last month I was fighting there against American troops.) They stayed on the Oder River, and when they started the Berlin offensive they had a ratio of eleven to one but the Russians could do it. This is the principle of massed attack. It is nothing new; they really do it today.

Drawing on his own World War II experience and observations, General von Kielmansegg argued for coupling of mobile defense and static defense:

The idea—and this again was a lesson from the Eastern campaign in World War II—was to rely only on mobile defense because static defense, even with strong fortifications, is nonsense.

The experience [which led to this conclusion] (and this experience is still 100 percent valid today) is that nowadays, speaking about conventional battle, if the other side has enough numbers and enough quality in a general way, then there is no line that cannot be broken through wherever he wants to do it, for a certain amount of time. How he does it, that is another question, but the first breakthrough is unavoidable, if you ask me, if he does not make mistakes. This again is a lesson from the Russian campaign of World War II.

Dr. von Hassell said that he disagreed with many in his country when he advocated the use of barriers as a part of NATO's defensive strategy:

There has been past discussion on increasing the emphasis on barrier defense. There has also been criticism that to do so you tacitly accept the demarcation line between the FRG and the GDR. Has this changed? We must do everything to prevent penetration. Forward defense/flexible response means that [plans for] all scenarios must exist. If we, for example, had a barrier of nuclear mines and a political solution achieving reunification were to be reached, then these could be taken out; they do not spoil the political chances. This has nothing to do with reunification. This is the task of guaranteeing our freedom.

According to General von Kielmansegg, one of NATO's strengths, compared with the Soviet-Warsaw Pact, lies in the flexibility and opportunity for initiative in the command structure:

It was *this*, this concept of mission tactics, that gives leaders on every level down to the platoon the freedom to decide at the very moment what he should do within the general framework. He has to know the mission, but as for what he should be doing at that very moment, he can do it alone. That is very difficult; it is very difficult to train the brain for this.

Such opportunities for initiative, von Kielmansegg pointed out, sharply distinguish NATO forces from those of the Warsaw Pact as a result of the nature of the Soviet regime itself:

It has been noticeable that with the various clients [the Soviets] have armed and trained, improvisation is practically nonexistent at the lower levels. I think that is not only the weakness of the clients, [but of] the Soviet system—it is their system of thought, the political system, and they cannot take this away, because otherwise the system would be in danger. This is one of our hopes, that after the first success, the Soviets will not act quickly enough to exploit it.

Ambassador François de Rose offered comments on what he regarded as the detrimental implications of the 1987 INF Treaty on NATO's ability to fulfill the targeting requirements of its follow-on forces attack concept, especially in light of the improvements in recent years in Warsaw Pact air defenses. He also discussed the potential for eventual denuclearization of the NATO-European landmass, arising from the post–INF Treaty security environment and the opportunities for Soviet political exploitation:

First, I think that by removing all weapons with more than a 500 kilometer range capacity, we impair considerably the capacity to implement the follow-on forces attack concept. Because the air-defenses over the Warsaw Pact are so great that its air space would be difficult to penetrate, at least until the Stealth airplane is deployed. I am not sure that the missiles which are sea-based will really play the same role. With regard to the shorter-range systems below 500 kilometers, I think that the Soviet Union will propose that they be eliminated in a short time. The Germans will be extraordinarily hard put to refuse this offer because of the pressure of public opinion. If you look at the figures, the Soviets have much more than NATO has, so it is going to be the same argument. They sacrifice more than we do. If they really go for the elimination of those weapons that threaten Germany, specifically, and if they get it, it would mean there could be only one end for them, which is the denuclearization of Europe.

General Gallois commmented on the discussion in France of alternative concepts for conventional defense in Europe. Gallois suggested that France is not prepared psychologically, in view of past military defeats, to fight a protracted conventional conflict. Hence the importance, from his perspective, of a strategy of nuclear deterrence designed in the first instance to prevent the outbreak of any conflict in which France's vital interests were at stake:

Pierre Lellouche [a French strategic analyst] has adopted Gen. Étienne Copel's thesis that France is planning for the wrong war. I think it is wrong. The Copel book [*Venter a Guerra: Outra Defensor, Outra Exercito* (Lisbon: Infueribo, 1984)] is just a return to the 1939 period. Copel believes that the French are capable of fighting a war, when they know that war is lost in advance, which is completely wrong. Copel is young, he did not see the behavior of the French in 1940. I tell you that if the French, in case of war, believe that they would be defeated, they would conclude immediately that to sacrifice life is useless and stupid and they would stop fighting. Gen. Étienne Copel wants to give every Frenchman a gun and a rocket and hope that they will fight a war; it is ridiculous. Gen. Guy Brossollet proposed a different system, very stupid also, but it was based on helicopters, which would be destroyed before they could be used. It is a return to the 1939 concept of war where the nation is involved entirely in a war, forgetting that in 1939 we thought that we were still the leading military establishment in continental Europe. Now we know that we were defeated in 1940, we were defeated in Dien Bien Phu, we were defeated in Algeria, we were defeated in Suez, we were defeated in Lebanon—we know that this is no longer true. Hence, from the very beginning should some military danger make its appearance, the French would immediately stop fighting and ask for negotiations. Hence, the Copel concept, the Lellouche concept, is baloney, nonsense.

Of major and continuing importance in the Atlantic Alliance has been the question of a NATO European and transatlantic market in weapons production and procurement. The lack of adequate levels of cooperation among NATO members has contributed to duplication and other forms of inefficiency, including a lack of weapons standardization and interoperability among NATO members. As secretary-general, Joseph Luns had numerous occasions to observe this problem. Although the United States spoke of the need to achieve a "two-way street" in which American forces acquired weapons produced in NATO Europe, while also continuing to sell armaments to allies, in practice the United States achieved little in this regard.

> Oh, on paper there is enormous [U.S.] support [for the two-way street approach], but in practice America sells an enormous amount of war materiel to its allies, but is very reluctant to buy hardware made outside the U.S.A. I once said to Secretary of Defense [Caspar] Weinberger, "Cap, we are building fifteen mine hunters, very modern [and] quite big for its class. Furthermore they cost less than half of what your ships would cost in America. Now I am not asking that you order from the Netherlands fifteen or twenty, but can't you order only two or three?" He replied, "I personally am in favor, but Congress absolutely refuses." Well, there are some hopeful signs. For instance, the Americans were prepared to buy, I think, fifteen thousand machine guns from Belgium. We do sell some of our excellent electronics to the United States. France, Belgium, and the Netherlands have agreed to build communally those mine hunters. France is building ten, Belgium also ten, and the Netherlands is building fifteen. This is a good thing. It is something, but we must do more in the field of European defense cooperation.

Former under secretary of state Lawrence Eagleburger told the following story:

> I think we have been consistently absurd in our mouthing the two-way street arms procurement and never meaning it. And I think we are going to pay a price, and that is driven as much by domestic political concerns and the blindness of some military types in the Pentagon as it is by anything. There are areas that you can pick out where in fact the domestic concerns have been dominant. I can remember a time when, I think it was Senator Levin [from the U.S.-automobile producing state of Michigan], who went into orbit when we were going to buy twelve sedans for use by the U.S. military in Europe—an Opel, I think—and he practically had a heart attack. [Another problem in this vein is] the amendments on the appropriations bills. Now those sorts of things are there but they do not impact immediately. Nevertheless, I think that the two-way street failure on our part over the long run is going to cost us.

The conventional defense of Europe by NATO is heavily dependent on the U.S. contribution to that defense. R. James Woolsey, assistant secretary of the navy from 1977 to 1979, commented on the U.S. component of NATO's maritime strategy by discussing differences between the staff planners in the Office of the Secretary of Defense (OSD) and the U.S. Navy with respect to the missions, respectively, of maritime power projection and defense of vitally important sea lines of communication (SLOCs). According to Mr. Woolsey, the United States, as a maritime nation, must have naval forces capable of operations in waters immediately surrounding the Eurasian landmass from NATO-Europe to the Pacific rim:

There was a big argument about that. Secretary of the Navy Graham Clayton and I tended to take the view that the navy had to be able to go into harm's way and confront any kind of sophisticated defenses. We never got to the point that we were making speeches about sending carriers against the Kola Peninsula early in a war, but one of the manifestations of our interest in having a Navy that would be able to take on any tough opponent, including the Soviet Union, was the interest in the all-F-15 fighter force and the outer air battle, and the Soviet Backfires. That was a very serious problem to deal with, and this all emerged philosophically because the staff in the Office of the Secretary of Defense put into planning documents things like the navy will "defend against" the Soviet Union, instead of "defeat the Soviet Navy." The OSD staff tended to emphasize SLOC protection, whereas we tended to emphasize taking the fight to the Soviets wherever they were. It tended to emphasize rather smaller deck carriers and F-19s, as if the principal mission of the navy would be to stand off Yankee station and refight the Vietnam War. We tended to think that those missions were of secondary importance and that we wanted to have a robust force of attack submarines and be able to send them north into Soviet home waters in the event of any hostilities. We generally agreed far more with our uniformed colleagues than with the OSD staff about this sort of "strategic planning" side of force planning. None of this—some of [U.S. Secretary of the Navy] John Lehman's suggestions to the contrary notwithstanding—has anything to do with how you would actually use a navy in wartime—that is operational planning. You use what you have and that is something that the Joint Chiefs and the secretary of defense do, and it is really beyond the purview of the service secretaries, and the business of buying things.

I think that passive navies lose. [The United States] is in a lot of ways an island country, and our situation is somewhat analogous to Britain's in the seventeenth to nineteenth centuries. We must be able to use the seas, not just deny them to the other side. We have to be able to use them in difficult places, like near Turkey and near Norway in the event of a European war, to and from Japan, and South Korea. That requires very capable systems that can have the logistics and the protection and the technology to fight in the Soviets' backyard. If we ever did have a general war with the Soviet Union, the only way for the navy to operate would be to try to come as close to keeping the Soviet fleet in port or on the bottom as it could. The principal system to do that with—and I am personally in favor of a substantially larger force than we now have—is the nuclear attack submarine. The submarine is becoming the new ship-of-the-line with the advent of the cruise missile and remotely piloted vehicles.

12
Nuclear Weapons and the Defense of Western Europe

A t the time of the founding of the Atlantic Alliance the United States was the sole possessor of nuclear weapons. Therefore, it was possible for the United States to offer an extended nuclear guarantee to other alliance members without threatening its own survival. The acquisition by the Soviet Union of its own nuclear arsenal ended the invulnerability of the United States to nuclear retaliation. Henceforth, the United States could only provide such a nuclear guarantee at great risk to its own survival. The result was a burgeoning debate about nuclear weapons and deterrence, the role of conventional forces, and the acquisition of national nuclear forces by other alliance members, namely Britain and France. In this chapter, strategists, policymakers, and military leaders, from both sides of the Atlantic, discuss important issues, including nuclear deterrence and the credibility of U.S. extended deterrence; tactical nuclear weapons—NATO's flexible response strategy, the Schlesinger Doctrine, the neutron bomb, and the double-track decision; U.S. strategic nuclear systems, focusing on force modernization; and finally, the Strategic Defense Initiative and its multiple implications for the Antiballistic Missile Treaty and for European NATO members.

Ambassador François de Rose begins with the issue of nuclear deterrence of conflict in Europe by noting several fundamental elements of this concept:

I have always felt that nuclear weapons have their greatest role in war deterrence. It is a point that I continue to make. I recalled having discussions with Robert Oppenheimer, scientific head of the Manhattan Project, on the dropping of the bomb on Hiroshima. Several times he asked, "Well, were we right in dropping it? Do you think we should have dropped that bomb on Hiroshima?" I always answered that if it had not been for the fact that it suddenly was revealed—that one man dropping one bomb from one airplane could kill 100,000 of his fellow human beings and destroy a city—neither the politicians, nor the military, nor the diplomats, nor public opinion would have understood what the scientists had a glimpse of. What was unnecessary was Nagasaki. Checking whether a plutonium bomb would do as well as a uranium bomb is really unforgivable.

But the 100,000 dead of Hiroshima was the price the human race had to pay to avoid World War III, and to live under deterrence. That gave birth to deterrence; I was convinced of that.

By the mid-1950s, the decision had been taken to deploy tactical nuclear weapons in Europe as part of the U.S.-NATO arsenal. Gen. Franz-Josef Schulze of the German Bundeswehr describes U.S. policy from his vantage point and, in particular, the course of action followed by the United States in the 1960s when Robert McNamara was secretary of defense:

It is very difficult to come to a valid conclusion on McNamara's policies. On the one hand, he was obviously guided by the perception that the Americans had to reduce the risks of extended deterrence. On the other hand—and some feel this is a contradiction, but it is not to my mind—we owe him the seven thousand tactical nuclear weapons stationed in Europe until a short time ago. Europe was swamped by nuclear warheads for artillery before we even had a valid concept to use them. Particularly in retrospect we can see that the direction in which the nuclear posture in Europe developed under McNamara was not well structured towards the aim of deterrence. We were on the way to correcting it when we started in the second half of the seventies with the INF modernization program, but even then we dealt first with increasing survivability and security and giving up nuclear air defense weapons. I pressed at that time for a better solution in the nuclear posture with respect to tactical nuclear weapons systems. There was growing concern, particularly in Germany, that the short-range weapon systems could be detonated only on German soil, and thus would contribute to self-deterrence rather than to deterrence. That is an argument which cannot be interpreted as a lack of courage, as some people obviously do.

There were other reasons as well. All of those short-range artillery systems require the authority of brigade and division commanders in the nuclear request and release process. I have so often seen in map exercises as well as in field exercise that, as soon as the battle turns in a way that the first release of a nuclear weapon becomes imminent, you did not find those brigade commanders where they should be. They were at their main headquarters because they cannot leave that grave decision to their deputies. However, exactly at that moment they should fight at the forward command posts, to do everything there in order to avoid having to go nuclear.

With the Montebello decision of 1983, we finally came to the conclusion that we should have a better mix of short- and longer-range systems. We still do not want to do away with short-range systems totally, but we do want a better mix, which would give us greater flexibility. If you have longer-range corps support weapons, you do not need as many as when you only have short-range artillery systems. If you want to keep enemy attacking forces under the nuclear threat, you need a larger number of weapons systems because their range is so small. If you have weapons with longer range, you can cover much broader sectors and achieve the result you want with fewer weapons systems. We could get the lower-level commands out of the request and release process, which would be a great help in fighting the conventional battle.

The military planning with regard to the use of nuclear capable artillery was so detailed that we had laid down a number of selective employment options for nuclear artillery, realizing that it would be much too late to start making plans in a deteriorating battlefield situation, but that had rather an adverse effect. At a time when the conventional battle will be at its peak and the first considerations begin as to whether to use nuclear weapons, I really want all the commanders to have their eyes looking forward, fighting the enemy and being as agile as possible. But then they start to think about the length of time it takes to get a release of nuclear weapons. Commanders were concentrating on where the enemy would be the next day so that they could target their nuclear weapons and did not concentrate on how you could push him back in the meantime. All this led me to conclude that we should have corps support weapons of longer range and fewer artillery weapons systems. That seemed to be a way to correct the nuclear posture which was mainly caused by McNamara's swamping the European theater with artillery weapons systems.

It took us a long time to realize that the Soviets cannot be deterred by risks put to their allies; they can only be deterred by risks you put to their own country. When I go back to the mid-1960s when we drafted the provisional guidelines for the first tactical use of nuclear weapons, the fifth meeting of the NATO Nuclear Planning Group failed because the American secretary of defense was unable to accept the phrase saying that follow-on use should go hand-in-hand with an expanded use in an extended area. When the guidelines were finally adopted one year later, there still was a clause stating that even at a later stage of follow-on use, Soviet territory should be excluded.

Gen. Pierre Gallois, formerly of the French Air Force, did not favor deployment of the enhanced radiation warhead, or neutron bomb. In his view, the purpose for which such a system would be deployed—to destroy Warsaw Pact armor—has lost significance as NATO's principal military problem:

Concerning the neutron bomb, I was always against it on many grounds. First, we would need plenty of these so-called neutron bombs because the radius of destruction is small. They are very costly; I do not think we can afford them, and spending money in that field to me is nonsense. The first point is that a great number are necessary, and we cannot afford that. The second point is that I do not think an invasion of tanks is the threat. I think that today the tanks are no longer the instruments for pushing through the front, if there is a front, but [rather the] SS-23s or SS-21s [are the primary threat]. Tanks, in my mind, are weapons to occupy a terrain which has been disarmed previously. The neutron bomb would have been very efficient against the German Panzers fifty years ago but not in the present situation. What is more, you should look at the map. You see that from Switzerland to the North Sea there is a block of interposition created by homes. There are 600 kilometers of homes along the Rhine, with a width of some 60–80 kilometers. You cannot send a tank division there. The plain of Europe does not exist anymore. The plain of Europe existed before 1939, but with the development of the economy of Germany, the plain exists no longer. There is a sort of natural Maginot line which has been created, which is for me an obstacle to tanks.

Thirdly, I think it is very naive to believe that it is better to use a weapon having a radius of destruction of 700 meters, instead of a radius of destruction of 1,500 meters. If such a war were taking place, I think it would be complete nonsense to select these weapons just to avoid hitting a village here and another village there. If you take the picture of the theater of operations, which is Germany, the density of the villages is such that whether you have a 700-meter radius or a 1,500-meter radius it is the same. This so-called neutron bomb has been created on the naive basis that we could destroy soldiers and not the people in the villages nearby. In the chaos and destruction of a war, with the millions of refugees, this is complete nonsense and I would not spend a franc for them, except for their use in an ABM system. In 1963, in America, the first neutron shells were studied for antimissile weapons—to destroy the incoming mechanism of an enemy warhead. This would be an interesting use for the neutron warhead, but not as an antitank capability.

General Schulze contended that the credibility of the U.S. nuclear guarantees could only be strengthened by the deployment of forces on NATO-European territory capable of striking targets in the Soviet Union:

You know, the years we are referring to are exactly those years when European doubts about the credibility of the American willingness to extend its nuclear umbrella were coming up again and again; and when Americans tried to find solutions to appease the European anxieties, like the multilateral force [MLF], the assignment of nuclear submarines to the supreme allied commander, Europe [SACEUR], and so on. European doubts regarding American extended deterrence are something which has recurred constantly from the beginning.

The problem was solved only once and that was with the double-track decision. It was the American willingness to station the Pershing II and the cruise missiles on European soil. Many people have said, not only military people like me, that this was the only time when this problem of confidence in the American willingness to take those risks of extended deterrence was convincingly solved. It was indeed the most important decision in the American-European relationship since the founding of NATO. It was a convincing demonstration of the American will to solve once and forever the problem of the credibility of extended deterrence. All previous attempts to solve this problem were not very convincing. The MLF is an example; although those, like General Norstad [SACEUR, 1956–62], who had conceived and supported the idea were of course very credible and convincing personalities, the solution was not.

According to Ambassador de Rose, NATO nuclear deterrence was reinforced by the deployment of systems capable of striking the Soviet Union.

One reason for deploying those missiles was that the manned airplanes would have had more and more difficulties penetrating enemy air defenses. But that was not explained in those years. The deployment of the missiles should have been based on those reasons and no other. But it was justified by the need to balance the SS-20. I will explain why missiles are necessary to implement NATO strategy. Attacking one main airbase takes thirty to fifty aircraft. With fifty main airbases in the Warsaw Pact, an attack to put them out of commission would have needed more than the 1,500 bombers that NATO has at its disposal. And how many would return to be available for later operations? A few missiles could do the job, with much better cost-effectiveness. [NATO's] mistake was the failure to justify the need for the deployment of the Pershings and cruise missiles on the basis of needing weapons capable of reaching Soviet territory. It was not done probably because politicians failed to realize it and because, for political reasons, it was easier to justify the deployment by saying, "We offered not to deploy our weapons. They refused but still want to deploy theirs, so therefore we have to deploy." That was fine so long as we dealt with Mr. Gromyko.

General Schulze also argued that the LRINF (Longer Range Intermediate-Range Nuclear Forces) systems played a significant role in NATO deterrence because of their ability to strike the Soviet Union:

It was clear to me from the very beginning that the Soviets would make any effort, support any opposition here in Europe, in order to defeat the LRINF decision. Indeed, the LRINF played an enormous role in their risk calculus. If people say today that the removal of the Pershing IIs does not create a gap, that the ability to deter can be kept up by other systems, then they may believe that, but the Soviets see it differently. In the Soviet risk calculus there is a great difference whether those systems which can hit the Soviet Union are stationed on the soil of the country the Soviets might go to attack (or put under pressure) or whether these systems are stationed at sea or are airborne. Even for the American president it is a different category of decision, whether he is going to release weapons from the strategic arsenal or whether he is going to release weapons which are stationed in the area under attack.

I wish people would not come up now with all the arguments that they turned down in the late seventies when we developed the NATO decision. At that time, particularly the Americans argued that systems stationed at sea would not have the same deterrent effect, and that ALCMs [air-launched cruise missiles] would not have the same deterrent effect as GLCMs [ground-launched cruise missiles]. The Soviet Union cannot be deterred by damage done to its allies. That is particularly true for a country that regards itself as being the guarantor of an historical process, the process of spreading Socialism worldwide. So any risk to their own territory deters them. Risk to their neighbors? No.

All this led then, finally, to the conclusion that we needed weapons which would put the Soviet Union at risk in case of an attack against Europe. That was the final reasoning for the long-range INF. But you cannot expect a politician to speak to a party congress and say we need weapons to put Soviet territory at risk. The tendency developed that those politicians who defended the NATO decision used the wrong arguments. They used the argument that the purpose of stationing of allied INF was to counter the Soviet SS-20. That was not the point. We would have needed those weapon systems—the Pershing IIs and the cruise missiles— even if there had been no SS-20s. The European-based LRINF was the instrument to couple the conventional and tactical nuclear weapons stationed in Europe with the strategic arsenal of the United States. Gregory Arbatov [director of the Institute of the U.S.A. and Canada in Moscow] had no difficulty to make clear in three sentences what the coupling argument was, when he spoke about direct retaliation against American soil and said that the Soviet Union would retaliate in exactly the same way as if those weapons had been launched from Montana. No one else has made it so clear that we had achieved the coupling of conventional and nuclear forces on the European continent with the strategic arsenal of the United States. Indeed, I have a lot of understanding for those people in the United States who saw the additional risks that the NATO decision brought to their own country. And I believe that, for example, the article by McGeorge Bundy, George F. Kennan, Robert S. McNamara, and Gerard Smith ["Nuclear Weapons and the Atlantic Alliance," *Foreign Affairs* Vol. 60, No. 4 (Spring 1982):753–768] against a NATO first-use may have been influenced by the awareness of the risks of extended deterrence.

The Americans had taken a new risk, the risk of direct retaliation to their homeland, and they had done so in the interest of European security and on European urging. Now, a few years later, the situation is reversed. I admit that the zero solution was a European invention and the number of people who claim fatherhood for that is growing. They claim it more loudly every time.

Lawrence Eagleburger was the under secretary of state when the GLCMs and Pershing IIs were deployed. He also served as political counselor in the U.S. mission to NATO. He offered a different perspective:

When Helmut Schmidt suggested [INF deployment] in the first place, the United States thought that it was totally unnecessary to deploy those weapons. We were not enthusiastic in the first place and only came to a decision to do it after a lot of persuasion. From a military point of view, no one in Washington was ever terribly convinced that it was a weapon that made any difference. I believed then and I believe now that if we had decided not to deploy them, we could well have made the argument— which we are now making—that we have other weapons that can do the job. That was the fundamental military argument: we do not need them. I would accept that.

It comes rather late to make the argument now. Because if that is the case, then why were we so interested in deploying it in the first place? My view of the INF issue was that it was far more important as a political-psychological question than as a military question. Point one is that you do want to avoid raising in the minds of Germans that they are the nuclear battlefield in the heart of Europe. Point two is that perhaps there is some merit (at least intellectually Henry Kissinger thinks it more than I do) to be able to say that the United States can respond to a Soviet nuclear attack from weapons deployed in Europe rather than having to go to strategic weapons sooner than it would otherwise. You could still make the argument that the F-111s are there and all sorts of things, but nevertheless it is valid, I think, up to a point, that we might barely be more willing to use them in extremis because they are located in Europe than if we have to shoot something from Nebraska. The reverse is clearly true. I think that those Europeans who particularly argue that we ought to get rid of them because we never would be prepared to go to nuclear war to defend Europe anyway could certainly ask why we would be more prepared to shoot something from Nebraska than we would something from Europe. There is an argument to be made that we would be prepared to put our money where our mouth is in terms of our defense of Europe with nuclear weapons more quickly if they were located in Europe than if we were going to shoot them from Nebraska.

Strategic nuclear weapons form the pinnacle of the nuclear force structure. They serve as an ultimate deterrent to Soviet nuclear attack against the United States and Western Europe. In the early years of NATO the United States adhered to a doctrine of massive retaliation: a Soviet aggression would be met with a swift and decisive nuclear attack by the United States upon the Soviet Union. Such a doctrine was deemed to be adequate as long as the United States held a monopoly in nuclear weapons. But as the Soviets built up their nuclear stockpiles, the United States concluded that it needed to adopt a new strategy for deterrence in NATO-Europe. In 1967 the alliance officially adopted the flexible response strategy, calling for a variety of options, including conventional and nuclear weapons, to halt a Warsaw Pact attack. Several Europeans spoke of their reactions to the change in NATO strategy. Kai-Uwe von Hassell was West German defense minister when flexible response was being formulated:

Massive retaliation was absolutely necessary at the beginning. If you look into history, before I came to Bonn—I had been in the Schleswig-Holstein Parliament in Kiel since 1950—both Adenauer and the Americans feared that the Russians would attack. [The United States] disarmed and the Russians rearmed and were able to march. Massive retaliation was absolutely the only deterrent; it was the only effective strategy. I was pro-massive retailiation. But as time went on, the Soviets developed their own weapons, and my opinion changed to the belief that soon massive retaliation would no longer be credible. The Russians must know that if they landed a probe in Lübeck or Braunschweig the United States will push the button. Credibility is critical. My view was that a new strategy was needed.

I was strongly in favor of flexible response from the very beginning. Also, it was coupled in the same period with forward defense. I could sell this package saying, "We have moved the line of defense forward. In 1947 it was the Pyrenees, then it was the Rhine when the United Kingdom built up the BAOR [British Army of the Rhine], and the third step was the river Weser. Now forward defense would mean defense on the Elbe River, not as massive retaliation but instead on flexible response. Flexible response means that a small attack is met with small weapons from our side; a larger one with more weapons would be met on a larger scale; a medium-size one, perhaps with atomic weapons. We will meet the attack with an equal level of forces." This was the new policy of forward defense plus flexible response.

We told the people that we do not build nuclear weapons to fight a war—the U.S. built them to deter and secure peace through deterrence. Inside our headquarters, we told [Secretary of Defense Robert] McNamara that we had to know what the United States was planning, what its targeting procedure was, what its philosophy was, and that he must consult us. The result was that we got the [NATO] Nuclear Planning Group with five permanent members and three rotating members. In the Nuclear Planning Group we discussed the philosophy for targeting, for release, and so on. We were consulted and informed, and this is what we wanted.

I know of no case when information was withheld, neither by McNamara nor [Secretary of State Dean] Rusk. We always got sufficient information. I could never complain about a lack of consultation as regards nuclear weapons. Although the opposition in the Bundestag accused McNamara of pressuring me, he never asked me to do something that I did not agree with. He never ordered me to do anything. There was never any hint of pressure on me. I informed my government (the chancellor and the foreign minister), and they were in full agreement because they could also see the credibility of the flexible response strategy and the lack of credibility of massive retaliation.

There was in NATO only one difference between France, before 1966, and the rest of NATO. France still adhered to massive retaliation. France argued that the Soviets must know that we would retaliate immediately. In targeting they still wanted to hit cities rather than military and industrial targets. De Gaulle said, "I can only deter the Soviets if the people are hit" (that is, countercity). McNamara did not want the civilian population to suffer; instead he wanted to strike military targets. It was a political discussion from a moral perspective. This was a philosophical question. Look at Dresden—one of the most dreadful events of World War II. They bombed a city without any industry. The people of Dresden were bombed, including 100,000 refugees passing through the city; this was countercity. Before that, the air war was directed against industry. But the Dresden bombing was countercity. The French also support countercity. This is a moral-ethical question, not a military question. Flexible response is a viable military strategy. It makes for credibility and has political effects. It removed the heavy burden of massive retaliation.

Joseph Luns was the Netherlands foreign minister when the strategy of flexible reponse was adopted.

Flexible response is an old concept. I think that when it was realized that massive retaliation would be dangerous because the Soviets had developed their own atomic weapons flexible response was adopted. I still think flexible response is a very good policy. Mind you, nobody knows whether in a conflict nuclear devices will be used; I myself doubt it very much. Nuclear armament is there in order to *prevent* war.

General Schulze was head of planning for Allied Forces, Central Europe (AFCENT) when flexible response was developed.

Flexible response is a military strategy [and] also a political compromise—this must be clarified. The military strategy concept is part of the overall strategy whose aim is to deter war. No antagonism should be construed between the military assessment and the political assessment. Any military force and any military concept is a political instrument. So flexible response is both in this case. Politically, I think many people started as early as 1961, and some even earlier than that—for example, Albert Wohlstetter [American strategic thinker who, in the late 1950s, warned of the vulnerability of U.S. Strategic Air Commnad bases to Soviet nuclear attack]—to ask whether massive retaliation was still a valid, credible concept. It was just not a sudden enlightenment; the development of the new concept of flexible response was a rather slow and lengthy process. Many people affixed the changeover from the strategy of massive retaliation to flexible response to the year 1967; this is simply not true. In 1963 SACEUR finally felt he had now enough forces to accept the concept of forward defense. He accepted that concept, put it into effect, starting with defense at the inter-German border, and that, of course, forced us to rewrite all our emergency defense plans. There you find already many of the elements of the later strategy of flexible response. If we had not had the debate [about massive retaliation versus flexible response] with the French, the concept of flexible response might have been put into effect as early as 1963. When France withdrew her forces from the integrated military structure of the alliance, we had to rewrite all our defense plans again, not only the emergency defense plan, but also the nuclear plans and the air defense plans, and we had to do that in a hurry because SACEUR insisted that AFCENT should be operational first (earlier than SHAPE) after the move from France. It was an excellent example of allied cooperation. We kept the crew very small—two people from AFCENT, two people from LANCENT [Land Forces, Central Europe], and two people from AIRCENT [Air Forces, Central Europe] under my direction—and it took us six weeks, but I must say six weeks day and night. Then we were able to brief SACEUR, General Lemnitzer. That was another step in the direction of flexible response. Then in 1967, when we were already in the Netherlands, we got the ministerial guidance for the strategic military concept of flexible response. The NATO Military Committee was asked to submit comments on the political guidance. General von Kielmansegg, then commander of Allied Forces, Central Europe, gave some very specific comments which were integrated into the final military document.

By the mid-1970s, increases in the accuracy of delivery systems led the United States to decide to build into its strategic doctrine options for selective use of nuclear weapons. This development, known as the Schlesinger Doctrine (after James Schlesinger, who was secretary of defense at the time), evoked criticism from Adm. Thomas Moorer, who was chairman of the Joint Chiefs of Staff:

I think many people have missed what actually happened. Two years before Schlesinger came in as secretary of defense, President Nixon came on television and stated that he would not be limited by only one nuclear option. So when that happened, we set up a group to work this out. It was hard to visualize. It started during a time of rapid change. We had [Melvin] Laird, [Elliot] Richardson, then Schlesinger as secretary of defense. Schlesinger publicly announced it, and it has since been labeled the Schlesinger Doctrine. This is a very complex subject. I have my own ideas as to its utility.

Nixon made a statement in a report that a president never should be restricted to a single option. It is difficult to have two options. However, the president has to do something. He has to retaliate or do nothing. It is a very difficult situation. I think it would be foolish to fire two or three missiles at the Soviets and ask them, "How do you like those apples?"

The "Schlesinger Doctrine" was more an addition than a change in targeting; we had new requirements. I think we need not more options but better options. Some of these options are simply dangerous, they are irritants. I cannot be specific, but it was a matter of taking some missiles and targeting some place on the periphery of the Soviet Union, not the command posts. You have to take a target they do not consider provocative, so they will not shoot at you.

R. James Woolsey, from his vantage point as a military analyst at the time, discussed the U.S. decision to deploy the multiple, independently targetable reentry vehicle (MIRV) on its intercontinental ballistic missile force. The need existed, so it was suggested, to forestall the ability of the Soviet Union to upgrade its primitive ABM systems, the effect of which would have been to blunt the capability of U.S. strategic forces.

The genesis of the MIRV program arose from the concerns that developed in the 1960s about the Soviets building an antiballistic missile system. If you started looking at what we needed to do to be able to penetrate an ABM system at that time, one of the most important things you needed to deploy was credible decoys. It turned out in the late 1960s that once you made a decoy that had the same characteristics to sensors as a warhead, the decoy may as well have a warhead in it. I think in a way the MIRV program in its beginning grew out of the decoy program, because ultimately someone is going to say, "Well, the Soviets are going to be able to discriminate between decoys and real warheads, and by the time the decoy is large enough, you may as well put a warhead in it and thereby make it unprofitable for the Soviets to discriminate."

By the late 1960s there were intelligence estimates based mainly, I think, on technical and theoretical capabilities rather than actual projections of what the Soviets were doing, which indicated that the Soviet Union could deploy a reasonable number of interceptors in a nationwide system. At that point, I think the MIRV program got a big boost because people felt that if you were going to have an actual Soviet ABM system deployed, that what you needed to do was exhaust it with large numbers of warheads, and that it would be the only tactic that a president or the country would have confidence in as a means of being able to maintain a deterrent. If you made any calculations or any assumptions at all about the effectiveness of the Soviet system, you needed a fair number of warheads to exhaust it. I think the MIRV program got a big boost from that. It also got a big boost at the end of the 1960s by the Soviet efforts with the SS-9; there was great debate at the time as to whether that was an MRV [multiple reentry vehicle] or an MIRV. But the very large Soviet system was clearly being tested with multiple warheads of some sort, so you had the mirror-imaging argument.

Finally, one reason which I think was laughed at then but which has ultimately proven to be the reason why you really need MIRVs—at least sea-based MIRVs—and the reason why they are probably necessary in order to maintain an effective deterrent, is the notion that surface-to-air missiles could be upgraded to become ABMs [antiballistic missiles]. There was a lot of talk at the time about the SA-5 Gammon system which was probably a very high altitude Soviet system designed against the old B-58 bomber that never got built, or maybe against Skybolt. It was deployed in rather large numbers, and it was a capable air defense system for its time. Many studies were run about what it would take to upgrade the SA-5 system to turn it into some type of reentry ABM.

Mr. Woolsey offered perspectives on the decision taken by the Carter administration, and by Secretary of Defense Harold Brown in particular, to build and deploy the Trident II system with highly accurate, counterforce-capable warheads:

> I think that to the Carter administration's, and particularly to Harold Brown's, credit we kept the Trident II program alive and well and moving along smartly. That was the key decision and strategic program in the navy. The only reason to have a Trident II, as distinct from a Trident I, is to be able to target Soviet silos. Brown knew that deterrence requires a survivable counterforce capability, and so, from my point of view, that was one of the key decisions. From the navy's point of view, that was really the only thing that was ever at issue in connection with strategic programs during the three years I was there.

In addition to modifications in targeting, the United States faced the need to modernize its strategic force posture. This became one of the Reagan administration's defense priorities. Richard Allen was President Reagan's first national security adviser. He set forth his perspectives on the Reagan administration's program:

> I believe that the window of vulnerability was a state of mind—a state of mind on our part and a state of mind on the part of the Soviets. They had to believe that we were absolutely serious in restoring America's defense posture. I felt, and I believe that that feeling has been validated, that almost certainly the momentum for closing the window of vulnerability, the underlying public support for the process, would sooner or later be dissipated. We made early commitments in the campaign, and I then made sure they were carried out. We were able to get Stealth and the B-1B at the same time because putting all the eggs in one basket did not make any sense to me. The only system about which I had grave doubts in the beginning and was opposed to was the MX. I believed that it would never work. I still believe that it never will work, and I became a strong advocate for Midgetman, which is now seen to be one of our saviors, but whose existence may be threatened. I have always believed that lots of smaller, very efficient weapons are infinitely better than very few, large nation

busters such as an MX. I just do not believe in them, particularly when they are sitting ducks and you do not have a suitable basing mode.

All in all, it was remarkable in spite of, say, David Stockman [director of the Office of Management and Budget, 1981–84] and his inherently pacifist tendencies. However, the argument was as fraudulently constructed by the Department of Defense as it was fraudulently contested by David Stockman. The numbers became meaningless, the mind numb. I sat through hundreds of hours of such sessions which were absolutely worthless to me. They educated me about nothing. I think they put the president into early sleep every day. Eventually, we knew that we could get enough money because the consensus behind Reagan was that America had been pushed around long enough. The boldness of the Soviet moves around the world—for example, in Angola, the Horn of Africa, [and] Afghanistan. America, the pitiful, helpless giant, was now a reality. There would be a long period of time, enhanced by Reagan's ability to communicate goals in simple terms, in which we would enjoy superior funding for this project of getting America renewed militarily.

Gen. John Vessey, first as vice chief of staff of the U.S. Army and subsequently as chairman of the Joint Chiefs of Staff, was in the center of the most complex debate that had been taking place from the Carter administration to the Reagan administration: where and how to base the MX missile. He described the difficult decisions that had to be made concerning the basing mode for MX:

Congress had told the president that he could not put the MX in Minuteman silos. This was the background of it, and the president himself had rejected the Carter administration's racetrack proposal, and Congress had then told him okay, but we reject putting them in Minuteman silos. So, the MX was due to be deployed in 1985–86. We were talking about December 1985 for the first MX, so there was some urgency in solving this problem because you had to get engineers and architects, contractors, and people doing work someplace which had not yet been chosen for a deployment system that had not yet been selected. We were behind the eightball!

A whole bunch of schemes were examined, and I do not recall the exact genesis of closely spaced basing [CSB] now, but it was proposed. Once the air force proposed it, the secretary asked a separate panel to examine it. The panel was headed by Dr. Charles Townes [University of Seattle physicist and Nobel Prize winner; the Townes Committee favored basing MX on a continuously airborne platform]. The JCS were also involved in examining it and gave their views to the secretary of defense in November of 1982. The chiefs spent an awful lot of time on the question. We listened to the air force layouts of closely spaced basing, but I must say that the chiefs were not brought into it as early as they should have been. The chief of staff of the air force made a mistake in not laying the plan out to the other chiefs early, but we had a change in air force chiefs that summer.

Closely spaced basing is one of those things that on first blush looks a little nutty, but the more you examined it the better it looked. The Townes Committee, a board of eminent scientists, said it would work. They said that it had value both from the dollars that would be invested in it, as compared with other means, and with the protection that it might give. The JCS gave their views to the secretary in writing. The JCS split on closely spaced basing; their split was based primarily on the belief that it was not salable politically. First, they did not understand it well enough technically. There was not enough evidence to support the view that it would work. It was not self-evidently sensible from the technical point of view, even though the Townes Committee said that it would work. The chiefs said, okay, maybe it will work, but it has some real technical questions on the face of it.

We were faced with the problem that the president had just cut the props out from under something that the Congress appeared to support, which was the Carter racetrack proposal, and the Congress told him that he could not put MX in Minuteman silos, and now we had to come up with another basic scheme that appeared to be nutty to the American people. We were again jeopardizing one aspect of the strategic modernization program, which the chiefs believed was necessary. There were some people in uniform, particularly in the army and navy staffs who did not support the MX and did not want their chiefs to support the MX, but all the chiefs did support it.

General Vessey recounted a crucial meeting of the National Security Council on the subject:

Then there was an NSC meeting on November 18, 1981. I had two special meetings with the chiefs, one on the night of the seventeenth when we went over my presentation very carefully. Some of the chiefs had some concerns about the words, and I worked through the night to make sure that the words expressed the views of the chiefs and my own views. We had another meeting on the morning of the eighteenth, and the chiefs agreed that what I was going to say represented the views of the chiefs. They continued to disagree on closely spaced basing, but they knew that their own views were being accurately represented. It was a long NSC meeting, and I think that no one expected the chairman to spend so much time, but I read carefully my handwritten words because I did not want to have any misunderstanding about the JCS advice in this very important NSC meeting.

It was the system working as it is supposed to work. That is, the president got the advice of the JCS and recognized that there were actually five different views, with the chief of staff of the air force and me agreeing to support closely spaced basing and the others not supporting it. I got a note from the counselor to the president [Ed Meese] after that meeting—a handwritten note which I have retained. It said, "Thank you, I believe that is the best example of a president of the United States getting military advice from the JCS that we have probably ever seen." It may have been a good example of the system working, but that was all lost in the trouble which ensued from the JCS disagreement.

I reported the NSC proceedings to the chiefs on the afternoon of November 18. A Senate Armed Services Committee hearing was called for December 8. Of course, the issue of the disagreement of the JCS came out, and the Senate rejected closely spaced basing. They declined to fund it as they had declined to fund MX in Minuteman holes. They did not vote against it; they just failed to fund it. The president set up the Scowcroft Commission [the Presidential Commission on Strategic Forces]. We told the secretary that the next regularly scheduled meeting of the JCS with the president should be on strategic forces. Judge William Clark [served as deputy secretary of State, 1981, and national security adviser, 1982–83] also sent a note to the secretary telling him that the next regularly scheduled meeting of the JCS with the secretary should be on strategic forces.

General Vessey spoke of a meeting that the JCS had with President Reagan:

We met with the president in December but on other matters. The JCS worked with the Scowcroft Commission. The chiefs met with the commission both individually and as a whole a number of times. I met with them separately a number of times. The JCS came to a set of conclusions that we wanted.

We went back through what the Soviets had done after the SALT II Treaty signing, and we pointed out the modernization that the Soviets had undertaken with their SS-18s and SS-19s. We told him that he had a political problem in that the Congress had told him that he could not put MXs in Minuteman silos, and that we had, by not being unanimous in our advice on closely spaced basing, contributed to his political problem, but we were not apologizing for that. Then we told him that he had a larger geostrategic problem with his strategic force modernization. It had to do with its interface with alliances, with the role that arms control negotiations would play in the national security of the United States, and that we wanted to make some recommendations.

We gave him a long briefing, and we went through Soviet strategic forces and what we knew about Soviet strategic objectives. We showed him that in our view the Soviets had been much more consistent than the United States in tying together nuclear force building and arms control negotiations. We showed him the Soviet General Staff and the relationship of it to the arms control negotiators and the relationship of the General Staff's Directorate for Deception. The strategic force building, deception, and arms control negotiations are all under the same head at the Soviet General Staff.

We had done a lot of analytical estimates; some very good guys at the DIA [Defense Intelligence Agency] had done some superb work at examining the whole issue. It showed Soviet negotiating positions, Soviet force building, and Soviet military plans laid out to show the consistency among them in Soviet policy. Then we took it to the president at the meeting on February 11, 1983. We told him at the time that we knew that he had commissioned the Scowcroft panel and that we were not asking him to make a final decision until he got the commission's recommendations. We told him that, insofar as we knew at the time, our recommendations were not inconsistent with the Scowcroft Commission's recommendations, but they were independently derived. We told him that our session would cover a general review of strategic forces and the strategic balance between the United States and the Soviet Union, but with some particular emphasis on the MX.

Vessey continued:

We went back to point out that the target base that we look at is about twice the size of the one that the Soviets look at, that it is about twice as hard as the one the Soviets look at. All to explain why we needed modernized nuclear forces, and particularly the MX.

Now, not to go through that briefing in detail but to get to the conclusions, we told him that we believed that he should announce that his basing decision was made in the larger context of where we are going with strategic forces and with arms control. He should not be trapped into saying with a press announcement; "I have decided to base the MX here," but it should be tied in to a speech that talked about larger issues, such as improved deterrence. We recommended that he stress the fact that strategic modernization had already achieved improved deterrence. We talked to him about improved command and control and the fact that we were now hanging the cruise missiles on the B-52s, that the improvements already made gave him a better negotiating position with the Soviets. He should stress improvements in the triad and the interrelationship with the triad and the security of the triad as a whole as separate from the vulnerability of any particular part of the triad. We told him not to be caught up in the argument about vulnerability of silos, as though silos were the only thing we had. We told him that the improvements in the command and control and warning systems were an important aspect of reducing the vulnerability of any part of the triad and improving the strength of our deterrence. And we went through the hard targets and the time-urgent hard targets, and we discussed it in great detail with him: the ability to move to part of the sea-based force as hard-target killers and by changing some operations concepts, by moving part of the sea-based force into time-urgent hard targets when the D-5 and the Tridents came along. We traced this thing through time to show him in great detail how his strategic forces worked over time in light of the changing Soviet target base.

We pointed out what we would be faced with when the mobile SS-24s and SS-25s were deployed.

Our second recommendation was that he announce that he was going to put MXs in Minuteman silos despite the fact that Congress had said that he should not do so, but that he should tell the Congress that he is going to continue to do research on more survivable basing modes for the land-based ICBMs, that he should look at a small mobile ICBM as part of the force. We pointed out both the strengths and weaknesses of the small ICBM, the weaknesses being the few warheads, and the tremendous cost per warhead there. We did not recommend that he go ahead and build one or do the research and development on it as the Scowcroft Commission recommended, but we recommended that he examine it. We came up with that recommendation independently of the Scowcroft Commission. We did not really know that the commission was going to recommend the small ICBM.

The third recommendation was that we look to increasing research and development on strategic defense and that we look toward the integration of arms control, strategic modernization, and defense for our security in the years ahead. We pointed out to him that the R&D on defense was way down in terms of its importance and that it was probably producing things that deserved closer examination at the higher levels of government. We said that we believed it deserved his attention, and Admiral Watkins, chief of naval operations, was the guy who used the phrase during that discussion, which the president later on used himself, that "it was better to defend ourselves than avenge ourselves."

So you see how differences within the JCS on closely spaced basing were represented as both the law and how President Eisenhower probably envisioned that they should be represented, and how that led to a set of recommendations which eventually grew into the Strategic Defense Initiative. I think we left that meeting with a president who had a better understanding of ICBM basing and the requirements for strategic deterrence.

R. James Woolsey, who played an important role in the work of the Scowcroft Commission and had the opportunity to participate in the planning process in the Carter administration, described the discussions about the alternative MX basing modes under consideration:

That decision is plaguing us still: where to put the MX, and whether to have a small ICBM, and all the rest of it. Whereas you have heard me be fairly critical of the Carter administration's unwillingness to spend money, at least with respect to the overall strategic concept of SALT II and MX and multiple protective shelters [MPS], I do not know whether to give it a *C*, a *C*+, or maybe a *B*−, but at least it was coherent. It was not great, it was not perfect or elegant, and it was not cheap, but at least it all hung together. With respect to what we are doing, or not doing, today on SDI and MX and so forth, I get the sense that there is no coherent policy. It is just a lot of people off doing their own thing. I attribute the fact that we had perhaps not an ideal but a coherent arms control and strategic program in the Carter administration principally to [Secretary of Defense] Harold Brown, who did not get involved in some of the angrier philosophical debates between Brzezinski and Vance, but rather kept himself as a neutral military and almost technical adviser.

We looked at rail-basing but discarded it because it was not survivable against a surprise attack unless you had it out on the rails all the time, and nobody thought they would do that. I still do not think that the administration or the air force would put it out on the rails in peacetime continuously. We looked at a small ICBM in helicopters, not continuously on alert but as a sort of grasshopper; since it could be launched from a high altitude, it could be a somewhat smaller missile than the 37,000-pound missile we now had. We looked at that, and we also got quite interested in the long-endurance aircraft, but they were just as easy to do with a big missile as a small one, so there was not any reason to go small based on an aircraft. We worked hard with Sen. John Glenn on his proposal to base them in grocery trucks, and everybody thought that was a great idea except for the public interface problem. That killed it. You cannot assume that any administration would keep ICBMs rolling around the highways.

We racked our brains and came up with the idea that later led to densepack, which said, suppose you tried to put the Soviets in a cleft stick by making the silos very hard and putting the systems so close together that if the Soviets attacked simultaneously they would have a fratricide problem. So we mentioned that in the Townes Committee report. There were some dissenters in Townes who did not want to go along with the MX at all; the majority of us were willing to go along with this solution if the MX could be made survivable. We thought that the long-endurance aircraft would probably work, but there was a lot of resistance to it in the air force so we wrote the report in such a way as to say that what you have to do is deploy one hundred MXs and one hundred vertical shelters expandable into an MPS system. We were trying to come up with a system that would get around what we were sure would be [Secretary of Defense Caspar] Weinberger's and the president's objection to deceptive basing. We did not have to decide at that point how to turn single shelters into multiple shelters, but you wanted to make sure that at least you had that option in case these other things did not work.

That was the one thing that Weinberger changed from the Townes Committee recommendations when he made the announcement in October of 1981. He talked about putting one hundred missiles in one hundred silos, not expandable, vertical shelters, and then working on these other things that might pan out in the long run. The problem with that was that it looked to Congress as if he planned on putting them in the silos and that he possibly planned on using them first. They would be vulnerable counterforce systems. The reason it did not fly then and it more or less flew in 1983 was that there was no long-run plan that people believed in for doing something different. The air force did not like the long-endurance aircraft, and Weinberger kind of did, but it looked to the outside world as if all you were really doing was putting one hundred MXs in one hundred vulnerable silos and then fiddling around with some R&D.

R. James Woolsey discussed the strategic logic that entered into calculations within the Scowcroft Commission about ICBM basing modes. He suggested that conceptually it was seen as useful to create a situation in which the Soviet Union would find it necessary to spend billions of rubles in order to maintain a semblance of counterforce accuracy against changing U.S. basing modes. To the extent that the Soviet Union would find it impossible to do so, it could gain an incentive to alter the structure of its force.

The underlying assumption of the ICBM survivability issue in the report was that, as much as you can, you want to try to move into a world in which the survivability of your own ICBMs is not dependent upon what the Soviets do. That is to say that they would be survivable regardless of the deployments that the Soviets choose to make and the direction they choose to go. That is the beauty of the small mobile ICBM—that you do not need an arms control agreement to make it survivable. Now if you stay in silos with a small ICBM, which is one of the options we left open in the report, you do need a de-MIRVing agreement, and you also probably do not need the assumption that neither side is going to use anything except ICBMs in a counterforce role. Once the Soviets are able to threaten your ICBM force with their SLBM [sea-launched ballistic missile] force, then I think the possibility of a silo-protecting agreement—even assuming single warheads, if you could magically say, "There will be no land-based MIRVs"—the possibility of protecting your forces with that kind of agreement is completely out the window. So what intrigued us so much about the small mobile missile was that the Soviets would have to use such a high proportion of their throwweight to barrage a small mobile missile on the southwestern military bases that an ICBM attack is a mug's game [something which cannot be profitable] for them. What is really likely to cut Soviet force structure in the event that the United States deploys a small mobile is not really an arms control agreement—which is part of the policy we stated in the report, and it has some utility, I suppose—but the thing that would really cut the Soviet force structure is that we should not give them many targets. There are not that many times that they could blow up New York. If they cannot put at risk any substantial share of the U.S. strategic force by building ICBMs, then the chances are that they would spend their money on some other systems. With small mobile ICBMs, the only strategic targets in the United States that are fixed would be the bomber bases and a few command and control targets.

At some point the cost-exchange ratio enters into this calculation, and it is radically easier for us to expand basing areas than it is for them to add throwweight. I mean, it is not a negligible thing for them to double their throwweight—that is, doubling the size of their whole force—and even if they could do it in the cheapest and most efficient way possible (that means putting it on SS-18s, even inaccurate SS-18s) still costs a lot of money. The survivability of the small mobile on the southwestern bases goes with area that can be covered. If you can require the Soviet Union to pay the price of using its entire existing throwweight to barrage three southwestern bases and they spend tens upon hundreds of billions of rubles to double their throwweight, and it costs us merely a fraction of that amount to increase the area that we would deploy on by going to another couple of southwestern bases or by going to Fort Campbell, Kentucky, or other bases in the United States and planning to flush off those bases on tactical warning—you are in good shape. We looked at the numbers, and barrage attack looked like such a mug's game for the Soviets that, in a way, you almost hoped that they would spend the money to try it because then they could not do anything else. The intelligent way for them to get the small mobile would be to do something that they have more trouble with than we—and we certainly do not find it easy—and that is to build a sophisticated surveillance, command and control system in which the warhead can be updated by overhead reconnaissance—we are talking twenty-first-century kind of stuff.

It would not work if it cost them a billion dollars to double their throwweight and it cost us five billion to add enough land to operate the small mobile, but one nice thing about the small mobile is that as long as you have about thirty minutes to flush them, and you can flush on tactical warning, lots of military bases around the country are available. The only reason that you need the southwestern bases is if you want to be deployed in peacetime so that with no tactical warning, or with just a few minutes' warning from a Soviet SLBM attack, you want to be able to flush to a survivable area, and adding large amounts of throwweight by building SLBMs is not easy. Warheads are not really the main measure of the ability to barrage. You go by equivalent megatonnage, which goes directly with throwweight.

Although the Scowcroft Commission addressed the issue of strategic aircraft, the focus of its work was ICBM modernization. It was assumed that the emerging force posture of the United States would include aircraft whose versatility was such as to make them usable in nonstrategic, nonnuclear missions, as in the case of the B-52 in the Vietnam War. Mr. Woolsey explained:

We did not even talk that much about bombers. The B-1 program was going along and the ATB [advanced tactical bomber] was going along, and some people, like those in the Carter administration, probably would have said, "If you do ATB then you do not need the B-1," and the Reagan people said, "You need the B-1 and you may need the ATB." But there was no reason to fight over it. We knew we were going to have a bomber force.

The B-1 happily was faster in getting away from its base than the B-52—which I think is the major bomber vulnerability—so you had an improved survivability coming into the force. The pace of it—and whether to supplement it with the ATB—these were kind of cost-effectiveness issues. Bombers were generally useful because they could, as in Vietnam, be used for things other than strategic nuclear war. Although people were willing to be diverted to haggling over the merits and relative advantages of the ATB and B-1, we did not see much reason to get into it in any detail. It was not an immediate decision that needed to be made; somebody else would decide it some years down the road. The immediate thought-provoking decision that had to be made was what to do about the ICBM force.

National security adviser to President Reagan at the time, Robert McFarlane argued that the Scowcroft Commission had significant political impact as well:

On the whole, I believed our electorate should be informed on fundamentals; ours is not. The Scowcroft Commission changed that a little. It changed it a *lot* on the Hill. The Congress has had a very superficial understanding of nuclear doctrine; the Armed Services Committees and Appropriation Subcommittees were the only people who really knew much about it. You can read the Scowcroft Commission Report, and while a lot of it is very sophisticated, much of it is in layman's terms, explaining deterrence, stability, why we can be reasonably confident against a first strike, how we get a synergism from the triad, and so on. Suddenly, even the congressional leadership had a better understanding of the matter. I think that Sen. Albert Gore really learned 90 percent of what he knows about strategic doctrine from the Scowcroft Commission, as well as Congressmen Richard Gephardt and Vic Fazio and a cadre of other people that I worked with in the House. Even some others who were sophisticates, like Les Aspin, had a much better grasp of these issues after the Scowcroft Commission Report.
At the same time, many of those who had shaped the modernization program in 1981 began to rethink some of the criteria. I think that it made life easier for people like Fred Iklé, who was a very sound analyst but felt compelled to defend very high targeting requirements for the JSTPS [joint strategic target planning system] and very demanding force requirements that JCS posed to him; he began to throttle back a little bit after the Scowcroft Commission. It was a very solid service.
So in addition to the educational function, which was probably the best part of the Scowcroft Commission, it did give us a program for [nuclear force] modernization—particularly in the land-based forces—that had some intellectual foundation to it. That had been missing from the Pentagon's budget appearances in 1981, 1982, and 1983. Suddenly it was there and you did not have to call the secretary of defense. You could call

all the members of the Scowcroft Commission, as they did finally in the 1983 hearings. The administration suddenly had—because the president endorsed it—some credibility on the Hill. The commission worked well beyond its report.

On March 23, 1983, President Reagan announced his Strategic Defense Initiative, calling upon the scientific community to ascertain the feasibility of deploying a defense against ballistic missiles. As chairman of the Joint Chiefs of Staff at this time, Gen. John Vessey presented perspectives on the president's decision and the events that followed:

> I think that the major role the JCS played was in that February 1983 meeting that we had with the president, when the JCS told the president that strategic defense ought to play a role in the future. We pointed out what the Soviets were doing in defense. We went into great detail, both in what they were doing in research for space defense, as well as their activities in conventional air defense, as well as the ABM defense. That was the major JCS contribution. I think that many other people were advising the president that strategic defense ought to play a role in the future strategic nuclear equation. It was bound to have an effect. It would be presumptuous for me to say that was a key issue, but it seems to me that if I were president, I would not announce a major change in our strategic military policy without coordinating with the JCS.
>
> The March 23, 1983, speech was constructed in the White House; the secretary of defense and I saw it before it was given, but it was very tightly held. The secretary and I were in NATO at the Nuclear Planning Group meeting when the speech was made. I do not recall whether the chiefs saw the text, but they knew it was going to be made. The JCS wanted to make sure that balance was kept, the SDI was not looked on as a panacea for all our defense ills, that if you solved the strategic defense problem, you still had tremendous Soviet conventional strength, which led us into the strategic nuclear business in the first place. So, the JCS wanted to make sure that the program was structured to be a balanced program. SDI did not take the focus off the need for both conventional and strategic offensive modernization in the short run, but it had long-run benefits that we ought to pursue. The chiefs were all supportive of the president's views and thought that they made a contribution to shaping those views.

R. James Woolsey points out that, in the period between the ABM Treaty of 1972 and President Reagan's March 23, 1983, address unveiling the Strategic Defense Initiative, the discussion about defensive systems within the defense community had as it focus the protection of limited, fixed sites rather than large urban areas or the entire nation.

> I think the world forgot about the idea of population defense between 1972 and 1983. People had worked on various ABM systems that were

terminal—to protect ICBM survivability. At the time I took the statement concerning potential withdrawal from the ABM Treaty to mean essentially that, if we in light of Soviet strategic improvements felt it was necessary to defend our silos, and we did not have an agreement that would effectively limit SS-9s and SS-9 follow-ons, that we would feel free to go ahead and do so. Indeed, the structure of SALT II and the MX and the multiple protective shelter system was one in which what one was trying to do was to negotiate sufficient limits on SS-18s that the Soviet Union would not have enough counterforce warheads to launch against all of the shelters in the shell game. But if the Soviets, by some fashion, were able to improve the accuracy of other systems, or violate the treaty, or even under SALT II to be able to put the shelters at risk, if we had to—and I have heard Harold Brown say this—we could rely on that escape clause in the ABM Treaty and deploy terminal defenses.

I think that from 1969 to March of 1983 very few of the people who participated in these discussions across a broad part of the military and political spectrum had thought about defense other than in terms of terminal defenses to protect ICBMs and possibly bomber bases. There were a few who kept the flame of population defense alive, but they were not really part of the negotiating teams or the government in either Republican or Democratic administrations.

Mr. Woolsey then discussed what he regarded as the priorities that should guide U.S. strategic defense program planning in response to the problems of force survivability and related issues:

The most important job for defensive systems would be to try to deal, first of all, with protection of U.S. strategic targets, and I would include in that things like air bases in Europe, and defenses against conventional as well as nuclear attack. An antitactical ballistic missile that would defend against Soviet nonnuclear or chemical warhead short-range ballistic missiles and which would protect NATO air bases is, in my terms, a strategic system. One of the most important strategic interests that the United States has is its alliances, and there is a certain degree to which all of this business is a seamless web between the conventional and nuclear levels. You want to try to deter a conventional attack as well as a nuclear one. So in a real sense, I would regard something like an antitactical ballistic missile defense in Europe as part of the U.S. strategic defenses. The term *strategic* does not just mean strictly the continental United States.

But in addition to something like an antitactical ballistic missile defense, I think that you ought to keep moving hard on the technology because something particularly interesting might turn up, and you want to try to stay ahead of the Soviets in all the defensive system areas if you can so that you are not surprised. But in addition to that, it seems to me that if you do everything you can to preserve the survivability of your forces without defenses, like having a small mobile ICBM, then you would want to look hard at deploying strategic defenses—without violating the

ABM Treaty if you can help it. Look first at any strategic defensive deployment that would take up slack in your defenses which cannot be dealt with by the other survivability measures, particularly our command and control and our bombers. I am assuming now that we have small mobile ICBMs, so I am not worried about the small mobile or the at-sea submarines. So our bombers in the normal day-to-day posture—not cockpit alert—and command and control seem to me to be potentially vulnerable to stealthy Soviet cruise missiles from submarines or to close-in Soviet SSBNs (Ballistic Missile Submarines, Nuclear Powered) firing depressed trajectory SLBMs. So in addition to an antitactical ballistic missile defense in Europe, I would look hard at warning systems and defenses against cruise missiles, and I would look hard at what types of ballistic missile defense deployments would be the most effective against things like depressed trajectory SLBMs.

The tendency now is to concentrate on the SS-18 attack, but I think that there is another way to deal with the SS-18, namely by deploying the small mobile ICBM. Silo-busting systems thirty minutes away do not have nearly as much strategic importance as if you were sitting in silos. The Reagan administration talked a lot about fast flyers versus slow flyers. The fastest flyer of all would be a depressed trajectory SLBM or a cruise missile that you could not even attack because you did not know it was there until it was detonating over the bomber bases. So if I look first at the military problems, I come up with defending main operating bases and the command and control nodes, and maybe the prepositioned equipment and ammunition stockpiles—nonnuclear and chemical. I would look at protecting command and control centers and bomber bases against a leading edge strike with stealthy cruise missiles, and quite possibly also seeing what you might need to do to protect command and control nodes and bomber bases against depressed trajectory SLBMs. Those would be my first priorities, not population defense, not accidental launch, and not SS-18s (using low–earth orbit boost-phase intercept).

Among the issues confronting the Reagan administration and its SDI critics was the interpretation of the ABM Treaty with respect to the development, testing, and deployment of systems based on "other physical principles" than those in existence when the treaty was negotiated, signed, and ratified. Mr. Woolsey presented his rationale for accepting the restrictive interpretation to the effect that the treaty placed constraints on such systems:

I think that the narrow interpretation is correct. Senator Nunn is right on this. I think that the best argument is one which is partly classified and has not seen much attention. It has to do with the fact that under the Vienna Convention on the Law of Treaties—which the United States has signed but not ratified, but which embodies the operating principles for the interpretation of all international treaties—the most important thing in interpreting a treaty is not its legislative history—which is the way one would proceed in interpreting a statute—the first thing one looks to in a treaty is subsequent agreements, and then to subsequent practice, and then finally to ratification. It is an interesting American political and constitutional point—I am referring to what people thought at the time the treaty was ratified and what they said—but the most important thing is subsequent agreements, and if you look at the history of the Standing Consultative Commission and the agreements that have been signed there, I would agree that Article 4 [of the ABM Treaty], which is the testing article, makes it pretty clear that the narrow interpretation is correct.

Joseph Luns was secretary-general of NATO at the time of President Reagan's March 23, 1983, speech.

It was discussed within NATO, but of course it was generally accepted that America had the full right to devise measures in order to defend America against an attack by intercontinental missiles. Nevertheless, there were some misgivings that if America was able, completely, to defend itself, then the bulk of the fighting would fall on Europe. But bear in mind that, first of all, the Americans do not know yet whether it can be done. Secondly, if it can be done, they do not know whether they can pay for it. Certainly the Russians are far less hostile now than they were about two years ago, and I do not understand why they did not accept the offer by the president that all the know-how would be given to the Soviet Union too, but there it is.

The decision of the Reagan administration to press forward with SDI gave rise to an intensified debate and discussion of strategic defense in Western Europe and in particular its implications for deterrence in the alliance. One French perspective was set forth by General Gallois.

Concerning the SDI, when I learned about it I was very interested for two reasons. First, I thought that the Americans may, because of their aim of the SDI, be capable of developing a completely new set of technologies, some of them militarily usable which have nothing to do with the existing weapons—including atomic weapons—based on new principles of physics. That was extraordinarily fascinating for me. This is why I went to discussions with General Abrahamson [Lt. Gen. James A. Abrahamson was director of the Strategic Defense Initiative Organization, 1984–89]. Second, I was delighted by such an effort mainly because I thought that the Soviet Union was doing it and it would be very dangerous to leave the Soviets alone.

Nevertheless, Gen. Pierre Gallois acknowledged that the decision of the Reagan administration to press forward with SDI gave rise to an intensified debate and discussion of strategic defense in Western Europe and, in particular, its implications for deterrence in the alliance. Many in France discounted the Soviet program in space and in strategic defense, for which he offered the following explanation:

> This is the result of a futile attachment to the past. You see, in 1939 we were attached to infantry. In the 1940s we were attached to tanks because we had discovered the tank. We finally have discovered the deterrent merits of atomic weapons, and we stick to that concept just as we were sticking to the infantry in 1939. For the French, the Americans and Soviets installing themselves in space is a vague threat against an established order which they finally like. They do not accept that technology is changing, and that policy must change according to technology. They were safe in an atomic world with what they have achieved: 6 submarines, 18 missiles on the Albion plateau, and 120 Plutons. Now we rest, and we do not move anymore. When it was a question of creating a shield against ballistic missiles, obviously the question is, what about us? Our weapons are not going to penetrate anymore. It is a catastrophe. We must be against it—as if it were possible to be against the technology. Human beings are what they are, but they always want to invent even if what they invent is not necessary or is dangerous. As soon as something can be done it is done. So it is useless to protest against it. The problem is to adapt ourselves and try to know what to do should a shield be created. This is why I was so interested in what [America is] doing.
>
> Through the money which is spent for SDI the Americans are going to catch up with what the Soviet Union has achieved. What the Soviets have achieved is not understood in Europe. When I deliver speeches in this country, which I do frequently, I say to my countrymen that for the past ten years the Soviets have launched a satellite every three days. They have discovered something which they say is not possible. To launch with success a satellite every three days, you need an organization, a scientific organization, a technical organization, which is extraordinary. When you have launched some 1,900 Cosmos satellites, then access to space, by rockets, not by shuttle, is already for the Soviets something of an ordinary action—everyday action at most. This is very important. It is for two reasons that I welcome the SDI—despite the fact that the SDI may, in the long run, destroy my own concept of deterrence.
>
> You see, what was important in the nuclear system in which we are living, based mainly on proportional deterrence, is that with few weapons we would be capable of achieving such great destruction that a few weapons have the power of intimidation, but if these weapons do not penetrate, they are useless. If you increase the number to such a rate that you return to a certain extent to the old system—that is, that you are a military power when you retain a great number of weapons. The more soldiers you have, the more guns, the more ships, the more aircraft, the more important you are. That idea was destroyed, as we say now, by the advent of nuclear weapons, and I always said that the equalizing power of atomic weapons

makes almost all nations concerned about their vulnerability. If you destroy fifty cities in the Soviet Union, forty in China, sixty in the United States, ten in Germany, and nine in France, you can do the maximum damage and always small numbers are used. But if [strategic] defense suddenly takes on an important role, to overcome defense you have to saturate and then you return to mass production. My point was that the industry producing the vehicles was becoming a small industry; an industry making the explosives was a major industry—but with the defense system the major industry would again return to the production of vehicles for a phenomenon of saturation. So there is a change, and I am not sure that we can follow it because of the immensity of the task which we have to face.

General Gallois addressed the question of defense against shorter-range missiles:

I have studied such a question, although it is very difficult because the information is difficult. And what is more, it is completely contradictory. Somebody said, "Look, with the short-range, generally they do not use MIRV, then it is easier to see it." That is a point of view. Some of us believe, on the contrary, that because there are only three minutes, it is very difficult to react. Some said, "Well, but you see that they are using a trajectory which is climbing relatively high, so detection may be easy in spite of the short time, and you may defend more easily some fixed targets." I do not think so. Finally, I think that it will be very difficult to protect targets in Europe, mainly because we have relatively few buried targets. That is a great difference between United States and Europe. We have on-the-surface targets, and this means that the accuracy is not going to have to be as great as it is and that the cone in which we have to intervene against an incoming missile is not a small angle, but a very large one because of the fragility, the vulnerability of surface targets. But again, against [a Soviet] saturation [attack] I doubt that if the Russians allocate ten weapons [to a target], a small yield probably exploding at various heights to neutralize an air shield, I doubt that we could protect it efficiently. I think that any static target is doomed.

To make weapons survivable, you need mobility and deceptive basing. To saturate a deterrent you need new devices, some for low-level penetration at high speeds. You see, we are studying the ASMP [Air/Sol Moyenne Portée] aircraft-delivered missile. We originated that at Dassault. It is an interesting weapon because it is thermal, hot jet concept and rocket concept combined. For the time being the range is limited to 300 kilometers, but we can imagine it having up to a 1,000 or 1,200 or 1,500 kilometer range. It will be very difficult to intercept, even with an SDI system in place. We would have been wise in the world if in the 1950s we would have been satisfied with the capabilities of taking hostage fifty cities on both sides and have, say, two countries, two big countries, ten submarines launching 160 [nuclear] warheads each, period. But unhappily, we have made a reasoning by analogy: those who have more weapons are stronger. That was the case in the conventional era, and we have projected the conventional era into the atomic one.

The SDI program is of great value to stimulate the development of a completely new set of weapons based on transport of the great quantity of energy on a light wave at distances the speed of light. I am sure that in fifty years' time you may have conquered a completely new type of weapon based on these new physical principles. That will be, for America, militarily speaking, positive. It may change the world. You may have a lot of satellites with these weapons, and they may control terrorism. They may destroy a terrorist in his house without warning the bodyguards who are in the other room; you can imagine anything in the future, in the distant future. Things will be changed. Strategies will be changed completely and possibly only a combined force of German-British-French-Italians and so on will be capable of being in competition with what you are doing and what the Soviet Union is doing. Possibly not. You see, possibly atomic weapons constitute the last technology in military affairs which can be mastered by a medium-sized nation.

Ambassador François de Rose presented other perspectives on strategic defense, deterrence, and arms control:

SDI, if it can work, would have diminished the chances of a disarming first strike. I think that if the Soviets were people that we could talk to, and if we were capable of speaking their language, it should be possible to use SDI to diminish that danger of a disarming surprise attack.

Let us suppose that we live in a different world, and that the Soviets and we agree that we are not going to wage war on one another, but nonetheless that we are afraid of one another. Talking in terms of general disarmament (which is absurd, because we are not going to give up our defenses since rivalries and competition go on in every field), we could offer another approach. Would it not be possible to have a sort of structure in which both sides would reduce—let us say to one thousand—the number of offensive weapons, whatever they are, missiles and airplanes. We would keep one thousand airplanes and missiles on both sides because we cannot give them up. But both sides deploy antiair and antimissile capacities redundant enough to stop not 100 percent, but let us say 70–80 percent, of the attacker's delivery systems. Why the other side will save his defense weapons, because he will only lose his offensive weapons. Therefore, the result of an aggression would be to leave the aggressor much weaker than the attacked. The first strike would be absurd. We could have the same also for the [Soviet] operational maneuver groups, land-based offensive systems, artillery, transport, and so on. In other words, to reduce the offensive forces and to calculate the defensive forces so that you would have enough to saturate and destroy the offensive ones, aggression becomes absurd and stability would, so to speak, result in the very structure of forces on both sides—not on the always questionable good faith of the other side.

I do not really know what the technology now is and would warrant, but they would have to be recognized as efficient. What would be important is to calculate the defenses, whatever they are, so that they blunt the offensive ones. The disarming offensive should be counterforce; but if one went crazy and wanted to make a strategic offensive against demographic and economic assets, the other party would have the same capacity to retaliate. So the defenses should be focused only on military targets, the ones by which you try to destroy the defense of your enemy. But massive retaliation as far as attacking civilians would still go on because it would be equally absurd for one to attack the other since he would know that he would be destroyed.

13
French Nuclear Forces

The Atlantic Alliance is unique in having more than one of its members in possession of nuclear weapons. The development of such capabilities by France and the United Kingdom represented a response to diverging strategic and political considerations in the transatlantic relationship, together with a perceived need, especially notable in the case of France, to acquire the means for independence. Therefore, this chapter focuses particularly upon the creation of the French *force de frappe* by addressing the Defense Program Law of 1960, French nuclear strategy (with emphasis on proportional deterrence), the impact of France's decision upon its NATO allies, and distinctions between French and NATO nuclear strategy. In addition, the chapter touches upon British nuclear forces, the multilateral force idea, and Franco-German nuclear coupling issues.

Gen. Pierre Gallois and Ambassador François de Rose were keen observers of, and participants in, the process that led to the creation of the French national nuclear force. They offer complementary, as well as contrasting, perspectives on the circumstances leading to the formation and ambitions of France's atomic weapons capability. They shed particular light on the motivation of President de Gaulle. General Gallois stated that the security of France could be assured only if it possessed nuclear weapons:

> I think that de Gaulle was convinced that after the last war France could not accept any more war. We were unable to conduct war operations on a great scale, completely unable. Cardinal Richelieu in the seventeenth century said that the French were not very keen on war because war necessitates organization, calm, and foresight, and these were not French qualities. [With] what took place between 1939 and 1945 when I was in Britain working in the Air Transport Command, I realized that we were completely unable to reach a similar military status. Hence, only one solution existed and that was to exploit technology. The new technology was a miracle, revealed by Hiroshima and Nagasaki. So, in 1945 I was already sure that since we were capable of mastering such technology, we would get the weapons to avoid war. So as early as 1945 I had begun to think about deterrence based upon this new technology weaponry.

You must understand the despair of a young man being the witness of such a blow to his country. In 1939 people thought that the French Army was the first on the Continent. Not me. Even the British staff believed it to be so. Suddenly, we discovered that in six weeks we were not. We were pushed to the Pyrenees. The roots of the defeat were obvious: lack of materiel, lack of a good strategic concept, lack of command, lack of fighting spirit, lack of money, and internal disorder. As a result, I had to leave my country and go to Britain to be under British command, to fly British equipment to bomb my country, to destroy some cities of my own country. When I returned to France in 1945, after four years of occupation, I knew the situation was still terrible. The people were accustomed to the black market, they were accustomed to hiding from the Germans, everything was in ruin; the country had the appearance of a ring of destruction and misery and so on. I was relatively young at that time. The idea was to do anything to avoid ever being put into such a situation again. This is why, starting in 1945–46, I began my campaign for nuclear armament. General de Gaulle did also—as soon as he returned to France in late 1944, he decided upon the creation of the Atomic Energy Commission of France.

General Gallois contended that France's displeasure with NATO played a role in the creation of the French nuclear force:

At the time of the Algerian War we were very disappointed by the attitudes of not only the Americans, but the allies in general. That may not be very fair but, after all, Algeria was composed of three French departments; Algeria was French territory. Hence, Algeria should be defended as any French territory within NATO. Naturally, the British and the Belgians objected and said, "No, this is not the question; NATO has a role which is in Europe against the Russians." That reaction was increased by the Suez crisis. During the Suez crisis, the American fleet was moving between Cyprus and the coastline to demonstrate that the Americans were against the British and French action. When Nikita Khrushchev made his famous warning in November of 1956 (threatening nuclear destruction of British and French cities at the time of the Suez crisis and Anglo-French military action against Egypt), we had the feeling that we were left without the protection of America. Thus, in December 1956, when the military budget was prepared by Parliament, all of its members except the Communists were in favor of France's development of atomic weapons, not as a weapon of independence, but in case of trouble for use as a last resort because we were not sure anymore of the American attitude toward us.

Because of these two facts, the attitude of the allies during the Algerian crisis and because of the Suez affair, French public opinion was persuaded to support an independent capability, even though a majority was initially against the French atomic weapons program. They thought that these weapons were just the weapons of great powers, that we were wasting our money and that it would be ridiculous to have just a few weapons.

They were not aware of proportional deterrence, but when the Americans demonstrated against us in the Suez crisis, and when they demonstrated against us in the Algerian crisis, the French people began to realize that they had been too confident of the idea of Europe and too confident of the idea of the merits of the capabilities of the Atlantic Alliance. From now on, we should provide for ourselves the means of our own defense. So 1956 was a turning point.

Ambassador de Rose added a few political considerations for France wanting nuclear weapons of its own:

First of all, the French government needed a platform to explain the program to the world. The British had a nuclear capability, and we would not drop out and let the British be the only ones who would have influence over the Continent through their possession of nuclear weapons. Secondly, there was the German factor. After the Second World War, there was concern that if Germany were to emerge as a great power, she would have to possess a nuclear capability. In that situation, the French were convinced that they had to have a similar capability to balance German influence.

General Gallois told of the role he played in getting his view across to the political leadership of France on the importance of nuclear weapons:

The prime minister was Mr. Guy Mollet [secretary-general of the French Socialist party, 1946–69, and last prime minister of the Fourth Republic, 1956–58]. Gen. Lauris Norstad [SACEUR, 1956–62] said, "You should go and see him and explain to him what you are doing. Your government must know." I said, "Sir, I do not think the politicians will understand. I am going to waste my time." He said, "You are wrong, Pierre, you should go." "Well," I asked, "could I take from the safe room some documents to convince him?" He said, "Yes, take the documents you need from the room," which I did. I went with Chaban-Delmas [Jacques Chaban-Delmas was president of the National Assembly, 1958–69, and prime minister, 1969–72], and one night, at Matignon [the office of the prime minister], I explained to the prime minister our new strategy. I showed him some charts which were convincing, and he said to me, "Look, Colonel, I made my political campaign on three bases. The first was peace in Algeria; the second, reduction of taxes; and the third, disarmament. I am fighting in Algeria. To fight in Algeria I am raising the taxes and now you want me to make a bomb." I said, "Prime Minister, as far as I understand, you have told lies to the French in your campaign because you are fighting in Algeria. You are raising taxes. So why not the last?"

He said, "Well, Colonel, it is not you who is going to face the electors, the voters." I said, "Prime Minister, according to what you said I think your political career is finished. So before leaving political office you have the chance to do something important for the country." He said, "You are right," and he asked me to telephone our minister of defense. It was two o'clock in the morning at that time. So we telephoned at two o'clock in the morning, and the prime minister told Yves Bourges [then minister of defense] that he should see Gallois immediately. The next morning I saw him, and we had several discussions. In July 1956, just a few days before the nationalization of the Suez Canal, a large meeting took place in the Ministry of Defense with all the French command and the political command, and I prepared for that meeting the charts, and I delivered my speech lasting probably two or three hours. Some were convinced, some were not. One French Air Force general came to me and said, "Look, you are very stupid, what you are doing with your bomb, you are destroying your whole career. With your system you do not need any men. Many officers, many men will never be promoted. You are mad." That man was General Giraud, the famous leader in Algeria.

General Norstad also urged Gallois to meet with General de Gaulle:

Then a few days after that meeting with Guy Mollet, Norstad said to me again, "Look, Pierre, you should see General de Gaulle." I said, "Sir, no, I have just seen the prime minister, but de Gaulle is nothing now, he is just retired. I said he will never return to power. I think that he, being the man of the offense, will not understand the new strategy. He will be against it because his mind is turned to the past." Norstad said, "You are wrong, Gallois, I read the translation of some of his books. He is a very intelligent person, and forward looking. You should go and see him." "All right, sir, may I take the charts?" "Yes, you can take the charts." I then asked for a meeting with General de Gaulle.

I went to the Hôtel Lapérouse; [the meeting] was there on the fourth floor at 9:30 in the evening. I brought some 40 kilos or about 100 pounds of charts. I was helped by a military policeman. We were meeting in a sort of library with Louis XVI furniture, and General de Gaulle was sitting on a large sofa. I put my charts next to the armchair and I began my briefing, which probably lasted for one hour and fifteen minutes. Not a word did he utter. Then he began to think, talking aloud about the impression he had from my presentation. I was very impressed. We used a new type of language that was particular to the atomic concept we were developing. Then I realized that de Gaulle was using almost the same type of vocabulary. For instance, he said that "we understand that with these weapons, numbers are losing their significance. It is not necessary to be strong or to have more or the same amount of forces as the other side; the problem is to be capable to tear off an arm or even a hand."

He understood that this was a way to give the country a status above its real situation. He gave me the impression that he understood that possessing atomic weapons was one way to give France a status much above its real situation in the world. Politically speaking we had no resources; no oil, no steel, no iron ore. But if we had atomic weapons, we would give

France a position in the world well above its material situation. I was very impressed by such a declaration. Then he asked some questions to refine some views which were not clear, and around two or three o'clock in the morning he suddenly said, "Gallois, it is late, you must have some rest." I said, "Yes, sir." Then we went together to the lift; so I entered the lift and he told me to get some rest. "I shall take care of your career." He was laughing. I went back home. This was April 1956. I went home to my wife and said I just left Louis XVI and we are on his private list. That was exactly the impression I had. This surprised me because a few months before, while delivering a speech at Strasbourg, he insisted on the necessity of France having fifteen land divisions—not a word about atomic weapons. I was disappointed. Now I was very impressed by the fact that he understood so rapidly. He was more advanced than we ourselves.

Ambassador de Rose played an important role in writing the initial draft statement setting forth France's nuclear policy.

There was one incident while I was at the United Nations which could have had consequences for the future. Every government got to make a statement of policy. I wrote the draft which was sent to Paris and approved. Before World War II, France was abreast with Britain in that field. Frédéric Joliot-Curie [French Communist scientist and Nobel Prize winner] was considered to be a man at the same level as the best of his colleagues. I wrote in the draft that France assigned the efforts of its scientists to purely peaceful objectives in nuclear energy, not minding that, in the decree by which de Gaulle had created the "Commissariat de l'énergie atomique" in 1945, that said that the mission of the commissariat was to develop all applications of nuclear energy, which included the military, of course.

I would not say that funds were made available under the supervision of the prime minister. We were very quiet about nuclear weapons officially. Our program dealt especially with the question of finding raw materials in France and what was still the French empire and developing the reactors that could produce plutonium.

General Gallois described what occurred once the decision to build a French nuclear force had been taken:

The decision was made to have an A-bomb in July 1956, in spite of the fact that a moratorium of five years was asked by the Socialist government, because the technicians said that France needed five years to implement the order. The fastest way to attain a nuclear cabability was to use an aircraft platform. We had to make a choice between the Dassault proposal [for the Mirage IV bomber] and that of a nationalized company in the southwest, a derivative of the Sud SO 4050 Vautour IIB aircraft. The two projects were examined during the month of October, and I believe that the choice was made in March of 1957. The choice was made by the technical authorities and the chief of staff of the air force. The decision was taken to launch a prototype, which flew in May 1959; de Gaulle was there at the launching.

Immediately thereafter, he prepared the Defense Program Law of 1960, in which fifty aircraft were ordered, and that was the beginning of the French *force de frappe*. At that time orders were given to study ballistic missile weapons which later would be deployed on the Albion plateau. Orders were also given to study a submarine capable of launching ballistic missiles. Already, in the Socialist government, a submarine propelled with atomic fuel was under study. The idea was to have atomic propulsion. It was a complete failure. The engine was too big; it did not work. It was only in the budget law of 1964 that we came back to the problem of nuclear-propelled submarines, deploying sixteen weapons, copying what we had achieved in Washington in 1960 and by the Russians later. As you know, the size of the submarine is dictated by the dimensions of the weapons it deploys.

General Gallois set forth his views as to why the *force de frappe* continues to be widely supported by French public opinion:

The French are very proud to have mastered with success nuclear technology, including for peaceful uses. This is why France has such a big program of civilian atomic energy. They understand that proportional deterrence plays a certain role in deterring. They realize that France was invaded in 1849, in 1850, again in 1870, and in 1914, and in 1940—five invasions, with the city of Paris occupied four times. They have lost any hope of winning a war, and some wise people here, there are some, believe that France's only hope is to have the means to intimidate in such a way that no one threatens it with invasion again. Finally, because of the French past, the French are very pleased to see a government, including the de Gaulle government, say no to the powerful nations, such as the United States. They believe that such freedom of action, to a certain extent, is a result of having atomic weapons.

General Gallois criticized U.S. opposition to the French nuclear program:

When President Kennedy came to office, the United States was very much against what we were doing. The press, the clubs, and groups of some small think tanks we have here used to go to the United States to take information and then get back and publish papers and articles, documents, against the nuclear policy of General de Gaulle. The political parties used this technical information and soon the idea was that for France to develop nuclear weapons was ridiculous. We would never have enough. It would be too costly, and we would never dare to use them. They said we were wasting money. I would say that the Americans, the British, and the Germans supported those arguments. I had many fights with American journalists, and battles with British people like Lord Chalfont [British foreign minister, 1964–70], for instance. Lord Chalfont was a very strong critic of the French effort even though he was himself in favor of the British nuclear force. He criticized the French Mirage IV bomber and said that the British Vulcans were better. Remember, in Germany there were people like Professor Richard von Weizsäcker who were against the idea of a French weapon. In Switzerland, there was opposition, in Italy, everywhere. I spent probably half of my time discouraging these attacks, fighting them and writing against them. It was, for me, very interesting, a very amusing period. But the policy was fixed by de Gaulle himself with mainly two laws: the Defense Program Law of 1960 and the Defense Program Law of 1964.

Ambassador de Rose also spoke about this point:

I knew that the United States was against it, but Gallois's view was that the United States was not really an ally of Europe. For a very long time he held the view that with nuclear weapons you could have no alliance. I think that he has slightly changed his views, but I disagreed with Gallois's views on that front, although he is a very intelligent man who has done a lot to convince the French that nuclear weapons are necessary. I did not agree with his theory of France being alone. Sometimes, he even says that we cannot cooperate with the Europeans because we have nuclear weapons.

In 1961 we were already well advanced on a nuclear submarine. We were also building an isotope-refining plant to produce enriched uranium. Where I disagreed with Gallois was in the conviction that we would make our cooperation with the alliance less strong, less intimate. The difference between me and the others was that I always felt that the primary guarantee of French independence and security was given by the alliance. Therefore, we had to cooperate with the alliance.

Certainly, we were not able to increase our authority. Other European governments were very much against the French development of nuclear weapons. President Kennedy called it an unfriendly act and Secretary of Defense McNamara said that it was useless and dangerous. It could hardly be both at the same time. That was the predicament; we would increase our prestige but certainly not the quality of our relationship with the others.

Our nuclear arsenal would be useful politically; it would put us in a different position in Europe. It would go well with our position as a permanent member of the UN Security Council. Militarily it would be useful as a deterrent only in case NATO failed. That was a reassurance for France, but perhaps only reassurance of not being invaded, not of saving her sovereignty if Germany were conquered.

Ambassador de Rose pointed to the problems that France faced even before the Kennedy administration's more intense opposition to the nuclear program:

France's nuclear power certainly did not require good relations with allies. Then there was the McMahon Act [prohibiting the export of nuclear weapons data and technology from the United States, but amended. in 1958 to allow Britain to gain access to such knowledge], which was tailored to suit the U.K.'s case and to exclude France. That was very carefully analyzed in France, and the lesson and the message were received. I think that de Gaulle, who said that states have no friends but only interests, knew that if he had had nuclear weapons and the United States had not, he would probably not have shared with them, so I think he found that it was all in the game—that states have no friends.

What we needed were certain pieces of equipment, like large computers, which were very difficult to obtain. There was almost an embargo on them, but eventually we got them. Then we wanted to be able to get more submarines, but there was almost an embargo on them. Eventually we got them. Then we wanted to be able to build nuclear-powered submarines; after all, the British had been given Polaris blueprints at that time. Subsequently, we tried to buy a nuclear reactor for a submarine, and that was refused. Eventually Admiral Rickover [who designed the first nuclear-powered vessel in the U.S. Navy, the *Nautilus*, in 1952] said, "Give them the U-235; they will not be able to do anything with it."

General Gallois pointed to other problems in the relationship between the Kennedy administration and President de Gaulle.

The relationship between Charles de Gaulle and Robert McNamara was very bad. This had an influence—a technical one—on the French nuclear development. We bought the U.S. license for a jet engine, the TF-30, which is the same engine now on the F-111s. We bought the license, and we got thirteen of these engines and transformed them into the TF-306. This engine was then installed in an aircraft prototype which was called the Mirage 3-V, for vertical lift. It was a ten-engine aircraft, according to a NATO program (the NATO NMB III in 1961–62). We were competitors with this engine, and the corresponding aircraft was built by Dassault. It was for use on aircraft capable of taking off vertically and achieving Mach 2 speeds. The trouble was that the consumption of fuel was such that to be efficient, the enemy had to be at the end of the runway; anyway it was a prototype. This aircraft was dropped. We developed another aircraft and we took that engine to put it on the new air frame. Then Mr. NcNamara wrote a letter to General de Gaulle in which he said, "We have a license, an agreement with you, and we sold to you thirteen TF-30s. They were for the vertical take-off aircraft answering the NATO requirements. I learned that you are using the same engine for a new aircraft. To this I object. You have not the right to do so." Defense Minister [Pierre]

Mesmer went to see de Gaulle and said that this is what McNamara said. De Gaulle went mad. "These Americans! I paid for that license, I paid for that engine, and I have the right to do what I want! Okay, you stop everything and the fourteen aircraft you have developed with French engines; I do not want to have any more American engines." That had great consequences because we had to develop a completely new engine and to drop these prototypes.

Whereas France was facing these difficulties in acquiring and using U.S. nuclear and other technology, the United Kingdom—as a partner of the United States in the World War II Manhattan Project—had acquired the means to build an atomic weapons capability. By the early 1960s, the Macmillan government saw the need to modernize Britain's nuclear force, which at that time was based on an aging bomber-delivery system. For this purpose Britain had planned to acquire an air-to-surface missile called the Skybolt from the United States. Such a system would have given the British bomber force a standoff capability and thereby prolonged its life. Without Skybolt, the British nuclear force faced imminent obsolescence. In late 1962 the Kennedy administration canceled Skybolt, which was to have been procured by U.S. forces. At the end of 1962, however, Prime Minister Macmillan and President Kennedy met and signed the Nassau Agreement providing for the acquisition by Britain of U.S. technology to build a new generation sea-based nuclear force consisting of submarines deploying missiles. Although the Labour party opposed the policy, after 1964, when Labour returned to power, the government of Prime Minister Harold Wilson decided nevertheless to deploy the new system. Lord Mulley, a leading Labour party defense expert and minister of aviation in the Wilson government, described the evolution of policy on this issue:

As you know it was the outcome of the failure of what was to have been a joint development of Skybolt that led to the generous offer of the United States to make Polaris available to us, and this had been accepted by Macmillan. I think that it was a mistake that he had not at least consulted the president of France on the problem, but anyway, he did not. And so the Labour government not only inherited the decision, we also inherited the commitment of quite substantial amounts of money on irrevocable contracts to build submarines and long-lead items for the others not already fully contracted. As you know, we were buying the actual Polaris missile system from the United States, but the submarines and the warheads we provided ourselves, and of course the contracts and expenditure had already been occurring for two or three years.

Our official party position was that we were going to seek to renegotiate the agreement that Macmillan had made on Polaris. So for two or three years Wilson was regularly asked questions in the House of Commons about renegotiation. But he always said it was not timely or found some way of saying there was not going to be complete renegotiation.

Denis Healey [then secretary of state for defense] and I were able to use the fact that a lot of money would be wasted if we just canceled the contracts and did not build the submarines. It could, I suppose, have been used for something else, but because money had been spent on four of them we were able to get a cabinet decision to go ahead with the four but not the fifth. This was a pity because it made the actual rotation more difficult when you only had four instead of five. But not enough money had been spent on the fifth for us to get away with that. And that is what we did, we went on that basis and it went through quite well.

Having had a seminal influence in the development of proportional deterrence as the conceptual basis for French nuclear strategy, General Gallois described its foundations and evolution:

The essentials had been laid between 1945 and 1960. After that we spoiled the atomic strategy. We have destroyed it with too many intentions, too much knowledge, too many discussions, too many books—everybody is going to write about it. The problem for me during these years is very simple. I was impressed by the book of Bernard Brodie [Bernard Brodie, ed., *The Absolute Weapon: Atomic Power and World Order* (New York: Harcourt, Brace, 1940)]—he was a good friend of mine—and some papers of Thomas Schelling [Thomas Schelling, *Controlled Response and Strategic Warfare* (London: IISS, 1965); also, with Morton Halperin, *Strategy and Arms Control* (New York: Twentieth Century Fund, 1961)]. I have never changed. These weapons are the weapons of a desperate situation. Why? I take my own experience in June 1940. I was on the airfield of Marseilles trying to find an aircraft that would cross the sea because the Germans were supposed to be in the hills just in front of us. I realized then that if some Mephistopheles would have said to me, "Look, Pierre, you see this is an atomic bomb. If you take it in your aircraft, and if you go and drop it on Berlin, the Germans are going to negotiate new conditions." It is for me, and it was always for me, a weapon of last resort, to use in extreme conditions. It plays a role, which is to inspire fear. The effect of the weapon is such that it can be used only when a nation is in a terrible situation. The consequences of such a concept are that it is very difficult to ask another nation to protect you with such a weapon because that nation may not be in that same situation that you are. It may have a different fear, a different threat which you have to consider. The consequence is that, to me, it has never been a weapon of an alliance.

Concerning the concept of deterrence, and its evolution, during the years 1952–63 it was very simple and it is still very simple. Unhappily, so much has been written about it, and so many people are interested in the problem that they have distorted the real function of atomic weapons for intellectual reasons as well as to give a role to the ground forces, to the navy, to the air forces, using these weapons as if they were ordinary weapons. Until 1960 it was clear, at least to my mind, that these weapons could be used only in despair and if the country was put in a very difficult situation—invasion, for instance. Only in that extraordinary extremity, would atomic weapons inspire such fear and intimidation and thus play their role of deterrence.

General Gallois expressed criticism for the U.S. strategy at the time of the Korean War, for in his view the United States could have detonated a nuclear device as a means of forcing mass troop formations to disperse, thereby diminishing the advantage of an attacking force:

I think that the Americans made a big political mistake. Truman made a big mistake. Having the monopoly of atomic weapons at the time, I think that the Americans should have at least kept their use in doubt, and not said, "We will not use it." That was a big mistake. When you have an enemy, you have all the advantages if you do not commit yourself to certain restraints—it is stupidity to restrain yourself if you know that you can do it. After the Chinese invasion of Korea with conventional forces, if the Americans had at that time dropped a bomb at sea, along the coastline, killing possibly some fish, no more, giving the impressions, telling them, if you carry on your offensive, I may be obliged to resort to these weapons. Then what would have been the reaction? Probably they would carry on. They would take the risk, but they would be obliged to disperse. The Americans could [then] regain tight order, hence, greater conventional firepower, then superiority. That aspect was not seen, and it was a big mistake.

General Gallois expressed approval of massive retaliation and opposition to flexible response:

I was a great admirer of John Foster Dulles, and a great supporter of this theory, of his concept of reacting with nuclear weapons from the onset of any aggression in Europe. That was, for me, a real position of deterrence. I was totally against the Kennedy administration and the Kennedy concepts. In 1962 in the United States, McNamara made his famous Ann Arbor speech about graduated response and was moving toward the adoption in 1967 by NATO of its new strategy. We were very angry about that speech. I discussed it with Pierre Mesmer, who was at that time minister of defense. When in May 1962 Mr. McNamara delivered a speech in Chicago, and which was later delivered at Ann Arbor, Michigan, I wrote a long paper attacking bitterly Mr. McNamara, explaining its contradiction.

Mr. McNamara said that a small nuclear force is prone to obsolescence and because it can only be directed at cities, its existence is tantamount to national suicide. He said that he was completely against these forces, and he was aiming at the French and the British forces at that time. My objection to his declaration was that, as Mr. McNamara knew very well, the U.S. nuclear submarine *Washington* had begun its trials at sea. The Russians are imitating the Americans. Mr. McNamara knew that it would be very difficult, in the near future, to destroy simultaneously the forces which matter, which are those of the alliance. Hence the strategy of counterforce of which Mr. McNamara wrote and said that it is the privilege of the powerful nations to have enough weapons to destroy the forces of the enemy. Such a strategy is doomed by the weapons that the Americans were developing themselves—that is, the submarines—because how can you destroy them if you do not know where they are? Then you are well obliged to return to the cities as strategic targets. The arguments of Mr. McNamara were not valid. That speech was hated very much by General de Gaulle and Mr. Mesmer.

According to Ambassador de Rose, the lack of sustainability of French conventional forces, compared with those of other alliance members in NATO's central region, lessens the prospects for effective participation by France in the forward defense. Within a short time of the outbreak of war, France might be forced to choose between defeat or escalation:

The "Inner Circle" is the protection of France proper. Well, I do not disagree with that idea politically. I agree in the sense that I do not think that we can give a blank commitment to use our strategic weapons in all and any hypothesis of an aggression across the Elbe. For the same reason, I believe that the United States had to give up massive retaliation. So, I think that it is true that our strategic weapons are designed to give us the fair assumption that we would not be invaded. In other words, that we might save for ourselves the status of Finland, which I prefer to that of Czechoslovakia.

The question of cooperation in the conventional field depends on where our conventional capabilities are different or the same from those of the alliance, that the alliance could fight at the conventional level for a month (they are building stocks for that contingency), while France could fight for only a few days and after a few days would have to resort to nuclear weapons, while the others could still fight at a conventional level. It would not make sense to unleash general nuclear war before it was necessary or engage in a strategic nuclear duel with the Soviets by destroying some of her cities at the same level. That's why I think it is absolutely vital now that France should have compatible capabilities with the alliance in the conventional field.

General Gallois took a different view of the doctrine:

I think that everything was said in 1960. Since that time we have distorted the deterrence concept. I think that the "Three Circles" concept is a distortion, and a very dangerous one. There are only two circles: one for which atomic weapons would be used, and one for which atomic weapons would not be used. There is no gray area between the two. By introducing the notion of a second circle, Gen. Lucien Poirier has done a very bad service to the country. Without realizing it, he has legitimized the use of atomic weapons over Germany. It is obvious that no government would ever use atomic weapons over Germany. They would never use them on France itself. So the concept of the three circles for me is nonsense.

General Gallois discussed the issue of nuclear war-fighting strategies as a result of improved nuclear technologies and accuracy:

People do not want to be buried; [this concept] has evoked the idea of trenches from [World War I]. They hesitate to be buried and they do not like it. It was a mistake to give the French Air Force their eighteen missiles deployed in the Albion plateau—to give an airman the command of these silos: they do not like it. The result is that the chief of staff paid little attention to these silos. Independent of their vulnerability, the role of these silos, as it was envisaged in 1960, was to confront the Soviet Union with a difficult alternative. If they attacked France without destroying these weapons, we could retaliate against their cities. To destroy them in a preemptive attack at that time would have required some 200 megatons because of inaccuracy, and 200 megatons makes a lot of radioactive fallout. We calculated that the radioactive fallout would have passed over Kiev. Thus, the role of the Albion plateau was the role of a mine. If you did not touch it, it is intact, but if you put a foot on it, it would explode. That was the role of the Albion plateau.

General Gallois described the problem of defending nuclear capabilities arising from the deployment of highly accurate counterforce capable systems:

The problem has been made more complex by two elements: first, accuracy, which reduces the yield necessary, and then reduces the fallout; and second, the development in America, as well as in the Soviet Union, of weapons capable of penetrating the earth and exploding later. The idea of some is that these eighteen silos may be destroyed without much fallout in the future.

The earth-penetrating weapons would have small nuclear warheads, and in that case the fallout would probably reach northern Italy. The role, the previous role, is not taken seriously anymore because of accuracy. Then the idea was to have mobile weapons, but France is a small country with a relatively high population density. I proposed to have mobile weapons in relative great numbers, moving permanently in what we call the pre-Alps and the pre-Pyrenees, above 1,400 meters where there are few or no inhabitants. You would probably have 10,000 square kilometers which could be used for that purpose without touching the inhabitants. That would have been possible. [President] Mitterrand, to whom I proposed it when I went to the Élysée, decided to maintain the silos on the Albion plateau.

When I discovered the capabilities conferred by accuracy, I began to warn my minister of defense, who was Yves Bourges at that time, about their potential effect on nuclear targeting. I brought to him several charts explaining that the Soviet Union could attack our conventional forces without collateral damage. Then, after our armies are destroyed, and we can hold on no longer, the only hope is the submarine. If we drop the bomb, we would be destroyed. Should we do nothing? Mr. Bourges did not understand the importance of accuracy. At that time I said that we should change our strategy. You must add to the capability of destroying cities the capacity to destroy some forces, to deter at the same level of violence. Naturally, you keep your weapons against your cities, just to avoid a hit against your own cities, but that is not enough. I also fought for developing the mobile SX, not thirty of these, as is the program now, but three hundred, in order to deter any action against our conventional forces. Not because I believed that these conventional forces are necessary to the country, but because I think that should these forces be destroyed, the will of the country would disappear immediately, and we would accept anything. Even today, this concept is not widely accepted. Very amusingly, Monsieur Mitterrand had been for twenty-five years against any atomic weapons, against the deterrence policy. As soon as he got to the Élysée he said, "Deterrence is me, I am the man who will push the button. I am higher deterrence." He uses that sentence in almost every speech as if he wanted to convince himself of the importance of his role. It is a naive attitude. He is so convinced of the virtue of the concept now that he does not want to change.

French nuclear strategy has looked to encompass what are termed "prestrategic" capabilities—namely, tactical nuclear weapons, shorter-range nuclear forces that would be employed as a precursor of any greater nuclear retaliation against the Soviet Union. Gallois comments:

In that conception of deterrence the tactical nuclear weapons, or prestrategic weapons, are intimately connected to the strategic ones. The air force had a bomber, the Mirage IV, which was the first to carry atomic weapons in its inventory. Then the navy came with submarines. A mistake was made by giving to the air force the silos on the Albion plateau; they should have been given to the army. The so-called tactical weapons would probably not have been necessary. But because there was a rivalry among the services, the army was in despair because it had no atomic weapons and the air force had some and the navy had some. The idea was put forward to give atomic weapons to the land forces. This is where the distortion began. It was necessary to give a role to these forces. The role of atomic weapons in the hands of the navy or the air force was very clear. In case of France being invaded, the frontier being violated, then the army, as a last resort, in a sort of spasm would react, attacking some main targets inside of the enemy's territory by combining the air force and submarine capabilities. But what about the army? The army, the land forces, had a difficult role in that perspective, probably no role at all. So the idea was to give some atomic weapons to the army, and to create a concept of nuclear land battle, which to me makes little sense. But, you see, we have had a land army for many centuries, and it is very difficult to change suddenly.

Then the idea was to try to devise a doctrine for the use of these army nuclear weapons. The first doctrine of use that was prepared by the ministry of defense (where they had a center for strategic perspectives), was that the army with its Plutons would create a *test* firing. The idea was to ascertain the intentions of the enemy, as if the enemy would be stupid enough to start a large war, create an operation of war against the West, without knowing its objectives. It was a purely artificial concept. We were crediting the Soviet Union with a good dose of stupidity. They would launch an operational war against us and suddenly, unexpectedly, receive Plutons on their heads and they would withdraw, sending maybe some telegram of excuse to the Élysée.

But imagine that the Soviet Union has decided to make a military operation—I do not know why, it is an assumption—directed against France. Then, if the Soviets take such a decision it is not to lose, it is to win at any cost, because they are very clever and they have examined all the possibilities and they know what the reaction of the French at this level would be. I do not believe that the Soviet Union would start something against us and, after receiving a few Plutons on their units, say, "Yes, we are sorry. We did not expect this response on your part. We retreat and we send our regrets." That is impossible for me to believe. This is, after all, the real concept of the "test" of force. To me, it is complete nonsense.

The idea before was that France would participate in the so-called forward battle from the edge of the front, with conventional forces. Before that period, a dividing line existed: combat with conventional means will probably take place, and should our troops be defeated, nuclear weapons would be used as a last resort. Because the enemy does not want to enter such a spiral, he would be deterred at a low level of violence; that was the first concept. The introduction of these atomic weapons was just changing the concept by crediting the enemy with a good dose of stupidity, but this is a mistake. We must always credit an enemy with the maximum of cleverness. What is important is to show that our leaders have the will to use atomic weapons against the Soviet Union. But the Plutons have a range of only 120 kilometers. Hence, the weapons would not be used unless they were moved across the French border, and still they would not hit Soviet territory. Hades, with its 300 kilometers to 450 kilometers range, is just as dangerous because it gives the impression that France is ready to use these so-called tactical weapons even if the French border is not in danger, but if the border of West Germany is in danger. That is a completely stupid and very dangerous position for France. I cannot imagine that we would use Hades against Soviet units threatening the Federal Republic of Germany without expecting an atomic reaction from the Soviets, which would trigger the use of our strategic weapons against the cities of the Soviet Union. The logic of such a decision is that a military incident takes place on the border of West Germany, destroy Moscow, Leningrad, and Kiev, which, obviously, we never would. It is impossible even to think about it.

In contrast, Ambassador de Rose saw merit in the development of pre-strategic systems:

Pluton was conceived under de Gaulle with the idea that it was necessary to give a nuclear weapon to the land forces, maybe for reasons that had to do more with politics than with military requirements. The land forces were under the shock of defeats in Indochina and Algeria. There was a complete revamping of the forces, and if it had not been for them receiving some sort of nuclear weapons then they would have been able to feel completely estranged from the building of the modern army. That was the paramount issue. Then the doctrine of "ultimate warning" was conceived, and set up to give them a raison d'être.

I think the ultimate warning makes sense in a way. Using strategic forces out of the blue would mean the immediate destruction of the whole of France. This is an extremely difficult proposition. I think it makes sense to say that before doing so, we will show that we are really determined, that we think that the issue is so important that we are ready to go nuclear to defend our interests. What would come next? Nobody knows. But certainly it is not irrational to have that capacity. In my opinion, since I do not believe that there will be a war in Europe, I do not conclude that our nuclear weapons are either useless or harmful—quite the contrary—I think their main utility is twofold: First, it presents the Soviet Union with a new unknown in the equation. What could these systems do? We do not know. But second and most important, it prevents us from being blackmailed. If we have a crisis and the Soviets say, as they did in the Suez Canal crisis, "What if we use our nuclear weapons?" we could say, "What if we use ours?" Therefore, from the point of view of not being the first that would yield—that would blink when you stare at the other fellow—it is very important. We and Britain are the only ones in Europe who can do this to the Soviet Union. It is very important that there should be in Europe two governments who in a crisis can keep their heads cool because they cannot be blackmailed.

This idea of multiple decision centers for nuclear use is in contrast to proposals in the late 1950s and early 1960s for a shared NATO nuclear force. As early as the years when Konrad Adenauer was chancellor of the Federal Republic of Germany, there was a view expressed by Adenauer himself that the deterrence of war in Europe rested on an escalatory ladder that included deployment of nuclear forces in or near the European continent capable of striking targets in the Soviet Union. In the view of Gen. Kai-Uwe von Hassell—West German defense minister from 1963 to 1966—this was a compelling rationale for the ill-fated multilateral force (MLF) of the early 1960s.

In the years before 1963, Chancellor Adenauer, who was always very well informed about all problems of strategy, defense, and security, told the Americans that in the entire concept of deterrence there was a gap in medium-range ballistic nuclear forces. He told McNamara, Paul Nitze [assistant secretary of defense for International Security Affairs, 1961–63; deputy secretary of defense, 1967–69; currently arms control adviser to the secretary of state], George Ball [under secretary of state, 1961–66], and the president that the Americans must fill this gap. He always spoke of a gap of some six hundred warheads in favor of the Kremlin so we needed some six hundred warheads.

Then, in January 1963, Ball came over and had a long talk with Adenauer. I was present when he produced the Nassau concept—twenty-five mixed-crew surface ships always on duty from the North Pole to the Mediterranean with eight missiles each to fill in the medium-range ballistic missile gap (like Polaris with a range of some 5,000 kilometers). Adenauer and I were strongly in favor because it filled in the gap and there were no political problems that would exist in placing land-based nuclear systems in Germany, eastern France, southern Belgium, or Italy. There would be no problem with deployment. It would solve the problem by introducing missiles without deploying them inside our countries. In addition, such a seaborne nuclear mission would create strong alliance cohesion because of the mixed crews on board and the common responsibility. Franz-Josef Strauss [chairman of CSU (Christian Social Union) and West German defense minister, 1956–62] wanted to be with de Gaulle's concept of *force de frappe* and was therefore against MLF. He said that surface vessels would be sunk in the first five minutes of a war. We did not agree. There were so many other ships that they could not be detected. Surface ships would be more vulnerable than submarines, but submarines cost as much as three to five times more than surface ships.

We met on board a ship on November 11, 1964. There were six different nations assembled there on the crew. They were all very good in English; they cooperated marvelously. They were clever and responsible. They were trained together and were a truly mixed crew. It worked marvelously. There were only three problems: the first was food, the second was pay scales, and the third was that the Germans had different ranks and this created problems. Similar ranks and pay would have had to be worked out, but the food was a difficult problem.

Since the failed effort to establish a multilateral force, the issue of Western European nuclear cooperation in some form or another has arisen from time to time. Ambassador de Rose addressed this aspect of alliance relations and Franco-German cooperation:

Franco-German nuclear cooperation is useful, provided it means that we discuss with the Germans what would be the targeting of our short-range forces. That is the position NATO members have taken in the Nuclear Planning Group [NPG]. Why not do between France and Germany the same as in the NPG? Mr. Laurent Fabius [French prime minister, 1984–86] and Mr. Jean-Pierre Chevenement [French minister of science and technology, 1981–82, industry, 1982–83; minister of defense, 1988–   ] both said that France should give a nuclear guarantee to Germany. What does that mean? Nothing—they are talking through their hats. They do not think profoundly in terms of what the problems are; they are toying with these ideas.

Ambassador de Rose recalled a meeting that he had with Valéry Giscard d'Estaing just after Giscard was elected president of France in 1974:

Giscard called me in and asked me to tell him what was the situation [for France in NATO]. So I explained our relations: that we still participate in the political decision making of the alliance and coordinate on a military level wherever it was possible. However, I told him that strategically there was a problem. The 1972 Defense White Paper, which had been published under Prime Minister Michel Debré, really called for us to use our tactical nuclear weapons on German soil—to nuclearize the conflict on German soil in order to [create a sanctuary in] French territory by combining a strategy of independence and neutralization. He said, "It is very difficult for me." I said, "It will not be easy to develop a real intimacy with the Germans while planning to launch a nuclear war on their territory in order not to have it on French territory." He said, "How could men who are intelligent and devoted to their country conceive of such inconsistencies?" But he did little to cure it. He realized that there was something there, and he is now the only one who advocates change in French strategy. And Mitterrand now says that French tactical weapons are not meant to fall on German territory.

I think they wanted to do something, and I wondered whether they realized that there was a contradiction in the strategy that would make it very difficult when they spoke of extended deterrence. It could have meant that we would not only use our strategic weapons in case there was a direct threat to French territory. They said that French national interests did not stop at French borders. They all say that, but none of them is bold enough to draw the conclusion that the strategy has to be changed. The strategy has to be changed because, if there is a war in Europe, then two things could happen. One, NATO uses its tactical nuclear weapons. If that happens, the French have no reason to use the Pluton, or even tomorrow their Hades, since the engagement would be between the U.S.A. and the U.S.S.R. Or second, if NATO would not use its nuclear weapons and therefore accept defeat in Germany, France could play her own game of sanctuarization by employment of a "last warning" strike, with her tactical weapons. Extended deterrence was designed to say that our nuclear forces would not simply cover French territory but part of Germany as well. But it could not amount to a guarantee that it should be applied as soon as Warsaw Pact forces might move westward.

General Gallois expressed strong opposition to the concept of "extended sanctuary," that is, an extended nuclear deterrence role for the French nuclear force that would encompass the Federal Republic of Germany:

Now you may realize a concept of French-German coupling. This seems reasonable, but in reality it is not, for the following reasons. Germany is divided, with a portion of its country in Soviet hands. In their constitution and in their lives they cannot accept, indefinitely, the partition of their country. As a result the Germans would never do something that would hurt the Soviet Union too much. They still hope for unification. On the contrary, if you follow Hans-Dietrich Genscher's [West German foreign minister, 1974–   ] line of thought, the Germans feel that in the Gorbachev era there is an enhanced prospect of closer relations with the Soviet Union. According to this line, the Germans, with their technical knowledge, may go to Siberia, invest in the region, and still sell their products to the Russians. So both get rich together. Possibly by doing so, they may facilitate conditions for the eventual reunification of Germany. This is going to be their policy for a very long period of time. Hence, suppose we want to create a real military force with the Germans; do you believe that the Germans are going to accept it if the Soviet Union objects? No. Secondly, the Germans cannot have atomic weapons. Now it is too late. The Russians would never accept German possession of atomic weapons, and [the Germans] realize this. You see that when they deployed the Pershing II the West German government refused the "double key." They want to be proected by you, the United States, but they do not want to be involved in their own protection. In case of something going wrong in Europe, the result for the Germans would be occupation by conventional forces. Our penalty would be destruction if we threatened or actually used nuclear weapons as part of an extended French deterrence concept that included the Federal Republic of Germany. The risk is not the same.

When Giscard came to power, the first decision he took was to reduce the number of missiles on the Albion plateau. In the de Gaulle era, it was understood that fifty-four would be deployed in silos. The project was delayed in 1968 by then president Pompidou because of lack of money, and later Giscard stopped at eighteen, although the planning was for fifty-four. Giscard also stopped the sixth submarine. Then we were supposed to have 250 tactical launchers, and he stopped at 120 or even less. Then he reduced the French naval forces and sandbagged some conventional army units. While he was doing that, he was extending deterrence, and he said that the French would extend deterrence to the eastern side of the northern theater in Norway and down to the south, suddenly upsetting the previous planning made in the defense budget law of 1964. Ten years later, we were certainly not protecting France but Europe. It was Giscard who decided in 1974 that we could not protect only France but Germany as well. It is complete nonsense, complete stupidity; I am against the extended sanctuary idea. I wrote this publicly, and Giscard had the tax people coming to check my accounts. Finally they stopped looking at extended deterrence and the idea lost momentum, until now when it has come up again. The idea of some politicians is to use all our defense means at any cost. It is because they are so scared of Genscher.

However, General Gallois expressed his firm belief that an extended deterrence concept will never become an integral part of French nuclear deterrence:

It is a national concept, and when you are a politician you may deliver a speech like that. But when you decide to transform the speech into a national program, you involve staff, headquarters, other people, and when the staff writes something, the truth appears. They cannot write something which is impossible to accept. You have to change your mind.

Finally, Kai-Uwe von Hassell provided his perspective on nuclear cooperation between Paris and Bonn:

The French believed that the *force de frappe* would guarantee the safety of France. We thought that in the calculation of the whole nuclear forces the French is only a limited one. We thought they would go their way and that there was no chance to stop them. They cannot take the responsibility to guarantee the security of Germany and as they are not ready to part with us. Franz-Josef Strauss believed that we would be able to join the French *force de frappe*. He believed that eventually it could be an instrument not only for France but maybe France would share it with Germany and perhaps for a European nuclear force. I opposed such a view from the beginning, because de Gaulle began the *force de frappe* not only as a military instrument but also as a political instrument. It strengthened his political power. France was acknowledged worldwide as a new nuclear power with all the importance of a nuclear power. I believe that de Gaulle was not ready to share his political power, this political instrument, with someone else—even with the Germans, his "friends" on the other side of the Rhine.

I have in all my experience, from the moment I first became acquainted with the French situation in the 1950s, not the slightest hint that there might be a readiness on the French side to share this *force de frappe* with us. There is not only, for instance, Franz-Josef Strauss; there is also still one important member of Parliament, Professor Abelein, who was the personal assistant to Dr. Krone [Heinrich Krone was a founding member of the CDU (Christian Democratic Union) and a member of the German Parliament between 1949 and 1969]. Krone was a Gaullist, and he visited de Gaulle in 1955 or 1956, and Abelein accompanied him as his personal assistant. He sat behind Krone in de Gaulle's office. Abelein once reported in the political group of 250 in Parliament [CDU-CSU] that it was wrong to go ahead with MLF: "We must try to get cooperation with the French with regard to the *force de frappe*. The French would be ready to do it." I objected and later asked him where he got this information. He said he was with Krone visiting de Gaulle. He believed that de Gaulle was ready to share it with us. I told him that he was wrong.

We had only one very dangerous problem. France not only went ahead with missiles of 3,000–5,000 kilometers, it also went ahead with short-range missiles like Honest John. If these missiles were part of the equipment of a French division stationed in eastern France and they wanted to fire a missile, it would not reach farther than Cologne or Bonn. It is very uncomfortable to know that the French stationed behind us have weapons which can only reach targets close to France. I asked Gerhard Schröder [minister of defense] to see to this problem because this would be a really dangerous situation for us. I told Mesmer that if they intended to develop and deploy these systems, we must know about it. For us, this would be intolerable. When the French deployed the Pluton in eastern France rather than with French regiments in the FRG, this caused great concern to us. At that time, the French only indicated that it was their intention to move ahead. I told them that we must do this together or not at all. They could station these weapons with their divisions based in Germany, but never with those based in France.

14
NATO and Arms Control

O ne of the most complex issues facing the Atlantic Alliance has been arms control. With increasing intensity since the late 1960s, NATO-European allies, as commentators in this chapter point out, have urged upon the United States a greater priority for arms control in relations with the Soviet Union. Yet these allies have often become apprehensive of the consequences of arms control accords negotiated between the superpowers. In Western Europe there is a pervasive interest in reducing East-West tensions without, however, creating a situation of what has been termed U.S.-Soviet condominium. As a result, the United States has confronted European criticism during periods of increasing East-West tension as well as in times of seemingly improved relations between Washington and Moscow. Therefore, this chapter elucidates such issues as European concern about U.S.-Soviet condominium, U.S. consultation with its NATO allies, nuclear force modernization and the 1979 double-track decision, negotiating strategies, and, finally, European perspectives on the 1987 INF Treaty between the United States and the Soviet Union. Lawrence Eagleburger presented perspectives on alliance relations and arms control:

> Our European friends and allies constantly expect to be saved from themselves by us. MBFR [mutual and balanced force reduction talks between NATO and the Warsaw Pact] is a classic example. INF is a classic example. I was in NATO when every European member of NATO and the Canadians were banging on us to push MBFR and we really ought to have it, and it is a good thing to do, and it was we Americans who were most reluctant. Henry Kissinger *was* reluctant; his reluctance was severalfold. First, he had real doubt whether we were able to manage that kind of a negotiation given the data base. Second, his reservations related to how do you deal with MBFR at the same time you are trying to deal with the nuclear issue—he was trying to separate them at the time. I think he was fundamentally a disbeliever in MBFR as a viable concept, for which I have had a certain sympathy, but that does not say that there does not have to be some conventional arms control. So he was holding it all. It was also all

being debated within the context of a European security conference [Conference on Security and Cooperation in Europe—CSCE] on which we were also very negative and in part because we wanted to get our own house in order with the Soviet Union first.

We were dragged kicking and screaming into MBFR, with the Europeans being the ones to push us on it, and their drive was not really because of the potential outcome, but rather the process. If we are in the process of negotiating with the Soviets, that would supposedly be wonderful and things would begin to change, we will educate them—and this is the Europeans now, not us. I was in the NATO Council when Ross Campbell, who was the Canadian ambassador to NATO and first class, sat there and said, "Why don't we adopt MBFR, because the Soviets will never accept it anyway." Half an hour later somebody came into the room and handed Secretary-General [Joseph] Luns a note that said the Soviet Union has just announced that it is prepared to negotiate MBFR. Now, no ambassador ought to be so discredited in front of his colleagues that quickly. Once the Soviets had said yes, we began to move toward it.

Mr. Eagleburger discussed the divergent views of mutual and balanced force reductions negotiations within the U.S. government:

I was back in the Defense Department, long since having left NATO, when Melvin Laird [secretary of defense, 1969–73] said MBFR will become a reality at some point, and it is time the Defense Department, for a change, was ahead of the game. He sent me off as a deputy assistant secretary with the deputy assistant secretary for systems analysis to work out the Defense Department position on MBFR, and it took us months. Laird had to fight against the Joint Chiefs because they did not even want to think about it, but we came up with a scheme, which by and large thereafter was accepted by the U.S. government. But when we first came up with the scheme and put it to the NSC, Henry Kissinger was violently opposed. This is an oversimplification, but to a degree it is an example of being driven into something by our allies, and once we are in it, the allies begin to worry about U.S.-Soviet condominium. INF is another example of our reluctantly moving into something the allies wanted us to do. And then we are faced with growing European concern that we might, in fact, do something.

In a speech that I gave in Switzerland a couple of months ago with Helmut Schmidt [former West German federal chancellor], I said that one of our problems is that for too long the Europeans have expected that we would save them from themselves, and we have, and they had better understand that is not going to happen any longer. It is correct that in the broad sweep many times the Europeans have advocated these things much more as a political gimmick in terms of their domestic audience than as a real need. They get terribly nervous when we start to take those things seriously and particularly when we move toward negotiations and agreements. But you have to understand that; it is frustrating and on occasion I used to yell my head off at them—if they do not like INF now, they have nobody but themselves to blame for it. It relates to a far more fundamental question, which is that as long as you are basically a client state, that is the price you pay, and we as the superior partner in the superior-subordinate relationship need to understand that this kind of thing is going to happen. There are ways, up to a point, to deal with it, but we do not always deal with it very well. But it is going to happen and the only long-term solution is the creation of a Western Europe that bears its own weight and that cannot happen until they organize themselves differently. It is not surprising; it should only be marginally irritating. Finally, whether it is surprising or irritating, it is the way it is going to be. I think that INF and Reykjavik all may have combined finally to scare the Europeans enough that the result is likely to lead to different policy approaches in the future which we may or may not like.

Several other Europeans, all of whom had important and unique vantage points, discussed the NATO double-track decision and the 1987 INF Treaty, and their consequences. In this context, Kai-Uwe von Hassell, former president of the West German Bundestag, assesses the issue of transatlantic negotiations, with special reference to the Reykjavik Summit Conference of October 1986.

We are on good terms with the Americans, but we criticize them because they did not consult us in advance. If they would have consulted us carefully before Reykjavik, we would not have learned in early morning that they had agreed on something vital for us. It would have been better if we had been consulted or at least informed beforehand. This is the main point, and I can give you some other examples. In 1962 after the Cuban crisis, which was managed excellently by the United States, the Thor and Jupiter missiles disappeared from Europe. No European was consulted when that decision was made. The multilateral force [MLF] was an excellent plan; yet it disappeared after President Johnson's election in 1964 without consultation. The neutron weapon—which was the best weapon to deter the Soviets—disappeared without consultations. The alliance lacks consultation. After Reykjavik, the Soviets have completely gained control.

According to Lawrence Eagleburger, however, the United States was less sensitive to NATO-European concerns and interests at the Reykjavik Summit Conference in 1986. Nevertheless, the issues that have confronted the alliance in the 1980s have their origins in an earlier era:

It is the Reagan administration that has most markedly achieved the great distinction of leading the Europeans to a view that we no longer can be counted on. All of the rest of it is cumulative. But this administration, that I was a part of and voted for and which is the one that has really accomplished what the rest of them may have tried to do but never quite succeeded in doing, is leading to some really fundamental questioning in Europe about our intentions and our coherence and our relationship. I happen to think that Reykjavik did a lot more damage in one fell swoop than those things taken over a twenty-year period. A president who stands around and talks about a world free of nuclear weapons is much more damaging than those kinds of things, although they also contribute to what I suppose you can call a growing distrust in Europe about what we intend. I have to qualify all of that by saying I have yet to know a time with Europeans when they did not distrust what we would do, and the most obvious example is Charles de Gaulle, who may have been right. He may have been a little bit ahead of his time, but he may have figured us out a lot better than most.

From my perspective, the Europeans began to get nervous not with the first SALT agreements, but thereafter. By and large they were anxious to see something on the SALT side. As seen from Brussels, while there was a desire to know what was going on, there was not great concern about U.S.-Soviet condominium, no great concern about whether we would be able to defend them after a SALT agreement. I say that in the narrowest context of the SALT negotiations. Where you began to see a reaction in Europe was the Year of Europe that was announced by the Nixon administration as a policy priority for 1973; that was almost not at all related to arms control, but very much related to whether Europe was a part of a condominium in which Washington had decided to spend a year worrying about Europe.

Mr. Eagleburger acknowledged that the United States, from his vantage point, did not fully consult with its NATO allies:

Our own efforts at moving toward a different relationship with the Soviet Union was not a subject we talked about any more than we had to at NATO. We would go through the litany of somebody coming back from a SALT negotiation and briefing the council and so forth, but it was almost after the fact and very tightly held, and since on occasion the SALT negotiating team did not know what was being done in other channels anyway, it was kind of hard to find out. There was a fair amount of discussion and "consultation" on SALT, on the Soviet negotiations, but at a level of abstraction that I think did not encourage great European involvement or advice-giving under the pressure of time when the Europeans were really substantially torn because they had gotten themselves all wound up on their own *Ostpolitik* and now found us involved and were not quite sure. This was really the first time they had had to deal with it. Therefore, they were not quite sure how to deal with it, and were kind of hoisted on their own petard. But the basic point I would make is that in those early Nixon years, if I had to make a judgment on it, it would be that NATO was told as little as we thought we could get away with, on the kinds of issues we are talking about.

It would seem that as the United States and the Soviet Union began more and more to negotiate, that there was great fear in NATO that we would make a separate deal with the Soviet Union that would maybe ensure our security. The fear was there; there was not as much said about what I am getting at in a way. There was not much said about it again in the council sessions or in ways that would be reported back to capitals as you might have expected. There was no question that there was fear [of a U.S.-U.S.S.R. condominium]. I think there is also no question that there was a fair amount of bilateral talking back and forth but not a lot in NATO. That is my recollection and impression; there may have been others who spent a lot of time dealing with it, and they would have a different view of it. We went through the ritual briefings. There was no question that there was fear and concern in Europe in general, and that there was fear and concern within NATO, but it was not something that occupied a lot of time.

I would also say that whatever definition you try to put on consultation, as much as they should have been consulted, I suspect that their definition would always exceed whatever limits we though we could accommodate. Some of that is sort of self-serving, but I would have to say as well that, in my judgment, the U.S. administration spent a great deal of time thinking about how not to let NATO know anything in any great detail. I am not sure how accurate it would be to say that the Europeans were not concerned about the details of the agreement or were not as concerned. Although I would also say in part that, at least within the NATO context on the political side, they did not understand it anyway. Now on the military side and the defense side maybe they did, but most of the NATO ambassadors were not conversant with the intricacies of nuclear negotiations anyway, not of the negotiations themselves but rather of the nuclear world in general.

It was pretty well handled outside the normal processes, including the Berlin negotiations with Kenneth Rush [deputy secretary of defense, 1972–73, deputy secretary of state, 1973–74, and ambassador to France, 1974–77], and Henry Kissinger and Richard Nixon. Most of the Soviet negotiations, as we know, were handled through other channels. Now that changed a lot when Henry Kissinger became secretary of state, but in that first term it was pretty much outside the normal channels and I do not think Henry Kissinger would dispute that. I think that he would admit it. In retrospect it probably was not the best way to do things, but, having said that, it is not the best way to do things if you have the right secretary of state and the president of the United States is comfortable with doing it through the secretary of state, and the obvious answer in this case is that neither applied. Bill Rogers is a nice fellow, but he was not a great secretary of state [1969–74].

As deputy national security adviser in the Nixon-Ford administration and subsequently as national security adviser in the Ford administration, Gen.

Brent Scowcroft played a role of importance in the formulation and coordination of U.S. policy in SALT II. He offered a somewhat similar assessment:

> There was no routine process of briefing allies on what was going on in SALT II. Periodically, someone would be sent to bring the allies up to date on developments in SALT. Normally, after every meeting with the Soviet Union, somebody like Helmut Sonnenfeldt [a senior NSC member responsible for Soviet and Eastern European affairs, 1969–74], for example, would make a tour and explain to our allies what had happened. But it was an ad hoc rather than a regularly scheduled briefing. I do not remember the allies being that restive about being informed on the details. This was a period, or at least much of it was a period, keep in mind, when our European allies feared a U.S.-Soviet deal from which they were cut out. As long as we kept them generally abreast of things, they were content; they did not have the preoccupation with the details that they later developed.

No arms control issue was more vexing and divisive for the Atlantic Alliance than the 1979 NATO double-track decision and the other events leading to the signing of the INF Treaty in December 1987. In December 1979, NATO members had agreed unanimously to deploy 464 ground-launched cruise missiles (GLCMs), together with 108 Pershing II ballistic missile systems, in Western Europe, unless agreement could be reached for the dismantling of Soviet SS-20 systems. Joseph Luns, NATO secretary-general at the time, offered a perspective on the NATO decision and the role of INF systems:

> It was absolutely necessary, because if we had not reached the double-track decision, the Soviet Union could have blackmailed Western Europe. There would have been doubt about the possibility of defense. The credibility of our defense would have suffered because we could not reply to those SS-20s, and the Soviet Union would have refused to come to the negotiating table. I always said that if we deployed they would come back to the conference table; we did it. It was a defeat for the Soviet Union and a victory for NATO and for America. Modernization of atomic weaponry itself is an American, French, and British issue because they are the possessors of nuclear forces. Other countries have no say in the matter. But, when it is a question of stationing such weapons systems, then it is a different matter.

Ambassador Tapley Bennett, U.S. permanent representative to the NATO Council at the time, saw the need for a commitment to arms control negotiations as a necessary prerequisite to consensus in favor of deployment.

> I think it was clear that if we were going to get the deployment decision, we had to come forth and meet the Europeans on their insistence on arms

control negotiations—hence the name double-track decision. It was always a "give to get." Our emphasis was on deployment, based on the original German sounding of the alarm. But the Germans, particularly Genscher, the foreign minister, have drifted more and more toward the—I do not mean to say Left versus Right in terms of politics—but in favor of arms control concessions to try to satisfy the Soviet Union. To me, Genscher is by no means as strong an alliance man as he was when I first knew him.

NATO Secretary-General Joseph Luns discussed the differing perspectives of alliance members with respect to INF:

> Some of the member countries, especially the northern allies, wanted to link INF deployments with an offer for negotiations. That became the double-track decision, which pleased everybody more or less. Dutch public opinion was divided, and the cabinet was divided too. Finally, after much hesitation, they took a rather weak decision, to wit, they would start deployment in 1988 if by then there was not an arms control agreement. Then it was to be in the form of a treaty so the two houses of Parliament would have had to agree to it. Furthermore, of the five atomic missions of the Dutch armed forces, two would be discarded. So what they gave with one hand, they took back with the other one. The United States was not very happy about the whole thing. There were very long debates before it was finally agreed.
>
> The Belgians did it in the following way. On a Monday at about eleven in the morning, the prime minister said to Parliament, "My government has decided to deploy the missiles. You can debate it next Wednesday." At twelve, an hour later, the deployment started. The prime minister said, "The government decided," and Parliament may approve or not approve. . . . Then, using very strong language, he persuaded all the members of the Christian Democrats to vote for it. So he won the debate, and furthermore—the Lord of heaven from time to time rewards his sons already on this earth—he handsomely won the election a month later.

In accord with the 1979 NATO double-track decision, the Reagan administration in 1981 developed and proposed the zero-zero option for INF systems. Robert McFarlane, then a counselor to Secretary of State Haig, recounted the gestation of this negotiating proposal:

> The [NATO] allies sought in the late spring and summer [of 1981] to ascertain the U.S. position on INF—what we were going to do to declare ourselves on the double-track decision of 1979, and especially that part of it that required that we engage with the Soviet Union in INF negotiations. An informal process was established through which State began to call meetings. The director of the Political-Military Bureau, Richard Burt, would call meetings. Richard Perle [assistant secretary of defense for inter-

national security policy] would sometimes come and sometimes not come, and that was a very interesting exercise because it brought out the worst in everyone. I thought we were not in a position vis-à-vis the Soviets to achieve very much, and yet we needed to take a position that we could sustain in INF while expecting very little from the Soviet Union and probably the more demanding the position the better. I thought, the tougher the position the better (bearing in the mind that the other restraint was the ability of allies to sustain the position in their own countries). The State Department position—Richard Burt, the European Bureau—was more interested in putting forth a position that was negotiable, that would not be an affront to the Soviet Union. The secretary of state generally was more of that persuasion. He did not want to create gratuitous squabbles within the alliance which Richard Burt persuaded him would occur if we took too tough a position that would seem to be nonnegotiable with the Soviet Union. That would have led you toward some concrete, finite set of numbers that we believed would have been a sensible balance for the INF forces, and it would have been something near the deployment levels we intended: 572 warheads on both sides.

The Defense Department, and specifically Richard Perle, felt differently. I should not cast that so much from the military point of view that, militarily, we need more warheads or fewer—that really was not what drove Richard Perle's thinking on the issue. For Richard Perle, the political sustainability of it was important. He did not want to do something irrelevant. But his point was to put something out that was very demanding of the Soviet Union, . . . has exposed Soviet bloody-mindedness about the whole enterprise and stressed them the most. In short, it would be most nonnegotiable—the least negotiable position. Richard Perle came in with the zero option immediately, and Secretary of State Haig was dismissive of it and of the affront that it would represent to the British, the French, the Germans, and everybody else (Richard Burt as well). It was a very ideological kind of thing for Richard Perle, but for the State Department much more a matter of avoiding conflict both with the friendlies and the enemy. The process was informal; as I say it went along in the spring and summer at the subordinate level.

I think that the president had a better sense of where he wanted to be in 1988 than any of us did. He did not say it, and that was what was so misleading to the rest of us. We thought that this very iconoclastic stance of zero-zero INF systems was a position of political expediency; it was not at all. It was a position of principle to the president that clearly expressed an idealistic vision, the means to which he could not see, but the end of which he believed achievable and that it had to start with a consistent position of zero. You had to carry it through. So he decided it, and I think, really, if Richard Perle even had not proposed it, we would have come to that meeting and the president would have said, let us propose zero-zero, because that was the nature of his view about nuclear power, nuclear weapons.

Additionally, Ambassador Tapley Bennett outlined his perspective on how the zero option was first developed:

I do not accept the argument that it was just thrown out by us as a convenient way to block progress on arms control. I am convinced it was and is a very sincere position on the part of the president and the secretary of state, and I have heard Vice President Bush on the subject. The zero option was a big issue at the Gleneagles NATO NPG [Nuclear Planning Group] meeting in October 1981. At that meeting, the Dutch pressed to include mention of the zero option in the public communiqué. Secretary of Defense Weinberger resisted, not because he was opposed to the zero option, but because, as he said, "It has not quite finished its bureaucratic process in the United States. We are not quite ready; it has not received the final White House stamp of approval as a position, although that is the president's position, but I am not really ready to make it a public NATO document yet." The Dutch made a major issue of it, and they were, as I remember, supported by one or two others. The Dutch kept saying that this would be so important to their public opinion. As I said, Mr. Weinberger did not want to put it into the communiqué; he may have known that President Reagan was going to deliver an address later, in November, on the zero option. At any rate, he kept saying, "We in the United States have not finished our bureaucratic consideration of it yet."

The zero-zero option was a logical outgrowth of the 1979 double-track decision itself. I think that our government deserves to be given credit for more sincerity than its critics have given it. I am convinced that our top leadership went at it very straightforwardly. We proposed the zero option because we wanted to move in the direction of reducing nuclear armament. Finally, after a lot of argument, Weinberger reluctantly conceded and agreed to put it into the communiqué; and so, now to be told that this was an American trick, after we had agreed to it on the most urgent Dutch pleadings, is a little bit ridiculous.

The discussion of the zero option was continued at each of the semiannual NATO defense ministers' meetings and, as appropriate, at the foreign minister's meetings, but the emphasis in those two years was on whether we were actually going to deploy, because that was the period of growing antideployment demonstrations. I remember going to Germany in the spring of 1983, to Stuttgart and then on to Augsburg, and having a lunch with all the press people there. That was during those days when you were having human chains against deployment all the way down from Stuttgart to Munich. I never doubted that the deployment would go through; but the press was regularly writing, our columnists were regularly writing, that the situation had gotten so serious we would never get it done, that this was the collapse of the alliance, and so forth. In April, I had given a lecture at Stuttgart and gone on to Augsburg. The editor there in Augsburg, the head man at this lunch—and there were several other newspaper people present—said, "Yes, I think it is going to go through, regardless of all this public opposition; underneath there is an understanding that it needs to be done and it is our protection, and you will see when the time comes that the Pershings will be deployed." Well, they were deployed. In fact, the whole program stayed right on schedule. I am not sure, but maybe the first Pershing was installed a little ahead of schedule. Despite all the public clamor and all the press comment that things were going to hell in a handbasket, that whole double-track decision never wavered; the deployment plan never lost momentum, never missed a single target date.

Ambassador Bennett discussed the political setting in NATO-European countries at the time of deployment, as well as the Soviet decision to walk out of the INF negotiations in Geneva after the first systems were installed:

These are peace movement people, the peaceniks, and all those who charged that the zero option was an American trick. This was street opinion, which sounds very impressive and looks massive when you see it on television. Yet, when you get to elections—the German, the British, even the Danish, certainly the Dutch recently—so far as I can figure, every election has gone in favor of those supporting NATO. Time after time, these big demonstrations which looked ominous on television did not turn out to be significant in the fact. After all, 100,000 people or even 300,000 people out of 50 million is not all that much. There was one big demonstration in Bonn where people were brought down in buses from Holland by the thousands. It turned out that each person was given the trip, plus the equivalent of thirty dollars to spend. Now who would not take a nice trip?

Then the Soviet Union made the mistake of pulling out of the negotiations because we had deployed. There again, there were all the shrieks and cries of alarms that we had offended the Soviet Union. We would never get them back to the negotiating table—all of that drivel. As soon as the Soviets realized that they were not going to be able to veto our plans and that we were holding to the decision and going right ahead with deployment, they came back to the table. The only way to deal with the Soviet Union, really, is to have a firm position and stick to it; the Soviet Union is very good at adjusting to realities.

In Holland, the money for antinuclear demonstrations was raised by the churches. There is no question that there is plenty of money in Holland; they did not need Soviet funds there. The German movement, as I recall, came to vigorous arguments within itself as to where the money had come from. I do not think you could say that we anticipated quite what it grew to be, because it developed on its own; but, having seen the amount of energy the Soviet Union put in on the enhanced radiation issue, I was not surprised at the extent of their determination to derail the double-track decision.

Obviously the Soviet Union is very active in various ways. One is that they want, it seems to me, to inculcate the feeling that here is this big, powerful, dangerous bear just over the horizon and you had better take him into account or things will not go well and you may be sorry. You can see that in their constant probings of Sweden, sending submarines there not only to find out what little needs to be known about the depth of Swedish waters, but even more for political effect. They have done it again and again after they were caught; you do not do that unless you are making a point of browbeating you neighbor. Certainly they have used that tactic on the Germans for a long time. At the same time, there is all of the peace propaganda they put out; they want the world, particularly Europe, to believe that the Soviet Union is committed to peace and disarmament at any price. Many gullible Europeans and some Americans fall in with this idea, and all the while the Soviets continue the frantic pace of their arms buildup, far beyond any reasonable needs of a defensive posture. It is a mixture of cajolery and threat, but I do not think the Soviets ever want the threat to be forgotten. I think it is in their nature to deal with their own people that way and with everybody else the same way.

There is no question that it is cardinal Soviet policy to try to split the Americans from the Europeans. That, I would say, is the most consistent strain in a Soviet foreign policy which is far more consistent than anything the West manages to mount and stick with over the decades. There is an awful lot of evidence—unfortunately too much of it without the kind of proof that would stand up in a courtroom—of their active involvement with these Western peace movements, both financially and otherwise. It was a known fact that at one point the Soviet ambassador at The Hague called in the representatives of some ten or twelve Dutch peace groups and said, "Now let us all get together, we are all working for the same thing." In other words, he took it on himself to try to coordinate and manage that peace movement. Now, most of those groups are not by any means Communist in their origin. I am distressed by what some of our church people do in this country. You cannot, by any stretch of the imagination, say that these movements are Communist in the majority of their membership, but certainly, at times, they serve Communist purposes. The Soviets play on those kinds of people with great calculation, sometimes subtly, sometimes not so subtly.

I could not cite any specific cases of direct Soviet funding for European peace groups, although I would think some of our intelligence people could. There again, you run against that intelligence program where, if you reveal what you know, you give away your source, so it is hard sometimes to make public the facts that you do have. Secretary-General Luns was always convinced of Soviet funding, and he, I think went a little further than the proven facts on occasion in some of the charges he made. We also understood that the Soviet ambassador at The Hague had been decorated in Moscow for his work with the Dutch peace movement, but we could never get the proof on it. Simonet came to me once when he was still foreign minister in Belgium and said, "Joseph Luns is always telling the story. Can you give me the exact facts because, if you can give me proof of it, I can use that very effectively." I never could get the actual proof of it, but there is so much of that kind of story that some of it must be true. It is an area that is very difficult to get at, but a lot of effort should be put into it. Dean Rusk tells the story of having been aware of a particular Soviet piece of disinformation, then it went underground. Five or six months later it surfaced in a European country—the exact same thing—he knew the origin of it, but he did not know all the channels it went through, but it came up as the statement of a perfectly reputable spokesman. That is the kind of thing that is so hard to trace.

In the early 1980s the United States was engaged in negotiations simultaneously for the INF Treaty and for a Strategic Arms Reduction Treaty (START). Drawing upon the experience of the previous decade in the Strategic Arms Limitation Talks (SALT), Lawrence Eagleburger drew some lessons for the present context:

It is easy to look back on it fifteen years later or however long and say that it should have been done differently or you should have thought of this or that. One of the obvious ones is that technology will find ways around almost any agreement. You have put yourself back into the time and against what was known (which was not much), particularly with regard to how do you negotiate on nuclear issues with the Soviet Union. Under those circumstances you have to ask whether you would have done it differently. The answer is intimately related to the general question of would you have done it differently.

I am of the view, to some degree, that the agenda of the negotiating team was not necessarily the agenda of the administration. That will get us into a wholly different subject, which is how American negotiate. There gets to be a dynamic in any negotiations where Americans who are doing the negotiating want an outcome. That is not to say that Kissinger and Nixon did not want an outcome, but it is to say that the forest and the trees are much more easily mixed up if you are there than if you are sitting back in Washington. Therefore, I guess that I would have to say that you do not necessarily have to do it the second time with the same negotiating team. I am not sure that Nixon and Kissinger were wrong to have largely managed the process—*largely* is wrong, but to have managed the process at critical times outside the context of the negotiating team.

If you are driven by that assumption, it follows that what you do with the allies becomes much more complicated. So, in the abstract, yes, we should have done more with the allies to jump way ahead. I am strenuously of the view now that we ought to put the START negotiations in the refrigerator until we have in fact spent a lot of time talking with the allies and ourselves about where we ought to be by the end of this century with regard to nuclear issues. Then, and only then, can you deal with the START negotiations. Now, I say that but I would also argue with you that it is a different time, a different circumstance, it is in the aftermath of SALT I, and a screwed-up SALT II and an INF.

Finally, Lawrence Eagleburger reflected on the INF double-track decision and, in particular, on his perception of the Soviet leadership in the years just before Gorbachev came to power:

> We created our own Frankenstein's monster in terms of the public demonstrations in Europe and everything else. Inevitably, no matter what we might do in the negotiations, until they led to an agreement, we were going to be charged in Europe with not doing much because what you wanted to do was get the weapons deployed. That is the scenario you could have written before we ever sat down. Having said that, we, I think, made the problem.
>
> For its part, the Soviet regime at the time was geriatric in the extreme. The Soviet decision-making process on the whole INF issue [of 1979–83] was very largely in the hands of the military and within the civilian bureaucracy, a bunch of very unimaginative hard-line types. But added to it, I think—and this was a misestimate—was a judgment on the part of a number of Soviet leaders that they had created such monumental problems for us in Europe that in fact simply by holding still they were making us face even more difficult problems. To a degree I suspect they believed, and I think wrongly, that it would almost be nice to see us begin to deploy because the public reaction would be so bad, and indeed if they walked away from the table at that point the reaction would be even worse. I think they misjudged the degree to which we and the Europeans were able to manage the process, although it was very unpleasant. But I think as much as anything, it was a combination of that kind of misjudgment and a not very well put-together Soviet machine where nobody was really in charge, and to the degree that anyone was directing this issue, it was a bunch of rather geriatric noncompromisers reinforced in their judgments by those who were saying that the Americans have a terrible problem in Europe now and this will just make it worse.

Based upon his experience with the alliance, Ambassador Tapley Bennett reflected on the problems confronting NATO and its members in countering Soviet active measures intended to disrupt the defense of the West:

> I am sorry to say I do not think we do very well. For the country of Madison Avenue, we have never sold our own national case very well. Part of the problem may be inherent in the circumstances, in that we are always having to defend the necessity of arms for deterrence and having to defend the reasons for deploying this weapon or that. The Soviets, with complete irresponsibility, can talk about global peace and throw out these impossible ideas of banning this or that weapon, knowing full well that we are going to say, "No, we have got to keep the deterrent there," and so on. They get marks in European public opinion because of that, because people do not bother to analyze the hard facts of a situation.

212 · *National Security Decisions*

In fact, all around the world, the thing that bothers me most about the Soviets is how mischievous and malevolent they are. I mean, in addition to their ultimate goals, which are so antithetical to ours in the West, they just seem to enjoy making trouble for trouble's sake. We may sometimes put our foot down wrongly, but it is generally with a good purpose behind it. We are trying to improve things, trying to make the world a little bit better. They hope to profit from disorder, they do not want to see a situation composed; so they offer to go out of their way to make trouble, obviously mainly for us as the leader of the West. It is an unequal contest to that extent, and I do not know whether any propaganda or any information program can remedy that fundamental difference in approach. After all, the burglar always has an initial advantage over the law-abiding homeowner.

But there is another problem: the members of NATO have never been willing to let NATO have its own information program, or what they could call an information program. It is standing policy on the part of everybody around the table that their own country, their own government, will handle the public diplomacy or public information program in their country. NATO as an organization really has its hands tied. Whether it would be any more effective than the individual governments, I do not know. It does do a certain number of films, and the *NATO Review* is published. For example, the selling of the double-track decision in Britain was a British responsibility, not a NATO responsibility; and that is the way the governments want it.

General Franz-Josef Schulze, who served as commander of Allied Forces, Central Front, offered his observations on the zero option:

The first thing to say is that the zero solution was a European invention and we have no reason to blame the Americans. The present government [of the FRG] intended continuity of foreign and security policy, particularly foreign policy toward the East, and repeated the formula of the zero solution again and again. I agree that it would have been difficult to start a new government at a time when the weapons had not yet been stationed by just saying, "Forget about the zero solution." That would have been politically impossible: we would have had another wave of protests.

The only possibility that European governments had to distance themselves from their own proposal was when the Soviets started to build up an alternative potential—modernizing the Frogs, Scuds, and Scaleboards [NATO designations for Soviet short-range missile systems], and so on—the whole potential of the SS-21s, SS-22s and SS-23s. At that time we could have told the Soviets, "Wait a minute, friends, that was not what we meant by a zero solution." All European governments and the American government failed to take that opportunity. We all knew that the zero solution would bring some adverse effects to our security policy and Minister of Defense Wörner had it in his speech at the *Wehrkunde* meeting in 1987—serious deficiencies in our defense posture. But on the other hand, I do not overlook the internal binding effect that the repeated claim to stick with the decision would have. So it was difficult and that was the only possibility. After having said all that, I must now say that the way in which the American administration handled it frightened me.

Joseph Luns expressed support for the 1987 INF Treaty. However, he would view with great apprehension subsequent negotiations that, presumably by removing any remaining nuclear weapons from Western Europe, would have the effect of dismantling NATO's deterrence capabilities.

It means only that [once] the INF is ratified and comes into being, we can live with it; but if it means the first step to further dismantling of our nuclear deterrent, then I would have some misgivings. I feel that we should be very cautious, so I give only cautious approval to the INF Treaty.

Finally, Ambassador de Rose pointed to some steps that the alliance should take in light of the INF Treaty:

The great change which first took place was the loss of the American monopoly and then superiority in nuclear weapons. When flexible response was first conceived of, and then adopted, American theater [nuclear] weapons were vastly superior to those of the Soviet Union. The Soviet Union had superiority in the conventional field. There was what I have called in other publications "a balance of imbalances," NATO being superior in nuclear weapons and the Warsaw Pact in conventional weapons.

The superiority of the United States in nuclear weapons progressively eroded while the Soviet superiority in conventional weapons remained. Therefore, flexible response was no longer really based on that "balance of imbalances." It was based on the credibility of an escalation process which would eventually make the Soviet Union itself a victim of a nuclear exchange. This was the process. The land contiguity between Europe and the Soviet Union makes it possible or even likely that the conflict will reach Soviet territory.

Flexible response is dependent on the presence of nuclear weapons and the risk of escalation; therefore I think that we should first of all refuse the triple-zero option. We should keep as many nuclear-capable aircraft as needed, as well as missiles on ships and submarines cruising not too far off shore. But I see that Mr. Gorbachev has already suggested that maritime platforms, whether they are submarines or surface ships, which have the range to carry nuclear weapons that can reach the territory of one of the two superpowers should be kept beyond the range of hitting that territory. So they are really very serious at this point. Still, I think we should say that it is out of the question [to do this], and therefore keep as many as possible, which will probably not mean a great number, in view of German reluctance. We should deploy more submarines with cruise missiles, or more surface ships with cruise missiles, that can reach Soviet territory even if this is much less reliable an option than if missiles are stationed on European territory.

With the INF missiles deployed, if the Soviets had launched an attack, those missiles would have been the first target that they would have to destroy. This is to say, a direct attack on the most important American positions throughout. Now that these weapons will be gone, they will have to attack American positions first. So NATO should have cruise missiles set aside and irrevocably under SACEUR command.

Among the reasons to resist a denuclearization of the NATO central region, according to Ambassador de Rose, would be the ultimate implications for the continued deployment of American ground forces there. Without such nuclear protection, the likelihood would increase that the United States would withdraw such forces.

Part IV
Soviet-American Relations and American National Security Decision Making

No foreign policy issue has dominated U.S. national security decision making since the late 1940s as has the issue of U.S. relations with the Soviet Union. Indeed, Soviet actions determined the creation of NATO itself. In part IV, our attention appropriately shifts to this paramount relationship. Chapter 15 elucidates U.S. policy toward the Soviet Union with emphasis upon the containment policy. Chapter 16 turns to the issue of arms control and to the ongoing efforts by the United States and the Soviet Union to reduce or eliminate certain weapons. Various verification approaches, negotiating strategies, and agreements are all covered here. An important factor in U.S.-Soviet relations over the past two decades has been American relations with the People's Republic of China; therefore, in chapter 17 participants speak about the Sino-Soviet rift, the U.S. opening to China, and related issues. Finally, in chapter 18 national security decision-makers speak about the global role of the United States, which is best viewed in the context of U.S. concerns about containing Soviet efforts to export Communism around the world, but extends as well to other U.S. national interests. Thus, U.S. policies in Latin America, Korea, the Philippines, Vietnam, and the Middle East receive comment here.

15
U.S. Policy toward the Soviet Union

E ach U.S. administration since World War II has confronted the need to shape a strategy toward the Soviet Union. Inevitably, each has built upon the work of its predecessors. Among the tasks facing successive presidents has been the containment of Soviet power in Europe, as well as in the Asian-Pacific area and, beginning with the Eisenhower administration, in the Middle East and the Western Hemisphere. Thus, this chapter includes an assessment of the containment policy; further, President Eisenhower's Solarium Project, the 1955 Geneva Summit, the U-2 incident, the Soviet invasion of Czechoslovakia and the subsequent Brezhnev Doctrine, Reagan's approach to the Soviet Union, and public diplomacy are dealt with here.

Gen. Andrew Goodpaster, who served as defense liaison officer and staff secretary to President Eisenhower, discussed the review of U.S. policy toward the Soviet Union undertaken just after the administration came to office in 1953:

> President Eisenhower set up the so-called Solarium Project in the summer of 1953, his first year. Three alternative lines of policy, particularly in relation to the Soviet Union, were examined and then presented, with the best case being made for each one. Separate small groups worked on each one, although the whole operation proceeded as a single project, with these lines of policy investigated over a period of five to six weeks. I worked on one of them, being called back from Europe to participate. Each group numbered six or seven. Admiral Connolly of the Naval War College handled one, George Kennan was called back from Princeton's Institute for Advanced Study to head another, and Gen. Jim McCormick headed the third one. At the end of the work, it was all presented to Eisenhower. He immediately summarized it orally, and set out what he thought made sense, in the presence of his whole security and foreign policy structure top establishment. To my recollection, there were nearly one hundred people in the room, out of which there were perhaps fifty or sixty in addition to the participants in the study. Out of that work, Eisenhower settled

218 • *National Security Decisions*

on a line of policy, which became the central policy for his whole administration. He had a very keen sense of the policy direction in which he
wanted to see us move.

General Goodpaster described the policy in the following way:

> It was containment, plus a positive and active policy of assistance, contact,
> help of many kinds, as well as diplomatic and political support to the
> emerging nations of the world. There was also, of course, support for the
> alliances that John Foster Dulles was working to create. I would say that,
> overall, the picture of Eisenhower that was given in the press and in much
> of the more scholarly literature was quite incorrect. Of course, what the
> press was looking for was to see him publicly involved in day-to-day affairs
> and details, and that was simply not his mode of operating. He personally
> assigned each individual participant to each of the three lines of policy—
> one being rollback, one being containment, the third being the drawing
> of a line (essentially spheres of influence, or spheres of interest)—and he
> wanted the best case made for each one. We all worked very diligently
> and then made our presentations. I would say that that was the end of roll-
> back as far as any serious thinking with regard to the basic policy was
> concerned.

While pressing for an appropriate strategic concept and military force structure, the Eisenhower administration evolved an approach to the Soviet Union
based on negotiations. The result was the Geneva Summit of July 1955, followed by Khrushchev's visit to the United States in 1959 and the abortive Paris
Summit Conference of May 1960. General Goodpaster recalled the discussion
of relations with the Soviet Union in the Eisenhower administration:

> Others in the government felt that Eisenhower, in particular, had a stand-
> ing in Europe and in the Soviet Union as well that could be helpful in
> establishing better relations. Eisenhower, I think, thought of this as a way
> of shifting from where you had the confrontation essentially in military
> terms to opening up discussions to see whether in fact there was agreement
> that could be found. Part of John Foster Dulles's concern was that the
> position of West Germany might be in danger. That was still to some
> extent an open issue, because in the sequence of things, the Western
> powers had finally taken arbitrary action without agreement to establish
> their own area in Germany, free from Soviet control or veto. Then, also,
> Eisenhower saw weight in what Churchill was saying—that "jaw jaw is
> better than war war"—although with some reservation that Churchill
> might be overenamored of the dramatic effect of the summit. Let me say
> that during the run up to the 1955 Geneva Summit, John Foster Dulles,
> in particular, was dubious that it would be of value and felt that it could
> be risky. He was thinking of the risk of confrontation.
>   Overall, Eisenhower came out with the feeling that this could indeed
> be something of value, recognizing that we would have a very hard time

with the Russians—as we did—on this subject of the European security arrangement. This is what they called it, but in a way it was really an attempt on the part of the Soviet Union to regain some degree of control over West Germany. That was a very difficult issue at the summit and, in fact, the last session was prolonged because agreement could not be reached on just this issue. You had a situation where the fact that the meeting had been held did ease world tensions considerably. At the summit, I think that a good deal was accomplished in terms of opening the kind of deliberation which was conducted with courtesy and dignity, although the positions were hard and demanding. There was no name-calling, or anything like that, and the respect that they had for Eisenhower certainly showed.

In the late 1950s, the Eisenhower administration learned that Nikita Khrushchev had an interest in visiting the United States. Eisenhower himself sought to attach conditions to any invitation that might be forthcoming. General Goodpaster described the circumstances leading to the decision to invite Khrushchev:

We had had a number of indications of interest from the Russians wanting to visit, and, as I recall, we had had visits from Mikoyan [Anastas Mikoyan as then Soviet chief of state] and Kozlov [Frol Kozlov was then head of the Leningrad Communist party] in about this period. All in all, they were giving very strong signals that Khrushchev was interested in making a visit to the United States. There is a little vignette on this: The State Department people came over and talked with Eisenhower—I think it was during the visit of Kozlov—and the idea was that perhaps an invitation could be conveyed. But Eisenhower said that it should be a conditional invitation—that is, that there would have to be progress with regard to the negotiations regarding the status of Berlin. Only then would the invitation be issued. In any case, the State Department people went back and issued the invitation through Kozlov, but without condition. Eisenhower was dumbfounded, to say the least, when he learned about this and felt that they had made a bad mistake. Having thought about it, however, and having reviewed it carefully, he felt that he was bound to honor the invitation that was made because it had been issued and accepted in good faith.

Well, you know the story—Khrushchev came, visited the United States, and apparently found it very impressive. It was kind of an up-and-down visit, some parts of it in a very good atmosphere and some parts of it very bad. Apparently, his greatest resentment was that he could not visit Disneyland out in California. I think he felt he had been treated with disrespect by the mayor of one of the major cities, either Los Angeles or San Francisco, and, in any case, Eisenhower sent UN Ambassador Henry Cabot Lodge, as I remember, to accompany Khrushchev over the rest of the visit. When he came to Washington and they met up at Camp David, of course a major part of the issue was the discussion about a summit meeting, and the Russians were continuing to propose this idea of the European Security System, to which we were not disposed to agree. But Eisenhower said that he did not want to go to a summit under the cloud of this ultimatum—that the ultimatum would have to be removed—and they talked and talked about that. Finally, Khrushchev said that he would be willing to do that—that they had not intended it as an ultimatum—but that this could not be announced until he was back in the Soviet Union. We were somewhat suspicious about that, but he said that we could be sure that he would announce it as soon as he was back in the Soviet Union, and indeed he did.

Our interpretation was that he had taken a major step without having taken it first to the Politburo. As a result he would be personally vulnerable and in danger. But in any case, their announcement removed the ultimatum, the time dimension on the situation that we were in. There was an agreement for a meeting at the level of heads of government on that situation and on the Soviet proposal for the collective security arrangement to which we were not disposed to agree. That is where the matter was left until the time of the U-2 incident and the Paris Summit meeting of 1960.

In June 1956 the United States had begun U-2 flights over the Soviet Union and Eastern Europe. Such missions made possible the collection of vitally important information about Soviet military deployments through recently improved technologies for aerial photography from the high-altitude U-2 aircraft. Just before the Paris Summit conference, scheduled to be held in May 1960, Eisenhower had authorized a U-2 flight over the Soviet Union in order to obtain up-to-date information about Soviet ICBM installations. The impact of the U-2 shootdown by the Soviets upon the impending Paris Summit is described by General Goodpaster:

Khrushchev continued to demand an apology and broke up the summit. Khrushchev, I thought, was under constraint, under pressure. This is my own interpretation. The fact that he had General Malinovsky with him at his side in Paris indicated to me that Khrushchev himself might be under personal pressure, because he had supposedly trusted Eisenhower and had been shown to be wrong, and that this was an insult to the Soviet Union for which Khrushchev was, in some way, responsible. Of course, there was great regret on Eisenhower's part because he was now unable to do anything constructive with the Soviet Union because of this through the rest of his term.

Dean Rusk served as secretary of state from the beginning of the Kennedy administration until the end of the Johnson era. He reflected on the problems that policymakers face in having access to adequate information at crucially important times in the decision-making process. Rusk addressed this problem, with specific reference to U.S. intelligence about the Soviet Union at the time of the Soviet invasion of Czechoslovakia in 1968:

> We have never been well informed about the relations between the members of the Politburo. They keep their mouths shut. We study it. They play the good cop/bad cop game—make concessions to strengthen the hand of those who want good relations with the United States. It is used as a diplomatic gambit. We come back with a similar gambit: we have to have the approval of Congress. We trade such things. We simply do not know some of the central things that it would help us to know. For example, the invasion of Czecholslovakia occurred on a Tuesday evening. We thought that the decision to invade had been made the preceding Saturday. When we asked our Soviet experts a week before about whether the Soviets were going to invade, they said they had the capabilities and assets deployed, but as to whether they would use them, they did not know. Our experts could not know because the Soviets had not decided yet. Sometimes you would like to have information which simply does not exist. I have spent a considerable amount of time trying to inform the Soviet elite how the U.S. constitutional system works, and I wish they would be a little bit more forthcoming on how their system works.

Asked whether, by the policies that it had followed, by omission, the United States was recognizing a Soviet sphere of influence in Eastern Europe, Dean Rusk replied,

> There is a difference between accepting a theory and being aware of the presence of the Red Army. We were not prepared to challenge it. After the Soviets moved their troops into Czechoslovakia, they announced the Brezhnev Doctrine. In early October 1968 I made the opening speech to the UN General Assembly. I addressed a series of questions to [Foreign Minister] Gromyko, who was sitting in front of me, about the meaning of the Brezhnev Doctrine with respect to independent members of the United Nations. Every delegate from Eastern Europe, with one exception, somehow got me a message, thanking me for making our speech.
>
> There is a kind of de facto division of Europe into spheres of influence because of NATO and the Warsaw Pact. We continue to believe that the peoples of Eastern Europe have the right to decide their own affairs, but there are limits to what they can do because the Soviet Union has the overwhelming power in that area. We had been embarrassed as a nation by the feeling among many that, through the Voice of America, the Hungarians had been encouraged in 1956 to revolt on the understanding that we would come to their help. One must not do that unless you mean business. I do not know to what extent we deliberately or inadvertently misled the Hungarians on that particular point, but many Hungarians that I have talked to say that they feel that they were misled.

222 • *National Security Decisions*

Speaking from a later date—as adviser to Richard Nixon on foreign policy in the late 1960s and subsequently to President Reagan before and just after the 1980 election, and as Mr. Reagan's first national security adviser—Richard Allen offered perspectives on Western analyses of the dynamics of Soviet decision-making:

> Over and above the question of structure, time problems, and the unfore-seen, there is also a kind of in-built hesitation to saying that the adversary has internal resistance. Instead, we say we cannot possibly know this, so we had better treat him as one single monolithic entity, and therefore pursue a one-on-one relationship. We could say, wait a minute, what are the destabilizing factors, what factional infighting exists, but when we come to the few moments when crisis decisions are made, there is not anyone willing to listen to that sort of thing. But you could always have a current inventory of factors of instability in the Soviet Union or Eastern Europe. For example, anyone who believes in the dependability of Eastern Europe as a safe passage or a clean route to the invasion of Western Europe ought to have his head screwed on in a different direction.
>
> In the U.S. government, everybody is always busy shuffling paper, and you have no part of the mechanism that consists of thinkers, no people with a clean desk. I know two or three people today whom, if I were presi-dent, I would put into the office to the left of the president's desk. I would go into this office and if I caught them with a piece of paper on their desk, they would have to leave. These would be people of great judgment who would understand the dimensions of the presidency and would be ready for the next action that came onto the desk. In a certain sense, that is what [Chief of Staff] Jim Baker was in the first four years of the Reagan adminis-tration, except he was—I do not want to abuse him by saying this—limited in his scope of knowledge about foreign affairs and national security issues.

As national security adviser from 1983 to 1985, Robert McFarlane had the opportunity to participate in the efforts undertaken by the Reagan administra-tion to shape and advance U.S. national interests. He described the world scene as it appeared to the administration at the end of the 1970s and into the early years of the 1980s.

> I told Secretary of State Haig that we ought to simply put our heads down and devote really the first term of the administration to restoring the strength of our economy, the strength of allied relationships, in short to repairing all of the underpinnings of power before we could have much expectation of being able to influence the Soviet Union. Consequently, I did not think that defining an agenda for action toward the Soviet Union in a diplomatic sense made very much sense in 1981. It is kind of a cliché, but I told him do not just do something, stand there, get our house in order. As it turned out, that was the president's natural inclination. The

president, I think as most of us understood, did not come to the presidency with a detailed foreign policy agenda beyond keeping the peace and restoring our strength. His instincts were extremely good. He did put foremost in his own mind restoring the strength of our economy for essentially domestic reasons, although he did understand that it had a foreign dimension to it: that unless your economy is strong, you cannot sustain military strength nor a competitive position in the global marketplace nor the other instruments of power, for example, security assistance, foreign aid, and so forth, without an economy that can underwrite it; repairing that economy was squarely his first priority.

Toward the Soviet Union, I think the president, Secretary of State Haig, and I clearly believed that it was going to take a four-year investment, *at least*, until you could provide evidence of renewal, of renewed strength and purpose, that would get the attention of the Soviet Union and make possible some more concrete framework for deterrence, stability, and any other goals you might want to set. As a consequence, Secretary of State Haig, I think, believed that we ought to do that and that his agenda for the first time ought to be in other regions and in other functional areas, and not foremostly vis-à-vis the Soviet Union, except in building these foundation items back up again.

McFarlane then discussed how the foundations that had been established in the first term were built upon in the second Reagan administration:

The military foundation was being restored as was popular support for political leadership and for a more assertive international policy. The Soviet Union could not have helped but be very impressed that here was a leadership very strong in its convictions, supported by its people, underwritten by great power militarily, and it had a very significant effect. It all came home, I think, to Gromyko, who was angry about it, who kind of grumped off and was kind of seeing the beginning of the end. He had been presiding over the ascendant power of the Soviet Union throughout his lifetime really as foreign minister since 1957, but suddenly he came up to this undeniable array of facts that the Soviet Union was not going to make it. Well, not that he was ready to capitulate, far from it, but he went back and began to stew about how to begin to chip away at these American trends. He had to acknowledge that the traditional Soviet stratagem of the threatening, of intimidation, of walking out, just had not worked. He decided that they would go back to another stratagem that has worked, and that is to get back into negotiations and try to beat us at negotiations.

It had been a real frustration of mine from the beginning that we had not established those one or two goals that we wanted to accomplish in the first term, although we had accomplished one very important goal, and that was the restoring of U.S. strength for the beginning of the investment quarter. And we had accomplished the second, which was restoring economic strength, which had its foreign effect, and another one, succeeding in the deployment [of INF]. So it was not trivial. But having spent

the first term—call it investing and gardening and tending the alliance—
what were you going to do in the second term? I thought that we could
maybe consolidate as a permanent fixture of U.S. policy that the Soviet
Union ought to be one of the two priorities in the second term—the Soviet
Union not in terms of an arms control agreement (although maybe that
would occur), but in terms of writing down the ground rules for behavior
and a true framework, a set of rules, for dealing with each other that were
designed to stop aggression, try to contain the expansion of Soviet influence, establish some criteria of how they treat their own citizens, bring to
bear some pressure for better human rights treatment. Perhaps at the end
of the day, regional problems also needed to be addressed, from Nicaragua
to Afghanistan. Finally, if we could do those three things, then perhaps
we could begin to cooperate in trading nonstrategic goods and services and
other kinds of East-West exchanges and so forth. But [the goal was] to
have [this set of rules] not only written down in treaties, protocols, but to
have it widely publicized in the United States and understood by Americans and based on a bipartisan consensus. That would be a worthy goal
for the second term.

There were so many ways in which détente in the early 1970s had
been oversold based upon really superficial judgments about the Soviet
Union and the assertion of convergence or the assertion of really nonexistent convergence. So we had to correct that and introduce a more
realistic notion about the Soviet Union—that we disagreed with them on
virtually every notion of governance. We disagree about the way that they
treat their own people, we disagree about the role of the state beyond its
own borders. We ought to accept that. Maybe we can influence it, maybe
we cannot, but the implication is for competition forever. The central
requirement is that the competition be peaceful, that we have enough confidence in the fact that our system works better, that we should not worry
about competition, and that it need not be violent. But to underwrite a
peaceful competition requires certain things: it requires strength, it requires
about 6 percent of GNP be spent on it every year (all the time, not cyc-
lically), and finally, that in such a climate of competition and of strength
you can engage in a dialogue across the board, and from a position of
strength you can expect to prevail in that dialogue in advancing U.S. interests in a peaceful way.

Lawrence Eagleburger, from his vantage point as under secretary of state
for political affairs, addressed the problems facing the Reagan administration
in the formation of foreign policy toward the Soviet Union by drawing contrasts
between the first and second terms of the Reagan presidency:

You can argue that the first Reagan term was incoherent on foreign policy.
I would argue equally strenuously that the United States was in a better
position to deal constructively, imaginatively, and creatively with the
Soviets at the end of the Reagan first four years than it had been in a

long time. I happen to feel fairly strenuously that Reagan's approach to the Soviet Union in the first four years created a very healthy climate from which to do some things. "Evil empire" never bothered me. Reagan's policies and rhetoric created an atmosphere, given the objective facts of the Soviet Union and its own leadership problems and its own economic problems, in which there was a real chance for creative diplomacy in the next four years. Now, if you want to take a deep breath, say okay, here we are, now what is it we are doing to take advantage of this set of circumstances in the next four years of an administration? What ought our strategy to be with regard to the Soviet Union, and what is it that we ought to uy to do, what are the objectives, how are we going to try to achieve them, what is it that we are trying to accomplish? Believe me, I will not argue with you for five minutes that that needs to be done.

As long as you permit yourself some flexibility, and as long as you are sensible enough to say that here is an issue we need to study and set some general policy framework for it. Recognizing all the time that events may throw that all off track, I am all for it. But it is extremely difficult to do with an administration in midcourse; it is not impossible, but the tragedy of it is that the people who make a difference are all busy answering telegrams, or running off to Geneva for this negotiation or that one. Henry Kissinger succeeded at it better than most, and I will not say that he was by any means right. Kissinger also spent, in my judgment, a lot of time in the first four years writing all of these studies on what we were going to do about this, that, and the other thing that by and large showed some intellectual capacity, but also became irrelevant very quickly. Your targets must be discrete. As you establish your targets, you also have to recognize that they relate to each other. That is very difficult to do. It is not ever accomplished by some grand design: we are not going to go out and set up a series of foreign policy objectives so that everyone will understand them and we will all be able to march off in lockstep. Our system does not work that way.

You need to recognize that doing it while the train is leaving the station is not easy. What you shall do is to sit down and spend a lot of time doing it before your president is inaugurated. Yet, by and large, either the people who are doing it do not know enough about what is going on, or the new president and secretary of state are so busy selecting personnel and getting themselves organized that they pay no attention.

According to Mr. Eagleburger, one of the policy interests of the Reagan administration was how to combat Soviet disinformation, a problem that the United States, in particular, faced in the controversy surrounding INF deployment in Western Europe.

I have a particular interest in disinformation. The Reagan administration came in arguing that it was going to reinvigorate—they did not call it "political warfare" then—our ability to deal with this arena. They believed that the Soviet Union was spending a great deal of time on these sorts of subjects, having looked at things like the neutron bomb campaign of the late 1970s. William Clark [deputy assistant secretary of state] was interested in this, and he got a Madison Avenue advertising friend of his to take a look at what we did and was horrified, as he should have been. We have all of these offices of public diplomacy and so forth now in the State Department, most of which I got organized only because I got interested in it. But I tell you, I did not have the vaguest idea what I was doing. I mean, I do not know anything about public relations and public diplomacy, and I also had eighteen other things to do. I think they have not really worked well. There was some attempt at it, but it was all kind of amateur hour. We did get some advice from outsiders. I will also tell you I am one of the few admirers of Charley Wick [director of the U.S. Information Agency, 1981–89], and, in a strange sort of way, he has understood the need of the government to communicate far better than it has in the past, to the point where he has put together some imaginative transcontinental, intercontinental television programs and things of this sort. It has really worked quite well. I knew what ought to be done, but I did not know how to do it. All of this was very much resisted by the Department of State, which thought it was not the way grown men should make a living.

Mr. Eagleburger concluded by giving an overview of the problems the United States faces in the public diplomacy area:

I think part of the problem was in the way the White House and the United States Information Agency presented the issue of how they were going to respond to Soviet disinformation. The USIA came out with project TRUTH. You see, part of the problem is to announce that we are going to take these things seriously, and then to ask a bunch of diplomats and others who have no experience in how you do it—without any help from the experts who hopefully know how to do something like that—is a formula for disaster. If somebody would tell me that I am now going to be responsible for responding to Soviet active measures, I would say, "Thank you very much, and if I find one I will do something about it." That is the kind of response you get. This is a case in which there has to be a lot of creative thinking about how do you manage it institutionally. I am not sure I know the answer, except that I think we have found a kernel of an idea which has largely disappeared. In the Department of State, at least, each bureau has to have somebody who is responsible for public diplomacy in that bureau. It would even be nice if they appointed somebody to do it who knew something about it.

What then are the policy options available to the United States in its relations with the Soviet Union or in American foreign policy more broadly? Donald Rumsfeld, secretary of defense between 1975 and 1977 in the Ford administration, discussed the implications of traditional American values, together with limitations upon available resources, for the formulation of a strategy designed to protect vital interests:

> You look at the alternatives to containment. On the one hand you can be a crusader and take your nuclear weapons around the globe and, with your power, try to make everyone else be like you. Well, we decided that is not our bag. Another alternative, if you want to be moral and pure, is not to have political, economic, or social intercourse with those who behave in a way which you find reprehensible. Well, if you do that, there are only about twenty countries in the world with whom you would have relations, and you would not have relations with them because they would have relations with the other countries anyway. So you would be all alone. [As a result], we are somewhere in the middle. We are not going to withdraw and we are not going to use force on everybody else. Therefore, what do we want to do?
>
> The containment idea had some merit and it had some success. The problem with it is that it is defensive, and a defensive posture is not a winning posture. If it is true that things do not remain static, then containment is a losing posture—not quickly, but eventually—one can make that case.
>
> It seems to me, then, that the way for this country to interact with the Soviets over time is to get ourselves out of the containment/static deterrent idea and think about the definition of the role for the United States in the world. That includes a very active political and economic "offensive" role. Not a military role in the crusader sense, but political and economic, which I think is accountable to the American people, as long as it is realistic. We have to couple that with the education of people to the fact that deterrence involves an active aspect to make the deterrent itself healthy, like the Libya action of April 1986. But even more than that, it involves a rollback, not in the sense of taking Poland, which would mean fighting the Soviet Union, but rather active in the sense that you are going to know consciously that you are going to have to do more than just hold ground. That means you have got to figure out ways to thwart the efforts of those that are in fact seeking to expand.
>
> However, one part of the doctrine suggests that we are going to weaken countries that, while offensive to us internally, are friendly to us externally. I do not think that we have the luxury to do that right now. If our power were superior in the world—politically, economically, militarily—one might say we could be more purist as we are with our environmental policy. We have enough affluence that we can take steps that are not cost-effective to preserve the environment. Try to impose that on Nigeria and it will be an underdeveloped country for the next two hundred years. Underdeveloped countries cannot live up to the same standards. So too if we had excess capability, we could live to a higher standard, but we do not have an excess of military power. It is very important that we use

those bases all over the world and not chop off countries just because we do not like the way they do certain things. Winston Churchill was able to deal with Stalin, not because he liked him but because he thought Hitler was worse at that moment because Hitler was the expansionist.

16
Arms Control

I n examining the Soviet-American relationship, this chapter focuses upon efforts to achieve arms control and strategic stability. After a brief account of the gestation of the U.S. arms control bureaucracy, recurring themes of arms control are articulated by policy formulators and practitioners alike, with emphasis on verification approaches, U.S. and Soviet arms control negotiating strategies, the critical role of intelligence assessments, rationales for seeking arms control, survivability problems, and strategic nuclear force modernization efforts, particularly detailed in the 1983 Scowcroft Commission Report. In addition—and integrated with these themes—accounts of actual arms control negotiations are provided, and here include the 1955 Geneva Summit, the 1979 Vladivostok Summit, SALT II, and START.

The Eisenhower administration, Gen. Andrew Goodpaster recalls, initiated for the United States the development of the intercontinental ballistic missile armed with a nuclear warhead. At the same time, however, Eisenhower pressed his administration's Atoms for Peace proposal and began to create within the U.S. government an organizational framework for the formulation of arms control policy. In General Goodpaster's words:

There is the well-known story, of how John von Neumann showed that the combination of the intercontinental rocket and the thermonuclear warhead would be a viable and significant weapon, given the forseeable accuracy and explosive force potential. Eisenhower authorized the work to go forward with the highest national priority. But then he constantly reflected and talked about it. He had long discussions and consultations with C.D. Jackson and Lewis Strauss on the Atoms for Peace proposal, reflecting his developing conviction that we were faced with something which in terms of security would be completely irrational in its potential impact. More and more he wanted to find a way to stop the increase in arms, to limit and constrain the confrontation between the United States and the Soviet Union, and to shift it from a confrontation that was expressed so much in military terms to a relationship which, though adversarial, would be conducted in other ways—diplomatic exchanges, political influence, economic development, and so forth.

He did not have an organizational instrument to deal with arms control in the Department of Defense, where interest was in stronger military forces, and it did not fit into the traditional pattern of diplomacy. So, as he very often did, President Eisenhower appointed a special assistant. That was a technique that he used a great deal. At that time Harold Stassen was serving as the head of the Agency for International Development [AID]. Eisenhower, decided to establish the position of special assistant for disarmament, and Harold Stassen, once named to the post, moved out very vigorously to study these problems. The NSC Planning Board had been involved in it, and now a group was set up called the Committee of Principals, a committee of department heads and the affected agency heads which then proceeded to analyze what steps might be taken in this area. The work began to take shape by mid-1955. They worked very hard at what could be done in the way of monitoring tests.

General Goodpaster continued his explanation of the establishment of an arms control bureaucratic structure:

President Eisenhower sought, and achieved, access to members of the scientific community in order for him to make appropriate policy choices, thereupon he convened this group of experts as the White House Scientific Advisory Committee, which assumed major importance in the Eisenhower administration. Following the reestablishing of the President's Scientific Advisory Committee, that body began to contribute to the arms control policy because they saw that security was not going to be achieved simply by the building of weapons for use in actual conflict. That was not going to be a solution, but there were nevertheless great dangers. The Science Advisory Committee was concerned about the possibility of a "knockout" blow against our bombers, for example, as the ICBM became a real and a viable system. It was not long until it became apparent that it would be essential to get into a dialogue with our allies and the Soviet Union on this whole issue.

Now this is the point at which one begins to see the basis of friction between the Stassen operation and the traditional State Department operation. The story is that John Foster Dulles felt that Harold Stassen, in some direct contacts with the Soviet Union, had gone beyond what had been authorized. This excited and alarmed our allies, and so it was an issue that had to be resolved. Eisenhower resolved it by putting Stassen under the supervision of the secretary of state, insofar as the diplomatic aspects of this thing were concerned. The important thing is that as a result of the Eisenhower initiative, an evolution was begun which gradually served to build up our substantive understanding of disarmament issues, together with initiatives with the Soviet Union. For example, we set up negotiations in Geneva between scientists to study technical issues related to surprise attack. On our side was Dr. Fisk from Bell Laboratories, and Dr. [Edward] Purcell, a physicist from one of the major universities. That was really one of the first times that we got into such discussions with the Soviet Union. I believe that this surprise attack issue was raised first in 1956 and then again later on.

All these things were coming together, and Eisenhower felt that it was incumbent on him as president to try to give leadership in this area in order to control and reduce these arsenals of tremendously destructive arms. Along with this he recognized, as he always did, that you simply had to have a strong military establishment that provided a nuclear capability in order to maintain deterrence, because there was a feeling at that time that the Soviets were going to push into every corner of weakness that they could find, and exploit divisions in every way they could. Now we would have to go down two tracks: the track of the arms and armaments on the one hand, and the track of trying to control, limit, and constrain on the other hand.

Among the Eisenhower administration's arms control initiatives was the "Open Skies" proposal. Goodpaster noted:

On the Open Skies proposal, when Nelson Rockefeller took over the position of special assistant for what had earlier been called psychological warfare, he set up a study group and they put together what was called the Quantico Study, in which Walt Rostow [deputy special assistant for national security affairs] and Max Milliken [professor of economics at the Massachusetts Institute of Technology], among others, were involved. In developing ideas for the Geneva four-power summit in 1955, they proposed an agreement between the United States and the Soviet Union to permit aerial photography overflights of each other's territory, along with an exchange of military "blueprints" showing the military forces and programs of each side, in order to build confidence and reduce the chances of war through miscalculation. Although this proposal had not been part of the planned presentations of the president at the 1955 Geneva Summit, while there he discussed it with his chief advisers, and finally presented it in one of the plenary meetings. The Soviet reaction at the table was equivocal. When we broke up and had tea, which normally followed the plenary sessions, Khrushchev came up to the president, wagged his finger sideways and said, "No, no, no." Eisenhower always said that at that moment he really knew who was in charge on the Soviet side, because that was the B and K [Bulganin and Khrushchev] period, where there was some uncertainty, but it was apparent then that it was Khrushchev who held the decision. Those were the main points in the way the Open Skies proposal developed.

By the time of the Nixon administration, arms control had become a principal concern to an unprecedented extent within the offical policy community of the United States. After the Limited Test Ban Treaty of 1963 in the Kennedy administration, followed by the Nonproliferation Treaty of 1968 in the Johnson administration, attitudes shifted to a focus on the Strategic Arms Limitation Talks (SALT), resulting in the 1972 SALT I accords, the ABM Treaty and the Interim Agreement on Offensive Systems. In November 1974 the Ford administration established with Leonid Brezhnev of the Soviet Union at the Vladivostok Conference a framework for a SALT II Treaty based on equal aggregates of systems. As U.S. representative to NATO, and subsequently as secretary of defense, Donald Rumsfeld recalled the arms control process in which he was a participant:

> I came back from Brussels in August on the day of President Nixon's resignation and was chairman of the transition team for about three weeks. Then I went back to NATO. I was in Chicago when President Ford later called and asked me to come back to Washington. He said he had to move Haig—it was not working—and I had to be chief of staff. I declined, and said I did not want to come back. I said I would go back to NATO and try to help him find some other names. I came back in October and went on the Vladivostok trip. The president had scheduled a full set of campaign speeches in the fall; President Nixon had been pardoned; and there were all kinds of staff problems. There were a number of President Nixon's nominations pending before Congress that had to be looked at. I was sorting through the White House staff. The resignation of a president had never happened before in history; so there was no roadmap for an unelected president.
>
> There is no question as to who was the dominant person; it was [Secretary of State] Henry Kissinger. To what extent [Secretary of Defense] James Schlesinger played or [Director of Central Intelligence] William Colby played, I do not know. There was no vice president to play a role during that period, and when one was appointed, it was Henry Kissinger's associate Nelson Rockefeller—who would have deferred to Henry. My guess is it was the president and the secretary of state, who was also national security adviser.

Briefly expanding on the issues discussed at the Vladivostok meeting, Rumsfeld suggested,

> It was clearly the Soviet position that the Backfire bomber was purely a naval forces weapon system and not a strategic weapon system. So it was inconvenient to have others in the process contend the contrary, that it was a strategic system, and if not a strategic, then certainly a potentially strategic system. I do not recall ever seeing a photograph of a Backfire during that period that did not have a refueling probe, and it struck me that the Backfire had to be included as a strategic system. The argument from State, and indeed from Bush [who succeeded William Colby in 1973] at CIA, was to the contrary.

General Brent Scowcroft described, from his vantage point as national security adviser, how Brezhnev and Ford related to one another in the Vladivostok Summit Conference in November 1974:

They were both very outgoing personalities, at least on the surface for Brezhnev. Everything you see was there on the surface. I think they responded to each other really quite well, probably more in a personal sense than did Nixon and Brezhnev. They were very different types of personalities. Nixon has a very reserved, formal kind of personality, and Brezhnev was the bearhug type and Ford responds much more to that sort of thing. I think that the two of them really hit it off quite well. However, the Helsinki meeting in 1975 was not a good meeting. It did not go well at Helsinki. We made no progress at all on any of the issues, but it has turned out to be very much in our favor and has been far from what the Soviets expected the outcome to be. Vladivostok was a different issue; Vladivostok went well. Those were the only two meetings they had.

Mr. Rumsfeld also reflected on his own position as NATO ambassador and negotiator and on the problems confronting President Ford in formulating a coherent U.S. arms control policy:

I remember nights when I would be at NATO meetings and would finish, handle some business, then call it a night, and go back to the room. Kissinger would be in Moscow preparing a brief on the final position to go to the NSC for the president. The NSC would have relayed it over to me in Brussels, and to George Brown, chairman of the Joint Chiefs of Staff. I would look at it, and think about it, and try to figure out what I thought was right, and then we would try to fashion a response and get it back to Washington. Henry was in Moscow trying to close the deal. The president did not have either one of us there to talk to. We came out differently on the issue at hand, and that was tough for the president. It is also tough for the person who knows that his position is inhibiting the deal because there is a natural dynamic of wanting, once you start the negotiations, to end them "successfully." I have no problem with starting negotiations as long as you have the strength and conviction not to end them on a basis that you think is unsatisfactory. I think it takes a lot of patience. You should never feel stampeded, and if you do not have that ability, you ought not to get into the negotiations in the first place.

Regarding the larger agenda—beyond military capabilities—of political issues involved in U.S.-Soviet arms control negotiations, Rumsfeld stated:

If you are looking at a broader picture, you end up making trade-offs between apples and oranges. It is hard to do that. It is not that you have got three apples and I have got three apples. It is a matter of two apples versus an orange, and what value you are going to put on those things.

Asked whether this approach to negotiation might be disadvantageous to the United States, Rumsfeld replied,

That is one outcome, but the other possible outcome is at the opposite end. In fact, you could have fashioned a web of connections in the multi-faceted relationships between nations, and because of the value of the process and linkages with other things, it could, over time, alter a relationship favorably. This would be notwithstanding the fact that to get there you had to agree to some things which, had they been taken in isolation, you might not otherwise have done. That is a fair position. It could come out that way just as easily as it could come out the other way. [This approach is not] per se invalid; it is a legitimate negotiating strategy.

Nonetheless, you have got to make value judgments as you go along as to the weight or value you want to give things which you might give up. You have to do it on an absolute scale, but you also have to do it on a scale of what signals it sends to the other side. If you are less vigilant on things that are hard and specific, and in exchange you get things that are theoretical, potential, retrievable, or changeable, it would be danger-ous. Second, you have to factor into the negotiation the asymmetries between the United States and the Soviet Union in terms of the absence of a free press, a congress, their secrecy, and so on. It seems to me that compromises—the things we get for what we give—have to be looked at in the context of those asymmetries, because there are certain dynamics that take over in one society and not in the other.

R. James Woolsey reflected on what he observed to be the fundamental dif-ferences in approach to arms control negotiations between the United States and the Soviet Union. In sharp contrast to those of the Soviet Union, American negotiators, according to Mr. Woolsey, have had a tendency to try to view the various proposals both from a Soviet and a U.S. perspective. In sharp contrast, Soviet negotiations have had an almost exclusive focus on Soviet national interest.

The Soviets have a very tough, very repetitive negotiating style—very much in need to send it all back to Moscow, very much in the posture of always exhorting the U.S. side to come up with new ideas and new propos-als which they could react to. Their tactic is to select small portions of a proposal that they liked and then reject the rest, urging us to try again. [Regarding] civilian-military strains, there was one bit of folklore. I think it was really a misunderstanding, but one of the Soviet generals at one point admonished one of the American generals for raising a particular issue, saying that this was not an issue that the civilians needed to know about, implying his own civilians, as well as ours. I think that the Ameri-cans from time to time tried to convince the Soviets to take with them what might be called the "man-from-Mars, two-sided, objective, analytical view" of the process. I think that the Soviets largely regarded all this as an interesting and humorous American affectation that we used from time to time. The Soviets then and now regard these exercises precisely and narrowly as undertakings in their own national interest. Whereas Americans do too. From time to time in discussions among themselves or in negotiations, Americans will lapse into the Mars perspective.

This "objective" tendency can lead, says Mr. Woolsey, to an ineffective and misdirected negotiating strategy for the United States:

> I would not negotiate a settlement to a lawsuit based on the principle that it is okay to have a flawed agreement because we are establishing a good relationship with an opponent in litigation and we will get it sorted out later. Similarly that is not the way to negotiate arms control agreements. The Soviet interest throughout the process has been very much tied to specific issues of national interest. I do not think that they ever lapse into this mode of "international objectivity," or "man-from-Mars" view. They are quite willing to talk that way if it is of assistance to them, but they do not operate that way except to come up with positions that enhance Soviet national power.
>
> During the time that I was involved in the talks, I do not think many people thought otherwise. Most had a pretty clear view of Soviet objectives, but there was a degree of optimism that, in spite of those, one might be able to strike bargains in which the net result was positive and would promote greater strategic stability, in that we would not have to worry as much about Soviet counterforce systems. It always came back to that—a way on the offensive side to put a limit on the Soviet ability to attack American silo-based ICBMs. The ABM Treaty eventually became something different, trying to preserve the ability to penetrate defenses and maintain a deterrent, but the offensive limitations issue always came back to a way to get the Soviet Union to limit its SS-9s.

At the time of the Ford administration, however, there was a debate of increasing intensity about U.S. détente policy and overall relations with the Soviet Union. Rumsfeld continued:

> You can look at overhead photography of where the Soviet Union is scooping out an acre or so around major residential and industrial facilities for civil defense and then covering it up again. A few months later, they have installed modern civil defense capabilities for what seems to be on the order of something like a third of their urban population; it gives one a sense of their doctrine. You cannot track the numbers of nuclear tests that they have had and not come away with a sense of their seriousness. You cannot watch them exercise chemical and bacteriological warfare, employing environmentally controlled army personnel carriers, and not have that

affect your assessment of their doctrine and intent as well as their capabilities.

On the subject of the trends of Soviet nuclear doctrine, Rumsfeld contended,

> My conviction is that it is unusual for a large, bureaucratic, highly centralized, dictatorial regime to build a submarine base where they can erect from the hull up something like ten and a half nuclear submarines. Why would they hire all of those carpenters and electricians and welders to build all that if they did not intend to use them, if not directly, then indirectly? So my assumption is that any country that devotes whatever it was—and there was a debate between Defense and the CIA over this as well—12–17 percent of their GNP going to defense, with a much higher portion going into procurement than the United States—demonstrates its seriousness of purpose and thereby reveals a lot about what it thinks and what it plans to do. Now does that mean that such a country could not change over time? No.

At the time of Rumsfeld's tenure as secretary of defense there was increasing concern within the U.S. government about the accuracy and adequacy of the U.S. intelligence assessment of Soviet military capabilities.

> Some have argued that our defense establishment is, and has been in the past, overly concerned with numbers of capabilities and has ignored the question of what is the purpose of Soviet weapons systems. When I was secretary of defense we were becoming more and more sensitive to the question of not just "What do they have?" but "What is their purpose?" Clearly during James Schlesinger's tenure as secretary of defense, there was an interest relative to our interests about our prospective goals in the world. There is no doubt in my mind that during his tenure there was interest, and there is no doubt in my mind, but that even today, despite all these efforts, it is imperfectly done. . . . There is no question that the United States should make certain that we know what our interests are and what commitments we have made. We must make certain we invest at certain levels and buy [weapons systems] that will enable us to have the capabilities to protect those interests. To the extent that arms control activities occur during that period, one has to assure that those activities do not adversely affect our interests and do not adversely affect our weapons purchases and deployment. That means that it has to be an intimate process. The problem is that the arms control process gains a life of its own. On the other hand, weapons investment and development. The tendency is to allow arms control a heavier weighting in the decision-making process and to have it drive other [aspects of security policy.]

Asked if Soviet weapons and Soviet military spending reflect a doctrine that calls for the establishment of superiority, and whether such a doctrine in fact calls into question some of the basic assumptions underlying the arms control process in the West, Mr. Rumsfeld replied,

> I look at the experience and see that we got into extensive discussions and debates within the Ford administration and between myself and Congress and the press, particularly on the issue of Soviet intent. I very simply stated that I am not a psychiatrist and that freedom is very precious. I said that it requires vigilance and that if you are going to err, you should err on the side of safety. I also stated that we know precisely what they are doing and have done. A trained ape looking at the facts has to come to certain conclusions to the effect that the Soviets intended to have done those things and intend to be doing what they are doing. I know it gives them options which are disadvantageous to us.
>
> The problem is that the lead times are very long and once you rely on intent as opposed to capabilities, you have positioned yourself so that they can change their minds in five minutes and you cannot—it would be too late. You cannot develop capabilities in five minutes, but leadership and/or intent can change in a day. Anyone who argues that we should base our force structure and capabilities on our perception of the other side's intent is wrong—we cannot. It is dead wrong to trust the Soviet Union or anyone else, or to risk our freedom on that speculation.

Mr. Woolsey offered perspectives on the basic accomplishments, as well as on the deficiencies, in the U.S. approach to strategic arms control with the Soviet Union since the beginning of SALT in the late 1960s until the present phase of START. In his view, the United States has been unable to negotiate limits in Soviet systems that would effectively restrain the ability of the Soviet Union to place at risk the survivability of U.S. strategic forces:

> About 90 percent, I think, of what arms control is about is survivability of silo-based American ICBMs. It has been a tough road, and it has ultimately proven unsuccessful. We have spent a lot of capital and effort and time and negotiating leverage since 1969 trying to hold down the numbers of Soviet SS-9s and then SS-18s and trying to limit fractionation and testing. All of these, in one way or another, pertain to trying to limit the threat to silo-based ICBMs so that one can retain them. It has been the case for twenty years now that the Soviets have cheerfully negotiated with us and, grudgingly, one by one, occasionally given us a limitation here and there on their counterforce systems, but at the same time they have gleefully been designing systems that have been a threat to U.S. silo-based ICBMs. With their moving from the SS-9 to the SS-18, improving accuracy and now, I think, getting accurate enough SLBMs, before too long, getting limits on SS-18s does not do much for you. I think that the limitations on Soviet offensive systems that we have tried to negotiate over the years toward this end have largely been a failure.
>
> Back in the late 1960s and early 1970s, people did lots of calcula-

tions—and I did them too—and had lots of hopes that one would be able to do enough to preserve the survivability of U.S. silo-based ICBMs; that by a combination of hardening and arms control, one would be able to keep silos survivable. I think that is what most of the offensive limitations were about. We have never had any hope in negotiations of doing anything to improve the survivability of U.S. bombers. There have never been deep enough cuts contemplated or limitations on Soviet submarines that would hinder the Soviet Union from putting a few submarines off the U.S. coast to attack the command and control of U.S. bomber bases. We have never used arms control to try to preserve the survivability of our submarines— that we do through our own antisubmarine warfare programs and quieting. Therefore, what arms control has largely been about is trying to preserve silo survivability and, from the U.S. perspective, the assured ability of ballistic missile warheads to penetrate Soviet defenses.

According to Mr. Woolsey, the approach to arms control based on constraints on technology, such as that symbolized by the nuclear freeze and the advocates of limits on missile test flights, is self-defeating. In his view, there is no known way to prevent by arms control agreements qualitative improvements in range and accuracy. Therefore, the key to strategic stability and the proper rationale for arms control are said to lie in unilateral measures, as necessary, to assure the survivability of strategic systems in a crisis situation.

A lot of people unlike me who support the nuclear freeze and ballistic missile flight test bans and other similar arms control measures look on technology in general as something you just want to choke off, and try to do it through arms control. I do not think that is a fruitful course. The most that one can do is to try, through arms control agreements, to establish some modest incentive to incline both sides toward systems that are not as effective in destroying or being able to execute a first strike against our own forces as would be the case in the absence of arms control.

We tried to do that for a long time by limiting the numbers and size of the Soviet systems, and that has not worked because you cannot really constrain accuracy and yield effectively, and over time, accuracy has gotten to be so good that there has not been any way that you can really preserve the survivability of silos. Some people have said that you could constrain accuracy with some sort of complete ban on flight tests, and then neither side would know whether its deterrent was effective. It seems to me that that is the wrong way to do it.

The right way to do it is to take unilaterally the steps that you need to preserve the survivability of your forces. The first objective of arms control, I think, is a sort of Hippocratic oath: first of all, do no harm— which is why I have been opposed to the mobile missile ban that the Reagan administration has in its START negotiating position. I think that if you are taking steps unilaterally to preserve the survivability of your forces, such as having a mobile Midgetman, then you may be able to use whatever leverage you have in arms control negotiations with the Soviet Union to accomplish other things. You do not have to waste all that effort in something you are bound to fail at anyway. This all points to what Paul Nitze (secretary of state for arms control matters, 1984–89] has called "crisis stability" [as the rationale for arms control].

People come up with other rationales for arms control, such as saving money and reducing the damage if war occurs, but those approaches almost always upon further reflection and analysis take a back seat to crisis stability, because people tend to realize that if you limit the role of nuclear weapons overall in the defense budget, then you are probably going to want to increase the budget, not decrease it, to pick up the slack with conventional forces, since the Soviets dominate in conventional forces. Indeed, the major rationale from the beginning for substantial nuclear deployments was to deter a Soviet conventional attack in Europe, and reducing the damage if war occurs is really crazy if you are talking about reducing from ten thousand to six thousand warheads. Even a few hundred warheads if they were targeted properly, or even a handful, can wreak incredible devastation on either country, at least on the civilian population.

Therefore the best way to keep damage from occurring is to prevent the war in the first place through crisis stability. I think that the effort to constrain Soviet offensive forces in such a way as to preserve the survivability of American silos, which is the main enterprise we were involved in with SALT I and II (SALT I on the offensive side, and SALT II in toto), has largely been a failure. It does not mean that we should not have tried, or that you cannot continue to work on arms control agreements, only that you ought to acknowledge that you are going to be preserving the survivability of your ICBMs in some other way.

As deputy national security adviser under President Nixon and national security adviser under President Ford, Gen. Brent Scowcroft helped shape U.S. arms control policy in SALT II. Here he reflects on the role of the NSC in that process, focusing in particular on the latter years of Nixon and then the Ford administration:

The NSC staff was really key in the development of arms control positions. While there was a very active and fruitful interagency debate and discussion managed by what was then called the Verification Panel, the intellectual leadership was clearly from the NSC. The development of SALT II stemmed from an attempt in the latter part of the Nixon administration to find a way to curb Soviet MIRVing. The last proposal while Nixon was still president was a suggestion for an asymmetry with the Soviet Union—an asymmetry which would favor the United States in MIRV and favor the Soviet Union in total delivery vehicles. The Soviets rejected that proposal. They probably would have in any case, but I think they were probably becoming somewhat cautious about Nixon and about the utility of making agreements with him.

The upshot of the failure at the U.S.-Soviet Summit in 1974 was an agreement to change the horizon of an arms control agreement from five to ten years, to look out farther to try to encompass more elements of strategic forces, to broaden its scope. This led to the agreement at Vladivostok. At Vladivostok we again were going to try to see if the Soviets were sympathetic to an asymmetrical relationship. We presented this to President Ford and he decided (partly as a result of the Jackson Amendment mandating equality at the aggregate level) to stick with the proposal for equality in both numbers and MIRVs, and therefore warheads. At Vladivostok we did develop the elements for an arms control agreement which subsequently ran into trouble primarily on two issues. After there was agreement and concurrence on equality of MIRVs and total delivery vehicles below the levels of the Soviet Union, we had a disagreement or misunderstanding on cruise missiles. Our interpretation of what had happened was that we had banned the development and deployment of ballistic cruise missiles with ranges over 600 miles, and the Soviets insisted that what we had done was to ban cruise missiles of a range of over 600 kilometers. We were focused on the strategic delivery vehicles, while the Soviets were focused on the overall cruise missile threat, so that the misunderstanding did not emerge at Vladivostok as a primary problem. It emerged in the course of writing up the memorandum of understanding after the meeting, and that is when the cruise missile issue surfaced. The Backfire bomber came up at Vladivostok, but at that point the Pentagon was not as exercised about it as it was to be later. It was not a primary focus of the discussion.

After Vladivostok, however, the two central issues of the SALT II agreement came to be the Backfire bomber and what to do about it, and cruise missiles and what to do about them. We went through a number of formulations, but we never did solve the problem. Indeed, it was one of the last issues left in SALT II for the Carter administration. They were solved, both of them, outside of the framework of the formal treaty itself. The last effort of the Ford administration was in January 1976, but Kissinger's efforts were significantly undermined by the Defense Department, which insisted strongly on the inclusion of the Backfire in the strategic force totals and the free run of cruise missiles. The Soviets, of course, would not accept it. At this time, January 1976, the Soviets did hint a willingness to take deep cuts in SS-18 levels, but they were unwilling even to talk about our formulation on the Backfire and cruise missiles. Our suggestion that we simply ratify the main elements of Vladivostok and set the others aside did not get anywhere. I think this agreement was a casualty of the Reagan decision to compete for the 1976 Republican nomination. Otherwise, I think that President Ford would have overruled the Pentagon and gone for an arms control agreement.

Expanding on the Backfire bomber issue, General Scowcroft noted that there was considerable disagreement about the capabilities of the aircraft, even within the American intelligence community:

> There was great difference in the intelligence community, and it related to whether there was a Backfire A and a Backfire B, and the general characteristics of each version. We got the Soviets very involved in this debate. One of the times that Brezhnev was most angry was at Helsinki when we disagreed with his description of the range of the Backfire. He had a general officer sitting in the room with him to describe the range of the Backfire. It dealt with its innate capability, size, fuel capacity, and so on, with the normal profile for a mission, all these kinds of things. The Pentagon, in the end, was adamant that, certainly on one-way missions with recovery in Cuba, for example, the Backfire was capable of carrying a strategic bomb-load and, therefore, had to be considered a strategic bomber. Our argument was that it was designed to replace the Badger. It was obviously focused on the peripheral mission, making it a big threat to Europe and around the rimlands, but it was not designed as a strategic bomber and therefore should not be counted as a full strategic weapon. That dispute went on for a decade. I think the Pentagon now admits it is not a strategic bomber, but at that time it was a big issue and it was a litmus test for conservative Republicans.

On the subject of the cruise missile, General Scowcroft discussed at length how and when that issue came to the fore within the Ford administration:

> It is an interesting story. In the summer of 1973 we were in San Clemente, and I had a call from Deputy Secretary of Defense [William] Clements saying that they were reviewing the defense budget and cutting out things to stay within reasonable constraints. He said that one of the things they had decided to eliminate was the cruise missile program. We went back to him and said you cannot do that. If we are going to eliminate the cruise missile program, we want to eliminate it in the course of negotiations with the Soviet Union to try to get something for it, [but] not as a unilateral U.S. decision.
> Well, having forced the cruise missile program down the throats of the Pentagon, they in general, and Bill Clements especially, fell in love with it. Bill was told that they were so cheap they could be turned out like sausages, and that they would, in fact, transform the strategic relationship. It was an issue by the time we went to Vladivostok, but we did not know how to solve it. What we had thought we were doing at Vladivostok was simply punting, and not dealing with the issue at that particular time because we did not know how to deal with it.
> I do not want to put words in his mouth, but my guess is that Kissinger, at that time, would have been prepared to trade it away for something

else like deep cuts in SS-18s or something like that. When Kissinger was in Moscow negotiating in January of 1976, and the issue of cruise missiles came up, we had an NSC meeting to review the report from Kissinger. The chairman could not come, and instead the alternate was Admiral Holloway, the chief of naval operations. In the course of the cruise missile discussion the president turned to Admiral Holloway, and said, "Well, now, what is your cruise missile program? What exactly do you have in mind?" Admiral Holloway said, "We do not have a cruise missile deployment plan. If we really were pressed, we might be able to find room for it on seven or eight cruisers." I have never seen President Ford as angry, because the Defense Department had been holding up the arms control agreement on this invaluable weapon for which at that point we had absolutely no deployment scheme. This was the kind of political infighting that was very divisive inside the administration.

As I recall, the cruise missile fit none of the traditional missions of the armed services. For example, the navy, in order to deploy cruise missiles on submarines, was reluctant to fit a cruise missile into the torpedo tube. From the air force's perspective, it had similar problems, I suppose, because of the role of the bombers, the leg of the triad, and then the ICBM leg of the triad. The air force was, at first, fairly relaxed until the beginning of the Carter administration, when President Carter canceled the B-1 and said we could do the job with cruise missiles, which the air force did not like. Later he prolonged the life of the B-52 to standoff in order to get the cruise missiles close enough to launch.

Asked whether the cruise missile could have been traded with the Soviet Union for a deep cut in SS-18s, General Scowcroft replied,

I think it might have been a plausible negotiating position for the United States. Whether or not, at that point, we should have agreed, under any circumstances, to give up the cruise missile is another point. Maybe we should not have. The Soviets did make some noises about a willingness, at least, to do what they say they are prepared to do now and that is to cut the SS-18 in half—down to 150—and that would have been worth something. Since SALT I, our overall objective has been to try to find some way of coping with the threat posed by this very large missile, which now, compared to the SS-9, was MIRVed, and the Soviets were developing the accuracy to make it a hard target killer. It was, by all odds, our most serious problem for which we should have been willing to pay something significant.

A major verification issue that confronted the Ford administration was the multiple independently targetable reentry vehicle (MIRV). Scowcroft commented,

The SALT I unit of account, the delivery vehicle itself, emerged quite logically, because it was the only thing we thought we could count with any degree of accuracy. For example, it was not too hard to count airplanes, not too hard to count submarines, and if you could ban silo reload (which is what we did) then, in fact, all you had to do was to count silos, which is not too difficult. Therefore, counting by delivery vehicles rather than by warheads—which at the time we had no idea how to count—seemed to be a reasonable thing to do. The problem came with the MIRVing and with the fact that the Soviets seemed to have—we found out through their testing and because they told us—a mixed SS-18 force, some of them being single warheads, some of them being MIRVed, and we had no reasonable way to distinguish between them. [The Soviets surprisingly bought the counting rule that] once a system is tested with a MIRVed bus, all missiles of that category would be assumed to be MIRVed, with the exception of the Minuteman 3, which had once been tested with seven but obviously was never going to carry seven warheads—it was grandfathered. It turned out to be a major breakthrough in MIRV counting, because until then we really did not know how to do it.

Robert McFarlane addressed the Reagan administration decision making regarding U.S. strategic nuclear force modernization which eventually led to the establishment of the Scowcroft Commission. He refers initially here to the Carter administration proposal for a multiple protective shelter (MPS) basing mode for a new ICBM.

The MPS system in the Carter administration was vulnerable on a number of counts. Yet the community of those involved in analyzing how to do better was dominated by a kind of an animus against the Carter association with this basing, and were (as a consequence of this kind of partisan overlay) driven in a rather antiintellectual fashion away from deceptive basing in deciding what to do. That is a long way of saying we just went off in any direction except MPS because it was a Carter system. The important lesson is that if you want to be partisan you can be, but to be analytically sound you have got to be able to put partisan considerations aside. That did not happen [in this case]; there was a very clear bias against multiple protective shelters and deceptive basing generally in the first year of the Reagan administration. We went in Pentagon excursions toward air mobile basing and ultimately toward closely spaced basing [CSB or dense-pack], and one or two other options were examined by the Townes Commission.

I think the secretary of defense must have a very solid grasp of strategic concepts. The time has passed when you could really appoint someone who does not have experience in these matters, because you are going to be faced with uniformed military analysis which—while sound—is understandably service driven and will have a certain amount of service self-interest included in whatever they may propose. The secretary ultimately has to deal with that and be able to determine what every component of a service recommendation really contributes in terms of value to deterrence or to lower order conflict resolution or whatever the issue may be. Secretary of Defense Weinberger really could not do that. His own familiarity with defense issues was born of his own service in World War II in the army—patriotic service—dated in time, however; nor was it separately informed by much depth in reading of history or any survey of postwar technological development or collective security history, whether it be NATO, SEATO (Southeast Asian Treaty Organization), CENTO (Central Treaty Organization), or the several alliance relationships. In short, [he had] no very clear grasp of the basic concepts of deterrence, of the ancillary components of doctrine, from sustainability to readiness to force projection. Unless you can deal easily with those several elements in the application of force, you are going to be very vulnerable to service arguments that may express a parochial interest when indeed they are talking about capabilities that are redundant or otherwise suboptimal for achieving your goal. [In sum, the] absence of grasp and of depth in these issues I think accounted for the lack of results at the strategic force modernization level in getting a sensible [ICBM] basing plan that could be promoted to Congress. There was another component too that the secretary must also be a politician. It is quite true. He must be able to go to the Congress and by dint of intellect explain the strategy, the doctrine, and how they correlate to the program you want to buy; he must also be able to do it in a way that is persuasive and succeeds.

We [relied] too much on the mandate [to increase defense spending at the beginning of the Reagan administration]. The mandate clearly was there that the public wanted a renewal of strength; but it provided a big hedge for flabby thinking when you know you have got the money. The flabby thinking is what leads you not to do your homework and to go up to congressional hearings and not be able to defend what you are seeking when criticized by well-meaning people like Sam Nunn who would question, "What is the correlation between the carrier battle groups that you want to buy and deterrence? What kind of war scenario do you envision, and how is it that fifteen, sixteen, twenty, or twelve carrier battle groups make much difference?" If you could not get really informed answers to those kinds of question—informed by history as well as opportunity costs—you are going to lose that struggle. We started losing it in 1981. I say that in the face of clearly increasing defense budgets for 1981, 1982, and 1983, but increasing far less than they might have. By 1983, I estimate we lost $60 billion simply by what the Congress was prepared to endorse when the budget was drafted versus how we ended up. Although we got an increase, we had less of an increase than we might have had. The frustration, I do not think, was fully partisan on the Hill. People I worked with in the Armed Services Committee—Sam Nunn, Scoop Jackson, John Tower—called me regularly and said, "We cannot cope with the way the Pentagon is refusing to engage intellectually on what all this hardware is for. Now it is true, we are all going to vote for it, but this is going to come back to bite you, because people are losing confidence in the intellectual honesty of your defense planners." Both [Democrats and Republicans] were calling to express these complaints as early as 1981. This ineptitude was translated into two formal iterations at trying to modernize strategic forces—specifically with the ICBM leg of the triad—that failed after the Townes Commission and CSB were shot down.

Another truism was emerging that it is going to be awfully hard to get interdepartmental consensus on any political-military policy in the Reagan administration because there was a clear animus extant between the secretaries of state and defense. The difficulty in terms of this process was also reinforced by the [inability to] define a sensible answer in the Department of Defense—by a lack of analytical and political competence that could, in terms of ICBM survivability, define a solution that was politically feasible, and engage in a political setting in the Congress to get it done. Part of that expresses some residual Democratic partisan criticism coming out of the rather abrupt dismissal of the Carter MPS program. There was going to be a cost paid by the ascerbity of the Republican criticism of MPS, but with good-will and analytical soundness, we could have overcome that; but we [had neither], and I knew that of the first two efforts [Townes Commission and CSB].

By the end of 1982 I was at the White House and sat down with National Security Adviser Judge William Clark and said, "We are going to be paralyzed here in forging any political-military policy consensus in our own house until we get Democrats and Republicans to give us two things: political and analytical agreement. We are not going to get it inside the administration; we are going to have to reach outside to do it." I proposed that he bring a commission [the Scowcroft Commission] into existence, and with the failing vote for densepack or CSB in early December of 1982 Judge Clark agreed to this and to Brent Scowcroft [leading it]. I called Brent and he said he would do it . . . We began to get some latecomers [on the commission] who saw that this was an opportunity for the expatriates to contribute usefully: Jim Schlesinger, Donald Rumsfeld, Melvin Laird, David Packard, and others began to help . . . The Scowcroft Commission was a product of my conclusion, by the middle of 1982, that the only way we were going to get something salable to the Congress was to reach out to a bipartisan community and outside the government.

General Scowcroft described his experience as chairman of this bipartisan commission to examine strategic force options for the United States in light of the continuing controversy about the MX and its deployment mode and the Midgetman single-warhead missile.

I do not know why I was asked to head the commission. I assume that Bud McFarlane had something to do with it. I initially turned down the request to head the commission. I agreed to serve on it but said I did not really have time to be chairman. The next day, the *Washington Post* printed that I was going to be the chairman. So, I agreed that if the administration would make a serious and good faith effort to find another chairman (and I gave them two or three names), if they could not find someone, then I would serve as chairman. Whether they tried or not I do not know, but that is how it ended up. I had some, but hardly decisive, influence on the membership of the commission. I did have something to say about the involvement of the former secretaries of state and defense as a kind of advisory body for the group.

The structure was basically wide open. Thomas Reed [a business executive] was the vice chairman, and the representative of the administration on the study. He had some ideas about how to structure it and how to organize the thing, but I had pretty much a free hand in it. The charter, unlike the earlier attempts to solve the issue of the MX, was an open one designed to "tell us what to do," not "what is the best deployment scheme," or "whether this deployment scheme is technologically feasible or not." What do we do with the MX, is basically the question that we were asked.

The commission was composed of people of widely varying relationships to the issue, from people who were immersed in it and had strong ideas about how to solve it and so on, to those who knew virtually nothing about it. The first task, I felt, was to bring everybody up to a level where the issues could be discussed on an equal basis around the table. That gave me the opportunity, I thought, to do what else I felt was important, and that was to avoid staking out positions before all of the data were in. There were a few people who had strong views about what the solution was. Not everybody on the commission supported wholeheartedly the MX, although there was nobody on the commission implacably opposed to the MX. I used the device of bringing everybody up to speed to delay a discussion of the solution to it, while we went into past efforts to solve the problem, the technical issues involved, the nature of the threat to the other elements of the triad which we were also asked to look at.

One of the other major organizational issues that came up was how do we deal with this [whole problem]. We were asked to complete this study in, I think, three months. We eventually took four. Tom Reed's position was that that really was not very much time and we needed to break down into subcommittees to do it. I had a gut feeling that if we did that we were in for a disaster. I opted instead for the commission always to operate as a committee of the whole and we never broke down into subcommittees. Sometimes a couple of people would go out and talk to somebody, some expert here or there, but we never broke down into subgroups, so that everybody had the same kind of information on which to come to a conclusion. The upshot was that by the time we had finished our examination of all of the relevant issues, we had a very strong consensus toward a solution. It was not a difficult job to put together where it was that we wanted to go. It was really amazingly simple, even with people as far apart ideologically as James Schlesinger and Roy Cutler, for example.

On the subject of the inputs to the commission from the departments and agencies of government, General Scowcroft recalled,

> The Department of Defense cooperated very well with us. We got inputs in terms of intelligence, in terms of detailed analyses of silo parameters, for example, of closely spaced basing, the whole issue of crater size and dimensions, including a study of that issue, which the intelligence community was undertaking. Every scheme, good or outlandish, for basing, which anybody within the Department of Defense had submitted to the department or in the defense industry, was examined by us. However, the commission was wholly independent and operated on its own. It had no staff for all practical purposes. We had a staff director, and we had a half-dozen captains who did runner work for us, but we did not have a staff, just people to set up briefings and so on. I kept Secretary Weinberger apprised of what we were doing, and nobody tried to fence us in. Mr. Weinberger and I disagreed quite significantly all the way along, but nobody tried to steer us. I think the commission idea came from the Congress. I think that in the defense report rejecting closely spaced basing there was a requirement to report back to the Congress with a new evaluation or something, and the suggestion that an independent, bipartisan commission might be a way to go about it. That is my recollection.

An issue considered at great length by the Scowcroft Commission was the Midgetman, or the small ICBM. This was a proposed intercontinental ballistic missile that would be mobile in its basing mode and would carry only the nuclear warhead. Scowcroft continued:

> One of the major questions for the small missile was whether or not one could develop a mobile carrier hardened enough to permit it to be based somewhere less than the whole United States. In other words, you needed 30–50 psi hard (pounds per square inch overpressure) per vehicle to allow it to be based, for example, on the larger military reservations in the Southwest, which we felt was an indispensable part of any mobile deployment to avoid public interface. That was an absolutely critical development. Another was how small could you make a small missile. We wanted to keep it as small as possible both to enhance the hardness of the carrier by making it not so bulky, and also to facilitate alternative ways to deploy it which people might think of in the future—helicopters, or whatever—so we got industry to say what is the absolute minimum cost for which you can build one of the carriers.

Asked whether strategic defense played a role in the consensus that the commission was developing, General Scowcroft replied,

> In fact, the president's speech came out on March 23 and our report was released early in April 1983. We looked seriously at strategic defense, not

at population defense, but strategic defense as an alternative to mobility for protection of the ICBM force. We urged a vigorous program of research into it, that it looked farther down the road in terms of point defense rather than the development of a hard, mobile carrier or a small missile, and that, especially, if one were to return to some kind of deceptive basing, that would give you the option for preferential defense, and thus as leverage it made good sense.

When it began its work, General Scowcroft related, the commission encountered a hostile response on Capitol Hill to the Reagan administration's strategic modernization program. According to General Scowcroft the commission failed the challenge of developing a greater understanding of U.S. strategic needs and of building a bipartisan consensus on which effective choices could be based.

One of the other things that we did at the outset was to try to get a solution that would work politically, not just strategically. The mood we found on Capitol Hill at the outset was just terrible, both toward the MX and toward the Defense Department. Indeed, I thought when I first accepted the chairmanship that it was a job to preside over the decent burial of the MX—things were that bad. We undertook a process of cultivating the Congress, both groups and individuals. One of the first people I talked to was Sen. Al Gore, Jr., for example, who had supported this notion of a small missile for a long time. I remember that in our first meeting we got into a big shouting match about the MX. Subsequently, of course, he became one of our strongest advocates. Both to find out what there was on the Hill, what one could do with it, and also to give them the sense that we were really interested in their views, we cultivated the Hill.

Then as we got along and began to know where we wanted to go, we had a series of breakfast meetings in Blair House [the vice president's residence]. Congressmen love breakfast consultations. We would have maybe twenty to thirty congressmen, usually in different groups, like the Armed Services Committee, or the freshmen of the House, and groups like that, and all or most of the commission. While we were eating breakfast we would describe the nature of the problem that we had to face and alternative ways to solve it, and not present a solution, but to try to deal with questions of those who we thought would be favorably disposed to what we knew we were going to come out with. This was not my idea, but I think it was highly effective, and in the end, what we tried to do was to put together a solution to the problem of strategic modernization, which was militarily and intellectually satisfactory, and which politically held out the promise of being able to provide a rallying point for a sufficiently broad consensus, which was an important and urgent problem that needed to be solved.

Everyone had to give a little in order to find a solution to the problem. Nobody could have his way all the time. I think by and large it worked.

There were people who were strong supporters of the MX who did not much care for the small missile but were prepared to acquiesce in the small missile if it saved the MX. There were people who thought the MX a bad idea, the wrong way to go, who thought the small missile was the right way to go, but if it took some MXs to get the administration on the right path of strategic modernization then they were prepared to do it. There were others who thought that the whole route of modernization was not a particularly good idea, that instead we ought to focus on arms control and stop Soviet progress, rather than have progress ourselves, but if going along with some kind of a modernization program would finally get the Reagan administration to engage seriously in arms control then it was worth it. We had these three disparate kinds of groups all agreeing on different parts of what we put together for different reasons, and in fact it was a consensus which got us through appropriations in 1983.

I think that our consensus foundered in the political climate of an election year of 1984, not so much on the merits but really over, I think, Lebanon and the fight between Speaker of the House O'Neill and the president. [Speaker Thomas] O'Neill thought that the president was playing unfair on Lebanon by blaming Congress. O'Neill had not supported our solution on the MX, but had kept hands off and had acquiesced and made sure there would be no Democratic caucus on the issue. We knew if there was a Democratic caucus we would lose it, that we would have party discipline turned against it to get at Reagan. They twisted arms brutally in 1984, and the number of MX procurements got cut back to fifty. Then the administration accused the Congress of violating the compact, and so on. So it worked in part, not wholly, and I think that the consensus is an incipient one, but it is badly bruised at the present time [1988].

It takes unusual circumstances for a commission like this to be effective. It takes an important problem, a consensus that the problem has to be solved, and some pressure or acknowledgment that it has to be solved in a short period of time. With all those conditions then I think it works. You can argue that we were a kind of catalyst—there was an impasse between the executive branch and the Congress on solving the problem. They both knew that the problem had to be solved, and we then gave them something to which both of them could agree. Without all of those elements, though, I think it probably does not work, and I think one of the best other examples is the Central America Commission: important problem, yes; a sense that it had to be solved, yes; time pressure, none. Thus, no one felt constrained to modify his own position in order to meet this kind of deadline. We had a deadline because if there was not a decision on production it was going to start costing the air force big dollars so there was really pressure to resolve it one way or another. There was none of that on the Central America Commission [the 1983 National Bipartisan Commission on Central America, chaired by Henry Kissinger], so there was no particular incentive for anybody to change his views, and without that, on these divisive issues, I think a commission is not going to solve the problem.

Finally, Robert McFarlane provided his account of the Reagan administration's emphasis on arms control verification as evidenced by the decision to develop reports on Soviet compliance with previous U.S.-Soviet agreements.

There was a separate, but important change that occurred under President Reagan in the East-West strategic balance, and it has to do with the adoption of the notion of realism. One of the reasons for the failure of détente was this willingness to paper over Soviet failings, flaws, faults, and crimes, and a willingness not to be realistic about what is true of Soviet leaders. The result is that when you engage with the Soviets as we did in the early to mid-1970s, if you downplay the reality of their system and their way of doing business and put this romantic gloss on it, you weaken your own position vis-à-vis the Soviets. It was very real that under Kissinger we would diminish or really softpedal the truth about Soviet violations of arms control agreements or about the treatment of their own citizens by thinking, I believe, that [he] would thereby engender a more favorable attitude toward the Soviet Union in the Congress and a greater willingness to give them concessions whether in trade bills or anything else. Reagan, to his everlasting credit, disagreed with that. He said, "You must tell it as it is. The Soviets do not respect people who ignore their faults, who tolerate their intimidation. So you strengthen yourself by telling the truth about it."

Therefore, starting in 1983 the Reagan administration began to put out compliance reports on arms control. It was a very agonizing process to do this, but it was very successful. In 1983, at the end of the year, Richard Perle had engineered a law, really; he had gone to the Hill and had people write into, I think, the fiscal year 1983 appropriations bill that the president would report on Soviet compliance with arms control agreements. There have been forty years of agreements and so we began to get to work and analyze this history and come up with breaches and examples of violations—to each of which the State Department would say, "No, they did not," and the Defense Department would say, "Yes, they did." I was chairing this catfight in the NSC and it was terrific. It was the most exhausting work I think I have ever done in my life, but it was just very good policy. We brought all these guys together to hammer out where people stood. The CIA was quite good in this role in being able to say, "Here is the evidence of what happened, here is the language, here are the facts—you make a judgment." CIA data was quite good, and they performed very well. The State Department would say, "If by your recitation of sins you create the image that we are just a bunch of irretrievable flat-earthers who are never going to have anything to do with them, you will have done the wrong thing." I said, "I just do not agree with that. You can say that you sinned at the same time you say sin no more and we can have a treaty with you. But at the end of the day, our system requires that you tell the truth and get on with what is in the national interest." So I tended to tilt more toward the Defense Department on it.

I got all this together and sent it up to the president and said, "Here are thirty cases where there is a question about their performance, and the Pentagon said it is all black and the State Department said, pretty much, that it is all white, and you have to decide; most of the time I think it is black, Mr. President." He came down saying, "Things are pretty black." It took a lot of guts to do that because the allies were saying that that would ruin a chance for harmony—the West German Green party on the Left and the press were assertive factors. But he did it and sent it up in January of 1984. In some place, the punches were a little bit pulled, but not much. I think he judged only six violations of the treaty. The Krasnoyarsk [radar] was one of them, and then there was a family of other defensive technologies where we aggregated them together and said that they are almost certainly violations (that somewhat qualified): relocatable systems, reload possibilities for the ABM system around Moscow, and the testing of radars and the SA-10 and SA-12 [surface-to-air missile systems] ballistic missile mode, that were almost certainly violations of the ABM Treaty. Several others [were included], such as the deployment of the SS-16 as a violation of SALT II. We went through all of these, and it was very solidly backed up. When we sent it up to the Hill and hearings were convened, the Left really could not argue very much with it because the data was there and the people that were standing there [to defend the data]—Richard Perle and the Joint Chiefs of Staff themselves—were competent. They had just gone through twelve weeks of excruciating pain to justify what they were saying, so they went up there loaded for bear and able to defend and promote judgments that were solid. This changed the nature of U.S.-Soviet relations and the way they are viewed by Americans in the Congress and by the allies too. To Reagan's great credit, he began to call a spade a spade. As a consequence, it provided a much more advantageous position as a basis for dealing with the Soviet Union.

17
The China Factor

The accession to power of the Chinese Communist Party in 1949 was followed by a long period of estrangement between the People's Republic of China (PRC) and the United States. The first decade after 1949 was a period of close relations between China and the Soviet Union. In contrast, the 1960s represented a decade of deteriorating Sino-Soviet relations, at the end of which Sino-American relations began to improve. In this chapter several observers of various aspects of China and policies toward China present their perspectives on such issues as the Sino-Soviet rift, the China factor in U.S.-Soviet relations, the Cultural Revolution, Taiwan, and the interests of the PRC.

Rolf Pauls went to China as the first West German ambassador. He recounts discussions with Premier Chou En Lai, with special emphasis on Soviet strategy as viewed from Beijing, and factors leading to the Sino-Soviet conflict:

After we opened relations with the PRC and I was the first ambassador there, I met Chou En Lai. He said, "Mr. Ambassador, you come late, but not too late." He spoke this in German. He spoke about Adenauer and then said, "I heard you were in the delegation in 1955 in Moscow." He asked if it was true that Khrushchev spoke Chinese, and I replied yes. I was standing behind [Secretary of State in the Foreign Office Walter] Hallstein and Adenauer, and Khrushchev said, "Mr. Chancellor, your late emperor wasn't wrong when he warned about the 'Yellow Peril.' " This was an expression of Wilhelm II, which no one else used. Khrushchev said, "Mr. Chancellor, we Europeans must stick together and defend ourselves against the 'Yellow Peril.' " Then Chou En Lai gave me a new and interesting interpretation of the Sino-Soviet conflict. He said that in 1955 the Soviets asked the Chinese about making a combined naval command in the Pacific with Soviet ships guarding the Chinese coastline. With the Soviet advantage in naval strength, the Chinese would have lost their independence, which they felt they had just gained from the West. In 1960 they repeated the offer and, Chou said, that started the conflict. Everything else was negotiable. I was a very interesting guest for the Chinese because I had been to the United States, and they wanted to know how the executive and legislative branches worked.

My Norwegian colleagues in the UN had been interviewed extensively [by the Chinese] on the workings of the UN. They were [also] very well informed about the structure of Soviet society, that the Soviet Union was the most class-status society, traitors to Communism. They admitted, however, that the Soviet economic system did not work for the same reasons the Chinese did not. As far as military matters were concerned, they understood our bilateral approach to the Soviet Union but were against a multilateral approach because it would shift resources against them.

As Ambassador Pauls saw it, the ouster of Khrushchev in October 1964, followed by the emergence of Leonid Brezhnev, seemed only to exacerbate Sino-Soviet tensions. He pointed to the Brezhnev policy of strengthening relations between the Soviet Union and India and the reaction from Beijing:

In fact, the PRC saw Brezhnev's overtures to India as an attempt to encircle China, and this led to Chinese moves toward Pakistan. Especially after Vietnam, they felt confronted with a new set of problems from a regional superpower.

Dean Rusk, as secretary of state during much of the 1960s, sets forth the views of the Kennedy administration on the People's Republic of China, and in particular those of President Kennedy, as Rusk observed them:

When I first joined the administration, President Kennedy and I had a long talk about China. He had in front of him a congressional resolution that had been passed two years earlier, strongly opposing the recognition of the PRC. Just before his inauguration, President Eisenhower told Kennedy that he would try to support him as much as possible on foreign policy questions, but he said he would oppose him over recognizing Beijing and allowing it to join the United Nations. President Kennedy decided that there was not enough advantage to change our China policy. So he told me not to think about changing our policy. I went back to the Department of State, and I did not even tell anyone about our meeting. I always supported the normalizing of relations with Beijing.

Asked about the continued anti-China perspective of the Kennedy and Johnson administrations, Dean Rusk denied that that had been a major part of the equation:

We never substituted China for the Soviet Union as our number one problem. We had in the Kennedy years dealt with Moscow in two very deadly crises, but we set in motion actions to move U.S.-Soviet relations away from open hostility. In the Test Ban Treaty and civil air agreements, we sought to find areas of common agreement which could reduce the range of issues on which violence might occur. With China, getting along with Mao was very difficult. They chose the United States as Enemy Number One. We did not think that they were going to move into Southeast Asia unless we approached their borders by invading North Vietnam. As a matter of fact, there were a number of signs that the Chinese had taken their losses in Korea very seriously. We did not replace the Soviets with the PRC as Problem Number One.

We can be sure that the PRC will act in its own interests without any regard for us. The Chinese see themselves as very special people from a very special civilization. We should work to improve our relations with the Soviets and the Chinese bilaterally and not think that we can manipulate them with the "China card."

The Nixon administration had initiated basic changes in the U.S. relationship with the PRC, leading from President Nixon's historic visit in 1972 to the establishment of full diplomatic relations by the Carter administration in 1979. Gen. Brent Scowcroft, national security adviser in the Ford administration, was an active participant in, and observer of, the policy process in the evolving Sino-American relationship of the 1970s.

I guess the overall preoccupation as we move from the period of détente up into the mid-1970s, and the latter period of the Ford administration, was an increasing sense of a Soviet Union on the move, both in the Third World and in its military programs; of a Congress preventing a U.S. response; of a China hopeful of some help in this period, but still of somewhat uncertain leadership. We did not realize until the end of the administration, I do not think, that the Cultural Revolution in China really was not over.

Asked how well the administration understood the nature of the Cultural Revolution in which China was engulfed at that time (from the late 1960s until the mid-1970s), General Scowcroft replied,

In retrospect you can see what the effect was and the gradual change from the high point of 1972, when Chou En Lai was pretty much in charge and things were going well and our relationship was going well, to the attack on him in 1973 (and also, of course, his illness) and his loss of effectiveness. However, I do not think we had the dimmest understanding of that at the time because, of course, the Chinese said the Cultural Revolution was over. As you look at some of the comments that Mao made in Ford's meeting with him (in November 1975, I guess), they foreshadowed some of the troubles that Deng Xiaoping must have run into. In any case, China was certainly a positive element in our assessment of the world.

General Scowcroft commented on the proposition that the United States, by developing a closer relationship with the PRC, could thereby exert pressure on the Soviet Union, in light of the deeply rooted Sino-Soviet hostility:

> I think our general rule of behavior was that we hoped to have better relations with both China and the Soviet Union than they could have with each other. That was the optimal relationship. There is no doubt that the Soviets were paranoid about the Chinese, and paranoid about the possibilities of a U.S.-Chinese coalition—whatever you want to call it—the Russians brought that up time and time again, how seriously they would view that possibility. I think that we had in mind a much more subtle relationship than subsequently developed; like playing the "China card" against the Soviet Union. We thought that letting the Chinese relationship develop on its own merits would be the best way to produce the satisfactory effects. It was not directly related to the Soviets, but implicitly, yes, it was.

Although the United States had imperfect information and assessments of the Cultural Revolution then sweeping China, in retrospect, according to General Scowcroft, its effects on Sino-American relations were substantial:

> The relationship—again, obviously in retrospect—was all caught up with the Cultural Revolution and with the hazards of being involved in the American relationship, which we did not see at all. We did not think the American relationship played a role here. It did, but we didn't realize that. I think that slowed down the evolution. What we saw were issues like Taiwan rising and declining as important issues between us, although I think Taiwan emerged as a kind of litmus of the state of the relationship. Henry Kissinger went to China in the summer or early fall of 1975 and had extremely difficult negotiations with Deng, almost to the point that we were not going to have President Ford go there. They were largely unrelated to the United States directly; they were instead manifestations of the Cultural Revolution inside China. It seems to me that when it did begin to clear up, which was really not until the Carter administration, then Deng moved very quickly to try to take advantage of the Sino-American relationship. Indeed, for a time, when they really feared the Soviet Union, they almost talked in terms of alliance relationships. That was when they were really scared.

During the 1980 presidential campaign, Ronald Reagan expressed concern about the downgrading of U.S. relationships with Taiwan as the price paid by the Carter administration for the completion of Sino-American normalization. In Reagan's view, the United States should have maintained an official relationship with the Taiwan government. There were indications that, once in office, the Reagan administration might seek to upgrade the U.S. relationship with Taiwan. The result, in the midst of the campaign of 1980 and just after the

Reagan victory, was an escalating rhetorical battle from Beijing concerning its view of the status of Taiwan, acknowledged by the United States and the PRC in the Shanghai Communiqué of 1972, and subsequently to be a part of China. Richard Allen was foreign policy adviser to Mr. Reagan at this time. He discussed the trip that he and George Bush made to China in the summer of 1980 and later events:

The approach to the PRC is interesting because, as you remember, George Bush and I took a trip which I had engineered just after the [Republican] convention in 1980. We went to Beijing where we had an enormous shouting match with Deng Xiaoping in the Great Hall of the People. We had some other sessions over there too. The purpose of going over there was to try to defuse the Taiwan issue once and for all as far as the campaign was concerned, and it succeeded beyond my wildest expectations. Although the trip was judged by the press to be a tactical failure, it was by no means a failure because on the way back I decided we would use this opportunity when Bush reported back to Reagan in Los Angeles to enunciate a simple yet somewhat complicated five-point plan of what the Reagan administration policy toward China would be. We were there in August. When we returned, and I had written this very elaborate statement—it was eight, nine, or ten pages— I gave it to Reagan and I gave it to Bush, who liked it.

The five-point plan's purpose, Allen notes, was largely one of clarification:

The net effect was that it sent a message to the PRC and in effect said, "Do not shout at us anymore. If you shout at us and threaten us, we are not going to forget it. We are not going to break relations with you, and we are not going to establish relations with Taiwan, but we are going to watch out for Taiwan's interests because there is something called the Taiwan Relations Act. It requires the attention of the president of the United States and his fulfilling its conditions because it is a law. It has the force of the Constitution." They tried shouting during the transition. Bush and I went to dinner at the Chinese embassy and the Chinese ambassador tried to keep him captive. After twenty minutes of reading a diatribe after dinner to Bush and to me, through his interpreter, I said, "Excuse me, thank you very much for the nice dinner, we are going home." He said, "You can't; I am not finished with the statement yet." I said, "You do not understand; this is a new era and you are addressing the vice president-elect of the United States, and you are not going to continue talking to him like that." "But I must deliver this message," he said. I said, "Deliver it in writing if you think it is so important. Thank you very much, and good night." And we left. I engineered the first meeting between President Reagan and Zhao Ziang at Cancun; he had never met a real live Chinese leader before, and that led them into a patient dialogue. We just kept telling them to stop shouting, do not shout at us. Everytime they shouted, Haig would say, "You are going to destroy the strategic relationship between China and the United States.'' You are absolutely right, this is a coalition. China is not an ally. We consider it a friendly, nonallied country today, and I consider its policy to be reversible and changeable. Witness only the extent to which Gorbachev is now trying to woo the Chinese, and do not think that that does not offer some modicum of prospective success for Soviet policy if it does. In fact, there never was a Chinese card. I think there is only an American card, and the Chinese and the Soviets can both play it.

18
The Global Role
of the United States

A s a global power, even the United States, under successive administrations, has found it necessary to make important choices about commitments, as well as about the types and levels of capabilities to be developed, deployed, and actually used on their behalf. Although every president necessarily inherits for better or worse the policies pursued by the preceding administration, it nevertheless falls upon each new incumbent in the White House to fashion a national security policy based on a strategy and defined goals. Here, various interviewees share their insights on topics ranging from Eisenhower's defense policy and global strategy to Kennedy's Latin American policy, Carter's proposals for U.S. troop withdrawals from South Korea, U.S. basing rights in the Philippines, and, finally, the impact of U.S. involvement in Vietnam upon NATO commitments, as well as the issue of NATO out-of-area operations. Gen. Andrew Goodpaster discussed the approach to the military component of strategy taken by President Eisenhower:

> In the area of strategy, he was not at all enamored of, or drawn to, brushfire wars. He simply did not intend to get involved and was rather skillful in finding ways of avoiding being drawn into that kind of thing. He had a feeling that if war should come with the Soviet Union, it would be all-out war, in the sense of using everything that we had. But he also felt that it would be absolutely irrational for such a war to occur.

General Goodpaster recalled a meeting early in the Eisenhower administration.

> Eisenhower gave his views on what we should have in the way of strategic bombing forces, air defense, the navy, NATO, and technology. Interestingly, he was rather vague and noncommittal, in the true sense of the term, in avoiding any commitment on actions in what have come to be called the Third World countries. After this meeting, Secretary Charles Wilson [secretary of defense between 1953 and 1957] called me and asked if the president's remarks could be put into a letter to him from Eisenhower, indicating that this would be helpful in an enduring way. I

spoke to the president, and after a grumble or two he said okay, that I should do that. I then drafted the letter and showed it to the people who had been there—at least to the secretary and the JCS chairman [Adm. Arthur W. Radford, 1953–57]. At this point the deputy secretary, as I recall, asked if the part about the Third World countries could be strengthened. So I strengthened it a bit and took it in and drew the president's attention to it, and he immediately took a pencil and lined it out and put back in, almost word for word, what he had said, which avoided this commitment. I made one more try at it—and I can still remember the second time I took it in and showed it to him—and he looked over his glasses at me and said, "Now, Andy, this can either be done your way or my way, and I guarantee you that ultimately it is going to be done my way." And I said, "Mr. President, I think I understand."

General Goodpaster had the opportunity to observe firsthand the evolution of the Eisenhower administration's defense doctrine. Having just extricated the United States from the Korean conflict, President Eisenhower embarked on an approach to defense based on a greater emphasis on nuclear weapons and the avoidance of protracted conventional engagements.

In setting up the military budget, Eisenhower had gone to the so-called New Look. He did not intend to get drawn into brushfire wars or anything of secondary importance, but said that in whatever conflict we did get drawn into, nuclear weapons would be available for use as just another weapon. This was in the early days of his administration. Part of the restructuring of the forces, in particular the limitations put on the army, grew out of that approach. Repeatedly, Admiral Radford, chairman of the Joint Chiefs of Staff, raised the point that if this is not what you mean, then say so, because forces are being structured that do not have the capability of sustained long-term conflict, and repeatedly, in the NSC deliberations and in the budget preparations, it was reaffirmed that that was indeed so. So this was implicit, I think, in successive crises.

Eisenhower's refusal to intervene in Vietnam on behalf of France reflected this approach to U.S strategy.

I learned after I came back to Washington in 1954 of the negotiations that had taken place between Admiral Radford and the French at the time, and between [the United States] and the British. I have never known whether Eisenhower really would have been prepared to intervene had the British agreed to go with us or whether this was the instrument by which he was able to avoid our commitment. He had no desire whatsoever for Americans to be involved in that struggle. The trauma of Korea was still fresh in his mind. We certainly did not want to be involved in it if the French were still in any way trying to maintain control. That was incomplete, but there is only one man who knew—and that is Eisenhower. I do not think

anybody else ever knew and, in any case, the condition which might conceivably have led him to take a positive decision never existed, which was
agreement of the British to join with us, and of the French to give Indochina independence. They never took a clear stand on that issue.

With the accession to power of Fidel Castro in Cuba in the final year of
the Eisenhower administration, Latin America came to occupy a role of increasing importance in U.S. foreign policy. Subsequently, the Kennedy administration sought, through the Alliance for Progress, to promote economic and political stability, and, by means of the quarantine of Cuba during the Cuban missile
crisis, to thwart Soviet strategy by political-military means in the Western
Hemisphere. Dean Rusk, secretary of state during the Kennedy and Johnson
administrations, reflected on the record of the Kennedy administration in support of representative governments in Latin America:

> I have just finished yesterday the calculations, working in the State
> Department library—in five-year periods from 1950 to 1980, there were
> more elected governments in office [in this hemisphere] in 1960 than at
> any other time—fourteen of them. So there were more targets for coups
> than there had been at any other time. In 1975 and 1980, there were six
> elected governments in office. And in 1955 there were only about eight,
> as I recall. But there were fourteen in 1960, and many of them were frag-
> ile, with no previous experience with elected governments. So that the
> Kennedy record is not as bad in historical perspective as it looked at the
> time. Plus, the fact that the Castro threat—and not only that threat, but
> what Castro was doing—was worrying people about the capacity of gov-
> ernments to hold the Communists in check. In addition, there was the fact
> that the Alliance for Progress had a left-of-center focus which had made
> the business community and the military unhappy. So that all these things
> were rather unusual pressures on what was a very unstable political soci-
> ety, an instability which goes back to Spain.

Edwin Martin was assistant secretary of state for inter-American affairs
under President Kennedy. He pointed to another difficulty in relations
between the United States and its hemispheric neighbors to the south:

> These people had never voted in an election; what was a mayor, what was
> a governor—the words did not mean anything to them. We had a contract
> with a Texas university, and they did drawings for illiterates on the elec-
> tion business, providing thereby a whole set of guidelines by color of the
> candidate's party. These were things that politically inexperienced and
> illiterate people could absorb. It was a necessary thing that just had to be
> done to prepare for this. I think it is hard to imagine how difficult it is
> to mount an honest election with people who have had no experience of
> what the word means. You also had some real problems with getting a

reflection of popular will when you have large numbers of people excluded.

As examples, he pointed to Brazil and Equador:

In Brazil, illiterates, which were at least one-third of the population, did not have the right to vote. For a long time women did not have the right to vote unless they held jobs of a certain kind. In Equador, they tried to take a census for laying out electoral areas and up in the highlands they shot the census takers because they thought they were out for revenue or conscripts. There is a backwardness to some of these areas that people who have only been to Rio or São Paulo cannot imagine.

Finally, he noted the shift that took place with the Johnson administration:

When Murat Williams was the ambassador to El Salvador [1961–64] he did a superb job of contacting the agents-of-change in accordance with Kennedy's slogan, "The only alternative to violent revolution is peaceful change." When Lyndon Johnson became president, the edict was: "The current power structure can best serve U.S. interests." Nothing much was done about population and related matters. And that is why we are where we are in Central America, in my judgment, to a very considerable extent.

David Newsom was under secretary of state for political affairs in the Carter administration. He outlined his concept of the post and the scope of U.S. responsibilities:

The under secretary for political affairs had been a post held by a Foreign Service officer. The secretary of state used that position in different ways. Henry Kissinger used Joseph Sisco [1974–76] pretty much as a high-level special assistant working on some of the same problems that Kissinger himself was working on, and to some extent Cyrus Vance in the first year did the same with Philip Habib. I conceived of the job as a kind of utility infielder on the seventh floor [of the State Department] following those things that the secretary was not following. I felt that if I could relieve his plate of some of the multitude of crises that it would be a benefit to him. So, for much of the period that I was there, I was shifting attention from one crisis to another, to do as much as I could to relieve both the secretary and Warren Christopher, the deputy secretary, of some of their responsibilities.

Newsom observed that U.S. foreign policy, if it is to be effective, must operate simultaneously on several levels:

When I came in, we were in the midst of the ratification of the Panama Canal Treaty. SALT II ratification lay just ahead, and Cy Vance spent a lot of time on that. Warren Christopher was the principal manager of the Panama Canal Treaty ratification. In Central America, if I recall correctly, the civil war had already started in Nicaragua, and in the summer of 1978, saw the beginning of the end of Somoza, and had the beginning of stirrings of discontent from Iran.

In addition to southwest Asia, and Iran in particular, the United States retained vitally important strategic interests in the Korean peninsula. Nevertheless, President Carter, as a presidential candidate in 1976, had committed himself to the withdrawal of U.S. ground forces from South Korea. Within and outside the Carter administration, this decision, never actually carried out, occasioned considerable debate and controversy. Gen. John Vessey, then United Nations commander in Korea, described the differences in the administration on the troop withdrawal issue:

> We had had a session that morning with Vance and Brzezinski and the president, again going over the withdrawal business. Both Brown and Brzezinski were opposed to the withdrawal. This was not the time to withdraw for Brzezinski in particular, and Harold Brown. I think Vance was a little more neutral, but Brown and Brzezinski sided with me. The president said, "When can we withdraw? If we cannot withdraw now, when can we withdraw?" I told the president that, in my view, if you looked at the broader strategic situation—the situation vis-à-vis the United States, the Soviet Union, and China, and where Japan and Korea were located geographically and strategically, and if Kim Il-Sung came down and kissed Park Chung Hee on both cheeks and told him that he was now a reformed democrat and capitalist—that he, the U.S. president, would still have to keep his forces on the peninsula because of our broader strategic role in the region.
>   The [South] Koreans, no matter how hard you tried to explain it to them, just could not see that anything good could possibly come from President Carter's decision. And it upset things inside the Park administration to the point where some were saying, "To hell with the Americans, you cannot trust them anyway; we are going to have to do this ourselves." The nuclear issue, whether or not to go nuclear, was clearly an option that they were keeping open. They had people who were working that problem. There was a chance that the Koreans would drift farther away from us and become more and more of a problem for the United States.

General Vessey pointed to a meeting he had with officials of the People's Republic of China as an example of the broader strategic setting of which the U.S. military presence in South Korea was a part.

> The Chinese said to me, "We will not support an attack by the North, and we will do all we can to prevent it, but if the North is attacked from the South, we must support the North, and we will support the North." I said

that that is a perfectly understandable position because it is almost exactly the same position that we are in. We will not support an attack by the South on the North, but as I told the Chinese chief of staff, "If the North attacks the South, we will destroy them, and he needs to understand that." And he said, "I do understand."

In support of its interest in and beyond the Asian-Pacific area, the United States has maintained an overseas basing infrastructure, of which the military facilities at Subic Bay and Clark Air Force Base in the Philippines are an important component. David Newsom, who was U.S. ambassador to the Philippines between 1977 and 1978, offered reflections on the political-psychological problems confronting the United States in the late twentieth century in preserving access to such installations:

> My feelings regarding the basing issue with [Ferdinand] Marcos, and perhaps with the [Corazon] Aquino government too, is that there remains a desire to terminate the agreement because it is viewed as the remaining symbol of American "imperialism." Juxtaposed to this is the desire of others in the Philippines to perpetuate the American connection based on the large number of Filipinos who have relocated to the United States. Paradoxically, however, Philippine politicians have often found it good rhetorical material to attack the American presence in public, all the while hoping that the demands will never really come to anything. There is more substantial support in the Philippines for the retention of those bases. I believe that resolution of the bases issue will inevitably affect our negotiations with the Philippine government. My impression of Marcos was that he was where he was because he was still the smartest and most astute politician in the Islands. He had a way of orchestrating the political process so that he was seldom seriously challenged. Benigno Aquino was imprisoned while I was there, and I was instructed several times to try to see Marcos to get him released. I would always get a sympathetic response: "Aquino is my friend but he has violated the law and we can't have the law violated." This was balderdash, of course, but Marcos was a very shrewd, astute man who, with Americans, took refuge in a legal approach. Mrs. Marcos was a disaster as far as I was concerned, because she was demanding. If you did not bow to her every whim, your relations with her were not very good. I think I established poor relations with her quicker than anybody before me because we had to turn down a couple of her invitations. I had the impression that Marcos was not bothered by that.

From time to time the United States has faced formidable problems reconciling its interests, capabilities, and commitments in one part of the world with those in another region. At no time was this difficulty more apparent than during the Vietnam War. The United States encountered opposition—official and otherwise—within the Atlantic Alliance to its policies in Vietnam. However, the United States was not without its supporters, including Joseph Luns, then foreign minister of the Netherlands:

> I thought the United States was right. The unfortunate thing is that it lasted too long for the Americans. The Americans are not accustomed to not having a 100 percent victory, so the internal support was dwindling. Your losses were very moderate. All your losses were less than one year's car accidents in the United States—I think about 55,000 killed. Yet, think of our postwar campaign in the [Dutch East] Indies—which lasted for over a year and half—and cost us about 35,000 casualties, of whom about 30,000 were Indonesians in our army. We killed off, I think, about 70,000 or 80,000 Indonesians. A big mistake of America was to allow the press on the battlefield. When we were fighting the gangs of Sukarno, we never allowed the press or the film people near the combat scene. Never. But when the public saw those horrors in Vietnam, it made a tremendous impression. War is always an awful thing.

Gen. Franz-Josef Schulze was a NATO staff officer throughout the 1960s. He observed the following result in Europe of the escalation of U.S. military operations in Vietnam:

> The reasons for concern became obvious very quickly, with the ever growing threat of American force reductions in Europe [and] the decline in quality of [U.S.] personnel over here.

Kai-Uwe von Hassell, who served as West German defense minister from 1963 to 1966, assessed the credibility of the United States elsewhere in the aftermath of the Vietnam War:

> U.S. credibility before Vietnam was not in dispute. As Vietnam went on and after Vietnam, the credibility of the United States in general was greatly diminished. Lebanon, for instance, never really could rely on the United States after Vietnam. The United States had security treaties with some forty states around the world and gave them guarantees in case of an attack. This credibility was questioned, but not as regards Europe. This is different. In Europe, it is their freedom which is at stake here. If the Soviets march into Europe, then there is an immediate danger to the United States. The freedom of Europe is of paramount interest to the United States.

According to Ambassador Luns, opposition in Western Europe (especially among elements of the Left) to the Vietnam War a generation ago had its counterpart in the 1980s in hostility toward the Reagan administration's Central America policy:

The American involvement in Central America was being criticized strongly by left-wing parties, not by right-wing parties. It is of course generally accepted that NATO and the European countries have no say in the matter. We can only comment on it. It is also a fact that the United States very fully informed its allies of NATO about the Grenada expedition. This was generally applauded. There are various opinions on Nicaragua and Honduras, but I belong to those who believe the United States is absolutely right not to allow Cuban-inspired, Communist dictatorships too near the home frontier. And the domino theory has some worth. When one falls, the other falls.

With specific reference to the Middle East, Dr. Luns offered a perspectiv on his advice to the United States in building support for its "out-of-area" policies among alliance members:

> The Middle East lies outside the [area of] responsibility of NATO. But of course we discussed it at great length but we did not have to make decisions. I always said to the Americans, "Do not ask NATO to do something; approach the individual countries, most of them will agree." Great Britain and the French took action in the [Arabian-Persian] Gulf, and therefore there was no real problem. But the American government does not always quite understand that they themselves bear a great deal of responsibility for the fact that Europe has so little influence outside Europe.

Asked whether he supported the decision of the Netherlands government in 1987 to send ships to the Arabian-Persian Gulf, Luns replied,

> We also put strong pressure on the Belgians, who finally did it too. We said, you may command the squadron, which they are very proud of because the Belgian navy is about one-seventh the size of the Dutch navy.

Part V
Crisis Management and National Security Decision Making

The final part of this book focuses upon international crises and the crucial decisions made during them to attempt to manage or control events and responses by adversaries. At core, a crisis is a turning point in the relations between or among states which invariably has far-reaching ramifications for the future. Chapter 19 sets the tone for part V by describing the nature of crisis situations through the firsthand accounts of key people in key positions during actual crises. The long-term effects of crises, their impact upon the U.S. president and upon decision-making structures, and the human element during crises are detailed in these pages. With these broad observations concerning the nature of crises in mind, the following four chapters provide insight into numerous specific crisis cases. Chapter 20 covers various Middle East crises, including the Suez crisis of 1956, the October War of 1973, the fall of the shah of Iran in 1979, and the U.S. involvement in the Lebanese imbroglio from 1982 to 1984. In chapter 21, the single case of the Dominican Republic crisis and the ensuing intervention by U.S. forces in 1965 is recounted in detail. Next, chapter 22 addresses the Hungarian crisis of 1956, the Berlin crisis of 1959, the Soviet intervention in Czechoslovakia in 1968, and the Polish crisis of 1981. Finally, in chapter 23 a key participant speaks about the Congo crisis of 1960–64 in which the United Nations was heavily involved.

19
The Nature of Crisis

The history of U.S. foreign policy and diplomacy, especially since the end of World War II, has been punctuated by crises, some of which have been between the United States and the Soviet Union, while others have had as their locus third parties in which one or both of the superpowers has had a greater or lesser interest. Some crises, including such superpower crises, have been periods of acute tension that have been deescalated without actual resort to military action. Other crises have resulted in war between the contending parties. Crises can be studied and analyzed from the perspective of the events immediately precipitating them or in a broader context that assesses background variables. In this chapter, the focus is upon how crises may have long-term effects outside the immediate zone of confrontation, the impact crises have upon the U.S. president and upon decision-making structures, and the human element during crises.

Crises can have longer-term effects outside the immediate zone of confrontation. Such is the context in this chapter for discussion of three different crises. The impact of the Six-Day War of 1967 in the Middle East had direct implications for the fall of the Libyan monarchy. The Greek-Turkish crisis of 1974 was a recent manifestation of a longstanding feud that continues to affect U.S. legislation and NATO cohesion. The *Mayaguez* crisis of 1975 can be seen as an outgrowth of the Vietnam War, since it occurred in the aftermath of South Vietnam's collapse following the withdrawal of U.S. forces.

To begin with, David Newsom described the Libyan setting of the late 1960s from his vantage point as U.S. ambassador to Libya:

> Libya is a country divided into three quite distinct provinces. There is a feeling of xenophobia in Libya arising from the Italian occupation as well as from the fact of a history of foreign wars being conducted on Libyan soil. Particularly in eastern Libya, in Cyrenaica, there is a strong, residual Arab feeling among many Libyans. As in any other Arab country, but perhaps tempered by a lack of direct involvement in the Arab-Israeli issue, there is a high level of emotionalism against the West. King Idris was forced on the Libyans as part of the independence arrangements after

World War II. He was not a Libyan. He was born in Algeria. He was chosen because he was the head of the Senussi movement, which gave him a certain caché in Libya. He had lived in Cairo for forty years and was much more comfortable there than he was in Libya. He did not have a single Libyan in his personal entourage at Tobruk. He had an Italian couple and two Palestinian women who were his secretaries. So there was a built-in distance between the old man and the Libyans which he bridged only occasionally when he got interested in something that was going on in the country.

As a result there was always a certain vacuum in Libya that was in danger of being filled by somebody else. Another element was that Idris had been born into the ruling family of the Senussi Order. As a child of eleven [years of age] he had been given another child (of another family) as his kind of aide, slave, and companion. His name was Ibrahim al-Shalhi, and he followed Idris to Libya when he became king. In 1952 al-Shalhi was assassinated by a relative of the queen, and Idris (who had only one son—who died in childhood—by a very early marriage) had no issue of his own. There was a nephew, a rather unimpressive man named Mohammad al-Rida who was crown prince, but Idris preferred to accept the al-Shalhi family as his own. Idris was fairly active in ruling the country in the early 1960s.

As Ambassador Newsom recalls, strains in the relationship between the United States and Libya appeared in the mid-1960s:

One of the issues that always periodically came up was that of Wheelus Air Base. We had a U.S. Air Force facility and a practice aircraft gunnery and bombing range about 25 miles west of Tripoli. Periodically, there would be some political demonstrations against the base, in part because it was right in the heart of an expanding Tripoli and you had aircraft taking off over population centers. You can understand their displeasure to some extent. So in 1966 we renegotiated and exchanged notes in which the United States agreed, in principle, to withdraw from Wheelus sometime in the future. At that time, the British also had a base in Tobruk.

The 1967 Six-Day War between Israel and its neighbors, I believe, was the beginning of the end for Idris. The country went into a state of trauma. Nasser was extremely popular, and his defeat was a tremendous psychological blow in Libya. You have heard stories like those about the printers who refused to set type until the editor of the paper came in and played a tape of Nasser's cease-fire speech. We evacuated all the American nonessential personnel and dependents out of Libya, and for about three months no Libyans would speak to us. With the agreement of the commanding general, U.S. Air Force, Europe, we stopped flight operations out of Wheelus. After a couple of weeks we decided to resume them on a test basis to see what would happen and picked two planes to take off one day. Nothing happened, and the next day a few more planes took off, until gradually operations were normalized. However, the Libyans deeply resented this, and it rubbed off on the United States because if you remember there was the so-called big lie that the United States had helped to provide air cover to the Israeli Air Force in bombing Cairo during the 1967 war.

Typical of this kind of resentment is a story about the governor of the Bank of Libya, who was a good friend of mine. He was an Arab, educated in Italy. One day, a couple of months after the Arab-Israeli war had ended, I passed him in the street—we had not seen each other for some time—and I said hello. He responded, so I answered that I would like to come and call on him at the bank. He said, "No, I will come and call on you tomorrow night at your garden." So he came and we sat in the garden, and I will always remember what he said to me. "I know it is hard for you to understand the reaction in Libya, but just because I accept in my head that you did not support Israel's attack on Egypt, in my heart, there is a different feeling. The humiliation is too great; to think that 2 million Jews whom we always considered second-class citizens could defeat 80 million Arabs." That was that. I cite all of this because I think that Libya before Khadafi has to be understood to understand Khadafi's rise to power and his actions. Khadafi, in a kind of bizarre way, is an embodiment of some of the more extreme manifestations of this rather strange, isolated, xenophobic people.

Ambassador Newsom elaborated on the impact of the Six-Day War on the fall of King Idris and the rise of Colonel Khadafi to power in Libya:

In the two years after the war, before the overthrow, Idris apparently lifted all constraints on the al-Shalhi family. There were five members of the al-Shalhi family. One had been killed so there were four. One was in the Libyan military, and the others were in business and became the middlemen for outside oil interests getting into Libya. They began to throw their weight around in the civil service and make themselves unpopular. Their unpopularity rubbed off on the king. We had always assumed, in the planning for events in Libya, that the Cyrenaicans would defend the king if there was ever a move against him. But the excesses of the al-Shalhi family, among other things, I think, really undermined the position of the king so that when anybody moved against him, nobody was really prepared to raise a hand to defend him. Before I left in July of 1969, I remember I went around and called on the principal political figures. Subsequently I wrote a final message to the department saying that I have the feeling that there is genuine malaise in this country and that something could happen to its leadership, but it is impossible to say from what quarter it might come. We did have fragmentary intelligence about groups plotting in the army, but we never had anything that mentioned Muammar Khadafi.

At the time of the coup that brought Khadafi to power, a political vacuum existed in Tripoli. Ambassador Newsom described the takeover in 1969 by Khadafi and his supporters:

272 • *National Security Decisions*

It is important to understand the vacuum because Khadafi had, I think, something like seventy men and forty armored cars which moved from the base, 140 kilometers east of Tripoli, into Tripoli through military road-blocks, and took over the city without any real opposition. The king was in Turkey, and we did not know who was in charge in Libya because Khadafi did not emerge as the central figure for about two weeks after-wards. In its first appearance, the revolution did not look too bad because the prime minister was a young Libyan who had been a lawyer for Esso (now Exxon), Dr. Suleyman Maghrabi, and there were other moderate people in the administration that was initially announced. Then, of course, they were all swept aside ultimately. That is the Libyan story.

As President Ford's national security adviser, Gen. Brent Scowcroft had the opportunity to observe, and to contend with, the political pressures unleashed by the Greek-Turkish crisis of 1974. The Ford administration found it neces-sary to cope with the vicissitudes of American domestic politics, including the Greek-American community, as well as demands upon U.S. policy within the Atlantic Alliance.

The crisis came at an extremely difficult time for the United States. It started a couple of weeks before Nixon resigned. Initially, we decided to let the British take the lead in trying to negotiate the difficulties between the Greeks and the Turks. It did not work. We invested enormous time and effort to try to seek a way out of the impasse on Cyprus because it was beginning to do material damage—both to the alliance, where the debates in the Atlantic Council were getting very acrimonious, and also domes-tically. One of the things we found out, which we had not known before, is that the Greek lobby was one of the strongest in Congress. We simply had a terrible time continuing aid to Turkey. I think there was no more intense lobbying effort on any issue that President Ford undertook with Congress. We had many congressional breakfasts. I think he probably had the whole Congress down at one time or another in fairly large groups. There would be a technical briefing by the Department of Defense on the role of Turkey in the alliance and its contribution to our own security, with its facilities that are made available to us and could not be duplicated anywhere else. The president ended up with a passionate plea for continu-ing aid to Turkey. When the vote was taken on suspending aid to Turkey, we had on our side the congressional leadership of both houses—the House and Senate leadership, and the committee leadership—and lost it decisively. The Greeks had one powerful lobby. We simply did not make any significant progress.

   The problem is not over to this day. It is now slightly below the sur-face, but Turkish aid is in trouble again. We cannot give Turkish aid with-out it being tied to a formula for giving Greece aid. It is a very difficult issue. I do not know whether we could have done it any other way. We were certainly surprised by the Cyprus invasion. Perhaps we should not have been, but it had not been a preoccupying issue. I do not know whether we could have done any better than we did. It is an important issue. It was important then, and it still is.

General Scowcroft also commented on the effect that U.S. policy, resulting from the anti-Turkish vote of the Congress, had on the alliance and on the domestic situation in Greece and Turkey:

> I think it probably helped to create the domestic problems that the Turks had thereafter. Probably it facilitated the anti-Americanism in Greece as well. It was a very difficult issue. I do not know what we could have done differently except perhaps not have taken a back seat to the British in the original negotiations to try to resolve it, but we did not have any brilliant ideas for resolving it. It might have gone somewhat better. The Greek Cypriot majority's suppression of the Turkish Cypriot minority had pre-cipitated the Turkish action in invading Cyprus and partitioning it between the Turkish and Greek populations. There was little leverage that the United States could bring to bear against the Turks, I suppose, under the circumstances, and certainly not much against the Greeks.
>
> It was a crisis in which we were severely limited in our ability to effect a positive outcome either way. We were just enormously frustrated by it. Whatever we tried to squeeze out of one party, the other would be unrequited by the other and so on. It was an extremely frustrating issue to deal with. Yet, it did produce the downfall of the authoritarian regime of the colonels in Greece. Until Papandreou, we had a fine Greek govern-ment. So there was that gain on the mainland of Greece at least, I suppose. I think that the colonels, who obviously had been aiding and abetting this coup, were discredited. For at least the short term, or perhaps for the long term, it produced an improvement, certainly in Greek domestic politics, but I am not sure whether it led to a growth of anti-Americanism on the grounds that we were insufficiently attentive to Greek concerns on Cyprus, which they think of as a Greek island.

General Scowcroft discussed the *Mayaguez* crisis, in which a container ship by that name was seized by Cambodian forces in 1975, and against which the Ford administration responded rapidly and decisively:

> I heard about it when I first got in to the office in the morning, at about 7:00 A.M. I mentioned it to the president when I briefed him about 7:30 A.M. and said we do not know whether this is fact or fiction, but if it is true, it could be a serious problem. At that time, Kissinger had a standing appointment with the president, I think, at 9:00 A.M. By 9:00 A.M. it appeared clear that there had been some kind of a seizure, so the president asked for an NSC meeting, which convened at about 11:00 A.M. The whole *Mayaguez* situation was a unique case for the NSC itself, which pretty much handled the crisis. There were no sub-

committee meetings. The NSC met three or four times in the course of a couple of days, and in fact resolved the crisis itself. It was a very interesting illustration. I think that by the time of the NSC meeting it had become clear that the ship had been seized by Cambodian military forces.

There were two principal considerations among those of us who felt deeply about the *Mayaguez*. The first was a perception of the U.S. role in Asia as a result of the evacuation of Phnom Penh and Saigon. What we feared was a presumption that the United States was withdrawing from Asia, and that this was an opportunity to demonstrate that we still had interests in Asia, and that even though we were out of Southeast Asia we were still a force and a power in the Pacific. The second concern was to avoid a repetition of the *Pueblo*, when we allowed the crew of the *Pueblo* to be taken off the boat and dispersed to somewhere in North Korea where we could not find them. [In January 1968 the American intelligence vessel USS *Pueblo* was seized by the North Koreans, ostensibly for violating their territorial waters.] So those two things were really what motivated the president and the NSC.

Nevertheless, there were a lot of different opinions about how to do things, but what we wanted to do militarily, if we could, was to prevent the crew from being taken off the ship and moved to the Cambodian mainland. So, early on we tried to isolate the ship from the mainland. One of the first options that we implemented, when we had some military force there, was to interdict traffic between the mainland and the island. It was very hard to know what was going on. We had very inadequate intelligence. We suffered from the fact that there was a twelve-hour time difference, and that when we were ready to go to bed it was just becoming daylight over there. That was hard to get accustomed to. We had no forces in the area able to do anything useful in a situation like this. We had some modest forces in Thailand, and a naval task force on its way from the Philippines to Australia, and, of course, we had marines in Okinawa.

We asked the Defense Department to assemble a task force, and they moved as quickly as they could into the area. We did what we could, first to locate where the ship was. At one point we thought the ship was heading for Kompong Som, Cambodia, and I actually called the president out of bed to authorize an employment of some fighters to try to divert the ship from going into Kompong Som. When it had stopped at Koh Tang island, we tried to interdict it. We sank quite a few boats in the course of our action. We were assembling the task force, which was composed of air force helicopters from Vietnam, a navy task force on its way to Australia, and marines from Okinawa—but these units had never worked together and before they could get to the area, some of the crew had been moved.

General Scowcroft details the rescue plan as it developed:

Our plan was to rescue the crew before it was moved to the mainland. This was to be accompanied by an assault on the mainland against enemy airfields and points of embarkation, and so on. This was a controversial issue within the NSC relating to the demonstrated use of U.S. power. We had not the foggiest notion that Koh Tang island was so heavily garrisoned. This was because there was a struggle between the Vietnamese and the Cambodians over control of these islands. There was no visible evidence and our reconnaissance people did not know, in fact, that the Cambodians had reinforced the island—not against us, but against a fear that the Vietnamese were going to assault it. The Department of Defense wanted more time, another day. We were afraid, again from the *Pueblo* case, that we simply had to move as quickly as we could. We told them they could not have another day, and we actually launched the first strike at a range that, if the aircraft carrier had stopped, the aircraft could not get back to it. In other words, they were at their extreme range, counting on so much travel on the way back to get back in. We did not notify the Congress until we had decided on the course of action, at which time the president called them down and told them what we were going to do. In addition, we had tried to forestall any such act in communicating with the Chinese through the UN to the Cambodians. We know that the Cambodians got the message.

An interesting example of modern command and control was while in an NSC meeting, I got a call from the National Command Center (NCC), which had had a call from the pilot who was traversing the straits to interdict them. The NCC said that the pilot reported that he had intercepted a motor boat. He had strafed it to try to turn it around, but he was unable to do so, and he was about to attack it when he saw what he thought were some Caucasians in the front of the boat, and he was asking for instructions. So, I went back in to the president and said, this is the situation, the question is whether or not this is the crew, or part of the crew. What do you want the pilot to do? The president said, "Have him strike as close to the boat as he can, but do not sink it." It turned out that it was the crew. Here is the president communicating with a fighter pilot out on a mission during a crisis situation.

The boat was headed to the mainland, and in fact we did not know it at the time, but the crew had been moved to the mainland. We thought some of them were still on the ship and the rest of them had been moved to Koh Tang island. So our assault was on the ship and on the island. We took the ship without any problems at all. We had a hell of a time with the island. We were under murderous fire and we could not communicate well. We had a command and control aircraft, a C-47, but it could not communicate with the marines. So, it was a very difficult military operation. I think that, in fact, the ship was not seized as a deliberate act of the Cambodian government and that the Chinese told the Cambodians not to get involved in this. Then, as you may recall, there was a radio message that was intercepted which suggested that the crew was about to be freed. It took place while the first-strike aircraft were on their way. We debated whether or not to recall the aircraft but we decided to proceed. We actually planned three strikes on the mainland, only one of which actually took place.

Increasingly, in crises since the Vietnam War, the Congress has played a role of considerable importance. The *Mayaguez* crisis, occurring shortly after enactment of the War Powers Resolution, provides an example of executive-congressional relations during crisis situations. General Scowcroft described the congressional reaction to the *Mayaguez* incident, as well as lessons learned from this experience:

> Subsequently, Sen. Mike Mansfield said, this was not a consultation, this was a notification, and there was rumbling that in fact we had violated the War Powers Act. However, in meetings there was not much grumbling and there was not any overt opposition. I guess that on the whole it was a successful operation. It was very difficult militarily because we did not have the needed forces in the area. We patched together a very haphazard task force. It certainly accomplished what we wanted, that in the larger sense we were still a force to be reckoned with in Asia, even though we had withdrawn from South Vietnam. The *Pueblo* simile did not work, because we were not able to isolate the crew, but I think it made sense to try.
>
> We succeeded in resolving the crisis far more quickly than the *Pueblo* crisis was resolved. It was a success compared to the *Pueblo*. Again, we were lucky. If the Cambodians had said, no, we are not going to release these people and every time you bomb us we are going to kill one or two of them, we would have been in a very, very difficult position. So we were lucky. But it seemed to me that the policy objectives were correct and that we used the best means we had at hand to accomplish those. There was not a breakdown of communications among the military. Instead it was incompatible equipment that created problems for us. You had naval forces with their own equipment, the marines with their own equipment, the air force with its own equipment, and a command and control aircraft, a "leftover" from Vietnam, where it was communicating with army troops on the ground, not with marine troops on the ground. To me it is a great object lesson on the necessity for interoperability in our military forces, because you never can tell when you might need to rely on a combined arms unit. Actually, I think the military did fairly well, considering everything.

The significant problem, contended General Scowcroft, was the tendency toward centralization that instantaneous communications had made possible:

> There is no question but that there is a dichotomy between the need for the president to manage these sorts of things, and the utility of the man on the scene being told what it is he is supposed to do and then letting him do it. As a military man, of course, I am attracted to the latter. As a practical matter, however, as I watch what is involved in these isolated kinds of military situations—I am not talking about a general conflict or anything—the president's political neck is on the line. As a matter of course,

he is going to be very reluctant to leave in the hands of some unknown military commander decisions which could have a great impact on his political well-being. Therefore, the military has to expect that it is going to be subject to intense scrutiny in carrying out crisis interventions. Whether it is optimally the better way to do it is almost beside the point—very few presidents are casual on this point. President Reagan perhaps is as relaxed about it as any I have seen. An incumbent president is simply not going to leave these things up to the vagaries of the local U.S. military commander.

Ambassador Tapley Bennett further highlighted this tendency during crises toward centralized decision making by describing the use of "special missions":

Well, there is a great propensity in Washington to send out special missions during a crisis, and now also in normal times. It is hard to say whether the ambassador's role is enhanced. He is the man whose name is on all of the cables as the crisis builds. On the other hand, he has got all those extra people who are suddenly flooding in.

My reporting as ambassador kept going, and my recommendations kept being looked at and acted on right through all of this no matter whether the national security adviser or the under secretary of defense, or the under secretary of state was there on the spot. Obviously, their opinions would have weighed more; they were senior Washington policymakers.

Nonetheless, Bennett encouraged such activity during crises:

You would want the key players from the other parts of the decision-making structure to see the crisis firsthand. I think that is useful in a major crisis; and our government has grown so big, I accept that you must have several people representing the different players. That is here to stay, I am sure.

Finally, Adm. Thomas Moorer, who served as chief of naval operations in the Johnson administration and subsequently as chairman of the Joint Chiefs in the Nixon administration, emphasized the human element in crisis decision making:

I hold that it is not the structure that determines the outcome of crises, but rather it is the people. It depends on whose ego is at risk, who feels he has been found to be wrong, who tries to evaluate the current events according to his political ambitions. I have been struck with that from the outset. For instance, the Constitution says the president is the commander-in-chief. I learned this in the ninth grade. But when you have a situation where the secretary of defense and the president do not agree, then the president (as Nixon did) goes directly to the chairman of the JCS and says, "I am the commander-in-chief, you do this." Then, when the secretary of defense saw this, he would become angry and I would have to tell him to call the president. So the system is caught up with who happens to be in the job at the moment. I cannot emphasize that too much. The structure is violated continuously.

20
Middle East Crises

I n many of the crises that have erupted in the Middle East since World
War II, the United States has had a direct interest. Until the mid-1950s,
however, it was Britain and France which had major military forces committed to the region. The failure of Britain and France in the Suez crisis of 1956
symbolized the decline of British and French influence in the Middle East. By
the same token, the enunciation of the Eisenhower Doctrine in 1957, the successful landing of U.S. forces in Lebanon in 1958, the de facto alliance between
the United States and Israel, and the vital significance of Persian-Arabian Gulf
oil all reflected the growing importance attached to the region by the United
States. By the early 1970s the West, as well as Japan, had become increasingly
dependent on oil from the Persian-Arabian Gulf states, thus adding yet another
dimension to the individual and collective interests of industrialized and
energy-dependent states in the region.

The Six-Day War of 1967, together with the October War of 1973, pitted
Israel against its neighbors. In the case of the 1973 conflict the United States
decided to mount a massive military resupply effort to Israel and, subsequently, to play an important role (after Israeli forces had pushed west of the
Suez Canal) in achieving a cease-fire and disengagement of forces. Upon this
diplomacy of the Nixon administration, and in particular the work of Henry
Kissinger, the Carter administration built the Egypt-Israel Peace Treaty and
the Camp David Accords between Egypt and Israel in 1978.

For the United States, the 1980s represented another series of crisis challenges emanating from the Middle East. The fall of the shah in 1979, the rise
of the anti-Western, Islamic fundamentalist regime in Tehran headed by Ayatollah Khomeini, the seizure of American hostages in the U.S. embassy compound (held hostage until the Reagan administration came to office), the conflicts in Lebanon (including the Israeli invasion in 1982 and the bombing of the
U.S. Marine Corps barracks in 1983), and various terrorist acts mounted by
groups under the direction of the Iranian government—all these created formidable problems for the Reagan administration. The Iran-Iraq War, which
lasted for more than eight years and produced more than 1 million casualties,

together with the multinational naval operation in the Persian-Arabian Gulf (initiated by the United States and supported by several NATO-European allies), formed yet another dimension of the commitment of outside powers in light of their interests in the region.

Ambassador David Newsom drew upon his extensive experience at various levels of the U.S. Foreign Service to describe the Suez crisis. He offered insights into its origins and into the unfolding controversy and mounting tension between the United States and Britain:

> There was an interesting prelude to the Suez crisis in a little-known Anglo-American confrontation over an oasis in southeastern Arabia called Buraimi. In that part of the desert, there were really no boundaries or hegemony over this oasis. A village was really determined by the desert ruler to whom the village paid its tax. There were nine villages in Buraimi, some of which owed allegiance to the sheik of Abu Dhabi, some to the sultans of Muscat and Oman, and at least some claimed by the Saudis. This was 1955, when the contest for oil in that area was on. You had a structure of petroleum concessions in the gulf that was British dominated even though the bulk of the ownership in Aramco (Arabian-American Oil Company) was American. Its properties extended all the way to the Strait of Hormuz. Five percent was owned by the Gulbenkian interests and then the rest of it was divided four ways between the Compagnie Générale du Pétrole, Socony (later Mobil), and British Petroleum. It was generally considered to be a British responsibility and on the other side you had the growing power of the Arabian-American Oil Company, Aramco. When the dispute arose over the Buraimi Oasis, Aramco, with a fascinating kind of geopetroleum strategist named James Terry Bruce, who was the vice president for governmental affairs of Aramco, plunged in on the side of the Saudis supporting the Saudi case in international arbitration. The other side was dominated by the British. In a minor way, this was a very acrimonious confrontation between the British and the Americans in the Middle East. In 1955, I think it was October, as a matter of fact, just a year before Suez, the British, with Omani scouts, went in and took over Buraimi in a military operation, thus ending the dispute. I have always felt that this was a kind of prelude to Suez.

At the time of the Suez crisis, Gen. Andrew Goodpaster was President Eisenhower's military liaison and staff secretary. He offered perspectives on the crisis as it unfolded and, in particular, on the different outlooks between the Eisenhower administration and the Eden government (Anthony Eden was British prime minister during the Suez crisis) in London:

> In the fall of 1955, after the meeting in Geneva, it looked as though a basis for better relations with the Soviet Union had been established. Of course, there was always hype about the "spirit of Geneva," which was very much

exaggerated, although that should always be expected. There was a great relief that at least we were in communication and in a different mode of dealing with issues than glaring at each other and building up armaments. But in September, as I recall—and this was shortly after Eisenhower's heart attack—the Egyptians, who had been trying to get arms, turned to the Soviet Union, and the Soviets [actually the Czechoslovaks] sent them arms. It really created a new and very unfavorable situation when Nasser decided to go down that route. We had tried to work with Nasser, and with Naguib before him. I have always wondered whether the president having that heart attack might have led others to conclude he was less able to take a hand in responding.

In any case, that started down a very bad road and then finally came the Aswan Dam affair, against the background of Nasser taking these military arms and generating a greater threat against Israel. Also, Secretary Dulles had been questioned hard about why we were supporting aid to Egypt to enable them to grow long staple cotton that would be in competition with our own cotton. But Dulles finally terminated negotiations over our aid for the Aswan Dam. That is one time when the president used a term that seemed to be somewhat critical of Dulles: he said that the action might be viewed as "abrupt," and Dulles wrote him a long memorandum explaining why it was not abrupt. I think he was hurt by that.

This started Nasser down the road of nationalization of the Suez Canal and work on the Suez Canal Users Group. The British in particular were saying that there was nothing there that would be acceptable to them. The exchange of messages between Eisenhower and Eden began with Eden saying, "If we lose this we will go down, and we will not go down without a fight." But Eisenhower went back and kept asking, "What end do you see to this, what solution do you think you can bring it to, and how are you going to bring it to a head?" He got the same answer back from Eden that if they did not hold their position in the Suez, Britain would go down and they would not go down without a fight. So it was unresolved. We were involved in a lot of busy activity in the United States at that time getting ready for the election. In retrospect we could see that everything had gone silent for a couple of weeks. The British ambassador was away. We heard nothing from the French or the Israelis, and then they went ahead with the attack. Eisenhower felt that their international positions were untenable, and that he could not and would not support them. He felt that the conflict should be brought to an end as quickly as possible, for otherwise the industrial democracies would alienate much of the rest of the world, and that simply could not be accepted.

Dulles at this time had his first operation for intestinal cancer and was out of commission, as I recall. Herbert Hoover, Jr., was acting secretary of state during all of this time. We felt the loss of Dulles. Herbert Hoover, Jr., stepped up to it awfully well and gave leadership, but did not have the background and experience of Dulles. Hoover knew what had happened in the Users' Group negotiation, but nobody knew it as well as Dulles, and as a result we were handicapped.

On July 26, 1956, President Nasser of Egypt had nationalized the Suez Canal Company. In the months leading up to the Anglo-French military operation, which was mounted in October 1956, the United States attempted vainly to find a diplomatic solution. General Goodpaster describes his part in the Eisenhower administration's efforts. Of special significance was the proposal developed by Secretary of State John Foster Dulles for a Suez Canal Users Association (SCUA), which would have served as a kind of collection agency for transit fees. As General Goodpaster recalled, this idea was acceptable neither to the Eden government nor to Nasser's Egypt:

Then came the nationalization of the canal and John Foster Dulles's idea of a Suez Canal Users Association. In these days, the administration of foreign policy was much simpler. Perhaps it can never be replicated again, but you had a secretary of state and maybe two under secretaries, and an assistant secretary for Near East and South Asian and African affairs, with one deputy. The real guts of the operation was in the regional offices under that assistant secretary. This was before Dean Rusk created the country director plan, which I have always felt was a mistake because it inserted still another layer into the State Department bureaucracy. Many of us dealt directly with the secretary when the issue was something that the secretary had involved himself in directly, so we spent a lot of time in Mr. Dulles's office on events leading up to the Suez crisis.

One day Dulles's office director, Frazier Wilkins, came into a Near East staff meeting and announced that the secretary had just had a great idea for a Suez Canal Users Association. There was dead silence because, I am afraid, most of us really did not quite see how this was going to work. It would be seen by the Egyptians as reversing the process of nationalization. They would see it as an affront to their capacity to run the canal. Nevertheless, Dulles took the concept to London, and I went with him. The British, as I recall, were wildly enthusiastic about it; Evelyn Shuckburgh, I think, was the man who was handling the British Near Eastern affairs at that time. A decision was made to try to sell it to the countries of the area. So I was sent out in August with Robert Anderson, the former secretary of the treasury, and a CIA man named Bill Evelyn, to visit the Arab capitals to try and sell SCUA. We did not come back with dramatic results. I think that the whole SCUA episode probably convinced the British that they had to take some other action if they were going to protect what they saw as their national interest.

I remember the Suez period vividly because there was a man in the British embassy named Willy Morris who used to come in almost daily to exchange messages with us and discuss the area. Suddenly he stopped coming, and I asked Willy several years later, "Why did you stop coming to the department just before the Suez Crisis?" He answered that they had "begun to get the most bizarre messages through London" to go in and tell the Americans things that they knew would just not help relations at all. They went back to London and queried the Foreign Office as to whether this was really what they wanted to do. They never got any answer until they heard on the radio about the landings; so, the British embassy was, to some extent, in the dark also.

During and immediately after the Eisenhower administration, the "conventional wisdom" of the day held that Eisenhower himself played only a passive role in the foreign policy process. Ambassador Newsom supports the assessment of more recent histories in commenting on the extent to which Secretary of State Dulles was in contact with President Eisenhower in the various phases of the formation of policy and the conduct of negotiations:

One impression I have from this era that has been confirmed by some recent writings was that Eisenhower was more of a player in all of this than a lot of people thought at the time. Dulles had a conference table in his office with a phone on it which we later discovered was a direct line to the president. I have never seen any other secretary of state who had that. During the critical days, which I would say were from October of 1956 to the end of 1958 when we were up in Dulles's office frequently, he would often pick up the phone and say, Mr. President, we are thinking of this or that. You never heard the other end of the conversation but you knew there was one. Certainly Eisenhower made the critical decision on Suez, and it was not an easy decision because it was, after all, just before an election.

According to Ambassador Newsom, the diplomatic wounds in the Anglo-American relationship inflicted by the Suez crisis were slow to heal.

For some time relations were still strained between the British and the Americans on anything to do with the Middle East. Some of the issues we were dealing with were the British decision to withdraw forces east of Suez, and what the future of the Persian Gulf was going to be, and how we were going to react to OPEC, which was just in its beginning stages. Another issue was how we were going to deal with some of the major changes in relationships between investing companies and the petroleum resources countries, now that we were getting into the production-sharing contracts. We also were getting into a growing pattern of threats to legislate unilateral changes in petroleum arrangements, although this did not come fully until later in the 1960s. You had the beginnings of a competition, with the major oil companies from independent companies moving into the area, including the opening of Libya after oil was discovered there in 1957. In the years after the Suez crisis the whole nature of the Anglo-American relationship with regard to the Middle East was changing quite dramatically. The British were becoming less and less the dominant player while we were assuming more and more of a major role.

In the years before the Suez crisis of 1956, Britain had played a pivotal diplomatic role in the Middle East. Among the British efforts to preserve pro-Western governments in Arab states in a region that was being transformed by the tides of nationalism was the Baghdad Pact. The United States had never joined the Baghdad Pact, although this security alliance consisting of Britain, Iran, Iraq, and Jordan had U.S. encouragement and support. In the period just after the Suez crisis, the United States developed what was termed the Eisenhower Doctrine. Ambassador Newsom discussed the evolution of U.S. policy in this period:

> In early 1957 after the Suez war, the decision was made that we would try to substitute for adherence to the Baghdad Pact a series of bilateral and executive agreements based on a joint resolution of the Congress. This is how the Eisenhower Doctrine was born. In March of 1957, Congress passed a joint resolution and with it an appropriations authorization for $200 million in assistance to countries that committed themselves to join with us in resisting Communist aggression in the Middle East. There were many times in my bureaucratic career when the original intention got twisted by political requirements. This was one of them. Our idea in the drafting of the doctrine was to give us an instrument that was sufficiently flexible so that we could respond to specific requests in the Middle East without going through the lengthy authorization and appropriations process in Congress. The $200 million was looked on as a fund that would be used over time to meet with specific crises. Immediately, however, the White House saw an opportunity to reward a defeated former chairman of the House Foreign Affairs Committee, Congressman James P. Richards, by sending him on a mission to get countries to commit themselves to the Eisenhower Doctrine and dole out $200 million. So instead of this being a flexible instrument of the executive, it became a kind of stand-up and be counted exercise of the kind that countries in the Middle East are very leery of. That is how the Eisenhower Doctrine was born.
>
> We were able to negotiate bilateral agreements with the members of CENTO (Central Treaty Organization). That was at a time when we still could negotiate an executive agreement and we did not have to fight the Congress. We did it under the umbrella of a joint resolution. It maintained our position and it was the legal umbrella under which we responded to the Lebanon crisis in 1958, when we sent marines into Lebanon. It also facilitated Robert Murphy's negotiation for a change in the Lebanese leadership, setting aside the very people who had invited us in but creating a leadership that had a broader base of support both in Lebanon and outside.

In 1958 the Eisenhower administration faced yet another crisis in the Middle East. In the aftermath of Suez, Nasser's position had been strengthened in Egypt and the nationalism that he symbolized gained in appeal elsewhere in the region. Religious-communal strife had broken out in Lebanon surrounding the

Lebanese presidential election. In Iraq the pro-Western government was over-thrown. Fearing that Lebanon would be thrown into civil war supported by revolutionary Iraqi and Nasserite forces, the United States responded to a Lebanese official request and landed about fourteen thousand troops. Ambassador Newsom described the U.S. decision to intervene and discussed how it unfolded:

> The decision to go into Lebanon in 1958 was a classical model of decision making with consultations, bringing in all of the players in a relatively short space of time. So far as I know, it was one instance in which all of the key players in the picture gave their support. I think that this crisis occurred on a Sunday. Crises usually seem to happen on Sundays and on holidays. It began on Sunday in the morning with a nine o'clock meeting at the White House. I was not there but I was putting the books together for people who were. Meetings and consultations went on throughout the day with Congress, allied leaders, and the appropriate military commands. By the end of the day, the decision had been made, Congress had been consulted, and the allies had been informed.
>
> I do not know whether that kind of decision making is still possible because of the fragmentation of Congress. You have a larger bureaucracy, but I think that with adequate presidential leadership, it probably is possible—but it never seems to work quite the same way. During the Carter administration that decision on normalization of relations with China had that pattern, except that Congress was not consulted, a factor that came back to haunt them later, and the time frame was not as constrained. On Lebanon, the decision was made to go; simultaneously, a decision was also made to set up daily briefings for the Senate Foreign Relations Committee and the House Foreign Affairs Committee.

Early on the morning of October 3, 1973, which was Yom Kippur in Israel, Egypt launched an attack across the Suez Canal against Israeli units occupying the Sinai, seized by Israel at the time of the Six-Day War in 1967. Simultaneously, Syrian units attacked Israeli positions in the Golan Heights, which Israel had occupied in 1967. In the weeks that followed, Israeli forces quickly turned the strikes against them into a highly successful counteroffensive, with a substantial resupply of military equipment provided by the United States. As the Egyptian Third Army faced the prospect of destruction by Israeli forces, President Sadat appealed for superpower intervention. The prospect of Soviet forces being dispatched to Egypt led to an intensification of U.S. efforts both to forestall such Soviet actions and to achieve a cease-fire and disengagement of forces. General von Kielmansegg, formerly commander of allied forces in the NATO central region, discussed the role of surprise in military operations, with special reference to the October 1973 War:

> An example of a successful tactical surprise is Yom Kippur [the Arab-Israeli War of October 1973], the crossing of the Suez Canal. Why it

was a surprise for Israel is very interesting. This [Egyptian] maneuver to go forward [across the canal] had been practiced and shown to the Israelis six times before. That is another method of camouflage, so the Israelis did not believe it. There was another reason. In one case, in May [1973] the Israelis had mobilized, and it turned out to be a false alarm. The Israelis could not afford to mobilize each time there was an alert. For Israel, mobilization is quite a problem, but this was coupled with the very good [Egyptian] choice of timing, Yom Kippur, and this was a very good reason for the success of the tactical surprise. I really do not know whether it would have been a surprise without this timing; it was not a strategic but a tactical surprise.

Gen. Brent Scowcroft, deputy assistant to the president for national security affairs between 1973 and 1975, recalled the initial reaction to the October War:

The first day or so there was broad expectation in the United States that this would be another 1967 war. Then, by about day three it began to be apparent, first in the White House and next in the Defense Department, that this was a far cry from 1967 and that, indeed, the Israelis could be in trouble. As days four and five rolled around, the Israelis were getting into increasing supply problems for some critical things, like 155-millimeter shells; they were in fact running out. They were being pressed very hard on the Golan, and the Syrian border, so we moved sharply into action with the airlift. The differences between the White House and the Pentagon on the airlift are another story.

We did the airlift for two reasons. The first was to make sure that Israel was not defeated, and also to demonstrate—somewhat to the Soviets, but primarily to the Arabs—that we would not let a victory by [Soviet] arms take place, and, therefore, they ought to turn to us to resolve the dispute because the Soviet Union could not do it. From there the strategy evolved between the first disastrous week and about the third week when the cease-fire took place. When we made the first Egyptian contact, it appeared that Sadat in fact had started war for reasons we had not understood, which was why we did not foresee it, and that here was a real opening to make strides. We had tended significantly to underestimate Sadat.

Adm. Thomas Moorer was chairman of the Joint Chiefs of Staff at this time. He recalled U.S. policy as stated by Henry Kissinger:

When we were discussing the Yom Kippur War in 1973 I said, "Henry, what is our goal? What are we trying to do?" He said, "We are not going to let the Arabs force the Israelis into the sea, and we will not allow the Israelis to humiliate the Arabs. That is what we are trying to do." He meant to restore a balance of power.

According to Gen. Brent Scowcroft, the Nixon administration feared as a "worst case" situation for Israel a military breakthrough, not by Egyptian forces in the Sinai, but by Syrian units in the Golan area.

> The worst-case scenario is that there could in fact have been a break-through by the Syrians. The Sinai has all kinds of padding; that was never a problem, and we did not ever calculate that the Egyptians had enough strength really to advance clear through the Sinai, although they could have. They could have tied down enough Israeli strength, which is what they did. Now the Israelis played it just right; they moved forces quickly, especially air forces, and secured the Sinai. In order to stop the Syrians, they redeployed equipment, especially aircraft, in a short period of time, to bolster the Syrian front because of Syria's close proximity to the Israeli heartland. I guess that is the reason we underestimated the situation.

Such apprehension contributed greatly to the U.S. decision to resupply Israeli military stocks, which were rapidly depleted in the days just after the October War broke out. General Scowcroft described the discussion within the administration, as well as problems that had to be surmounted:

> Secretary of Defense Schlesinger felt less concerned by a threat to Israel in the early days than did others in the White House. He felt more deeply about the foreign policy loss that the United States would suffer by a visible moving to the Israeli side with military equipment. He therefore wanted to hold back. Henry Kissinger was probably at the other extreme, feeling that not only for military reasons—because none of us understood in the first couple of days what the problem was—but for diplomatic reasons we had to intervene to demonstrate to the Arabs that we were not going to permit this to happen, that if they wanted to solve this problem they had to come to us. So there was a different perception between the two of them.
>
> The first Israeli shortages were ammunition shortages. The first scheme was for them to send some El Al planes here with the insignia painted out, and they would land at American air bases and load up ammunition. That did not work; they landed in New York to have the "El Al" painted off the side and somebody saw that happening. In the meantime, it quickly became apparent that the whole capacity of El Al was insufficient to deal with the problem. Then I looked next at contract [aircraft]. It quickly became apparent that it was not going to be possible to contract out without government guarantee because the insurance companies would not cover the planes going into a war zone. Next we looked at the CRAF, the civilian reserve air fleet, and the possibility of mobilizing them to get around the insurance issue. For twenty-four hours we looked at that problem.
>
> In the meantime, the situation was deteriorating more and more,

288 • *National Security Decisions*

until finally the president said, "Okay, let's go." Then we started to seek advice from major airports, and learned that one of the complicating factors was that we needed landing rights from the Portuguese for the Azores. They were very reluctant, and nobody else would cooperate at all. The Spanish would not cooperate for air refueling, the Greeks would not cooperate, nobody would help us except the Portuguese, who finally agreed to do so. It would have been very difficult without their agreement. The C-5 could, in fact, make it to Israel, but not with any kind of a payload. That was basically the way the thing developed. There was a different perception between Defense and the White House, and different perceptions of our foreign policy interests and a different perception as to how rapidly the situation was deteriorating. Nobody in the government was disposed to let Israel be overrun, regardless of what happened.

We knew that the Arabs had threatened an oil embargo. There never was an oil shortage. One of the results of all this, however, was the emergence of OPEC [especially OAPEC, the Organization of Arab Petroleum Exporting Countries, a subgroup of OPEC] as a real political force, together with the realization on the part of the Arabs that if they worked together, they had an awful lot of clout.

Admiral Moorer recounted the role played by President Nixon himself in persuading Portugal to permit the United States to use its military facilities in the Azores in support of the resupply effort:

I saw him operate in the Yom Kippur War in 1973 during which none of our allies would let us land a plane in Europe and the only chance we had to get supplies to Tel Aviv was through the Azores. He had to get permission from the Portuguese prime minister. To do that President Nixon had to use some pretty strong words.

Because the United States drew from its NATO stockpiles, it encountered opposition from European allies. As General Scowcroft suggests, the resulting transatlantic frictions were set within a broader context. The Nixon administration had designated 1973 the "Year of Europe," a decision itself made allegedly without adequate consultation between Washington and NATO-European capitals. Taken together, the events of 1973 created for the Nixon administration a series of major difficulties in the alliance.

The Kissinger-Jobert [foreign minister of France] relationship was a very difficult one, partly as a result of personalities. They just loved to bait each other. That was an outgrowth of our widely, and mistakenly, proclaimed "Year of Europe," which, I think, was really well-intentioned but looked to the Europeans, or was received by the Europeans, as a kind of a condescension on the part of the United States. Michel Jobert, who, I think, frankly was not as well disposed toward the United States, and some of the other leaders, like British prime minister Edward Heath, took it very poorly. The October War further exacerbated the problem. Our European allies have always been less attached to Israel than we have, and more concerned with the Arabs, where they have much greater contact than does the United States.

It arose first of all in the notion of our resupply to Israel. We had some very severe drawdown problems, and we did not have the equipment readily available to replenish at the unbelievable rate at which ordnance and equipment were being used up in that war. So we had to use some equipment from our NATO forces stockpiled in Europe. We went ahead to do that, and the Germans found out about it and voiced strong opposition. The issue was over the dedication of U.S. forces and equipment to NATO or whether the United States had the right, in fact, to pull them out and to use either forces or equipment in another theater. It was part and parcel of a dispute which had developed throughout 1973 from the time of Kissinger's speech on the "Year of Europe." The October alert and the crisis further exacerbated it. We did not give the Europeans much notice, and we debated whether we should notify them in the respective national capitals or through NATO. My recollection is that we decided to do both. I think that one or the other did not work right, and so some of them, in fact, did not know about the alert until they read it in the newspapers. One of the things we badly miscalculated was how soon the news would get out. We did not publish the fact that we had gone on alert. We thought that the general public would find out about it gradually; in fact, they found out about it immediately because people's leaves were canceled, and people were calling home saying they could not come home—all sorts of factors which we had not thought about when we called the alert.

General Scowcroft recalled the reaction within the Nixon administration as the Israelis succeeded not only in reversing the attack against them by Syria and Egypt but also in nearly destroying the Egyptian Third Army. Henry Kissinger flew to Moscow to discuss with Soviet officials a proposed cease-fire. General Scowcroft discussed both the general problems of communication between Kissinger and Washington and the goals of U.S. diplomacy as the situation unfolded:

When the war started, we communicated, by and large, with Egypt through the Soviet Union. By the end of the war, we were doing direct communications and we had a fundamentally different relationship with Egypt than we had had at the outset. Only a few days before the alert crisis, Henry Kissinger had flown to Moscow to meet with Brezhnev and to work out a cease-fire, and in fact, had worked one out. There are a lot of interesting details about that: we had a major communications failure. Kissinger could not communicate back with us. Something happened to the embassy communications; whether the Soviets were doing this or not I do not know. The airplane, which we tended to use anyway, had two

communications points. One was in Ethiopia, where we had a major communications center (there was a tropical storm over Ethiopia, and communications were out). There were three or four hours where we had absolutely no communications with him, and he did not believe we could get
through. I was sitting here with the Israeli ambassador in my office, and
he did not believe it. He thought that this was a condominium at the
expense of smaller powers. There was a cease-fire in place worked out
between Kissinger and Brezhnev which Kissinger then flew directly to
Israel to transmit to [Prime Minister] Golda Meir. Soon after it took effect,
it broke down, with the Israelis claiming that the Egyptians started it.

Israeli general Ariel Sharon decided that this was an opportunity that
they could not bypass, and decided to complete the encirclement of the
Egyptian Third Army; the Israelis moved to complete that encirclement.
That would have made the Soviets and the Egyptians look bad, and it also
was not in our interests because what we were really working for, as a
result of this conflict, was to change the situation in the Middle East to
facilitate negotiations. We felt that before 1973 the Arabs could not negotiate because of the humiliation of the 1967 war, and what was really needed
was to restore their sense of confidence and their pride, if you will, and
give them a rationale for coming back to the table. The Egyptians had
made some progress in the Sinai. They were being forced back, but it was
not yet a rout, and this was a point at which both sides could claim victory.
Therefore, it was an ideal situation to have restored the Arab sense of
pride. They had fared well against the Israeli armies, and now they could
negotiate from a position of self-confidence. To have lost the Egyptian
Third Army would have destroyed what we were trying to do.

We were as interested as the Soviet Union in preventing the Israelis
from completing what they—for their own purposes, of course—wanted to
do. It did not help U.S.-Soviet relations because there was a whole question of whether or not the Soviets knew about the October War, since they
went through with their evacuation three or four days before its outbreak
and did not tell us. Perhaps the Soviets, giving them the benefit of the
doubt, wondered whether the alert was not a way for a president in trouble
to show that he was a strong and viable president. It did produce some scar
tissue, but it was not a fundamental problem between the United States
and the Soviet Union. The Russians tried to warn us at the San Clemente
Summit in 1973 that this was going to happen, and could result in problems for détente.

Admiral Moorer offered his perspectives on the issues facing the Nixon
administration at the time of the Israeli military victory against Egypt, and on
the U.S. military forces alert as a diplomatic signal intended for the Soviet
Union:

Towards the end of the October War, we had the odd situation where the
Egyptian forces were on the east side of the canal and the Israeli forces

were on the west side of the canal. In negotiating with the Soviet Union, a cease-fire was arranged, but it was violated by the Israelis in local areas, and this prompted Brezhnev to send a threatening message, at which time we raised the alert condition from four to three. I should note that we had been in alert condition three west of the 180th meridian for several years, because of the Vietnam War. At this time, we were also concerned that Israel would cut off water to the Egyptian troops on the western side of the canal and leave them stranded in the desert. As it turned out, the Israelis did not cut off the water.

General Scowcroft provided additional insights into this aspect of the October War, and in particular the military alert, as it unfolded:

The crisis developed fairly suddenly. Somewhere around eight o'clock in the evening Henry Kissinger called and asked if I could come over to the State Department. I went over there, and he had this communication that Anatoly Dobrynin [Soviet ambassador to the United States, 1962–86] had given him about joint action to save the Egyptian Third Army. The precipitating issue was the surrounding of the Egyptian Third Army by the Israelis in a breakdown of the cease-fire. There was great fear on the part of the Soviets and the United States that in fact the Israelis might destroy the Third Army. The question was what to do about it. The Soviets proposed a joint military action, and if we did not see our way clear, they may have to do it by themselves. I looked at the memo, and we decided we had to have an NSC meeting. So, I went back to the White House and talked to Al Haig and sent out the call to the principals for a meeting. I did not communicate directly with the president; Al Haig did. The president said, go ahead, convene the meeting without his presence. Thereafter the actual title of the meeting has always been in doubt, whether it was an NSC meeting without the president, or whether it was a meeting of the subgroup without the president, but all the principals were there except for the president.

We had a lengthy, serious discussion about what was happening, about interpreting the Soviet note, whether it was just a language problem, or whether it was a serious problem. At the same time we underscored the seriousness with which we took it based on our own intelligence information, which revealed significant Soviet support of the Egyptians. At the same time, during the day, and especially in the evening, we got evidence that the Soviets had started the resupply effort and that aircraft were already on their way from the Soviet Union to Egypt. We had no idea what the aircraft were transporting. There were also indications of a higher state of alert within the Soviet Union, especially some of their airborne units, which tended to underscore the seriousness of the crisis. So we did all the usual things, but in the end it came down to how to demonstrate to the Soviets that we were serious and that we strongly objected to them moving independently. The one thing we felt we could do to demonstrate that point quickly and unmistakably was to put our forces on alert. We knew that the Soviets would pick up the dramatic increase in communications activity and would understand the gravity of the situation.

That is basically what we decided to do, and in the meantime we crafted a response to Brezhnev. Haig checked with the president on both the response and the recommendation that we had drafted. The president okayed both. Then we decided on the timing. This was maybe two o'clock in the morning. We decided that we would hold the response until about 5:00 or 5:30 A.M., at which time I would call Dobrynin and tell him I was sending this over by messenger, thus giving time for the Soviets to have picked up a change in our communications and alert status. That was basically the strategy that we followed. There was a lot of talk, including by some of the principals, about the nuclear alert as a threat to go to war. In fact, it was designed that way. We debated whether or not we ought to include SAC [Strategic Air Command] in the alert, since they were already at one level of alert higher than the rest of the forces around the world. We decided that we should. I think, frankly, it was partly because of an ancillary issue—that is, that Jim Schlesinger, who was secretary of defense, had been trying to pull back a wing of B-52s from Guam for a long time and we would not let him pull them out. When we decided to go on alert, he argued that we had to have those B-52s back in the United States. This was not, I emphasize *not*, a nuclear threat to the Soviet Union. What we were trying to do was to dramatize to the Soviet Union that we were very serious in our response, which essentially was, "No, we are not going to send forces, and you should not send forces." I think it worked quite well, with some reservations. This was not a dramatic provocation on the part of the United States to test Soviet resolve. I do not know that we will ever know what the Soviets had in mind, but it was a preemptive action to try to avoid something that, we all agreed, we would have to respond to if Moscow had decided to move.

Admiral Moorer recalled the same communication from Leonid Brezhnev via Dobrynin that was received in the White House situation room, the effect of which was to lead the United States to raise the alert status of its forces:

At almost midnight we received a message from Brezhnev that arrived in the situation room. Eagleburger called me on the phone. I directed the Pentagon watch officer to alert the JCS chiefs to come to the Pentagon. I joined William Colby, director of the Central Intelligence Agency, Schlesinger, and Kissinger in the situation room. We studied the message from Brezhnev. We decided at this point that we had to raise our readiness posture. We wanted to make some kind of move. So we decided on Defense Condition (Defcon) 3. That process took less than an hour. I went from there to the Pentagon where the JCS asked "what if" questions.

Building upon his thesis of surprise, General von Kielmansegg discussed the intended signals to the Soviet Union provided by the United States in placing units assigned to NATO on alert:

> The Russians took the opportunity to assert that "this [the Soviet guarantee of the cease-fire] is the best way for us to bring troops in there legally." The United States said, "No, we do not like this. We will look for other means." Then the Russians started off again [moving their airborne troops] and again—surprise. Yet, actually, it was no surprise. Why? Because this was detected by the NATO early warning net. The first thing we observed were the unusual flight patterns.
>
> At this point, the Russians were planning to go into Cairo and into Egypt, generally. Then came this warning given out from NATO. . . . In Germany I have been asked, "Why did they alert the Seventh U.S. Army [stationed in Germany] and not just SAC?" I said, "It is quite clear: without alerting the Seventh Army, the alert was not credible to the Russians." In Germany nobody had seen this point.

In the immediate aftermath of the cease-fire, which later was honored by Israel and Egypt, the United States embarked on an extensive diplomatic effort designed to achieve a disengagement of military forces and to furnish the basis for a more permanent political settlement. General Scowcroft assessed the accomplishments of U.S. Middle East policy negotiated by the end of the Ford administration, as well as issues that remained for his successor:

> Kissinger continued the strategy that had developed in the war, which was more or less to separate the Egyptians from their Soviet host, and indeed, to do the same to the extent that one could in the whole of the Middle East. The first device to accomplish this was the international conference after the war in which the Soviets were participants. It was nothing more than a shell, the initial meeting—at least it evolved that way; whether Henry Kissinger realized it, and planned that it would be precisely the way that it happened, I do not know, but he took full advantage of it and gave the Egyptians enough maneuver room to cooperate with the United States. Without that, it would have been much more awkward for the Egyptians, in fact, to shift from the Soviet Union to cooperation with the United States.
>
> In theory, the Middle East settlement was to begin by removing the important points of confrontation and the sparks which could easily produce another conflict, and that was by attempting disengagement agreements around the periphery of Israel. The first was with Egypt, followed by a much more difficult one with Syria on the northern front. In this case, also, I think this international conference, which had been set up, gave President Assad enough maneuvering room to do what he did, grudg-

ingly. I think in retrospect that in the Middle East, one of the most serious mistakes we made was after the disengagement agreement on the West Bank. (Lebanon was not an issue at this early time.) I remember Israeli foreign minister Yigal Allon coming to the United States, and he and Henry Kissinger and I went up to Camp David and had a long discussion about what to do next.

Without identifying people, there were arguments that the next step had to be disengagement on the West Bank. There was just a new Israeli government—Golda Meir had just resigned as premier and Rabin had just taken over. Allon's opinion was that a disengagement on the West Bank was different from either the Sinai or the Golan Heights and it could not take place without elections in Israel. This was heartland property and it was just premature. It was too tough to ask Israel to do that. In the end, Kissinger felt that with Israel at least moderately opposed to this step it was too much to ask a brand new President Ford to take on this issue and to insist on disengagement from the West Bank. So we went back to yet another disengagement, a further disengagement in the Sinai with Egypt. I think it was probably one of the most serious mistakes we made. Had we been able to move on the West Bank, even modestly, it might have changed the character of subsequent events in the area.

In the latter part of the administration Lebanon blew up. It was a difficult problem, one which we worked, actually fairly closely, with the Syrians and the Israelis. By the time of the end of the Ford administration, we had a fragile—and what proved to be very temporary—settlement, with Syria in de facto occupation down to a certain point in southern Lebanon, with Israeli insistence that they would not accept Syrian forces closer than ten or twenty miles from the Israeli border [with Lebanon]. This was a serious mistake. I think if they had let the Syrians come down to the border, subsequent events in Lebanon, perhaps, never would have taken place. I do not know; that is a guess. It is a fact, however, that there are no terrorist infiltrations across the Syrian border [with Israel], and I think by leaving this "no man's land," if you will, in southern Lebanon, they prepared the way for the infiltration of the PLO and subsequent problems of the area.

What would have happened in a next Ford administration one does not know. Ford was the first one ever to suspend aid to Israel, in 1975. We had a period which we called the reappraisal, because of Israeli intransigence, during which we had a letter signed by seventy-six of the one hundred senators, asking us to restore aid to Israel unconditionally. This gives one an indication of the depth of the political problem in moving on the Middle East in any way which has a chance to be really productive. The way the 1973 war eventually came out and the subsequent negotiations afterwards proved to be the basis on which President Carter was able, with great perseverance, to bring about a peace between Egypt and Israel, fundamentally transforming relationships in the Middle East. It has fundamentally changed the military balance in the area and thus the whole character of the situation.

According to Ambassador David Newsom, policymakers usually do not focus on the most difficult problem, including international crises, until they have no alternative but to do so. In taking what they deem to be necessary action, political leaders often find it necessary to rely on intelligence reports that are incomplete or inadequate. Moreover, information that is available may not be adequate or accurate. Such problems are said to have hampered U.S. foreign policy at the time of the Iranian crisis.

My impression is that people under pressure of several problems simultaneously are not prepared to focus on unthinkable possibilities until they are forced to do so. Much has been written about intelligence failures. My feeling is that there are certainly failures in getting information, but the greater failure is the unwillingness of people in high places either to accept the full implications of intelligence or to know what to do about it if they do accept it. It is politically unrealistic to suggest that in the summer of 1978—when you had reports of Iranian unrest, and for policymakers to conclude that the shah was in danger of being deposed and the United States had to act. Given the porous nature of Washington, it would not have been long before that rumor would be out and that rumor in itself would have its own effect upon the situation in Iran and the international scene. It is nice in hindsight to suggest what might have been done.

I was dealing with the rest of the world while everyone was up on the mountain dealing with the Middle East, but Iran came into that. I think Anwar Sadat [president of Egypt, 1970–81] spoke to Carter about information he had received that the shah was in difficulty. Consequently, Carter phoned the shah from Camp David, if I remember correctly, to tell him that we were with him. This was after the September 1978 rioting in Tabriz and to some extent in Tehran as well. So Iran impinged briefly on the Camp David talks between Carter and the leaders of Israel and Egypt, Menachem Begin [prime minister of Israel, 1977–85] and Sadat. Then things unfolded in January 1979. I became involved in finding a home for the shah, which led later to dramatic developments. I was also continuing to manage the interagency group which was seeking to remove the Americans from Iran. At the same time I was overseeing a remarkable bit of negotiating that went on when a representative from the Defense Department went out and negotiated with the last cadre of the Royal Iranian Army, resulting in an agreement that disposed of some $12 billion in equipment that the Iranians had ordered and which was being manufactured in the United States.

One of the other tasks of the under secretary is to review the press guidance that goes out every day at noon to the spokesperson. The guidance during January, as the shah was in the final days of his throne, was particularly tricky because if the press officer says one thing different from what he or she had said the day before, if they leave out a word, immediately the press is on it [to determine] the significance of that. Hodding Carter [President Carter's press secretary] and I used to confer every day, and we would look at the events as they were unfolding for about ten days. He said exactly what he had said each day before, which made him seem to a lot of people a little ridiculous. However, if he had said, "Yes, we support the shah today," he would have been asked, "Do you mean not tomorrow?" We were aware that the press officer's comments could have an effect on efforts to put some kind of regime together in Iran. The other thing I recall from that period was George Ball's report [Ball was a former U.S. representative to the United Nations] concluding that the shah was in real difficulty. He proposed creation of a regency council of the shah.

As the prestige of Ayatollah Khomeini grew, the Carter administration considered, but rejected, the idea of direct contact with the enigmatic Iranian leader. Ambassador Newsom sets forth the factors leading to the administration's decision:

The proposed mission [for Ambassador Theodore Eliot, first secretary, U.S. embassy, Iran, 1963–66; Iranian country officer, State Department, 1966–69; and ambassador to Afghanistan, 1973–78] was an idea that was developed in late 1978. It had its origin in the evidence that Khomeini was a factor to be reckoned with. We had had some contact with his group outside of Paris—between the embassy in Paris and Dr. Ibrahim Yazdi, who was in the Ayatollah Ruhollah Khomeini's entourage and later became foreign minister. We had the impression—that if this was going to lead anywhere in terms of getting more of an impression of just what this man was all about—we should perhaps send somebody to see him directly.

By that time, we had the full impact of the dissemination of the tapes that were sent back from the ayatollah's headquarters in Paris to his representative, the Ayatollah Beheshti in Tehran, who was later killed in a bombing. The impact of these tapes was becoming more and more apparent, and, therefore, we in the State Department thought that it was perhaps prudent to try to establish some kind of link with the ayatollah. We felt it should be somebody who was not now in office, and therefore we suggested Ambassador Theodore Eliot as someone who knew the region, but the idea was not received with favor at the White House and was subsequently dropped. You can argue that it might have been a disaster (on the basis of the way the Khomeini subsequently treated visitors from the United States). Whether Eliot would ever have seen him or whether [he] would have been humiliated by the ayatollah's receiving him, lecturing him, and then walking out, which is what he did with the papal envoy and with the Soviet ambassador, is questionable. So the idea of the mission was based on a feeling that here was a country where we had a lot of major interests and there was something to be said for establishing a relationship.

In the waning days of the shah's rule, the United States sent a mission headed by Gen. Robert Huyser (then deputy chief of U.S. Forces in Europe) for discussions with the Iranian military. Ambassador Newsom comments on this mission:

The Gen. Robert "Dutch" Huyser mission was conceived to rally the Iranian armed forces against the ayatollah. It was never clear to me whether this was the objective of [Secretary of Defense] Harold Brown and David Jones [chairman, Joint Chiefs of Staff, 1977–85] in dreaming it up. By the time Huyser got there, the disintegration of the Iranian armed forces had already begun. We had made two assumptions about the armed forces of Iran without looking very deeply into their actual structure, which was far weaker than we had realized. We had not focused on the fact that one half of the armed forces consisted of conscripts, many of whom came from the same religious base as did the ayatollah. Further, the shah, for understandable reasons, never created any real commander in the army. He was the commander, and when he was not longer there, there was no clear voice of command; you had an inherently weak structure.

There was the famous telephone call of early February in which Zbigniew Brzezinski asked me to ask Bill Sullivan [U.S. ambassador to Iran, 1977–79] whether option C (a military coup), or whatever it was, should be put into effect. Sullivan made it very dramatically clear that he thought that was a lousy idea because Gen. Philip Gast [chief, Military Assistance Advisory Group, Tehran, 1977–79] was at that moment in a bunker dodging fire between the cadets and the Imperial Guard. So if there ever was a possibility of the Iron Fist (military option), it had passed by that time. Also, there was a certain amount of unreal talk about whether the United States itself actually had a military option to save the shah. We did not have any forces anywhere near the area. It could not have been done with naval forces that were in the vicinity. The logistics of moving any other kind of force there were enormous. At that time we had no base in Oman, so the options were very limited.

Huyser did as professional a job as one could do under the circumstances. I saw his messages and Sullivan's, which did meet at the upper levels of the government, and this again was illustrative of the kind of operation at the second level. I would be in touch with Bob Komer [under secretary of defense for policy, 1977–79] and Frank Carlucci [deputy director of CIA, 1978–81] about Huyser's messages and Sullivan's messages to try to bring various channels that we had together, but I do not see in retrospect what the Huyser mission could have accomplished, whatever its principal purpose. If you read the transcript of the conversations that Bill Sullivan and Tony Parsons, the British ambassador, had with the shah all during this period, you find an indecisive man, reluctant to use force and probably conscious of the fact that it was not a real option—that it would have been a very bloody affair and perhaps not successful. You see, instead, the unfolding of a Shakespearian drama in which everyone played a part to a tragic end.

In the aftermath of the Iranian Revolution, the Carter administration faced the need to open channels of communication with the new government in Tehran and, at the same time, to assist the shah, in failing health, to find suitable refuge in exile. Such problems, together with events leading to the hostage crisis, are discussed by Ambassador Newsom:

After the shah left, you had the Shapour Bakhtiar [Iranian prime minister, January–February 1979] government. After we got the embassy back from the February invasion, the decision was made that we should try to rebuild our relationships with whatever government was established in Tehran. It was concluded that, whatever the nature of the revolution might be, it was not a Soviet instrument. The Soviets were as baffled in some ways as we were by these developments, and in many ways disturbed by them because of their own Central Asian [Muslim population] problem. We felt that there was merit in trying to establish commercial relations and other avenues through which we could build a relationship with the new authorities. We also had a compelling reason for keeping a mission in Tehran after the February events, and this was in order to be of as much help as we could to the Jewish and Baha'i communities in getting them out of Tehran, which is why we also kept the consulate in Tabriz.

When the shah left Tehran, we had indicated to him that he would be welcome in the United States. That was on the assumption that he would come directly to the U.S. He decided to stay in Egypt; we probably still entertained some idea that we or someone would put him back on the throne—a possibility also very much in the minds of the Khomeini people, complicating even more our relations with them. Then Sadat became uncomfortable with the shah's presence or the shah became uncomfortable in Egypt, and he and his family moved to Morocco. That was short-lived, and then we had to find another haven.

I worked with an aide to David Rockefeller [chairman of the board, Chase Manhattan Bank, 1969–81] and with Joe Reed, who was also on Rockefeller's staff, to try to find a refuge for the shah. By this time I think we had concluded that if we were going to build a new relationship with the revolutionary government in Tehran, it would be unduly complicated if the shah came to the United States. It was clear that Khomeini still entertained the idea that we intended somehow to put the shah back on the throne. When he was moved to Mexico in early October 1979, we were also dealing with the Soviet brigade in Cuba and the fall of Somoza.

Late in 1979 we got word that the shah was ill, and Joe Reed alerted me that there might be a request to bring him to the United States for medical treatment. Now President Carter stated in his memoirs [Jimmy Carter, *Keeping Faith* (New York: Bantam, 1983)] that he had not been fully aware of the shah's condition and had been confronted with it suddenly. He implies that he was asked to make a very difficult decision, but his hands were tied. That is my impression of President Carter's feelings. We did have an earlier warning that this might happen, and I consulted with Gary Sick [an NSC staff member during the Carter administration who specialized in Iranian affairs], who I presume also consulted with people in the NSC. My recollection is that we went back to Joe Reed and said that bringing the shah in for medical treatment would be a very serious decision. Obviously we could not let the shah die in Mexico. I remember talking about it with Gary Sick, and we mutually concluded in late September that a president of the United States really could not be responsible for refusing to admit someone if there was a dire and demonstrable medical need. We did not hear anything for several days until Joe Reed called and said the shah's jaundice was worsening and they were going to ask Doctor Keen, who was somehow associated with the Rockefeller establishment, to come down to take a look at him because of the difficulty in diagnosing the cause of the shah's jaundice. Then we had a further call from Reed saying Keen had met two French doctors who informed him that the shah had been under treatment for lymph cancer for six years, and that there was a desperate need for a CAT scan to determine the degree of blockage of the shah's bile duct. Because there was no CAT scan equipment in Mexico that could do this, we agreed to the shah coming to Sloan-Kettering [hospital], in New York, for this treatment.

Newsom then described the effect in Iran of the U.S. desire to allow the shah to come to the United States for medical treatment:

We alerted Bruce Laingen, chargé d'affaires in Tehran. I had written Bruce a letter in July saying that we had had some indication that the shah might be ill. If that was the case, we might have to consider letting him into the United States temporarily for medical treatment. We advised Bruce and asked him to advise the [Iranian] authorities that this was a temporary stay, given that there were no alternative medical facilities. Dr. Ibrahim Yazdi [Iranian deputy prime minister for revolutionary affairs, February–April 1979, and minister for foreign affairs, April–November 1979], with whom we were dealing at that time, came back and said that they would accept this if they could send two doctors from Iran to confirm this diagnosis; but the shah was adamant that he did not want to be examined by any of the ayatollah's doctors. We realized that this was a very critical point, so we worked out a scheme by which [the American doctor] would meet with an Iranian doctor and share with him the medical reports. That just never came to pass because of events, but we did try to deal with that aspect. But the suspicion of our association with the shah and the recollection of 1953 [when the United States and other Western nations supported a coup against the government of then prime minister Dr. Muhammed Mussadeq, who had nationalized the oil industry] were just so strong that whatever we said would have been discounted by many of the people around Khomeini.

So the shah was admitted in late October, and then on the fourth of November the U.S. embassy was invaded again. Bruce Laingen and two others were in the Foreign Ministry at the time. We thought that we might again get the support of Bazargan [prime minister of Iran, February–November 1979] and Yazdi to recover the embassy, as they had helped us recover it in February, but Bazargan and Yazdi were in Algiers at a conference, where Brzezinski was also present. Brzezinski, on his initiative, met with Bazargan and Yazdi. That meeting enabled opponents of the prime minister and Yazdi to undermine them with the ayatollah, so that when we turned to them for help when they returned from Algiers they no longer had the clout to be helpful. Consequently, we were in for a long siege.

In the days immediately following the onset of the U.S. hostage crisis, Newsom outlined steps taken by the Carter administration:

We tried to communicate with Bazargan and Yazdi after the hostages had been held for about twenty-four hours, and it was clear that Yazdi and Bazargan were not going to be able to recover the embassy. The decision was made to send Ramsey Clark [U.S. attorney general, 1967–69] and William Miller to Tehran with a presidential message. We had hoped that they could sneak out of Washington without notice. We had had some contacts with the Iranian Foreign Ministry which had indicated that they would be willing to receive Clark and Miller. Then the fact that they were leaving for Tehran leaked, just after they left or just as they were leaving, and the whole tone of the Iranians changed. Originally, we had requested that they receive Ramsey Clark and the American aircraft and indicated that it was an aircraft large enough to take the hostages out. After the thing leaked, the first news we had of trouble was when a man from the [Iranian] Foreign Ministry said, "We will still receive Ramsey Clark, but not with the large aircraft. You will have to get a smaller aircraft." So then we scrambled to find a C-12 or a Lear jet to pick up Ramsey Clark in Istanbul and take him into Tehran. Then they called back and said, "No American aircraft; you can come in by charter." Well, then Ramsey Clark and Bill Miller did get to Istanbul, but they never got the clearance to go into Iran.

I think that was a critical moment in the whole hostage business. The pressure on a president in a moment like that to do something is very heavy, and particularly a president who feels the heat of the political campaign. You cannot just stand there, you do something; [the United States] does not have the capacity for subtlety in its diplomacy in situations like that. One can argue that it would have been better to have done nothing or to have made some ambiguous statements about how we will be prepared to talk with the regime when the hostages are released and be very equivocal about what we would do if that did not happen. I think that at the time, there was still great uncertainty in the ayatollah's mind about what our true capacity for action was. But it is very hard to maintain that uncertainty because if the president says we are studying the options— "We will talk to the Iranians when they release the hostages"— immediately the press is going to be looking for and speculating about military moves. Such speculation is often read as having some official endorsement, and so your capacity to deal with that kind of a problem is very limited. I think after the first seventy-two hours and after the failure of the Clark mission, it was clear that we were in for a long hostage period.

Saddeg al Mahdi [later the prime minister of the Sudan and a man who had helped Khomeini draw up his constitution] came through Washington in early January 1980, and I met with him just to get his sense of the ayatollah and the situation in Iran. He said, "You are not going to get the hostages out now until Khomeini has the institutions of his constitution in place and he can transfer the responsibility for a decision to release the hostages to those institutions." Actually, that is exactly what happened. But, again, our system does not permit us to wait out a situation like that; we had hoped that the Parliament might be in place in March and it was not in place until July.

So we did a lot of, perhaps inevitable, unnecessary, wheel spinning in the first few months of 1980, using an interesting Argentine-French couple, and other would-be intermediaries. That period ended with the failed rescue attempt. I came to the conclusion during that period (that came back to me again when I read about the Iran-contra crisis) that many of those who put themselves forward as credible intermediaries in that kind of a situation were playing a game in which they sought to gain favor with the ayatollah by claiming their ability to get something out of the Americans in the hope that if Iranian-American relations did improve, they would benefit from that improvement. It really was not until Khomeini sent his message to the Parliament in July, and [Deputy Secretary of State] Warren Christopher met with Tabatabai in Germany, I think in late August, that we for the first time had a feeling that we were meeting with someone who spoke for the ayatollah.

Ambassador Newsom presented perspectives on the negotiations that eventually succeeded in the release of the American hostages:

Warren Christopher's meeting with Tabatabai, which might have been followed up sooner had it not been for the outbreak of the Iran-Iraq War, was one of the several darker moments in all of this. Ultimately, through the Algerians, the negotiations were started in Algiers in which a three-man Algerian delegation talked with our people and then went to Iran. That negotiation was primarily a financial negotiation on the disposition of the assets. The ayatollah's original four-point message called for the return of Iranian assets, which they claimed to be $52 billion that were supposed to be in the United States. They subsequently reduced it to $25 billion. The Iranians also wanted a guarantee that we would not interfere in the internal affairs of Iran, and an agreement that we would redress Iran's grievances against the United States for its past involvement in Iranian internal affairs. So in the negotiations, we had to deal with each one of these.

We had made it very clear from the outset in all discussions, even before Tabatabai, that we were not going to return the shah as Tehran had originally demanded. By September 1978 his health was deteriorating. This became less and less of a point, although the Iranians continued to reiterate it.

The Algerians did an impressive job in getting the Iranians to understand that we did not have in our system an accounting of all foreign assets in the United States. If the shah had bank accounts around the United States then there was no way that we instantaneously would know about it, and if the Ayatollah's government wanted to recover these assets, they would have to do it through the American courts. The negotiations then centered on the $12–13 billion of frozen Iranian assets and their disposition, as well as on the American claims against Iran. We reiterated that we had no intention of interfering in Iran's internal affairs. The real negotiations were over the frozen assets.

I do not know whether when all of this was going on the Iranians deliberately delayed the conclusion of the crisis until Reagan got into office or not. On the night of January 18, [1981], we thought everything had been wrapped up, and then the Iranians discovered that one of the American banks had given what they felt to be false information on the rate of interest that they had been receiving on the Iranian assets. That threw the whole thing open again, and the last frantic hours were spent trying to resolve that issue. That is really what held up the final solution, but I just do not know enough about all of the intimate details to know whether there was in all of that an Iranian desire to release the hostages on Reagan's watch so that the Reagan administration would also be committed to the deal.

Later, in June 1982, the Israelis implemented their contingency plans and invaded Lebanon, ultimately pushing to Beirut in an effort to inflict a decisive defeat on PLO forces in Lebanon. Once again, the United States became involved in the Arab-Israeli conflict. First, in conjunction with France and Italy, the United States sent a small marine unit to Beirut to assist in the negotiated removal of PLO combatants from Lebanon during July and August 1982. U.S. troops left quickly once this was done. Gen. John Vessey was chairman of the Joint Chiefs of Staff at this time; he shared the JCS view of this mission:

Here is the situation in Lebanon: we have got Mr. Habib [Philip Habib, U.S. special envoy to the Middle East] over there, and we are probably going to be asked to interpose U.S. forces between Israelis and the Palestinian fighters. That in the larger, strategic sense, is a mistake: for the

United States to put its forces between the warring factions in Lebanon. The chiefs supported this, and we respectfully asked the secretary to convey those views to the president urgently—that we not get American forces involved in Lebanon.

We made our views known, but then things went downhill. We understood the decision to go, we didn't agree with it, we didn't want to do it, and foresaw problems. But we recognized that the box the president got caught in, both in the beginning to get the Israelis to withdraw from Beirut and to get the Palestinians out.

Then, with Israeli units just outside Beirut, Lebanese Christian elements converged on Sabra and Chatilla Palestinian refugee camps in southern Beirut in September and commenced massacres of remaining Palestinians. Robert McFarlane—then deputy national security adviser—conveyed the sense of revulsion of President Reagan, and the felt obligation to reinsert U.S. Marines in Beirut in late September 1982.

One of President Reagan's weaknesses was a deep revulsion at the loss of human life and a very strong vulnerability to visual images. The president saw the images on television of all these atrocities that occurred, and he was just revolted by it; it had a profound impact on him. Television and films portraying suffering children and women bring to the fore his sense of chivalry and humanity, and it has the power to influence his behavior all out of proportion. It leads him to do something even if it is wrong. But I did not intervene or seek to persuade him away from the decision to reinsert U.S. Marines. For, in fact, I did believe that if we could bring the secretary of state and defense (by then we had a new secretary of state, George Shultz) into a sensible political-military strategy that the marines, with French, British, and Italian cohorts, could serve a useful function in preserving order in Beirut, while we did one very important thing and that was to determine whether or not within Lebanon, the Lebanese prevailing party, the Christian Maronites, were willing to change the status quo with all the other confessional groupings in the country.

Frankly, that was wrong-headed on my part. We do not have any vital interest in Lebanon. The U.S. interest in Lebanon was to reduce its role as an avenue of conflict between Lebanon and Syria. Our interest in Lebanon was to have a coherent Lebanon, with Syria out of it and Israel out of it, but otherwise we had no interest in Lebanon except as a buffer. We should have limited ourselves to trying to get Israel out and Syria out, and I said that at the time, and Judge Clark [William Clark was then national security adviser] said that very emphatically at the time to George Shultz, and Shultz agreed with it. We disagreed on how to do it. The disagreement was that Philip Habib, U.S. special envoy to the Middle East, believed we could take the Saudis at their word. The Saudis had a habit of discourse with the Syrians, and they were subsidizing the Syrian government to the tune of about $350 million a year. The Saudis said that they had been assured by Assad that Syria would withdraw when Israel withdrew. Phil Habib felt that he had run the string out, not of his own volition, but he had no more credibility with Assad. So Habib was willing to ignore Syria. That was a very fundamental disagreement between Judge Clark. The judge and I felt that we cannot ignore Syria. You have got to go deal with Syria while Syria is weak. Phil Habib and George Shultz believed instead that we can concentrate on Israel, and Syria will take care of itself afterwards.

Well, why put the marines back in? It is true that Judge Clark and I believed that the presence of the marines there with the British, French, and Italians could help to stabilize the climate right in Beirut while you negotiated the withdrawal of Israel and of Syria from Lebanon, and to enable the government to function without the persistent threat of more massacres and atrocities. Well, this is very imprecise. How? By patrolling, by interposition, by a phased withdrawal, by more forces, by just what? Well, the president, Shultz, and I really expected the Pentagon to define the scheme of maneuver and always said that the marine force was to be a presence supporting the government of Lebanon and providing for stability with the other MNF [multinational force] countries while Israel and Syria withdrew. Now, that is a very uncertain mission that was left to the military to interpret as they saw fit. They saw fit not to undertake this broader set of tactics that involved maneuver and being in fact a policing force, but simply to be a kind of physical barrier around the perimeter of southern Beirut, and were very unenthusiastic about the mission. I thought, forlornly and wrongly, that in the course of the fall of 1982 and early 1983 that we could persuade the secretary of state and secretary of defense to work together to forge a more activist U.S. role that would involve maneuver with Italians and British and divide up the problem into pieces—that we would first get withdrawal from the Beirut-Damascus highway and move British and French forces down that road. Then we would get Israeli forces out of the Shouf Mountains and move U.S. forces there. We would get further Syrian withdrawal into the Bekaa Valley and more Italian forces, and so forth and gradually create a larger enclave around the Beirut-Damascus highway, in parallel with a basic reconciliation of elements within Lebanon, with the Maronites acknowledging that they would give up power and part of the economic pie to the Sunnis, Shiites, Druze, and so forth.

General Vessey also commented on the decision to reinsert U.S. Marines after September 20, 1982:

Then, after Sabra and Chatilla, he was caught having to go back in. There was a long sort of history of the JCS (the secretary did not want to be in there either) trying to get us out of there and trying to find a way to be neutral in this operation. Not be on the side of the Israelis or not be on the side of those opposing the Israelis, but to try and create the sort of image that the United States was there in support of the Lebanese people and that we were looking to help them end the miserable situation they had been caught in for the previous ten years.

McFarlane then discussed some of the obstacles that the United States faced in trying to achieve the objectives of stabilizing Beirut and Lebanon as a whole while simultaneously seeking withdrawal of Israeli and Syrian forces from the country.

One failure among many was that, first of all, we could not get cooperation between George Shultz and Cap Weinberger. It was a very defensible judgment on Cap's part that all you are going to do if you start maneuvering out there is expose yourself more easily to great vulnerability to terrorism, snipers, and all that, and it puts us into a very different context of being activists/participants in a very uncertain political climate, and he was dead right about that. The second fault, however, was that our diplomacy was going toward the wrong direction. Judge Clark and I both felt that it ought to be oriented toward getting people out of Lebanon. The State Department and Philip Habib came quickly to the point of view by October or November of 1982 that the purpose ought to be to see if we cannot negotiate a settlement between Israel and a second Arab country. They had one with Egypt, the Camp David Accords. Now, let's add one with Lebanon. This became a matter of bitter disagreement between the White House and the Department of State because I thought (and I was intemperate in this; Judge Clark was much more conciliatory, but he was strong) that it is self-evident that Egypt is not Lebanon. Egypt is the preeminent Arab country by dint of its cultural tradition, its homogeneous population, its centuries of excellence in science and the arts, and its 50 million people also. Lebanon is not a unified country, and Amin Gemayal is not even a Bashir Gemayal—he is a rather feckless, well-meaning, inexperienced man. I just thought it was a wasting effort for us to engage in trying to get an agreement that the Lebanese could never enforce.

But there were two central flaws in our Lebanon policy, and the first one was to misjudge the important goal. It should not have been a second treaty between Israel and anybody. It ought to have been withdrawal of foreign forces, starting with Syria. The second mistake was to become preoccupied with an internal resolution of the Lebanese political problems. By the time I got out there, you know, nobody had even dealt with that problem, which was a sine qua non of withdrawal. I put it very squarely to Gemayal—and not very diplomatically—and I said, "Look, demographically, things are very changed, aren't they, since 1940, and you can see things far better than I can that it is unstable here, that the Maronites are a minority dominating the economy and the political portfolios, and you are the president, and a Christian overlay of dominance in this country is inconsistent with the demographic facts of life and not just demographics. I mean, you have got the highest per capita weapons count in the globe here, so unless you do two things, there is no point in our being here. Number one is that you have got to change the 1943 compact that when the president is a Maronite Christian and the prime minister is a Sunni Muslim and the speaker is a Shiite Muslim, you have got to change all of those portfolios and divide it up so that the percentages correlate roughly to the demographics. Secondly, you have got to share the economic pie more equitably, instead of the Maronites dominating the ports. Finally, I think that you have to decentralize; get the government less into Beirut—you have to give the minorities greater autonomy.

"But finally, Mr. President, all this is from an American. We do not know beans about this. You have got to decide what it is that will bring stability to Lebanon and step up to it. If you cannot do that, I understand. But there is no point in us being here. We cannot do it for you."

Gemayal kept saying, "What do you want me to do?" I felt very pathetic in this situation. I said that I can tell you what seems logical; I cannot tell you what to do, I am not Lebanese. I do not know what will fly over here. This seems sensible to me, but if you do not think you can do that, then I do not know what to tell you. I said that I would do my best to get a cease-fire here to where you would have got at least enough calm to be able to try to do something, and we did.

In July 1983 McFarlane moved from his position as deputy assistant to the president for national security affairs (under National Security Adviser William Clark) to succeed Philip Habib as U.S. special envoy to the Middle East. McFarlane was now on the scene negotiating in Lebanon, Syria, and Israel. As the civil war in Lebanon—then in its eighth year—continued, the United States was increasingly perceived as a partisan to certain internal Lebanese factions; the U.S. embassy was car bombed in April 1983, and violence against Americans in Lebanon steadily increased. McFarlane steered a course of increasing U.S. military response to Lebanese attacks; the United States became directly involved in the September 1983 battle of Suq al Gharb, a village in the Shouf Mountains above Beirut. He described his role in U.S. policy at the time of the Suq al Gharb battle:

There were wild cards in the mix, and we Americans did not quite know where to affix responsibility for the periodic shelling that would come out of the Shouf on the marines, the British battalions, and all over Beirut; but it would come out of the Shouf, and we did not have either the means in terms of radar or human intelligence to know whether it was Syrian and Druze or both or some other force. We began to get intelligence of the arrival of Iranian-sponsored Shia extremists, and it was not clear from intelligence whether they were Iranian or they were homegrown and Iranian armed. But wer were told that at least in part whether they were Iranians that the Syrians were allowing to come into the Bekaa Valley from Damascus and on into the Shouf Mountains. But not knowing precisely who it was for sure—all we could know is that it ended up exploding and killing Americans, French, British, Italians, and coming down into the diplomatic compound of the U.S. ambassador's residence there.

Because we did not know, I could see that our days were really numbered there, unless one of two things happened. On the one hand, that Gemayal really did make a dramatic gesture at a grand compromise (that I talked about already) and called in Jumblat, the Druze leader, Sabsalam, the leader of the Sunnis, Nabih Berri, the leader of the Shias, and said, all right, we are going to redraw the political map of Lebanon. That was one possibility. The other possibility was that back in Washington we could get the secretaries of state and defense and the president to agree on a political-military strategy that involved political reconciliation in Lebanon, withdrawal of Israel and Syria, all under the prod of the effective use of force by the United States. But it had to be a willingness to use violent force to assure the withdrawal of Syrian elements. Now I doubted if that could happen.

The next month, in October 1982, a terrorist car-bombing attack against the U.S. Marine Corps barracks near Beirut Airport resulted in 249 deaths. The U.S. forces had been deployed in Lebanon as a part of a multinational peace keeping effort. There was widespread criticism of the security arrangements and command structure for U.S. forces which had allowed such an incident to occur, as well as discussions of the policy goals of the United States in placing military units in Lebanon. Gen. John Vessey was chairman of the Joint Chiefs of Staff at the time. He offered perspectives on the bombing attack on the U.S. Marine Corps facility and the broader issues in Lebanon:

It was like watching a bad dream that you had had come to life. It was like having a nightmare and then going out on the street and having it duplicated in real life. We were caught in a situation that we should not have been in. On the other hand, the bombing at the barracks should not have taken place. We should have been able to prevent the bombing of the barracks, and that was a local security problem.

The problem with second guessing that thing now is that we had a presidential commission that was appointed to look at it, then reported their findings. It was a good report. In my view a good part of it was lack of attention to security detail on the part of the marines on the ground, and their immediate supervisors in the task force and the fleet. I hate to say that because I have great admiration for the marine corps and great sympathy for the marines that were put over there in a lousy mission, in a poor position. But in fact a terrorist drove through the local security into the area and into the barracks in which several hundred marines were. As Adm. [Robert Lyman] Long and his commission pointed out, many factors made it difficult for the marines on the ground—principally, just being there and becoming the target, but the terrorist came through the local security.

But I stress the fact that our people were targets; that was no secret to anyone. Two days before—the barracks was bombed on Sunday—but on Friday, the JCS went through another hand-wringing session about the security, looking at the intelligence and looking at the threats to attack and looking at the way the situation had changed from the time we came into Lebanon. Our forces were first greeted with open arms by the Palestinians after Sabra and Chatilla, by the Lebanese Christians, and by almost everybody. But now that situation had deteriorated. Now we had become the target, because people had painted us as having been associated with the Israelis. And just two days before the bombing, at the JCS meeting on Friday, there was again one of the almost weekly sessions about concern for our own troops and bringing the intelligence people in and are we passing the warning of these threats of terrorist attacks, and has CIN-CEUR (Commander-in-Chief, Europe) looked at security of the forces, and so on. There were all these assurances up and down the line that yes, this has been done, and suddenly on Sunday we lose the troops. It was certainly the grimmest day of my chairmanship.

The U.S. role changed from the time the marines first went in in the fall of 1982 after Sabra and Chatilla. After the fall of 1983 dramatic changes had taken place in Lebanon. We certainly were not as forceful as we should have been, although we thought we were being reasonably forceful in explaining to the president and his advisers these changes as we saw them affecting the security of military forces. Although I must say, I thought we did not hide our feelings. There was a split in the administration; there were many who believed that by applying a little more military power that we were close to making some substantial progress toward solving the Middle East problem—that we could do that by applying a little more military power. I believe that both Bud McFarlane and Don Rumsfeld believed that. Then there were those who said we have no business being there at all. Probably none of us were serving the president as well as we might. We were in Lebanon and we had to deal with the situation that existed.

Following the October 1983 bombings of the French and U.S. multinational force contingents, joint U.S.—French contingency planning for retaliation began. McFarlane related how the U.S. participation unraveled:

The president was just—as you can imagine—livid when this explosion occurred and all of the lives were lost—all of us were—and he directed Bill Casey [director of Central Intelligence], Cap Weinberger, and the NSA (National Security Agency), and everybody to turn every collection asset on what we had anywhere to try to find out who did it. And we did. We found the headquarters in the Bekaa Valley. [McFarlane affirmed that it was in Baalbek, Lebanon.]

There was an unmistakable association with the Hizballah [Party of God] in terms of both communications intelligence intercepts as well as evidence on the ground in training for this operation. So we had it wired.

Now it is true that there were civilian facilities nearby (about a quarter of a mile away), and for certain aircraft attack axes, if you had a long or short munition drop, you would have hit some civilians, it is true; but not for all axes. But we had an NSPG [National Security Planning Group] meeting where all that information came back in, was considered, and with high confidence on the part of Bill Casey and NSA pinpointed that that is the place where these people are commanded, and occasionally live, and probably are today. It is true that we were not certain that they were always there, but that was always the headquarters, whether they were there or not. So the president said, "Well, let's go after it. Let's plan the mission, get ready and quick, and if possible do it with the French. But do it." And the directive I wrote and sent to Cap Weinberger said, "Please undertake military-to-military contacts for an early attack in the Baalbek area."

It came down to a reconfirming meeting in November, between the tenth and the twelfth or thereabouts, where the president reconfirmed, "Yes, go do that. You have the authority, Mr. Secretary of Defense." Later, after their meeting, Cap left, and John Poindexter and I, being a little leery of the fact that this might go off the rails, John sent a cable over to his French counterpart, the general in the Élysée Palace (he was a military adviser to President François Mitterrand), saying that the president had given his authority. The appropriate naval authorities got together, and they planned it all out and it was agreed: the aircraft sortie times, the integration of the two forces, and the French carrier in the area. The next morning, it was to occur for some reason at about first light our [Washington, D.C.] time; that sounds crazy to me because that would have been about noon or later, local time, but that was the time because when I got to work, it was the time when it was supposed to happen, and I arrived at my office and within minutes, about 6:30, Cap called and he said, "Well, I have decided that we really ought not to go ahead with this. There are complications." A very ambiguous answer. I said, "Cap, what has gone wrong?" He said, "No, Bud, there are just too many factors here that are uncertain and I do not believe it is prudent to go." Well, you ought to hear his side of it; there may be something I just do not know about, but I do know that the French got airborne and went ahead and conducted a mission, but they were mad. I do not think they have stopped being mad today, and I think that is why we did not get overflight rights in the April 1986 raid on Libya because they had not forgotten that, three years before, but they were good and mad.

McFarlane then described the decision finally to withdraw with the U.S. Marine contingent of the multinational force from Lebanon.

I could not blame the JCS about it. I had come to the conclusion by about Christmas 1983 myself that neither of the two conditions that I thought had to obtain was going to be obtained. Gemayal was not going to reach out for reconciliation, and the secretary of state and the secretary of defense were not going to be able to work together, so it was unreasonable to keep those marines at risk. So I came to agreement with secretary of defense that it was all right to pull them out, and we convened a meeting in early February [1984], and I do not really recall the circumstances except that the governing elements were, I had concluded and Cap had, and the two of us together with George Shultz (out of town on a trip to Grenada, as a matter of fact) convened the NSC, and everybody around the table, the vice president, Cap, and I, the only odd man out was the deputy secretary of state at the meeting—well, no, the president was not there. The president was on his way to the West Coast, and the vice president chaired the meeting, and we came to the recommendation to the president that we should pull them out, simply because the secretaries of state and defense could not get along with each other. Now, Cap would not give you that same version. Cap's proposal was that we redeploy, this kind of fig-leaf notion that they were still going to be there at hand and able to intervene if called upon. But once they had left the beach, everybody knew that they were not going back in, that it was a fig-leaf cover for an embarrassing retreat.

21
The Dominican Republic Crisis

I n 1961 President Rafael Trujillo, whose authoritarian rule had dominated the Dominican Republic for thirty-one years, was assassinated. During the period of intensified political turmoil that followed, Juan Bosch, who had lived abroad during the Trujillo years, and who therefore had had little direct experience in the politics of the Dominican Republic, was elected president. After only several months in office, Bosch was overthrown in a military coup that installed a government headed by a civilian triumvirate. In turn, in April 1965 pro-Bosch forces revolted against the regime headed by Donald Reid Cabral. The deteriorating political scene of the early 1960s in the Dominican Republic provided fertile ground for the growth of Communist influence in the elements supporting Juan Bosch. In order to foreclose the possibility of another Castro-type state in the Caribbean and to protect U.S. and other foreign nationals caught between the warring factions in the civil strife sweeping the Dominican Republic, the Johnson administration not only played an active diplomatic role in the Dominican Republic, but also ordered direct U.S. military intervention. Dean Rusk, who was secretary of state during the Kennedy and Johnson administrations, discussed the crisis as it unfolded and the planning that was undertaken first by President Kennedy and subsequently by President Johnson:

When Juan Bosch was elected president of the Dominican Republic, we invited him to come to Washington. We received him with high honors and told him that we wanted to be as helpful as possible. We thought that the Dominican Republic was getting off to a fresh start. But at that time three of his closest friends in the embassy—Luis Munoz Marin of Puerto Rico, [Romulo] Betancourt of Venezuela, and [José Figueres Ferrer] Migarez of Costa Rica—told us that Bosch would not be able to organize a government. He was a poet; a dreamer. He had no concept of how to build an administration. We tried to get him to turn to these friends in putting a government together. He did not do that.

Then there developed the anarchy. The armed forces, the police, various revolutionary groups, brought down the government and fell to fighting each other. In that process, American and other foreign nationals were in real danger. This brought us to the first phase of the Dominican affair—the concern for foreign nationals. We had been told by the chiefs of the armed forces and the police that they could not be responsible for them. There is a great desire for the United States to appear to be within the parameters of complete acceptance rather than standing up and saying we are preventing the spread of Communism. There was an inherent defensiveness in Johnson because of the way he had been treated by Bobby Kennedy during the Kennedy administration.

I think that it is also a result of his attitude to Congress. At the time, I believe that Congress would have supported action to prevent another Castro. The Organization of American States (OAS) had thrown Castro's Cuba out on the grounds that Marxism-Leninism was incompatible with the traditions of the Western Hemisphere. During the Cuban missile crisis the OAS had said that the missiles were a threat to the whole hemisphere and demanded that they be removed. In 1964 Castro was caught red-handed landing men and supplies on the coast of Venezuela, and the OAS imposed sanctions on Cuba. There was strong consensus in the hemisphere against the expansion of Castro-type regimes. This is the problem with the current situation in Nicaragua—we have allowed it to become a unilateral affair. Even at the time of the Bay of Pigs—that terrible mistake—my impression was that the hemisphere was not so much upset with the attempt as with the fact that it failed.

Former secretary of state Rusk discussed the controversial tenure of John Bartlow Martin as U.S. ambassador to the Dominican Republic. Martin had been appointed by President Kennedy. He was replaced early in the Johnson administration by Tapley Bennett. In this interview, Mr. Rusk alluded to differences between Ambassador Martin and President Johnson over political trends in the Dominican Republic and, in particular, over the government headed by Juan Bosch.

I think that he had different views than President Johnson did. He was emotionally inclined toward the Bosch approach. I just do not know what he would have done, but he did have different views on the affair.

Asked if he would have taken a course different from that chosen by President Johnson in 1965, Mr. Rusk responded,

President Johnson used a plan that had been developed on the orders of President Kennedy. He sent the marines in to safeguard the safety of foreign nationals. We sent in a lot of marines because there were pockets of Americans in many different parts of the country. We thought that it might be necessary to organize expeditions into the interior. When we got ashore, various individuals came out to our lines to inform us about the situation inside Santo Domingo. These people included the head of Bosch's own political party. We got the picture that a violent struggle was taking place that might lead to the establishment of a Castro-like dictatorship or a Trujillo-type dictatorship. Both of these alternatives were unpleasant. The OAS had already applied sanctions on both of them.

This ushered in phase two. Through the OAS we helped to organize an interim government, a police force, and elections for a new government. In essence that was what that was all about. We had no problem with international law. We landed marines for the protection of foreign nationals where no government existed to take such measures. There was an international police force during the second phase, but not for the initial landings. Nationals were threatened, and so there was no time for diplomatic maneuver. Someone had to act.

President de Gaulle could be magnificent in times of crisis. He blasted us from the rooftops for going into the Dominican Republic. But privately he asked us to move the marines four more blocks to pick up the protection of the French embassy. We did that. He did not thank us and in fact continued to blast us from the rooftops.

I think that I would have taken the same action. I felt very strongly against the spread of the Castro regime to other parts of the hemisphere. When Castro first came to power, he was invited to Washington, and we tried to work things out, but Castro sold out his own revolution.

In 1965 Ambassador Edwin Martin was serving as head of the Latin American Policy Committee and, as such, worked closely with the OAS's Special Consultative Committee on Security. Here he recalls one session of the Policy Committee in 1963:

We had one rather unique discussion, an unfortunate one, in September of 1963. There were lots of rumors out of the Dominican Republic that the newly elected president, Juan Bosch—from an election which we were very proud to have helped arrange after thirty years of the Trujillo dictatorship—was being threatened with a coup by his military who were dissatisfied with his performance, particularly the fact that he had been having interviews with known Communists, or participants in Communist party activities in the Dominican Republic.

There were also press reports that this movement by the military had been encouraged by the U.S. defense attaché and the military assistance mission in the Dominican Republic. So we called them back for a meeting of the Latin American Policy Committee to cross-question them. They had denied it by cable, but there were those who wanted to cross-question them very sharply on the validity of this; there had been suspicions in some other cases. They were rather effectively denying any role in this when I was called to an overseas telephone call from our embassy saying the coup had just taken place. The aircraft carrier *Boxer* was there in case there were problems, as it was in one or two other cases. We had it deployed off Port-au-Prince [Haiti] at one time, which was not publicized.

When we went for the inauguration of Bosch, it was offshore because Vice President Johnson, who was head of our delegation, may have needed a *Boxer* helicopter overhead to rescue him if there were any problems. So the *Boxer* was active in the Caribbean at this period.

Ambassador Martin recalled a conversation in which President Kennedy asked Betancourt for his assessment of Bosch. According to Martin, Venezuelan president Betancourt did little to inspire U.S. confidence in Bosch's ability to lead the Dominican Republic out of its then existing turmoil:

> I should say two things. One is that Bosch, who had lived abroad for thirty years, had had no political life—he ran in the recent elections and came in third, beaten by one of his predecessors before that time, Belaguer, who had been deputy to Trujillo. But I remember that just after his election, President Betancourt of Venezuela made an official visit, and I sat at the table with him and President Kennedy at the dinner in the White House. Kennedy asked him what he thought about the Bosch election—I think we all felt that Bosch was in a sense a part of what I called the Caribbean mafia of left-of-center political leaders. He had participated in a lot of the meetings and I think lived for a while in Costa Rica in connection with this group of social democrats or democratic socialists. Betancourt's answer was, "He's a very good novelist." After the inauguration, I talked to Betancourt and Figueres, knowing that they had been meeting after midnight with Bosch. I asked them about their meetings with Bosch. They said every time they tried to suggest anything, he would say, "I've been elected since you have, by a larger majority than any of you were. You cannot tell me things; I will tell you things." He was "innocents abroad" in a very real sense. As Betancourt said, "If he just knew the tricks of handling the military the way I did in Venezuela—where they had been dominant and were a threat—he might have survived, but he had no sense of that." And he did other ridiculous things. To prevent corruption, every voucher for a payment of over five dollars he had to sign personally. He lived in the house he had lived in before, he got up at six o'clock, and received people who would like jobs as ditch-diggers, or something like that, and interviewed them. And when we talked about political management, and use of the cabinet and the legislature, he said, "I am the president, I was elected by everybody, I do not have to bother with all these little people."

Ambassador Edwin Martin discussed the circumstances that led to the military coup against Bosch and how, in his view, and partly as a result of his own impression, the *Washington Post* misinterpreted an interview with him. The result was an article erroneously suggesting that the Johnson administration in fact had favored the military move against Bosch.

> I wanted to make a point on this; it may be the reason the literature is this way, is that I made a mistake. I was called up before the Senate Foreign

Relations Committee to testify, and the major question was, Why did the military do this? And I described some of the incompetence, and some of the leftist connections—Bosch had had some leftist connections—the *Washington Post* story about this election referred to him as the Marxist candidate. We did not think he was now a Communist, or would make any serious concessions to the Communists. And I tried to explain this whole situation to the Senate Committee. They were aware of our general policy and they understood that we had tried to prevent it, despite Bosch's difficulties.

But the next day, or the same day, I got a call from the chief editorial writer of the *Washington Post*, and he asked me, why did the military move? So, on the phone, I told him what we thought. I was a little busy; it was a hectic period. I did not explain how wrong we thought it was—and they were—and how much we tried to stop it. And so he wrote an editorial alleging that the U.S. government was friendly to the action. That was my mistake; I did not cover the ground the way I should have in that interview.

Dean Rusk recalled Ambassador John Bartlow Martin's style as U.S. envoy to the Dominican Republic, as well as the circumstances that led to his departure from this post:

Ambassador Martin was an interesting character too. He had joined Bobby Kennedy's campaign as a speechwriter, had had no experience of any kind in the diplomatic world, which was not unique, of course. But he fairly quickly was not speaking to his deputy chief of mission (DCM]. For a noncareer ambassador not to be speaking to the career deputy chief of mission was an unfortunate situation. I made a very quick trip and immediately sent the DCM to be consul general in Guayaquil, and brought the man from Guayaquil, Spencer King, up to the Dominican Republic. They got along fine. Second, Ambassador Martin never wrote telegrams. About once a month, he would write me a four- or five-page letter, which was fascinating, beautifully written, full of interesting information. But current up-to-date information was not there, and it was often quite difficult to distribute to the other interested agencies what was in this letter. Third, he was ambassador to the Dominican Republic and the Dominican people. He never would have anything to do either with the American community (business or otherwise) or with the diplomatic community, who often can be sources of information. He never went to diplomatic parties or receptions. I went there and wanted to have breakfast with some American businessmen who were having trouble in the sugar fields, and his response was, absolutely not; we never will have them in the embassy, they are not on my business.

So you can see that it was not all smooth going. He also got ulcers and refused to do anything about them. I was told this, I think, through a CIA contact. So I flew down again and had a navy plane ready in Miami to come over and pick him up, because they were bleeding ulcers. The doctors there said he had to get treatment. Well, he would not go off right away. He wanted to spend twenty-four hours talking to me first. Until, finally, Sunday afternoon, he did fly up to the naval hospital in Washington. They decided that they did not have to operate but put him on very stringent treatment. Thereafter, they always knew when his jeep was coming because the back was full of pails of milk.

John Bartlow Martin's successor as ambassador to the Dominican Republic, W. Tapley Bennett, Jr., held this appointment as the domestic situation deteriorated and the crisis unfolded that culminated in the use of U.S. military forces by the Johnson administration in April 1965. Ambassador Bennett begins by noting the major factors that shaped the Johnson administration's response to the situation:

> The Dominican problem had been with the Johnson administration—indeed, with the Kennedy administration—from almost the beginning. And it is a problem that goes back much further than that. The Dominican Republic has been a problem almost since Columbus landed there in 1492. It has alternated in its history between strong-man, dictatorship-type governments—Rafael Leonidas Trujillo being only the last of several—and things dissolving into complete chaos, which is what happened in the spring of 1965. The longest period of democratically elected government the Dominicans had had in their entire history lasted about four and a half years, and then Ramon Caceres, a good man, was assassinated. That was early in this century. So, from the beginning, first in the Kennedy years, and then under Johnson, you had this problem. The Kennedy era had a lot of starts toward "establishing democracy everywhere," and sometimes that policy was overblown and overenthusiastic. I think that is what happened in the Dominican Republic when the hated Trujillo was finally dispensed with. We played, I believe, a commendable role in holding things together there after this departure and in easing his would-be successors, including his son, out of the country. Then came the election in which Juan Bosch was elected. Bosch turned out to be—no matter what his political orientation was—a miserable governor. He had no knack for governing.

Ambassador Bennett addressed the question of whether the United States was surprised by the course of events in the Dominican Republic and, in particular, by the outcome of the election that had brought Juan Bosch to office:

> I think that is accurate. I do not know whether "caught by surprise" is the right phrase. It is a dramatic way to phrase it, but I think all the indications had been that the Viriato Fiallo would carry the country. He was a man who had a great deal of background and experience, and I think he obviously would have made a better president. He did not win, so to that extent, it was a surprise.

According to Ambassador Bennett, his predecessor, John Bartlow Martin, had left a controversial legacy:

He has been frank about me, so I guess I can return the favor. Well, as far as the everyday business of running an embassy was concerned, and as far as tending to all the things that need attending to, he was not a very effective ambassador. I think that is one reason he was pulled out in such a hurry. He was pulled out to show our political disapproval of what had happened, obviously, but he was also very anxious to go back to Santo Domingo, and neither the White House nor the State Department was ever willing for him to go back. His record had been very mixed, whatever his good intentions were.

For instance, I got there and found that in all his months there he had never once had a staff meeting. We began having normal staff meetings, and someone said, "We never had anything like this when Mr. Martin was here." Well, he was very much an individualist; he was a loner. He was a journalist; he had never run anything; he had never met a payroll, to use that famous phrase. I mean, he had never had a staff around him, so I suppose it was not natural for him. The embassy was not regarded by Washington as having been very well run, however much he was a sturdy figure for the democratic government. And I will say he had no hesitation—and this I say in tribute to him—in calling attention to the Communist influence in the 1965 uprising, even though it meant breaking with his own past. He told me, "This will ruin me with my liberal friends forever after." But he had no hesitation. In fact, he perhaps went further than I would have in casting the revolution in full Communist colors. He was courageous in facing up to what the real problem was, despite the fact that it was going to cost him politically among his natural friends and constituency.

Ambassador Bennett reflected on the overthrow of Bosch and the consequent fears in the Johnson administration that the eventual outcome of political trends in the Dominican Republic would be a Castro-like Communist government:

It did not really come before the Kennedy administration, because Bosch had been thrown out during those last months of Kennedy's incumbency. The next government, the civilian triumvirate, which was badgered and very much hindered by the military, was a well-meaning but very inexperienced government. Donald Reid Cabral, president of the triumvirate, had been an auto salesman. His father was a Scot who had come there as a banker and married into one of the old Dominican families, the Cabrals. On his mother's side he had a lot of political blood in his veins, but he had not had any political experience himself. He was erratic in many ways as a political leader, although his intentions were of the best; but the military were on his heels the whole time, and the economy was so bad. That was the combination that really brought things down in the end.

None of us ever said that Bosch was a Communist; but he was soft on Communism, and he thought he was smarter than the Communists. However, what we did say—and what I would maintain to this day—is that there was very strong Communist influence, small but key, in the revolutionary circles. I think they were already well on their way to controlling the street crowds—in other words, seeing that this and that happened in those days of general chaos. My own firm conviction is that Bosch would have been put in power by that group, and then a few months later he would have been discarded, as they have done in so many other countries where they have taken control. He would not have been a reliable vessel for them.

As Ambassador Bennett related, the rise of Communist influence was gradual, building on a narrow base of support and attempting to take advantage of evolving circumstances:

I do not think it had anything to do with the original coup. In fact, the planners themselves later said that they stumbled into revolution. They had not meant things to break out so early. They were not quite ready, but once it got started, it just grew like wildfire. The Communist group, which was a small group, simply saw the opportunities and began to exploit them. To that extent, it was a growing thing, but it was growing with regard to influence, not with regard to increasing numbers of committed Communists. One of the things that I have always thought should be given more emphasis than it has been was the Czech publications some months later. It is a sort of a confession on their part on how this thing got away from them, how they meant to control it, and how we stopped them by moving. You always have to be careful of anything that is written from those sources, but this seems to be pretty sincere—a beat-ourselves-on-the-breast about what we Communists did wrong. This is worth looking at.

I think that concern was growing with regard to Communist influence, and it was always shadowy. We made the mistake of letting ourselves get hounded by the press into putting out a list of Communists which, as usual in such situations, had some inaccuracies in it. It was put together in great haste, and we should not have done it, but we did. There were fifty-one names, or something like that, and one or two turned out to be dead, and a few others were wrong, and that attacked its credibility, obviously. We would have been smarter if we had refused to be quite so specific that early on in the game, because we were not really in a position to be. But most of the names stood up, and as Dean Rusk remarked during one of his press conferences, Hitler started with only seven men around him. The fact that there were only a few did not bother Rusk, because they were the few disciplined voices who knew what they were trying to achieve, and who went after it, in an atmosphere of complete breakdown. They were able to accomplish a great deal. And Capt. Francisco Caamaño Deñó—well, he was just a big bluff military man with no brains at all. He was easily manipulated. He had a certain hearty charm; he would have been good on a platform, and to call the troops forward—that kind of thing. He was useful to them, but obviously just a tool.

Although there were differences in emphasis, Ambassador Bennett suggests, both he and Ambassador Martin considered the problem of Communist influence in the Dominican Republic at this time to be an important issue. Bennett clarified his differences on the Communists with Martin:

> All I said was that Martin is an emotional man, and when he saw the Communists in this, he went further than I would have in saying that it was completely under their domination. I do not think I ever thought that. I just thought that the danger was very real, and was growing, and was going to be decisive in a very short period of time after this group took over. I still think that. Now I will say, and I am frank to admit it, that some exaggerated reporting came out of the embassy. We were accused of that, and it is true. One of our political officers was very excited in his reporting. I could not possibly see everything that was going out in those days. My name went on every cable. I have always stood by everything; I have defended those people who were attacked. But there were cables that came out of there that I would not have written myself. I would not have agreed with some of the estimates. But that is neither here nor there; they were sent out under my name, and I stand on it.

He continued:

> But let us get at Martin's statement that "Bennett maintained the traditional ambassadorial role of staying out of internal political affairs," and that "indeed, he told me at Christmas, 1964, he had never talked politics with Donny Reid." I find that statement astonishing because there was no way you could avoid talking politics to Donny Reid. I was accused by the local opposition, as the American ambassador always is in a country like that, of being "too close to the government." Well, it was not a question of my wanting to be; it was that people like Donny Reid wanted to come over and sit on my lap every day and talk politics. I saw a lot of Donny Reid, and I believe we had mutual respect for each other. I have sat on his veranda with him, and he on mine, and talked little else than politics. The difference between Martin and me was that I maintained a position of noninterference, while he became intensely and emotionally involved, convinced that he knew best what the Dominicans should do about their internal affairs and trying to get them to do things his way. He was always insisting you should do it this way, you should do it that way.
>
> Well, that is not, as he says, the traditional role of an ambassador, nor do I think it is generally an effective role. Ellsworth Bunker [former ambassador to the OAS] and I used to talk about that, later on. We could give the best of our advice; we could put on pressure; we could cajole; we could argue; we could urge, we could demand. And at the end of a twenty-six hour day the Dominican colonels and others were going to make the decisions on the basis of little electric signals going back and forth inside *their* brains, out of their experience, which was considerably more primi-

tive politically than ours. We did not really control it. Sen. J. William Fulbright can say, "Well, why don't you make them do so and so, you control them"—we do not. This is the situation in many countries and on many problems today. You can give your best efforts, but in the end the decisions are made by the local people, made on the basis of *their* internal calculations. You can influence the situation, but you do not control very much. If a man or a political group considers that it is their country, it is their future, or maybe their lives at stake, then they are going to make their decisions on their calculations of what is *their* interest, not on what might please us. Sometimes they will do things to please you, but that is not a very satisfactory relationship for the long term. When it comes down to the hard decisions, they are made on the basis of their own interests as they see them.

So, on Martin's comments about my talking politics with Reid, surely we discussed situations, but I did not try to insist that he do this or that, unless I had instructions to take a given position. That was the difference between us. The essence of diplomacy is to persuade the other fellow to your view of preferred course of action, not to dictate to him.

According to Ambassador Bennett, in the Kennedy administration it was feared that Bosch had little understanding of Communist strategy and tactics, and that an effort would be made to subvert the revolutionary forces sweeping the Dominican Republic to create another Castro-type regime:

I think the impression of Bosch as soft on Communism was gained quite early on in the Kennedy administration. There was great frustration in the Kennedy White House, as well as in the State Department, over dealing with Bosch because he turned out to be such an ineffective governor. He was, as I say, soft on Communism, in his underestimation of Communist objectives and in his feeling that he could outwit them. He was going to use them, and instead, they ended up using him, as so often happens in that sort of circumstance. That was what President Kennedy had warned him about.

Ambassador Bennett described the deteriorating political scene that he encountered upon his arrival as ambassador to the Dominican Republic in 1964:

You see, when I got there you had this faltering, inexperienced triumvirate, you had a worsening economic situation, and you had a military which was thoroughly corrupt, untrained, and illiterate politically. I have always described it as a three-legged stool: a weak government, a bad military, and an economy gone to pot. In the week between Christmas and New Year of 1965, sugar fell below three cents a pound. I remember saying—I think I reported it at the time, I certainly wrote it in my own diary—the days are numbered here; it just cannot go on this way. It was touch and go from the day I arrived there as to whether they could survive politically or economically or, if you will, militarily.

Obviously, there was a great sensitivity as to whether there were Castro elements in the situation. This was certainly a major factor in Lyndon Johnson's calculations; he was not going to allow another Cuba to be established. I do not think we ever said that the Castro elements were fundamental in bringing this on. Obviously, they moved to take advantage of it once things boiled over. And, certainly, Radio Havana was very busy exciting it with all the wildest type of Communist rhetoric during the revolutionary days. But I doubt that there were Castro people in on the original kickoff. As I say, they just stumbled into the revolt. It was mainly military, with some civilian plotters who hoped to gain from it in the usual Latin American way.

If I had one word to describe the Dominican Republic at that time, the Dominican way of handling things, I would say feckless. Nothing turned out right; everything went wrong. And this was as much a problem with running an embassy as it was in the political life of the country. We had a lot of trouble just making average machinery go.

Among the candidates in the Dominican Republic election scheduled to be held in the autumn of 1965 was Reid, who held power in the leadership group that had been established after the military coup against Bosch. Ambassador Bennett described the political setting in the early months of 1965 leading up to the crisis that resulted in U.S. military intervention:

An election was scheduled for the fall. Donny Reid was determined to run. By that time there was a duumvirate, Reid and one other partner— Ramon Caceres. He was the grandson, or great-grandson, of the man who had been assassinated after four and a half years of democratic government. He was a very honorable young man from a well-known politically established Dominican family, but he was quite inexperienced himself. I still get letters from him.

Donny Reid was determined to run for president. All the soundings that you could take in the polls showed that he had little public support. He meant well. He was a feisty sort of fellow, who had great self-confidence, but he was without a great deal of experience to back that up. We knew the military were plotting, and that Donny was there on their sufferance. The military was very corrupt. It being an island country, they were great on smuggling. They would use air force planes to bring in clothes and goods to sell on the black market, and so forth.

These were the kinds of things that I went back to Washington to talk about. As I said already, in early January I had felt that the outlook was ominous. There was a bad drought that year, and we had reports in March or April about, not riots, but disorders up in the poorer parts of town because people did not have water. The hot season was coming on, and it was obviously a society in disintegration. There was no government with experience to handle it, and a corrupt military was standing there grabbing what it could. So that was why I went home. I also went home because my mother was seriously ill; she died later that year. So it was a mix. It was time to go and talk in Washington. Secretary Rusk had told me when I first went out, "You know, you are not very far away, and you are going to a troubled country." He said, "It is a lot easier to work on these things face to face. Do not just send telegrams; get on the plane, and we will talk about it here when you have some problem." Well, by the end of April it had become quite clear that the time had come to talk, so that is why I was there. In fact, I remarked at the time of my departure that it was probably the first week I could safely go away. I turned out to be wrong by a week! I went to discuss whether we should go along with the plans for an election—support the holding of the election—or whether we should work for postponement of the election until things got a little better composed. I was going to explain that Reid was determined to run, even though he had no real support; that was clear. Nobody in Washington or anywhere else wanted to see Bosch return.

At this time, the Johnson administration had severe reservations about the leadership group headed by Reid but could not readily find a suitable alternative. There was no support for a return to power by Bosch.

There was no question about it. He had proven to be such a miserable governor, feckless and extreme. No matter what his politics were, he had just done a miserable job in trying to run the country. Martin is more effective in describing that than anybody else could be; he does it with great detail and I think with great expertise.

As Ambassador Bennett recounts, the U.S. Embassy in Santo Domingo had mixed feelings about the prospect for elections in late 1965 in the Dominican Republic:

We had not ever actually come to a decision; that was one of the things I was going to discuss in Washington, what attitude we should take. We were accused of backing Donny Reid to the hilt, and for lack of a stronger reed—pardon me for making a pun—we were. He was honest, and he was trying to do the right thing, although at times he tried—perhaps understandably—to use us for his personal political advantage. But he was not involved with the usual corruption and that sort of thing. So to that extent we supported him as the only government we had!

Ambassador Bennett was in the United States for consultations in Washington when the fighting in the Dominican Republic escalated to the point at which the Johnson administration moved to send U.S. military forces to the troubled country.

Consultations in Washington at the end of April would have been very significant had they ever taken place. You see, I was at home with my family in the country, in Georgia, on Saturday afternoon—no, I was driving there. A half hour before I got there, on the car radio news, I heard there was a shooting in Santo Domingo. I thought, oh no, I may not get through this weekend. But I went home, and a few hours later I got a call from Washington. They said, stay where you are because we do not know what is happening, what is unfolding. Then, on Sunday morning, I got a call from Under Secretary of State Tom Mann, who was then effectively running the details of Latin American policy. We had worked together before. He said, you had better come on up. I got to Washington sometime Sunday afternoon.

Everyone was thrashing around, and nobody knew what was happening. Sunday evening I was over at the State Department. That was in the days before all the high-powered task forces of today. Monday was still uncertain. We had a noon meeting at the White House with the president, the secretary of state, the secretary of defense, McGeorge Bundy, and two or three others. At one point in the conversation the president turned to the secretary of defense and said, "Mac, I think you had better set up a plane and get the ambassador back to his post." I left Washington at about 5:30 in the afternoon on one of those little jet stars. We flew to Puerto Rico and landed at our air force base there on the northwest corner of the island, and I spent the night there. The next morning I was very anxious to get on, and they kept delaying; I did not know why. It turned out later to be because the airport in the Dominican Republic was under fire. I finally got over: I was lifted by helicopter from the airport out to the deck of an aircraft carrier. Again I was delayed; it turned out there was shooting where they would have taken me in to shore. Finally I was lifted in, at about 2:30 in the afternoon, landing at Haina, a little port about seven miles west of town. As we came toward Santo Domingo—I can still see in my mind's eye the palm trees blowing—the first cars of the people we were evacuating passed us on the road. So I finally got back to the embassy on Tuesday afternoon.

A military attaché met me at Haina, a very fine marine officer named Heywood, with whom I am still in touch. So I guess he was the one who gave me a quick rundown during the ride into town. And it was not very long after that before the Molina Urena group came to see us. It was a very quiet moment. There had been shooting, street fighting and all that, and both sides were at that moment exhausted or recharging their forces or whatever. In this quiet period Molina Urena and that group came to sue for peace. The situation turned up and down several times; it seemed just like a seesaw, and they were very down at that moment.

It has never been quite clear what happened that evening to turn on the fighting again. According to reports, Caamaño himself was ready to give up, and his brother or somebody kicked him in his rear and said, "Get out there and fight, don't be a coward." And suddenly the fight did turn, and the next morning the rebels overran a police station, where they got more arms. That was a very ominous development.

The warring loyalist faction, led by Molina Urena, came to the American embassy to ask that the United States play a mediating role in the conflict. Ambassador Bennett explains his negative reaction:

> I was not authorized to mediate, nor was it my place to mediate. So when they wanted me to support their cause with the other side, that was not in the cards. I will be frank too; there was a certain feeling on the side of the embassy, and of our government, that these people had precipitated all this violence and killing through their action, and now they were coming to us to pull their chestnuts out of the fire. Well, it was not our position to do that. Nor do I think it would really have had any effect in regard to stopping the course of events as they were then heading. So I did not mediate, and I was backed up by Washington. I have always been supported on that by the State Department, because they know what mediation is. When you undertake mediation, you take on yourself the responsibility to solve the problem. This was something Dominicans had to solve between themselves.

In the fluid political situation of this period there were problems of communication at a variety of levels. They included difficulties in sending messages from one loyalist group to another, and between the U.S. embassy and American forces, and among the U.S. units themselves, once they landed.

> It was terribly hard for people to communicate. It was very hard to find out what was going on. The loyal forces were in separate parts of the city; they could not communicate with one another. This was, of course, one of the reasons that the request for American intervention was late in reaching us, an incident that has been so kicked around without much regard for what the facts were. All that was part of the communications problem. We had the same problem after we landed our own forces: trying to keep in touch with the situation. The problem first became apparent that morning when the police station was overrun—that would have been Wednesday morning. And when Wessin's troops [the armed forces] moved, would that have been Tuesday night? That same night there was supposed to have been a column at the other side of the city, but the other general never did what he was supposed to do, and that is when things began to fall apart. They had no communication between them, that was one problem.

In the rapidly deteriorating situation of this time, the United States moved quickly to embrace a policy of support for a temporary military junta as the only basis for deescalating the civil war.

> I guess by that time we had become convinced that some form of temporary military junta was the only way to restore any order and stop the killing. That was what we were trying to do, stop the killing. There was a lot

more of that than was ever admitted. The Red Cross itself said that 200 people had died around the Ozama Bridge. And that was not all. It was a tremendous casualty toll for a small place. Consider the fact that we evacuated some 4,400 people. If that had happened in Bangladesh, it would have been world news, as it was a year or two later, with only 700 evacuees. But this was on our doorstep and it got very little attention.

I remember Sen. Paul Douglas of Illinois who, at that time, was a very prominent senator. He was there during the Christmas season of 1964, and we had him and his wife to dinner. We saw a fair amount of them. He at the time was complaining that American public opinion and decision-makers tended to look *over* the Caribbean to farther places. The interest was farther away, whereas these places were right on our doorstep, and terribly important to us. We considered it important to restore some kind of order as soon as possible. Then we could sort out the politics. But first you had to stop the fighting and the killing and the looting. We established the military corridor, which at least insulated that area—kept the virus from spreading beyond the old city. It was touch and go in many of the Dominican communities around the country. Others know much more about that than I do because I was busy right there in Santo Domingo. The Inter-American force checked every car going through the corridor lines, and they would find rifles hidden even in the door frames of cars, not just in the trunks—that kind of thing. There were several communities where it was touch and go whether they were going to erupt as Santo Domingo had. I think it was a good thing that we kept all that from happening. Santiago in the north, second-largest city in the country, was a very tender spot. San Francisco de Macoris in the east was apparently ready to go just like that. Now there are many people who were involved down there who know about those things. Some good work was done keeping that fire from spreading. In a country like that, where you have so many underprivileged people in poverty and so forth, there are always people with plenty of grievances and reasons to erupt. They figure that they are not going to be any worse off if they do destroy everything; that is why it is so difficult.

Ambassador Bennett outlined the U.S. military operation:

There were two stages in our military operation. First we called in the marines to evacuate American citizens. That came shortly after lunchtime, after the takeover of the police station and all the other reports that were flooding in about looting—I have a lot of pictures taken by the Episcopal rector there which are very graphic as to the kind of disorder there was. This man was incredible. He went around with his clerical collar on, snapping pictures everywhere. It was about that time that we decided we needed to bring in some forces to protect Americans and manage the evacuation of private citizens. And it was not just Americans. We took out citizens of more than thirty countries, including the Belgian ambassador, who had to be carried out on a litter because he was ill. And then there was the Chinese community, which was a fairly large community. They were the small merchants, and the mobs quickly took their revenge on them and looted their shops. They were all trying to get out, and that became something of a problem because, as I recall it, there were over a thousand of them; it was a very large group.

In keeping with these two stages, American military units, Ambassador Bennett recalled, were landed in two phases:

The first landing of American forces was strictly a rescue operation. We believed that American lives were in danger—and the lives of other foreigners as well. Certainly those people thought they were in peril. There had been the incident of Wednesday morning at the Embajador Hotel, when a number of American families were assembling there to be transported to Haina port for evacuation. A group of Dominican rebels appeared and terrorized the Americans. These were not soldiers, just young toughs—hooligans armed with guns which had been handed out to the populace by some of the military in revolt. These soldiers had opened up armories and distributed guns to all and sundry in the streets, including some as young as eight- and nine-year-old boys. This was one of the most irresponsible things done by the rebel forces, handing out guns without any controls whatsoever. Well, in the incident at the hotel that morning, the rebel group separated the American men from their wives and children, and lined them up against a wall of the hotel. Then they fired their weapons, not directly at the men, but over their heads into the wall above them. You can imagine the panic of those families! No one was actually injured in this incident, but this sort of behavior certainly did not inspire any confidence as to what might happen next. I have pictures taken by that Episcopal priest of the wives and children hiding under tables and chairs at the hotel and of the young rebels brandishing their guns. One picture shows a gunman ripping down the curtain from a big hotel window.

We had one clear purpose in mind in that first landing of U.S. marines. Our concern at that precise moment was to save American lives, and to safeguard the evacuation which had already started by the time the marines came ashore a little after six o'clock in the evening. By that time we had begun burning embassy documents in oil drums on the embassy lawn. We did this because we considered that the small embassy marine guard—every embassy has a regular guard, usually a dozen or so marines—was in danger of being overrun in the chaotic situation and general violence that had developed. It is pretty serious when you get to the point of burning official documents. But that is how far things had gone. Actually, some of the marines later complained that the light from the burning documents had exposed them to risk by silhouetting them against the darkness—night comes early in the tropics—as they approached the embassy from the nearby sports field where they had landed by helicopter from the carrier offshore.

With respect to the actual evacuation, Ambassador Bennett discussed the magnitude and nature of the problem facing the United States, and its role in shaping the U.S. policy of military intervention in the Dominican Republic:

Now with respect to the evacuation, bear in mind—this evacuation was entirely voluntary. No one was told he had to go. More than four thousand people from over thirty countries asked to be taken off that island. These were people who in many instances had lived in the Dominican Republic for many years. They were leaving their careers, their homes, all their possessions. These were individual or family decisions to leave, based on their own estimates of the danger they were in. This was serious business. There is no doubt as to the rationale for the first landing of American forces in 1965. It was to protect American citizens who considered themselves in peril and whose government considered them in peril. The later landings of airborne forces had other purposes. By a couple of days or so later it was clear that the local situation was not stabilizing. In the capital city things had fallen apart completely into general violence and chaos. There was clear danger of the violence spreading to other parts of the country. There was increasing evidence that extreme leftists were taking advantage of the disorder to seize control of events—behind the scenes if not out in front. I am not clear myself as to just when and how the decision was made to broaden the intervention. That was a decision made in Washington, and I was not told a lot about it. But I certainly welcomed it, and I thought it was the right thing to do.

I will tell you a sideline story because it is rather amusing. Mobs began roaming the streets and looting, and one came to the British embassy, which was upstairs over the Texaco Building, on the second floor. They were about to rush up the steps and invade the embassy, and the chargé was at the top of the stairs. Suddenly, in a commanding voice, he said, "Don't you step on those stairs, they belong to the queen." And the mob turned around! There was another incident. The Guatemalan embassy was about to be besieged. Some of the government people had taken refuge in the Guatemalan embassy, one or two people, not a huge crowd. The mob had heard that and was assembling in the street before the embassy. The Guatemalan ambassador's wife, who was quite a character, saw these people coming and gathering outside and they looked very threatening. She went out on the porch: she had let her long hair down and looked very agitated as though something terrible had happened. The crowd yelled, "Who's in there?" She pointed down the street and cried, "They went that way! They went that way!" The mob all raced off that way, and those two people were never found. Those stories have nothing to do with the course of events, but they provide a little atmosphere. There were some serious mob situations, and people were caught up in them. It was not funny at all.

One of the defining characteristics of international crisis is the extent of direct participation by policymakers at the highest level of government, including the president and his key civilian and military advisers. Tapley Bennett discussed this aspect of the crisis from his vantage point as U.S. ambassador to the Dominican Republic:

> At the time people said to me, "Don't you resent having all these top-level people come down here and looking into things?" And I said, "I don't resent it at all, because the sooner those people get here and find out they cannot solve it either, the better I feel and the better it makes me look." And that is what happened. I did not feel that my position was cut back. Ambassador Ellsworth Bunker [U.S. ambassador to the OAS] and I had separate functions, and I had the greatest admiration and respect for him. We worked in very close harmony, and we had either lunch or dinner together almost every day of those nine or ten months he was there. I invited him to stay with me in the ambassador's residence. He thought it was more appropriate for him to stay separately in the hotel. It probably was, since he was there on an OAS mission.
>
> It was similar with General Palmer [who led the American intervention forces]. We are devoted friends to this day; we see each other quite often in Washington. The three of us would sit together, usually at my house because my cook made Florentine eggs which Ellsworth liked, with a bed of spinach under the eggs. In that way things were extremely well coordinated, once we got through the revolutionary phase and into the rebuilding. Minor problems were dealt with at the lunch table before they got to be major ones. General Palmer did stay in my house a week or so at the beginning, and then he got his own quarters. Those months of close association with Bunker and Palmer were one of the richest experiences of my life from the human point of view.

Reflecting on the role of the Organization of American States (OAS) during the crisis, Ambassador Bennett commented,

> First the OAS sent a fact-finding mission. The crisis had become something of a divisive issue in the OAS. Mexico traditionally opposed military action. But I guess one of the principal causes of concern was the Chilean government. And Eduardo Frei Montalva—his was a very hopeful democratic government [1946–70]—and Chile took a contrary position, which was difficult for a lot of people. However, we carried the situation in the OAS. They decided to send a mission down to get the facts, with the United States, Colombia, and El Salvador as members. When they came later to the full rehabilitation mission, Colombia was replaced by Brazil. Anyway, the three representatives came, and were extremely helpful. It was the Colombian ambassador who said, "Why shouldn't we land troops here? Are we supposed to stand on the balcony as at a bullfight and watch people being killed, and do nothing?" That was about as trenchant a comment as anybody could make. They set up shop over in the Embajador Hotel, which was without lights and without elevator service. They were

in the penthouse, which meant they had to climb up twelve flights of stairs, with flickering candles on each landing to light the way. The OAS mission was very successful in establishing facts. The Colombian government is a government that traditionally enjoys respect throughout the hemisphere. So when their ambassador took a strong position of that sort, it was useful. And, of course, Bunker was absolutely superb in his role.

Among the lessons of the crisis not readily understood in retrospect, Ambassador Bennett contends, was that of the Inter-American Peace Force, within which the military intervention took place. Although, of the seven nations represented, the United States contributed by far the largest force, the result was to give to the operation a multilateral imprimatur.

One opportunity that was lost in this crisis, which we should have built on for the future, was the extremely effective way that the Inter-American Peace Force operated. The bulk of the troops were American, but you had troops from seven countries involved there. The general from Brazil was made the commander-in-chief, and Palmer worked very effectively and smoothly with him. There were more than one thousand Brazilian troops; it was not a small contingent. And you know we had fought together in World War II, and the Brazilians were still proud of that record. There were seven countries involved, and that is what you ought to have for future crises. This great opportunity was lost by the muddled reporting and distortion of the true facts there. Instead of having that as an Inter-American achievement to build on for the future, it was, well, considered just something to cover the Americans. That was the way our press played it. But it was not, and it need not have been. It obviously had the helpful effect of supplementing the original U.S. effort, but it was more than that. It was another stone in the Inter-American structure.

Ambassador Bennett offered this perspective on other political figures who played various roles in the crisis, including especially Romulo Betancourt (president of Venezuela), Luiz Munoz Marin (governor of Puerto Rico), and José Figueres (president of Costa Rica):

They were helpful. All three of these highly respected Latin American democratic leaders knew Bosch very well. They were realists and they saw with clear eyes. They were helpful in clarifying facts in the situation, the sort of person Bosch really was. One such person who needed better understanding of the facts was Abe Fortas. Fortas was operating as a private agent for the president, and he was there in Puerto Rico. Then there was Jaime Benitez, then chancellor of the University of Puerto Rico, who came over and stayed in my house for a while. He complained constantly while he was there that he was not getting his eggs properly coddled and all that sort of stuff. Here we were in the middle of a revolution, and he was arguing about whether his egg was two minutes or three minutes.

He was fanatically opposed to the U.S. action; he was very pro-Bosch. So those three recognized paragons of Latin American democracy were enormously helpful in establishing the basic facts of the situation.

Ambassador Bennett discussed the work of Abe Fortas, who served as one of President Johnson's key advisers, and who came to the Dominican Republic at the time of the crisis:

He came down, and was helpful in getting the initial cease-fire between Dominican forces. I think he has taken a little more credit to himself than he deserves, although he was helpful. I do not think it was entirely his handiwork, as he likes to believe. He was quite courageous in facing up to the facts of the situation, even though it cost him politically, and he knew it would. It made him break with a lot of his liberal friends. I cannot remember now how long he stayed, but it might have been as much as a week, or maybe four or five days. He was just heartbroken because he was very emotionally committed to the Dominican Republic. As is sometimes the case with political ambassadors, he sort of thought it was his country, because that was the place where he had served. So this descent into carnage and killing in a country in which he had worked affected him very, very much.

In the process leading to the formation of the temporary junta, the United States entered into negotiations with Antonio Imbert. Ambassador Bennett discussed the problems that he encountered in establishing contact with Imbert in the unsettled political circumstances of the Dominican Republic at that time:

It was not official U.S. policy, but we all dealt with Imbert—Imbert was on the right side of the fence at the time. He had his own ambitions, of course; he wanted to end up being the head of the country. Cyrus Vance, deputy secretary of defense at the time, and I did some midnight maneuvering with Imbert which has never been told. We made several trips to him on dark nights to try to get some reasonable responses on things. Imbert was one of the two assassins of Trujillo who had survived. Each of them was allowed to have his own private militia—army is too big a word—but he had a force of about thirty goons around him, and these guys were real gorillas. He lived in a large house out in the western part of town. Imbert came from an old-line Dominican family and had a certain social prestige. He was not one of the raw military people who had just come out of the caves. His wife was an attractive woman of Dominican society, that sort of thing. They lived in a big house with extensive grounds, and up on the top of the second—or maybe it was the third—floor was this single room. That was his office, his stronghold. Everything was pitch dark; there were no streetlights or anything. Vance and I would go out in the car. There was a fair amount of shooting at night in those days, just desultory shooting, not strong attacks. You would get out there and these gorillas would suddenly emerge out of the bushes, and you never knew whether they were going to shoot before they looked, or what. They were all armed to the teeth with submachine guns. Then we would climb the steps up to his area on the top and try to reason with him.

At one stage we were trying to get a counterforce to curb the violence. There was a danger that the rebel forces were going to break through the northwest section of the city and go out toward Santiago [de los Cabelleros], and he was helpful in damping that down. At other times we wanted to get Imbert to work for the common good—this was mostly at a later stage—and stop trying to use us to catapult himself into leadership of the country. There came a time when Martin's "creation of Imbert's junta," of which he was so proud, came to be an obstacle in the effort to find a middle-of-the-road provisional government, and we had to damp Imbert down.

Among the goals of U.S. diplomacy at this time was finding a suitable candidate to serve as provisional president for the period leading up to elections. Ambassador Bennett described this difficult process and the selection of Hector García-Godoy:

The second OAS mission, with Ellsworth Bunker as the chairman, interviewed over one hundred individual Dominicans, trying to find somebody suitable to serve as provisional president—a president who could gradually, with our support, lead the country toward elections. García-Godoy emerged through this winnowing process as the one man who could do it. Now, he happened to be a very good friend of mine from my earlier days in the Dominican Republic, twenty years before. We had all been bachelors together and used to go to dances and that sort of thing. There was not a politically cleaner man on this globe than García-Godoy. He had served as Bosch's nonpolitical foreign minister, which made him acceptable to the Left. At the same time he came out of the Dominican establishment and was known to be a man of probity and high learning. So, after long discussions over several weeks, the OAS committee finally decided that he was the best man.

Among the attractive features of García-Godoy, according to Ambassador Bennett, was the fact that he had never been associated politically with Bosch:

He was never a Bosch man in political terms, although he had been in Bosch's diplomatic service. He was one of the few nonpartisan people in the country. He was sworn in as provisional president on September 3, 1965, and I presented my credentials to him that day. There followed over the next several months a tug-of-war between him and the military. There were many nights when Ellsworth Bunker and I would sit in one room in his house and the military were in another and García-Godoy would shuttle between us. The military would be pressuring him to do this or that, and we knew that was the wrong thing to do and we would try to stiffen his back. He was a completely honorable man. He was not the strongest man in the world, but he had every other good quality. After all, it is not easy to be strong against people who are pointing pistols at you.

Regarded as crucially important to the future political stability of the Dominican Republic was the finding of suitable alternative employment, preferably out of the country, for key members of the military who had played important roles in the junta since the overthrow of Bosch.

It was important to get Gen. Elias Wessin y Wessin [who had commanded the loyalist forces] out of the country by making him consul general in [the United States]. Getting people out of the country was important, and the military dug in to oppose that, particularly the ones who were ticketed to go. Caamaño was sent to London. Some of us, and I am not saying myself, had doubts as to whether he should be treated so well. But it was one way—and I think García-Godoy understood his own people on this—of getting the troublemakers out by giving them what seemed to be rather cushy jobs abroad. So Caamaño did go to London, and the British knew just how to treat him; they ignored him. He later just disappeared, reportedly into Cuba.

The U.S. military intervention in the Dominican Republic had coincided with the escalation in the Vietnam conflict. According to Ambassador Bennett, as might be expected, events in Vietnam helped shape U.S. perspectives, including those in the military, with regard to the Dominican Republic intervention:

It was very much in our minds there. We had two or three generals—I remember one particularly, Bob York—who had come back from Vietnam. York was one of those who was terribly frustrated over the way he considered our military's hands had been tied in Vietnam. At one point the troop level in the Dominican Republic was just a few thousand short of Vietnam. That was before the big escalation in Vietnam had come. We had about 22,000 in the Dominican Republic. That was criticized as being too many, but I would rather have too many than too few. Although I do remember one time, just after the marines landed, I looked out the window and saw what looked like the biggest tank in the world clanking down the street—it turned out to be an armored personnel carrier. I said, "We do not need anything like that here; all we need are a few good marines with guns to protect us and get these people out of here." Well, they replied, "When you call in the marines, you get the whole package."

Asked if President Johnson regarded this as one of the crises that was successfully managed, Ambassador Bennett responded,

Oh, very much so. He hit his highest point of approval in the polls just after he took the Dominican action. His book [Lyndon B. Johnson, *The Vantage Point: Perspectives of the Presidency, 1963–1969* (New York: Holt, Rinehart and Winston, 1971)] has a chapter on the Dominican Republic, and he comments favorably on the way things were done. He was quite satisfied with it, as was Secretary Rusk. As I have always said, it was a controversial action, and my role was controversial. I suffered a good bit of Calvary in the press. But I never had the slightest problem in the quarters where it counted, with the secretary of state and the president. After all, I was a rookie ambassador and could have easily been tossed overboard without a trace. Any ambassador is expendable in the national interest. But they were always on my side and gave me full support. Dean Rusk said to me once, "Well, now you have disproved the theory that with modern communications ambassadors are just messenger boys."

As Ambassador Bennett recounts, President Johnson on occasion engaged in hyperbole in describing events with which he or his administration was associated. The Dominican Republic crisis of 1965 was no exception.

There is no question that in a press conference he exaggerated that business about the 1,200 people with their heads cut off, lying there in the streets. That was obviously hyperbole. People who knew Lyndon Johnson knew that he talked in exaggerated terms. But the press took that remark in particular, along with several others, and used it against him.

I remember when I went to Washington to see him in August of 1965, after the troops had settled in, he said, "I want you to get me some pictures of people with their heads cut off. I do not like people calling me a liar." I replied, "Well, Mr. President, there was some decapitation." We knew of three cases. And he said, "You see what you can find for me; I don't like people calling me a liar." Well, we did get some of the most grisly pictures; they were so grisly that I did not even want to keep copies of them at the time. If you were pro-Johnson and pro-action, you tended to excuse that saying, well, everybody knows LBJ is a Texan and talks tall, too tall sometimes. But if you opposed the action, you took that as an example of an effort to pull wool over the American people's eyes.

Asked about the military lessons of the Dominican crisis, Ambassador Bennett offered a terse comment on the nature, magnitude, and effectiveness of U.S. military power deployed in support of American diplomacy at this time:

You would have to ask a military man on that. From my point of view, I called the marines and they came. I would emphasize that they left thirty days to the hour. I have the plaque to prove it. The marines like to get in and out; they do not like to stay in a place. That is one of the problems we had in Lebanon in 1983; they got caught there. In the Dominican Republic they were replaced by the airborne force. The airborne stayed on, and elections were held—free elections, so attested—and our troops were gotten out a month or two earlier than the original schedule had called for. I look on the Dominican action as helping a small neighbor back on the road—they had gotten off the road—and we helped them back on the road to democracy.

The result of the 1965 intervention is that the Dominican Republic has now, some twenty years later, enjoyed the longest period of stability of its entire history—a period in which the average person, whom we are all supposed to be interested in, has had room to expand and make his or her own lot a little better. If we could override our sugar lobby and allow Dominican sugar to come into this country, then they might live happily ever after.

22
Eastern European Crises

A mong the international crises of the last two generations, several have
had Eastern Europe as their locus. In particular, the Soviet Union in
1956 in Hungary, and in Czechoslovakia in 1968, intervened with
massive military force to oust governments threatening Moscow's hegemony.
In 1981 Poland faced the prospect of change unacceptable to Moscow. The
result was a crackdown by the Polish military, thus averting the need for the
Soviet Union to use its own forces directly in Poland. Gen. Andrew J. Goodpaster, who was President Eisenhower's staff secretary, describes the reaction
of the administration to the Hungarian crisis in 1956:

> Our first hope was to avoid the Soviet use of force against the Hungarians.
> We saw the revolution in Hungary as responding to inherent forces and
> the desires of the people to assert their own nationality and regain
> measures of sovereignty and extend greater personal and national free-
> doms. We were concerned that it would get out of hand and develop to
> a point where the Soviets would intervene by force.
> It took no time at all for Eisenhower to decide that there was no pros-
> pect of American military intervention. What we were hoping for was that
> there could be improvement in the situation in Hungary without bringing
> the Russians in. When we got the word that Prime Minister Nagy spoke
> of leaving the Warsaw Pact and joining NATO, I recall talking with Presi-
> dent Eisenhower and feeling that Nagy had perhaps signed his own death
> warrant. It would be very dangerous for him to attempt to go down this
> road. In fact, we discussed the possibility, the question, of whether there
> was any way we could get word to the Russians that we had no interest
> and no intent of trying to draw Hungary into NATO because we felt that
> would certainly tip the scale and that the Soviet Union would, in all
> likelihood, intervene. Whether that word got to the Soviets and, if it did,
> whether they believed it, I do not know—and I suppose we will never
> really know. There were some who felt that it was a lost endeavor, or not
> likely to succeed in any case, but I still think that once the Soviets saw the
> issue in those terms, that triggered their decision. They may, of course,

already have made the decision, and may just have been holding back to a time of their own choosing. Once they had started to intervene, I think that it was clear from our standpoint that there was no prospect of doing something to save the Hungarians.

General Goodpaster noted that the Eisenhower administration was not surprised by the Soviet move:

We saw a process going on there and saw the possibility that it would occasion Soviet intervention. I do not recall that we thought it would break out into this strong assertion of independence that did in fact occur. Subsequently, there were insinuations and charges in some quarters that the Hungarians had been led to believe that if they would take that stand for independence we would intervene on their behalf. We made a careful review, the result of which was that they had not been given that assurance. But I think we all had some question left in our minds as to whether, by implication, they had been led to think the United States might intervene. It was just an utter tragedy and, of course, brought terrible harm to the Hungarians. They spoke of a possibility of joining NATO. My own feeling—and I think others shared it—was that once that came into play—that is, that they might go beyond neutrality to something hostile to the Soviet Union—the odds that the Soviet Union would intervene then became very great.

There has been criticism of a different nature, that other people have said that the very fact that the U.S. government—Dulles twice, and Eisenhower at one point—would come out and say that we do not have any intention of making Hungary a military ally of the United States in effect gives the Soviets carte blanche, freedom from worrying that the United States might do something, whereas they might have been concerned about a U.S. response and backed off. I do not think so. We felt that the Soviets were making decisions on the basis of a fair assessment of their own interests—that if they felt threatened, they were going to go in—so I do not believe that aspect of it, that particular implication of it, was ever seriously considered.

One of the Soviet tests of the resolve of the Eisenhower administration came in 1959, when Nikita Khrushchev threatened to give control of the access routes to West Berlin to the East German government. At that time, the United States and its Western allies, notably Britain and France, as the other occupying powers of West Berlin, did not have diplomatic relations with the German Democratic Republic. By this proposed action, Khrushchev would have forced the West to alter its policy toward what it regarded as a Soviet puppet regime. At the same time, the East German government, it was feared, would be under no obligation to observe Soviet commitments to the West regarding land access to West Berlin. In turn, a change in the status of West Berlin to the detriment of the West would have a far broader political-psychological effect on the Federal Republic of Germany and the Atlantic Alliance. General Goodpaster described the problem from his vantage point in the Eisenhower administration:

> I think it was very clear that the Soviets were firmly determined to maintain a strong military force in East Germany and that they would be seeking to reestablish some degree of control over West Germany. This collective security framework that they proposed in place of existing alliances would have had that effect. And, of course, that has remained the Soviet approach to security to this day—collective security. They were being bled by the flow of people out of East Germany to West Berlin and wanted to assume control. The Russians said to us that they were going to give control of this to the East Germans and that was what triggered the crisis. We then entered into negotiation or discussion with them. Secretary of State Christian Herter was involved in this and took the active part. We did not receive firm support from the British and the French; as a matter of fact, their positions were rather soft. So it was a difficult situation for us.

At the time of the Soviet invasion of Czechoslovakia in 1968, François de Rose was French ambassador to Portugal. He told of a meeting that he had with Portuguese president Salazar:

> It was around the first of May 1968, just at the time of the Prague spring. I had visited Prague the previous fall. I said, "Most interesting things are taking place right now." He said, "Monsieur Ambassador, this will end like Budapest. There are provocations that a great power cannot put up with." And I found it extraordinarily interesting that a man whose whole life had been a fight against Communism, was so much a man of the nineteenth century that he had the concept of the hierarchy of nations, that the Czechs—by being provocative to a big power—were going to get smacked and that it was inevitable. I think that of all the European statesmen, Salazar was the least surprised—just as revolted, but the least surprised—when the Russian troops marched into Prague.

General von Kielmansegg was commander-in-chief of Allied Forces, Central Europe at the time of the Soviet invasion. General von Kielmansegg discussed the warnings of the impending Soviet military intervention and the assessment of escalating crisis within NATO from his vantage point:

> As far as strategic surprise is concerned, in contrast to the time of World War I, I would say today it is nearly impossible, but *tactical* surprise is nearly always possible. That is my experience from the example of Czechoslovakia in 1968. We were not surprised at all. In the middle of April 1968 we had the first signs that something abnormal was going on. [The

Soviet invasion took place on August 21.] We were then following the situation and had an exact picture of the Soviet deployment. This picture was so clear that in the West we were quite aware that it was not anything against us, not even the famous trick of turning around out of a maneuver [for an invasion]. You can do this, but it needs weeks, not days, and it would be absurd. On the second of August, Gen. Lyman Lemmitzer, supreme allied commander, Europe, gave the NATO Council his daily commanders' evaluation. The very last sentence of that day's evaluation was, "Now they only need to say, ''Go.' '' They invaded on the twenty-first of August; so there was no surprise at all, except for the date. It was because our picture was so clear that the governments did nothing. They should have done something, because we were not in any danger, not at all. This example is a very good one for crises in the future. . . . We have worked on the Czechoslovak crisis, and our conclusion was that the Soviets even deliberately leaked information in the weeks preceding the invasion in order to test Western reaction—not only to test, but to try to get their desired result without invading.

Gen. Franz-Josef Schulze commanded a brigade at this time. He also commented on the Czechoslovak crisis:

NATO was not threatened; the threat was clearly posed to Czechoslovakia. This is the reason why the Soviets, and later on all participating Warsaw Pact forces, made all their preparations so openly. If you want to intimidate someone, you have to do that demonstratively—and so they did. They took a tank division out of the Baltic military district, brought it down by rail and road, and then marched up to the Czech border and back. Then they had a logistics exercise around Czechoslovakia, and every time they hoped that by now the Czechs will be so intimidated that they will give in. That was clear from the very beginning, but I still believe that NATO did not react in the way it should have. NATO did not want to heighten tensions or contribute to the escalation. So an exercise which was planned in the south, in the CENTAG (Central Army Group) area, close to the Bavarian forest, was withdrawn and was played near the Black Forest. I think that was wrong.

The danger was that the Soviets, if they finally came to the conclusion that they had to invade Czechoslovakia, would run the risk that elements of the Czech army would defect; and that then Soviet forces would follow them in hot pursuit. Indeed, the Soviets themselves have seen that risk. That was the reason why they made that swift movement along the border out of the southwestern edge of the GDR, that very swift move with GDR and Soviet forces. That was something we should have taken into account beforehand. Until then, it was a Czech affair. But at the moment when Soviet forces would have crossed our border and violated the integrity of NATO terrain, without being countered, we would have lost forever any deterrence capability. The same is true as far as the Czech Air Force is concerned. There was a danger that some of the pilots would try to get away from Czechoslovakia and the Soviets would follow them in hot pursuit in violation of NATO airspace. So our air forces in that area should have been in the highest state of readiness; indeed, all our own air defense forces. That is a lesson to be taken from the Czech crisis. Most people rather like to think that we reacted very wisely because we were so cautious to not react at all.

Former secretary of state Dean Rusk commented on the U.S. position regarding the Soviet invasion:

The attitude of the West since World War II has been that however disagreeable we find these regimes in Eastern Europe, whatever they do to their own people, it is simply not an issue for war between East and West. It is very important not to bluff in these situations. When the Soviets moved, we immediately took another step to deter an expansion to Romania and Yugoslavia. We had some military talks with the Yugoslavs about supplies that they might need. In Czechoslovakia, one of the key issues came to be the monopoly on power by the Communist party. That was a point that the Soviets were very sensitive about. Romania, while slightly independent, had a tight Communist regime. The Yugoslavs had demonstrated that they were able to fight in World War II. I think that the Soviet Union has a major problem with the peoples of Eastern Europe. One sees increasing signs that these peoples have strong nationalist feelings and cultural links with the West. This is a difficult problem for Moscow to overcome.

I do not believe it is possible for the United States to display the necessary body language to the Soviets to convince them that we are willing to undertake a certain action to deter them from doing something unless we are serious. I do not think we can fool the Soviet Union. I always assumed that we were penetrated. Even at a meeting of the NATO foreign ministers, I always assumed that the Soviets would be fully informed. Indeed, I once used such a meeting to send a message to Moscow, thinking that it would be more credible if they received it that way than if I had given it to their ambassador.

In the summer of 1968 Richard Nixon was campaigning for the presidency. Richard Allen was Mr. Nixon's foreign policy adviser. He comments on the perception of the Czechoslovak crisis from within the Nixon campaign, as well as his perception of the principal reason for Nixon's unwillingness to condemn harshly the policy of the Johnson administration at the time:

In the case of Czechoslovakia I shared or suffered a small internal setback as a result of making an accurate prediction myself. In 1968, as I was coordinating the Nixon foreign policy operations, I firmly believed that the Soviets would invade. I had come to this conclusion by June. In my preparations of the candidate for that event, which I felt was certain, I sent him a memorandum either in late June or early July to the effect that I concluded that the Soviets would invade Czechoslovakia, that it is a matter of time, and that contrary to all the talk about it being an impossibility because the Soviets would never be able to sustain the damage done in the court of world opinion (whatever that is or wherever it is located) and all of the reasons that were being deduced why the Prague Spring would never be reversed, and that Dubček was on an irreversible course, struck me as phony. I was part of the community at that time that was temporarily detached from Stanford, at the Hoover Institution, where I was doing the *Yearbook for International Communist Affairs*. I had come to the professional and instinctive conclusion that the Soviets would have to act. All you had to do was think, at least temporarily, like a Marxist-Leninist of modern persuasion and you would have to come to the conclusion that an invasion would be the only way to do it. The problem was that the media was simply sticking it in the eye of the Kremlin every day. Such things as Dubček on the cover of *Time* magazine did not help, it hurt. Rather than permitting Dubček and his crowd to creep away slowly from the Soviet Union, they were looking, hoping, for some lurch to democracy.

On the night of August 21, I was in the office and I learned of the invasion of Czechoslovakia. Mr. Nixon had been out on a campaign swing. I awakened him from a sound sleep, with a special number to call him that I had, to tell him that the Soviets had invaded Czechoslovakia. He said, "What, what, goddamn them; what are you saying?" I repeated it, as he was waking up. It was early in the evening, about 9:30, 10:00, and he said, "Get over here right away." I hotfooted over to the apartment—Pat Buchanan [who was then executive assistant to Nixon] went with me—and I was there as he took the call from Lyndon Johnson. Lyndon Johnson had called Nixon at the apartment and obviously asked him to softpedal it and not go out-of-sight. Let's remember that we were then in the latter stages of the first period of détente which had begun with the Test Ban Treaty of 1963 and the debate surrounding it and the conclusions we had come to; the idea that fat Communists were less dangerous than lean ones was a lie in every sense; Khrushchev's "goulash" Communism, consumerism, and so forth.

He continued:

We released essentially the statement that I had prepared, but it was toned down. Nixon never spoke as harshly as he might have about the failure of the United States to react. I think I later learned why; it formed part of the deal that Nixon had with Johnson because Johnson really believed that Hubert Humphrey was too soft. As a matter of fact, I believe that Lyndon Johnson ultimately came to the conclusion that Nixon was better for the United States than Hubert Humphrey. That really changed my appraisal of Lyndon Johnson as a president. None of this is on paper; it will always be denied, but I believe it to be the case. Later this experience led to some newspaper leaks, alleging that at a subsequent staff meeting

I viewed my memorandum predicting the invasion of Czechoslovakia as some reason for taking yet another hard-line step toward the Soviet Union in our policy-making during the campaign. It was unbelievable, because I never did. I never, never mentioned the memorandum again. It had been circulated among other people.

This led me to the formulation of Allen's third law. I have a number of laws, proven in experiencing history, like laws of chemistry and physics. Allen's third law holds that it is always wrong to be right too soon in public circles. The person who is out first on the block with the correct prediction will always, ultimately, be ridiculed because the masses of policy analysts will only catch up to it later. Johnson had had his Glassboro Summit in June 1967, just fourteen months earlier. He still very much wanted to be invited to the Soviet Union, so I think that this accounts in a large measure for his inability to step up the condemnation of the Soviet Union that ought to have been delivered, much less take preemptive or any deliberate action. Someday we will know what the intelligence flow on that really was in those days. My feeling then was that a clever, insightful, and courageous president would have blockaded and invaded Cuba right away. Would there be costs? You bet, but the Soviets would have their hands full in Czechoslovakia. Moving swiftly on Cuba in August would have been Lyndon Johnson's monumental contribution to world peace, and it would have solved a problem created by Kennedy.

In 1980 the Solidarity trade union movement in Poland grew in strength and boldly challenged the authority of the Communist government. David Newsom, under secretary of state for political affairs from 1978 to 1981, noted that the Carter administration took an active role in discouraging any Soviet military move:

Poland loomed large in the Carter administration's thinking because the end of the 1970s was the height of the Solidarity period [at that time, before the events of the late 1980s that catapulted Solidarity to power in Poland]. Over that period we frequently had delegations of Polish-Americans visiting the State Department, often with quite different views about what should be done. Some advised us to have nothing to do with the Polish leadership, while others urged that now is the time to use our influence. Somewhere in this 1979–80 period we also had the increase in Soviet troop strength around Poland and were faced with the very real concern that the Soviets were thinking of going into Poland. The administration not only sent strong signals to the Soviets, but also did what they could to enlist the efforts of Western European countries in dealing with the Soviet Union on the Polish issue. Whether those efforts were instrumental in keeping the Soviet Union from going in or whether the Soviets on their own decided that the cost of trying to retake Poland was just too great, we will never know. Subsequently you had Gen. Wojciech Jaruzelski come in, the declaration of martial law and sanctions, which carried on into the Reagan years.

The feeling was that we took the mobilizations around Poland seriously because the Soviets had shown that when they felt their interests were threatened, they were not afraid to move militarily even if it caused them some problems in world opinion. Moreover, there is the history of Soviet military intervention: in Hungary in 1956, in Czechoslovakia in 1968, and it was twelve years later now. If there is any pattern to Soviet military intervention, it came in Afghanistan and not in Poland. This was not looked at in quite this way, I suppose. However, I may not have been in on all of the philosophical discussions on this. In my recollection it was regarded not so much in terms of the Brezhnev doctrine, but in the context of Soviet interests. Poland for them represented a special problem because Solidarity was really challenging the primacy of the Communist party and that was unacceptable. I think it was considered a very serious possibility.

At this time, Tapley Bennett was the U.S. permanent representative to NATO. He described the discussion within NATO on the crisis in Poland:

As to the Polish question, that was very much an issue at NATO. We devoted many hours and many days to meetings, just the members of the council—no back-up team or anything of that sort—in trying to divine what might happen or estimate what might happen and what should be done. That was in marked contrast to the past because I went back and got the records, and I also heard from Harland Cleveland, who had been U.S ambassador to NATO at the time of the Czech crisis. There was hardly any consultation then at all; we did not share any information on the Czech situation—this was 1967 or 1968. In contrast, on Poland, we went at it for weeks and months. I tend to believe, and it is a self-serving belief, that the great concern shown by NATO was one of the factors that may have kept the Soviets from acting militarily because they knew—it was made clear—that there was great Western concern over how they were handling the Solidarity issue.

There is a regular exchange of information within NATO at several meetings each year. The Political Committee follows political developments all year long, and the council discusses those reports. There would have been that kind of discussion. We followed that from the beginning, and as it got worse or more tense in Poland, we got more interested. It was not an easy consultation because the Europeans were extremely nervous about Poland, in contrast to the earlier Soviet move on Afghanistan. We could not get much European interest in Afghanistan, although I took occasion at the time to point out that with modern transportation, Afghanistan is no farther away today than Danzig was in the 1930s. But it did not make much impact on the Europeans; they did not want to get involved. They saw Poland as an immediate threat, and their memories of Poland and its role in precipitating World War II were very strong. So you did not have to work to capture their attention on Poland, but that did not mean they wanted to do much. They were very nervous. The Germans, being next door, were particularly cautious about agreeing on any specific measures, and the German ambassador was constantly trying to put his heels down and put on the brakes.

A whole range of specific diplomatic measures was discussed— whether to withdraw ambassadors, whether to express disapproval, whether not to attend the birthday party or the national day reception of this or that country. These are small slaps on the wrist, but in diplomacy they are the first steps. Then economic sanctions, where we were always more enthusiastic than the Europeans, were discussed. And then what kind of military reaction. We discussed the whole range of options, and we drew up papers and had several pages of possible contingencies and contingency actions. This is not military planning. This is political planning which envisages certain military moves. However, the damper was on from the beginning, and several people got their knuckles rapped for public statements that NATO would do this, or that, or that NATO would certainly move militarily if the Soviet Union moved militarily. That was always a no-no. The uncertainty of NATO's response was one of the points. [Joseph] Luns was a very strong believer in the effectiveness of a policy of uncertain response: that so long as the other side knows that you will react, it is better not to be specific on how you plan to react. That was implicit in the consideration of the Polish question. It was accepted from the beginning by everybody that Poland is absolutely vital to the Soviet Union. All the Soviet supply lines to Germany run through Poland, and so forth. So it was clear that the Soviets would take whatever action they thought necessary to contain the situation if it got seriously out of hand and that they were not going to let Poland slide out from under their control.

Now there was always a great question as to whether they could handle it through the Polish government or whether they would actually have to use their own troops, many of whom were already quartered in Poland. Then there is the commander of the Warsaw Pact forces. He was in and out of Poland all during this period. But as to what kind of force they would use, that was hard to say. In December 1981 Secretary of State Haig had been in Brussels for the scheduled NATO ministerial meeting and was leaving that morning to go somewhere in the Middle East. I had been scheduled to come home for Christmas. As I was getting dressed, I heard a news report on the radio that troops had moved into Poland. I thought, "Uh oh, here goes the trip." But my wife and I went and got on the plane. We got to Paris, and it was clear by that time that I was not going on to the States. I had to turn around and go back, but I could not get a plane back to Brussels for three or four hours. So that trip was an error on my part.

I got back rather late in the light of events then in motion. Haig had canceled his departure and stayed on in Brussels for another day or two. I did not get home for Christmas at all because it was too tense all during those days. I just stayed right there. Then finally I came over—I was due home on leave and had a very involved program over on this side, with speeches, a dinner with Vice President Bush and so on—I did come over but that promptly got quashed. I had a total of only four days of home leave because they called a special NATO meeting of foreign ministers back in Brussels on the eleventh of January. So I flew right back and Secretary Haig came back again; and we had an enormous snowfall the morning of the meeting. I was to host a breakfast at my residence for Haig and the other "big four" foreign ministers. The snow continued, but people gradually drifted in. West German Foreign Minister Genscher never got there because of the weather, but it was an exciting day. There was a feeling of genuine crisis about Poland. The very fact that NATO was seen to be so active on it was, I think, one element in deterring the Soviet Union from going all the way and intervening with its own troops. I might mention one other thing in connection with Poland. France always insisted on playing a large role in the Polish discussions, because France considers that she has a very special position in Poland—long-standing emotional and political ties. France is very possessive about Poland, more than the British are. But it was the Germans who worked the hardest on softening the language on Poland. It was general German nervousness about the tense border and the East German situation and the fact that they are on the front line. After the December 13 moves, a one-day meeting of foreign ministers enabled us to reach a satisfactory arrangement. After all, we at NATO had been preparing for months for just this sort of crisis, and we at the U.S. mission were generally satisfied with what came out of that meeting. It was Haig, if I remember correctly, who called for the meeting, but there was no hanging back on having a meeting. Everybody was quite ready to meet on it.

23
The Congo Crisis

A mong the issues confronting the Kennedy administration in the months after it came into office in 1961 was the rapidly deteriorating situation in the Congo (now Zaire). In 1960 Belgium had granted independence to the Congo. The immediate result was the outbreak of tribal strife and the eruption of secessionist movements that, had they succeeded, would have fragmented the new state. The Kennedy administration was committed to the preservation of a Congo state and the integrity of the borders that had been established during Belgian rule. The U.S. ambassador to the Congo during much of this turbulent period was Edmund A. Gullion, who set forth his perspectives on the policy issues, within the broader context of U.S. foreign policy at the time:

> The Congo crisis was the first foreign affairs test for the Kennedy adminis-
> tration. It is hard to look back on those days and recognize the tremendous
> concentration on the Congo problem. It was a major test for the new
> administration, at all levels, including the president, Congress, and the
> press. The administration's concentration on the Congo was as intense as
> that on Vietnam later in the Kennedy administration. The president had
> major stakes in the question. A defeat in those days would have been as
> important as a defeat in Cuba. Indeed, the Bay of Pigs was a contempora-
> neous event. However, in retrospect, the defeat in the Bay of Pigs proved
> to be more serious than a failure in the Congo would have been.
>
> The problem in the Congo was complex. When I arrived there, the
> Congo had not one secession, but two concurrent secessions under way.
> There was the Katanga secession, led by [Moïse] Tshombe and backed by
> the Belgian Union Minière Company, which sought to protect its invest-
> ment and people. There was another and perhaps more serious conflict in
> the Orientale province in the northeast. There [Antoine] Gizenga, the
> chosen man of the Soviet Union, had set up his own secession. With the
> support of the Soviet Union he was creating his own state, with foreign
> representation from Eastern bloc countries. If the Congo was to break in
> pieces—as it appeared at the time—it seemed likely that there would be a
> series of secessions and a predatory power would pick up the pieces.

Again, after Vietnam and many years later, it is hard to recognize now that the Cold War was then at its peak. We had the Eisenhower Doctrine, which I regard as a high watermark in the confrontation. We had the Vienna Conference in which Khrushchev had thought he had taken Kennedy's measure. And it was evident that Africa and the less developed world fell within the arena of contest. I think it was already appreciated that a contest in Central Europe was not something the Soviet Union desired. We felt that the Soviets knew that the road to Paris would lead not through Berlin, but through the outer markings of the civilized world. There were some sixteen countries that had their independence since 1960.

It was declared Soviet policy that once the "dead end of capitalism" was removed from those countries they would rise up against "foreign exploiters" and throw them out, in Marxist textbook fashion. Africa seemed to present exactly the kind of paradigm on which the Soviet dialectic was based. There was an uneven distribution of wealth, to an extent which made strife throughout the entire continent not entirely unlikely. Thus, the Soviets felt that all they had to do was to guide this process according to the laws of Marxist dialectics and Africa would fall into their hands. Gizenga was their instrument—after Lumumba's death—to achieve this.

The Soviets also had to support the idea of a unified Congo, but outside of the United Nations framework. Their position was that the entire United Nations action was a sham, an instrument of United States policy. The Soviet Union seemed to be under the impression that we, the United States, owned the Congo, and that we had a great interest in maintaining a strong position there. This, of course, was not true. The United States, at the time, had more of a missionary interest in the Congo, but the Soviets did not believe that. They offered to give aid to end the secession to Gizenga and other factions, alleging that the United States really supported the remnants of colonial interests. They played this line with Lumumba, as well as with Gizenga. Lumumba accepted some Soviet aid, but generally it was done through surrogate states, most notably the Arab countries, but on the whole, the Soviet presence was never strong.

The Soviets also suffered from a paradox. While supporting the central government of [Cyrille] Adoula, they had to try to thrust him leftward or throw him out of office. While attempting to influence Adoula, they also maintained their support for Gizenga.

The Belgians were the colonial power. Their interest was largely commercial. They did not have a long colonial tradition. It was typical for Belgians to come to the Congo not to stay for generations, but to make their money and leave. The Congo and especially Katanga province were very rich in mineral resources. The Belgians obviously wanted to protect their influence over the colony, which was their central asset in Africa. Hence, the Congo played a very prominent part in Belgian policy. Just as an illustration, I remember two maps hanging in the Leopoldville [now Kinshasa] guest house of Sabena, the Belgian airline. One of them showed Belgium, the other the Congo. Both were of exactly the same size. This says something of the mentality of the Belgians.

Within the context of the global role of the United States, Ambassador Gullion discussed the perspectives held by President Kennedy, concerned as he was with the need for the United States to separate itself from European colonialism then in its waning years. This dimension of U.S. foreign policy created problems for the United States in relations with NATO-European allies.

First of all, President Kennedy saw the Congo case as a cascade of colonial power. His views were considerably influenced by his experience in Indochina. He thought that the Congo case afforded the United States an opportunity to show that we supported anticolonial aspirations. This produced a strain with the colonial, or ex-colonial, powers, a recurrent theme throughout the entire episode. Our relationship with the British and French had already suffered due to the Suez crisis. Kennedy's own psychology was brisk and decisive. He was not patient with a great deal of Stevensonian philosophizing and hesitation. On the other hand, he had powerful sympathies with the British. In fact, he had close personal ties with the British. Throughout the Congo period these two feelings were in conflict. The sympathy for concerns of the allies and his understanding of anticolonial aspirations had to be reconciled somehow. We used to see this inner tension quite frequently. At times he would accept strong position papers on the Congo, but then waver in his approach after consultation with allied representatives.

I remember having dinner with Chip Bohlen [ambassador to the Soviet Union in the Eisenhower administration] just after the inauguration. Bohlen asked me what was Kennedy's character in terms of action. I answered that I interpreted Kennedy as a sort of "go for broke man," which he really was, but there were also these other pressures on him. In the White House we saw the seeds of the conflict between the formal policy formulation agencies, the Department of State, the NSC, and the White House. Then there were divisions within the White House. The advisers, Adlai Stevenson, Dean Rusk, George Ball, Averell Harriman, Ralph Dungan, McGeorge Bundy, and George McGhee would disagree among themselves and change positions frequently. These changes in position occurred particularly during the final round of the operation in the Congo. The big issue was whether the United Nations operation should proceed involving the use of force. Some backed down on the issue, including Harriman, as I recall. The McGhee mission in the final round is another indicator of the softening in attitudes. McGhee wanted to prevent an armed clash by once again attempting to draw Tshombe into negotiations—an attempt that had proven futile numerous times already.

I myself knew pretty much what ought to be done in the Congo, after I had been there for a while. There also was hardly any disagreement within the mission. The lone dissenter was Consul Hoffacker in Elisabethville, who developed an affinity towards the cause of Tshombe. In large part, I had to make sure that at home everybody stayed in line. At times I could appeal to the president himself. At times I had to compete with other people for influence.

Ambassador Gullion described the bureaucratic relationships during the Congo crisis, as well as U.S. decision making and the importance of the U.S. diplomatic mission in the Congo:

At the time we had a powerful White House not prepared to delegate executive authority on the issue. The result was that policy really had to be hammered out both with the State Department and the presidential staff. This, in a way, was a forerunner of today's situation. Today we are faced with a continuous proliferation of adversarial relationships within the American government, brought about on purpose. Of course, we need checks and balances within the government, as guaranteed in the Constitution. But in the nuclear age, with minimal warning and reaction time, such factional decision making is not always advisable.

In our case, even the smallest things had to be referred to the highest authorities. I remember one occasion when [Moïse] Tshombe [provisional premier of Katanga province in the Congo] wanted to come to the United States. I felt that would be a very bad idea, but we have freedom of travel here. So all of us, including the secretary of state, discussed the matter at length. Finally, it was decided by the president himself that Tshombe should not get a visa. Decision making on the spot, however, was more independent.

Another important point to bring out is the role of timing in our diplomacy. Part of timing is forecasting. In a way there had been a premonition on the structure of the postcolonial period. Nevertheless, it could have been forecasted more clearly. No policy had been formulated in response to the challenges of the postcolonial era which I myself had anticipated already in the early 1950s.

And just at the time of Kennedy's election a large number of countries had gained independence. These countries seemed to be likely targets of Cold War competition. Kennedy responded by sending out chiefly younger people to head the U.S. missions in those countries at that point. It was felt that this was a timely move to ensure that the younger African leaders who came to power would have counterparts with whom they felt comfortable dealing.

Let me emphasize the importance of local missions here. Most of the newly independent countries had very poor communication systems. Perhaps amateur radio, but nothing effective. Of course, these countries have missions abroad, but generally they will address the foreign representatives in their own capitals. They deal with the United States through the local mission. There you really are the American government, a point clearly driven home in the Congo affair. The idea that diplomatic missions matter little today is nonsense in light of this experience. You really have to exercise initiative. I was appointed when—mistakenly—it was felt that the crisis in the Congo was nearly complete. What was called Operation Rumpunch had just been concluded. I really was left with freedom of action, under the rationale of "act at [your] own initiative unless otherwise directed."

The interests of the two principal NATO-European allies, France and Britain, differed from those of the United States, as Ambassador Gullion relates:

France wanted to control the transformation of its colonial empire by itself. By no means did the French want to have it done by someone else for them, certainly not by the United Nations. In respect to the Belgian Congo, the French wanted to play it both ways. They wanted to be represented in rebellious Katanga and at the same time maintain close ties with the government in Leopoldville. Their own particular stake in the Congo was not so great, but the French under de Gaulle seemed to feel that it was necessary to avoid an increase in American power projection in newly independent nations at the expense of their own influence in those areas. France, therefore, was not overly happy with the strong involvement of our government in the Congo question.

The British had more at stake in the Congo than the French. They had large investments, not only in mining but also in plantations. They also wanted to preserve their freedom of action with respect to the decolonization of their own empire. In Britain, pressures were very strong in favor of a conservative policy regarding the colonies and the Commonwealth. The British saw their mission in the Congo mainly to modify American action, which they perceived as impulsive. They might have had a somewhat paternalistic attitude towards American diplomacy at the time. Also, both the British and the French were still feeling the shock of the United States' position in the Suez crisis. A closely coordinated policy, according to the much cherished "special relationship" between the United States and Great Britain, just did not develop.

24
Conclusion

National Security: Structure, Process, and Policy

Just as the witness to an event such as an automobile accident sees only a part of the totality of an observed phenomenon, so the decision-maker in major national security issues holds in his or her memory only a portion of what actually occurred. Moreover, human memory is fallible. Hence, oral history can best be used in association with other streams of evidence, available from a variety of authoritative sources, in any effort to understand how decisional structures were used and what the process was by which decisions were made leading to a particular policy choice. Although structures shape the process and the resulting policy itself, there is abundant evidence in the preceding chapters of this book to suggest that personality variables hold an important key to the development of policy and to an understanding of how policy is formulated. Many of those whose interviews are represented on the preceding pages, from former chairman of the Joint Chiefs of Staff Adm. Thomas Moorer to former secretary of state Dean Rusk, pointed to the abiding importance that personalities, egos, ambitions, mind-sets, and agendas for action have in shaping the decision-making process and rendering organizational charts inadequate in themselves as a guide to the policy process and its outcome. This concluding chapter provides an integrative survey designed to summarize, synthesize, and compare major themes discussed elsewhere in this book. Given the diversity of the materials and issues included, it is impossible to encompass in one concluding chapter all of the topics examined. Nevertheless, several focal points, based on the structures, processes, and policies discussed, encompassing national security decision making, alliance relations, international crises, and arms control, are delineated. Such topics form a basis for drawing from the interviews excerpted in previous chapters key points for comparative analysis.

The National Security Council and Its Uses

It was only during the Eisenhower administration that the National Security Council first assumed an important role in the policy process. According to

Gen. Andrew Goodpaster, Eisenhower as president wanted to participate in NSC deliberations before making decisions; he saw this process itself as valuable to "crystallize the issues." From Adm. Thomas Moorer's perspective, Lyndon Johnson as president took a different approach. He effectively made decisions at Tuesday lunch meetings that he held with his secretary of state, secretary of defense, and national security adviser, after which he called National Security Council meetings. From his vantage point, David Newsom suggested that the "lunch of principals" phenomenon has its disadvantages. Such meetings, without the presence of note-takers or prepared papers, make it necessary for subordinates to get together separately to "negotiate out" what the principals had said to each other because "they occasionally reported back somewhat different versions of [their] conversation." This may lead to disjointed decision making or—more likely—poor decision implementation. However, Tapley Bennett described how President Johnson, in deciding upon an approach on issues such as negotiations with North Vietnam, had a propensity to "poll every man in the room" in order to "have a range of options to choose from." The Nixon NSC had many of the same features as that of the Eisenhower administration, except that Nixon liked to receive a series of clearly delineated options or alternatives that he could use in making his decision. According to Brent Scowcroft, President Nixon made decisions "based on written input rather than discussions." Moreover, Nixon emphasized organizational centralization for foreign policy formulation. He wanted U.S. foreign policy to be developed in the White House by the president with the direct assistance of his national security adviser. As Lawrence Eagleburger suggests, President Nixon and Henry Kissinger, as his national security adviser, viewed the Department of State as incapable of developing adequate strategic concepts and as plagued instead with excessive "clientitis."

In a formal sense the National Security Council structure of the Ford administration represented a "direct continuation of that of the Nixon administration," according to Brent Scowcroft, except for the fact that, unlike Nixon, President Ford made decisions "as a result of the give and take of debate." From the vantage point of David Newsom, observing the NSC in the Carter administration, power flows to that group, in this case the NSC, that has control of crisis management. According to Newsom, the prominent "role of the NSC in the conduct and the making of policy was inevitable." From the experience of the Reagan administration, Robert McFarlane drew a distinction that has confronted previous presidents in the national security process: between the formulation and implementation phases of policy. In McFarlane's view, planning must be managed at the White House level, while operations or implementation of policy should be conducted by the Department of State. The "NSC system ought to be an invisible manager, and the State Department should be the visible protagonist, advocate." However, Lawrence Eagleburger concluded that "there is no natural place for the policy formation process."

The locus of decision making will be wherever the president wants it to be. An ideal NSC is a "staff that ensures that the president gets a comprehensive picture of alternatives, of options"; he does not believe that the national security adviser can be "a eunuch and not have views on the subject" at hand. Instead, the national security adviser should play the devil's advocate role in an effort to pierce the "hermetically sealed environment of the White House" so that the president obtains a "broad picture of the various landmines that may be around." Richard Allen viewed the organizational structure established early in the Reagan administration as detrimental to his ability to serve the president satisfactorily as national security adviser. He argues against interposing a White House staff person between the president and the national security adviser because the president needs direct and timely access to national security policy, and the national security adviser should have the status conferred by such access in order to perform his duties and to deal effectively with the bureaucracy. According to Donald Rumsfeld, the NSC role in policy formulation is crucial because "few issues are single department or single agency issues." Therefore, it is not possible to "turn things over to a single department or agency to carry out a directive." Only the National Security Council provides the framework for the integrated consideration of the many perspectives—diplomatic, military, economic, psychological—that must be brought to bear in the policy process for decision by the president.

The Department of Defense and Its Role

In addition to establishing the National Security Council to be a coordinating mechanism in an increasingly complex policy framework, the National Security Act of 1947 provided the legislative basis for the Department of Defense, itself designed to bring closer together the respective armed services of the United States under appropriate civilian leadership. According to Donald Rumsfeld, the principal responsibility of the secretary of defense is "to assure that there is an appropriate national concensus on defense investment." An effective secretary of defense should decide which issues are most important and work on such policy questions personally, while delegating those of lesser importance. The secretary of defense must decide how he wants to measure progress on those issues deemed to be of the greatest importance. Such priorities and criteria are vital because, Rumsfeld observed, "the Pentagon is filled with people who are still suffering from the trauma of Vietnam," during which time the military image was tarnished by the failures of American policy. The result is the existence of a defense establishment shaped by cautious tendencies.

Integral to U.S. defense policy since the National Security Act of 1947, moreover, has been the Joint Chiefs of Staff. According to Andrew Goodpaster, President Eisenhower wanted the "JCS to function as a corporate body"—that

is, "to take the guidance he gave them and solve their problems" by joint deliberations and action. Eisenhower was often frustrated that the JCS did not act
in such a collegial and unified fashion, but instead "they were pursuing [paro-
chial] service interests." In the Defense Reorganization Act of 1958, President
Eisenhower took steps to create vice chiefs of staff for each of the services.
Their function was to deal with problems within respective services so that the
chiefs could "give primacy to their joint role," as Andrew Goodpaster recounts.
Eisenhower sought integrated, joint forces in the operational chains of command by establishing the unified and specified commands. According to Goodpaster, Eisenhower "wanted to withdraw the service headquarters in Washington from that operational role."

Organizational problems persisted into the 1980s, during which time there
was protracted discussion leading to the Defense Reorganization Act of 1986.
According to Gen. John Vessey, the fundamental problem related to improving
JCS advice to the secretary of defense in order to enable him to perform his
duties more effectively. Layers of competing staff, created for the most part
since the Eisenhower administration, were diluting, delaying, duplicating, and
confusing JCS advice to the secretary of defense. It was John Vessey's view that
it was a "mistake to make the chairman (rather than the Joint Chiefs of Staff
as a corporate group) the principal military adviser" to the president. This was
a perspective shared by Thomas Moorer, who asserted that the chairman
"should not be the sole adviser" to the president.

The Function of the State Department

Although the locus of American foreign policy lies ultimately with the president, he is necessarily dependent on the State Department, especially in the
implementation phase but also in the negotiation and representation of U.S.
interests abroad and even in the formulation phase. According to Dean Rusk,
the planning of policy is an enormously complex task and dynamic process. He
suggests that "planning cannot be the monopoly of the [policy] planning staff,"
but instead every Foreign Service member must also be a planning officer. At
the same time, as the ingredients in decision making have become more complicated, Dean Rusk discerned a tendency in the State Department in which
"geographic bureaus compete with one another for influence" and "senior
officers seek to define national interest in terms of their geographic bureau."
Although the effect of the jet aircraft and instantaneous communication has
been to centralize the decision-making process in Washington, there has also
been an expansion of overseas responsibilities and activity. Both Tapley Bennett
and David Newsom noted the growth of bureaucratic structures not only in
Washington but also in the field. Tapley Bennett saw the burgeoning departments, agencies, and staffs in the executive branch and Congress adding new

complexity to the formulation and implementation phases of policy. David Newsom observed that "the growth of the foreign affairs bureaucracy with a number of new players" affects "the whole task of representing the United States" abroad. Tapley Bennett suggested that ambassadors in the field often miss "what happens [in Washington] in the corridors between the meetings and who influences whom." Dean Rusk concluded that policy implementation in the field tends to be faithful "to the direction that they receive" from Washington. Yet, as Tapley Bennett noted, the effect of technology on communications is such that "the temptation of Washington agencies to do their own negotiating through delegations sent abroad" rather than using the ambassador is increased. The ability to travel quickly from one capital to another "elevate[s] major negotiations to the level of foreign minister or secretary of state" more readily. Hence, expectations in foreign capitals concerning the appropriate level of representation at such meetings is raised. The growth in numbers of multilateral organizations increases the personnel requirements of the Foreign Service and adds to the travel schedule of the secretary of state. Among the effects, moreover, of the proliferation of participants in the decision-making process and its greater centralization is the fact, according to David Newsom, that ambassadors are more the "mediator[s] among representatives of conflicting agencies" than the "commanding officer[s] in embassies." In Tapley Bennett's view, the country team concept in U.S. embassies represents "an effective means of coordinating U.S. activities in a country." As a result of those forces that have shaped the framework within which policy is formed, a premium is placed upon the ability to understand the policy environment in Washington as well as in the field. As David Newsom asserted, the best ambassadors are "those who [understand] Washington as well as they [understand] the country in which they [are] working."

Executive-Congressional Relations

Especially since the Vietnam War, the role of the U.S. Congress in the national security policy process has been greatly expanded. The need for more extensive consultation with Congress on the part of the president and members of his administration, together with legislation, namely the War Powers Act and the proliferation of congressional staffs and subcommittees, has led to criticism of Congress for "micromanagement" of defense and foreign policy. As Andrew Goodpaster recounted, however, the Eisenhower administration was a relatively tranquil period in executive-congressional relations. Eisenhower was conscientious in consulting with Congress "on actions such as might involve a foreign commitment of force." Nevertheless, an "interesting reversal" often occurred. Members of Congress who previously complained about not being consulted would tell the president that "we look to you to make these decisions." In Eisenhower's view, according to Goodpaster, some in the Congress were "small-minded, and simply unwilling to look to the larger issues." Eisenhower believed Congress to be "too niggardly" with U.S. foreign assistance programs, trade issues, and public diplomacy appropriations. Eisenhower was critical of "various congressional leaders [for] pressing for military programs beyond what was necessary." Comparing the more recent period with the Eisenhower administration, Goodpaster saw congressional intrusiveness as having "almost run wild," with large congressional staffs "constantly intruding into the executive branch under the cover of oversight: "Every member of Congress tends to think of himself as a secretary of state; Congress is so powerful in the foreign policy field that it can usually find ways to give expression to its interests." According to Tapley Bennett, Congress could be efficiently served with "several thousand fewer people" on its staffs.

Nothing more fully symbolized the determination of Congress to play as full a role as possible in national security policy than the War Powers Act. Brent Scowcroft saw the War Powers Act as "preordained" under the "impetus of Vietnam . . . and the weakness of the president" resulting from Watergate. In this situation, "the presidency lost some of its strength and the Congress moved in to take it over." The act coincided "with the collapse of congressional discipline" and a "fundamental change in the make-up of the Congress" (increased power of congressional staffs, declining authority of committee chairmen) which work together to decrease "the possibility of a reasonable and cooperative relationship with the Congress."

On other issues as well there were expressions of concern about trends in executive-congressional relations. On the Clark Amendment (cutting aid to UNITA in Angola in 1975), Richard Allen saw the Congress as having grown accustomed to "usurping foreign policy functions, even micromanagement functions, that it was very difficult to reverse." John Vessey suggested that, in defense policy, the decision-making system has become disconnected. There is excessive emphasis on the front end of the process (deciding what weapons to build, what forces to maintain, and what budget allocations to make) and not enough time on "reviewing what did we get for what we decided to to." He sees a large part of this problem resting with Congress and the growing numbers of committees and subcommittees having a direct role in the defense budget and military procurement. In Vessey's view, Congress and the administration should reach agreement on a "mission-basis budget," and the congressional line-item appropriation power should be eliminated. Last but not least, Tapley Bennett saw value in congressional travel, which enlarges "Congress's understanding" of often delicate and complicated issues. Since foreigners usually do not fully understand the important role played by Congress in U.S. foreign policy, such trips have the value of enabling members of Congress to explain the functions of the legislature in the policy process.

Bureaucratic Interaction in Washington

The concentration of decision making in Washington, to which numerous policymakers and other observers have often pointed, extends to the very top of the policy pyramid—to the ability conferred by technology on the president himself to manage detailed aspects of crises, as noted elsewhere in this book. Nevertheless, beneath the president lies a vast bureaucratic structure, together with a proliferation of congressional committees and staffs having an interest in national security decisions. Thomas Moorer recalled how for the Vietnam War certain "decisions . . . were not made by formal means" as a result of the "different kinds of environment we were operating in" and changing public and congressional attitudes toward the war. Describing Henry Kissinger's policy style, Brent Scowcroft suggested that "back-channel diplomacy," designed to circumvent the bureaucracy, accorded with what was Kissinger's greatest strength—a strategic mind. Kissinger had an "ability to see events and patterns in a comprehensive whole, and to plan his reaction to individual events in relation to individual events in relation to their contribution to where you want to end up." To act strategically it is essential to have the elements of surprise and secrecy, features that are not characteristic of bureaucratic structures.

Domestic Factors in the Foreign Policy Process

In the second half of the twentieth century the impact of domestic factors, including a powerful electronic media and other groups having a direct interest in foreign policy, has grown substantially in the United States and in other pluralistic societies. Political leaders face the difficult problem of reconciling their role *as leaders* with the need to reflect and represent the interests of constituent groups on whom they are dependent ultimately for electoral support. The greater the scrutiny of an inquiring media and the more extensive the role of domestic factors in the foreign policy process, the greater is the problem of conducting in secret those governmental affairs for which the full glare of publicity is deemed either unnecessary or undeniable. In 1960, for example, President Eisenhower had authorized an intelligence-gathering surveillance flight over the Soviet Union just before the Paris Summit Conference. According to General Goodpaster, when the aircraft was shot down over the Soviet Union and the pilot captured, "we all came to the view that the moment the president himself said something it had to be true . . . Subordinates could do other things, but the president himself had a position such that, if he made a public statement, it had to be true." According to Richard Allen, President Reagan "always sought to lead public opinion" and to do so by an ability to choose issues carefully and then to communicate with the American public. In the period leading up to the first summit between President Reagan and General Secretary Gorbachev, Robert McFarlane recounted, the White House made a concerted effort to convey the themes and issues that could be discussed to the public through the media. The purpose of "promoting the policy by press" was to strengthen the hand of the president as he went into the summit meeting by building through the media as broad a base of public understanding and support as possible.

Electoral politics, together with the demands that seemingly are imposed on incumbents and candidates alike, sometimes shape the approaches taken to national security and the foreign policy process itself. Thomas Moorer related, from his vantage point as chairman of the Joint Chiefs of Staff, that President Johnson wanted to convey the idea that the Vietnam War was being deescalated in the days leading up to the election of 1968 by temporarily halting the bombing of North Vietnam. In the weeks leading to the election in 1976, President Ford, according to Brent Scowcroft, faced a formidable challenge from Ronald Reagan in the Republican primaries. Ford attempted to head off this threat by moving to the right on foreign policy issues—in Scowcroft's view a mistake. Instead, he suggested, Ford should have made an effort to build a coalition of moderate Republicans and Democrats.

Such events and pressures as are associated with the role of domestic factors in foreign policy are usually played out in the media. Moreover, the press and television can provide the catalyst for personnel changes as a result of statements made by subordinates about policy issues which run counter to existing policy. When President Carter sought to fulfill a campaign promise that he had made to withdraw U.S. ground forces from the Republic of Korea, he encountered opposition in the United States and Korea. A statement by Gen. John Singlaub, chief of staff to UN Commander General John Vessey, reported in the *Washington Post* and critical of the Carter administration's policy, led to Singlaub's recall and removal. According to General Vessey, this incident nevertheless "served as a lightning rod to draw attention to the Carter administration's plans." The debate that ensued, together with new intelligence estimates showing the extent of the continuing North Korean military buildup, led President Carter eventually to abandon plans for any U.S. withdrawal of ground forces from Korea.

Reflecting on the "fourth estate," Gen. Pierre Gallois viewed the media as "another form of government" that is more powerful than the executive, legislature, or judiciary. The media has a powerful effect on public opinion: "When there is a movement of the public opinion, the government changes its mind." However, Gallois continues, "you cannot have a foreign policy based on emotional, instantaneous movement of public opinion; it is impossible." Finally, on the issue of the media and its overall relationship to the government, David Newsom put forward a theme that was discussed by others as well, namely, that there has been a dramatic shift in the overall approach of the media toward political authority to the role of adversary, especially pronounced since the Vietnam War. For the first time, television brought into the homes of millions of viewers an instantaneous replay of the war. Such was said to be the role of the audiovisual media in shaping the domestic factors in the foreign policy process.

Foreign Policy: The Atlantic Alliance

In U.S. foreign policy the most extensive and complex extended security relationship since World War II has encompassed the North Atlantic area. To a certain extent the transatlantic relationship has mirrored the problems facing the United States itself in developing consensus based on domestic factors and international considerations in foreign policy. Most of the other leading pluralistic societies with representative political institutions are located in Western Europe and hold alliance membership. It follows, therefore, that an alliance composed of such entities represents, par excellence, all of the difficulties that beset decision-making processes under conditions of diversity, competing interests, and variegated domestic constituencies.

Throughout its history, spanning more than two generations, NATO has confronted many challenges to its cohesiveness. At the time of the U.S. involvement in Vietnam during the 1960s, questions were raised in Europe about the ability of the United States to achieve its goals in Vietnam, although American credibility regarding NATO-Europe remained unquestioned. Among the major problems facing NATO, moreover, has been the participation of its members in out-of-area conflicts, such as Vietnam, but also in other regions. Having earlier opposed such actions on the part of the NATO-European allies, notably Anglo-French intervention at the time of the Suez crisis, the United States itself later, as in Vietnam, sought European support for American policy. According to Joseph Luns, "The American government does not quite understand that they themselves bear a great deal of responsibility for the fact that Europe has so little influence outside Europe." Among the reasons for de Gaulle's decision to withdraw France from the NATO integrated command doctrine, according to Pierre Gallois, was the use by the United States of NATO facilities located in France without prior French approval at the time of the U.S. military intervention in Lebanon in 1958.

Among the other motivations leading to de Gaulle's NATO decision was, first and foremost, a quest for independence of action, especially in the development of a foreign policy that would elevate France's position on the international scene. François de Rose suggested that de Gaulle withdrew from the NATO structure in order "to embark . . . on a policy of détente with the Soviet Union." As a power remaining a signatory of the North Atlantic Treaty and thus benefiting from its security guarantee, France could pursue a policy that was not directly linked to that of the United States. Such independence was seen as psychologically important because, de Rose notes, World War II and its aftermath represented "the first time in the history of Europe that the fate of France [as] either winner or loser did not decide the fate of Europe." France's quest for independence carried explicitly the need to maintain its own military establishment, leading Tapley Bennett to observe that France "has never hesitated to spend the money on defense that she considered necessary."

A large number of other issues highlight the nature of the Atlantic Alliance as a pluralistic association beset even by enduring conflicts between certain of its members, such as that dividing Greece and Turkey, which has led to severe restrictions on Greek participation in the alliance. In 1983, moreover, NATO was increased in membership with the entry of Spain, but only after a deeply divisive domestic debate, the effect of which has been to place severe limits on any Spanish military integration into the alliance. According to Tapley Bennett, the United States was "pushing too far and too fast to bring Spain in" to NATO. Spain would be a more difficult partner than even France. In Tapley Bennett's view, Spain will "dine à la carte from the NATO menu just as the French do."

Especially since the 1970s NATO has faced increasing pressures from domestic political sources to temper military modernization programs with a greater emphasis on arms control. Such choices have posed formidable problems for alliance relations generally and for certain NATO member governments in particular. In 1978, for example, the Carter administration offered to deploy an enhanced radiation warhead capable of penetrating Soviet armor and thus reducing the effectiveness of some of the most modern and powerful components of the vast Soviet land force. Having obtained West German support for such deployment, President Carter abruptly reversed himself. According to Tapley Bennett and others, Carter's decision resulted in a loss of U.S. leadership credibility among NATO-European allies. According to Lord Mulley, the United States, as alliance leader, faces a major dilemma. Allies will "complain that they are not getting leadership from the United States, but then when they get such leadership, they say they have not been consulted." Joseph Luns viewed the United States as crucially important to holding NATO together and giving the alliance overall direction. In this perspective, "the great advantage of NATO for the European members is that even the smallest of them—Luxembourg—knows that what they are doing is of use." Luns sees the U.S. role in NATO, including the deployment of ground forces in the central region, as a manifestation of vital national interest and not as an example of U.S. generosity or philanthropy to Western Europe.

Although other alliance members embarked on their own policies toward the Soviet Union and its Warsaw Pact allies, to no country in NATO have such approaches been more important than the Federal Republic of Germany. Reflecting a perspective deeply held by Chancellor Konrad Adenauer, Kai-

Uwe von Hassell suggested that the best *Ostpolitik* is one "built on a strong basis in NATO and the Western world." In his view, the effort to achieve a gradual normalization of relations with the East embodied in *Ostpolitik* began in the years following Chancellor Adenauer's visit to Moscow in 1955, and in particular during the early 1960s. For the future, however, is the question of reconciling the need to explore avenues of opening with the East, with that of preventing a situation in which in Franz-Josef Schulze's words, *Ostpolitik* "would very quickly lead to an erosion in the threat perception, and that could only be to our detriment" if our defenses are dismantled while the causes of conflict remain unresolved.

The Conventional Defense of Europe

In the early 1950s, especially after the outbreak of the Korean conflict in 1950, the United States and its NATO-European allies pushed for the deployment of conventional forces capable of withstanding at least an initial Soviet offensive. Such a defense, forward deployed, could only be mounted with principally NATO-European participation, including German rearmament. This led to discussion of the appropriate European framework for a military contribution by the Federal Republic of Germany. The result was the proposed European Defense Community. As Andrew Goodpaster recounted, Eisenhower favored European unity for defense because "real defense could only be achieved if [the Europeans] achieve some degree of unity." Once the decision was taken to allow West German rearmament and entry into NATO, the Federal Republic faced problems of the size and structure of its new military units, together with French fears of the possible revival of German militarism. According to Kai-Uwe von Hassell, "The lowest possible level for integration was the corps, and we developed our plans for German units according to this idea." As part of the agreed-upon plan for German rearmament after the failure of the European Defense Community idea, West Germany was limited to twelve divisions placed under NATO command, with, according to von Hassell, NATO members asserting that "we must control Germany." As the question of West German rearmament was being debated, NATO in 1952 established at the Lisbon ministerial meeting conventional force goals, which were never met. Instead, as Pierre Gallois suggested, the failure of the Lisbon plans led SACEUR, Gen. Alfred Grüenther, and Field Marshall Montgomery to develop a new strategy that included tactical nuclear weapons, culminating in SHAPE 345 being adopted by the NATO Council in 1956.

Although France feared German rearmament, to the extent of thwarting the formation of a European Defense Community in 1954, almost a decade later France and West Germany signed the Franco-German Treaty of 1963. Among its provisions, as Kai-Uwe von Hassell pointed out, was "cooperation between

France and Germany mainly for research and development for military materiel." However, von Hassell argued that important choices should have been made at that time to develop joint prototypes of such items as tanks and other weapons systems for later coproduction. At a broader level, the problem facing Bonn was always to reconcile its need for close ties with both Paris and Washington. West German policy, in von Hassell's words, "was always to tell the Americans that they must stay [in Europe] or else we will never be able really to deter the Soviet Union." By the same token, "it was not Bonn-Washington *or* Bonn-Paris, but always with both; inside the alliance it is necessary for the FRG to have a relationship with France because they are in the rear and we are on the front."

Among the more recent NATO conventional force issues discussed was the decision in 1987 to form a Franco-German brigade. François de Rose viewed the concept as a "symbolic gesture" and as a "small unit that raises big problems." Among the issues to be resolved is the fact that French soldiers "are committed to the strategy of national deterrence, and the German soldiers are committed to the strategy of flexible response." In de Rose's view, in such matters of Franco-German defense cooperation, "we always come back to that problem: the inconsistency in the strategy of France and the strategy of the alliance." However, de Rose sees flexible response as "less credible and more difficult to implement" at the present time because "conventional capacity is becoming more and more important." Therefore, in his view, France should work with NATO to reach agreement on an assessment of Soviet strategy for the 1990s and then agree on a common alliance strategy. According to Kai-Uwe von Hassell, there is utility in the Franco-German brigade idea to the extent that it will increase the number of French officers training at a West German military academy, of French officers in German units, and of common staff exercises.

In discussing NATO strategy, General von Kielmansegg offered insights into the question of mobile versus static defense concepts, based on his long military experience. As a defensive alliance, NATO can guard against being confronted with Soviet strategic surprise. He stated his belief that the Soviet Union will always rely on the principle of massed attack in mounting an offensive and that the Soviets will not initiate offensive operations "until they [have] a superiority of five-to-one in divisions, and seven-to-one in tanks." General von Kielmansegg viewed a strictly "static defense, even with strong fortifications," as "nonsense." In his view, "there is no line that cannot be broken through whenever [the Warsaw Pact wants] to do it, for a certain amount of time." Nevertheless, he argued that "we must do everything to prevent penetration." He suggested that "defense without attack is no formula for success." Hence, NATO must be able to encompass in its defensive posture tactical surprise by means of the "secret behind mobile defense." A counterattack can surprise the enemy with respect to time, location, strength, and direction.

Although the achievement of Soviet strategic surprise would be measured by the denial of warning time to NATO, Joseph Luns stated his belief that the alliance would probably have substantial indicators of any impending attack. The question would be the willingness or ability of NATO countries in fact to reach needed conditions of readiness and mobilization for fear of further escalating the East-West crisis.

Nuclear Weapons and Deterrence in NATO-Europe

Central to NATO strategy from the beginning of the alliance has been the role of nuclear weapons as an ultimate basis for deterrence. According to Franz-Josef Schulze, NATO has always needed "a better mix" of short- and longer-range tactical nuclear weapons in order to "give us greater flexibility." The problem with NATO's nuclear artillery, he maintains, relates to the fact that division and brigade commanders are involved in the request and release process for these systems. This condition diverts such commanders from actively prosecuting the conventional war "at the forward command posts" and compels them to remain at their main headquarters waiting to give the decision to go nuclear. The focus on nuclear artillery, with its battlefield range, has the "adverse effect" of compelling commanders to have "their eyes [looking] backwards" instead of "looking forward." Therefore, Schulze contends, NATO "should have [nuclear] corps support weapons of longer range and fewer artillery weapons systems." Moreover, NATO should have in its inventory systems that possess ranges sufficient to strike the Soviet Union: "The Soviets cannot be deterred by risks you put to their allies; they can only be deterred by risks you put to their own country."

A similar perspective was advanced by François de Rose, who discussed the NATO dual-track decision of 1979. In his perspective, the decision to deploy ground-launched cruise missiles and Pershing IIs should have been based on the fact that manned aircraft were facing "more difficulties penetrating enemy air defenses." NATO made a mistake in "the failure to justify the need for the deployment of the Pershings and cruise missiles on the basis of needing weapons capable of reaching Soviet territory." General Schulze perceived that a gap was created by the removal of the Pershing II because "in the Soviet risk calculus there is a great difference whether the systems which can hit the Soviet Union are stationed in the area the Soviets might go to attack (or at least put under pressure) or whether these systems are stationed at sea or are airborne— particularly nonstrategic systems." In contrast, Lawrence Eagleburger stated the view that originally the United States believed the INF deployment to be "totally unnecessary" because "we have other weapons that can do the job" and the "fundamental military argument [was] we do not need them." Instead, Eagleburger suggested, "the INF issue was . . . far more important as a political-psychological question than as a military question." However, he concluded that the United States "might barely be more willing to use [nuclear weapons] in extremis because they are located in Europe than if we had to shoot something from Nebraska."

The acquisition by the Soviet Union of nuclear weapons capable of striking the United States contributed decisively to a rethinking of U.S. strategy as well as NATO's nuclear employment options. In 1967 NATO officially adopted the strategy of flexible response based on a force posture in which an initial conventional response to a Soviet–Warsaw Pact attack would be mounted. According to Kai-Uwe von Hassell, flexible response means that "a small attack is met with small weapons from our side; a larger one with more weapons would be met on a larger scale; a medium-size one perhaps with atomic weapons. We will meet the attack with an equal level of forces." The adoption by NATO of flexible response, as von Hassell recounted, capped an acrimonious debate in the 1960s between de Gaulle and the United States which was resolved only when France left NATO's integrated command structure. In the view of Joseph Luns, flexible response is a "good policy," although he doubts "whether in a conflict nuclear devices will be used." From Franz-Josef Schulze's perspective, flexible response is "a military strategy and also a political compromise," based on the fact that it necessarily embodies a consensus among NATO's diverse membership.

As it was preparing in the 1960s to leave NATO's integrated military structure, France was in the process of building its own national nuclear capability. According to Gen. Pierre Gallois, he, among others, was thinking as early as 1945, at the end of World War II, about "deterrence based on this new technological weaponry"—atomic bombs. He believed that France could master such technology and thus acquire "the weapons to avoid war." As a result, Gallois began his "campaign for nuclear armament" at this time. By the late 1950s, according to Gallois, French policy toward the acquisition of nuclear weapons had been influenced sharply by the policies of its principal NATO allies, especially the United States. At the time of the Suez war of 1956, American policy stood in opposition to Anglo-French military intervention after Egypt nationalized the Suez Canal Company. The Soviet Union had threatened France and Britain with nuclear devastation. The French felt "left without the protection of America." Therefore, there was broadly based support in France for "the development of atomic weapons, not as a weapon of independence, but in case of trouble for use as a last resort because we were not sure anymore of the American attitude toward us." According to François de Rose, France decided to build its own atomic capability because "we would not drop out and let the British be the only ones who would have influence over the Continent through their possession of nuclear weapons." What de Rose termed "the German factor" also contributed to France's nuclear decision. Gallois had discussed with French Socialist premier Guy Mollet in 1956 the need for a French nuclear force. Furthermore, Gallois had been greatly impressed with President de Gaulle's grasp of the significance of nuclear weapons in modern deterrence—that "numbers are losing their significance" and that the deployment of a nuclear force "was the way to give the country a status above its real situation." Ambassador de Rose discussed the context in which France's Commissariat de l'énergie atomique was established in 1945, as well as the effort to develop French reactors that could produce plutonium for nuclear weapons. General Gallois suggested that the French decision to produce an atomic device was taken in July 1956, together with the decision to develop aircraft capable of delivering such a weapon. The production in 1959 of the prototype, followed by deployment of the Mirage aircraft, represented the beginning of the *force de frappe*, followed by the decision to develop and deploy a submarine-launched ballistic missile (SLBM) system.

It was essential, in Gallois's estimation, that France develop its own nuclear force as an ultimate hedge against the possibility of a future invasion. Yet such weapons are to be used only as a last resort. Their role is to "inspire fear." Because they can be justified for use only "when a nation is in a terrible situation," it follows that "it is very difficult to ask another nation to protect you with such a weapon because that nation may not be in that same situation." Therefore, nuclear weapons, Gallois asserted, have "never been a weapon of an alliance." According to this logic, it is not credible for any state to offer extended deterrence with nuclear weapons to other nations, for example in the Atlantic Alliance.

The Formulation of Policy toward the Soviet Union

It was the challenges presented by the Soviet Union, of course, that led the United States and West European nations to join together in the formation of the Atlantic Alliance. By the time of the Eisenhower administration, the United States had begun the first of a large number of reviews and reassessments of its policy toward the Soviet Union. General Goodpaster recalled how President Eisenhower had set up the Solarium Project in 1953 in order to examine policy alternatives toward the Soviet Union. After considering three alternatives (roll-back, containment, and spheres of influence), Eisenhower chose a policy of "containment, plus a positive and active policy of assistance, contact, help of many kinds, as well as diplomatic and political support to the emerging nations of the world." Although Secretary of State John Foster Dulles, according to General Goodpaster, was "dubious that [the 1955 Geneva Summit Conference] would be of value and felt that it could be risky" because of the possibility of future and renewed confrontation, Eisenhower believed that such a dialogue was of possible value in easing East-West tensions. What is significant in Goodpaster's assessment of the Eisenhower administration is the extent to which

Eisenhower himself, contrary to the assumptions of the 1950s, was at the center of the foreign policy decision-making process of his administration. The president was far from the passive, detached figure depicted by many of the contemporary pundits who purported to understand his style of operation. By the late 1960s, nearly a decade after the Eisenhower administration, the United States had passed through the sharp deterioration of U.S.-Soviet relations marked by the Cuban missile crisis, followed once again by a thaw, only to be faced in 1968 with the Soviet invasion of Czechoslovakia to oust the reform-minded Dubček regime. According to Dean Rusk, U.S. intelligence knew in advance that the Soviet Union "had the capabilities and assets deployed" to invade Czechoslovakia, but did not know if or when the Soviets would move. Rusk believes that "our experts could not know because the Soviets had not decided yet. Sometimes you would like to have information which simply does not yet exist." Nor did he believe that the United States could have taken any action that would have prevented the Soviet Union from deploying military forces in Czechoslovakia. In his perspective, "the attitude of the West since World War II has been that however disagreeable we find these regimes in Eastern Europe, whatever they do to their own people, it is simply not an issue for war between East and West. It is very important not to bluff in these situations."

In the early 1980s the United States confronted yet another period of deterioration in relations with the Soviet Union after the détente of the Nixon administration a decade earlier. The approach taken by the Reagan administration, as Richard Allen discusses, was to restore American power in the first term in order to be able to negotiate from a position of strength. Robert McFarlane recalled that President Reagan "did not come to the presidency with a foreign policy agenda beyond keeping the peace and restoring our strength." McFarlane stated his belief that the Soviet Union should be "one of the priorities in the second term . . . in terms of writing down the ground rules for behavior" at the superpower level.

Arms Control

Much of the substance of negotiations between the United States and the Soviet Union has had arms control as its focus. In the Eisenhower administration, for the first time, a special assistant for disarmament was appointed. Moreover, in the National Security Council, as General Goodpaster recalled, "a group was set up called the Committee of Principles . . . to analyze what steps might be taken in this area," particularly "in the way of monitoring [nuclear] tests." Eisenhower established the White House Scientific Advisory Committee to gain "access to members of the scientific community in order for him to make appropriate policy choices." One of the immediate consequences of the appointment of Harold Stassen as special assistant for disarmament, according to

General Goodpaster, was bureaucratic friction with the Department of State. Eisenhower attempted to resolve this problem by placing the special assistant for disarmament under the supervision of the secretary of state.

The most controversial of the arms control initiatives of the Eisenhower administration was the Open Skies proposal. This idea came from the Quantico Study, produced under the leadership of Nelson Rockefeller as special assistant for psychological warfare. The proposal for each side to permit aerial photography of the territory of the other and to exchange military blueprints showing the location of forces on each side was intended to "build confidence and reduce the chances of war through miscalculation." As Goodpaster recalled, when the plan was presented at the 1955 Geneva Summit Conference, the Soviet reaction was "equivocal" at first, but then Khrushchev said to Eisenhower, "No, no, no." Summing up Eisenhower's approach to national security policy, Goodpaster states that he believed in the necessity "to go down two tracks—the track of the arms and armaments on the one hand and the task of trying to control, limit, and constrain on the other hand."

By the 1970s American arms control policy had helped to produce not only several agreements, such as the Limited Test Ban Treaty of 1963 and the Nonproliferation Treaty of 1968, but had led also to the opening of the Strategic Arms Limitation Talks (SALT). According to Donald Rumsfeld, there is in the American approach to arms control a "natural dynamic of wanting, once you start the negotiations, to end them successfully." There has been a situation, in Rumsfeld's view, in which "the arms control process gained a life of its own." Like many other observers of and participants in the U.S.-Soviet arms control negotiating process, Rumsfeld noted that "the tendency is to allow arms control a heavier weighting in the decision-making process and to have it drive [other aspects of security policy]." In similar fashion, R. James Woolsey compared and contrasted U.S. and Soviet approaches to arms control. In his view, the Soviet Union focuses narrowly on its national interests, while the United States tends to take a "man-from-Mars" approach based on an objective, analytic assessment of both sides' interests.

The central problem to which SALT and subsequently the Strategic Arms Reduction Talks (START) were addressed was the survivability of the land-based strategic nuclear forces. In Woolsey's view, the "limitations on [Soviet] offensive systems that we have tried to negotiate over the years [in an effort to limit the threat to silo-based ICBMs] have largely been a failure." Such deficiencies may not be remedied by means of arms control agreements. According to Woolsey, "The most that one can do is to try, through arms control agreements, to establish some modest incentive to incline both sides toward systems that are not as effective in destroying or being able to execute a first strike against our own forces as would be the case in the absence of arms control." Furthermore, an approach such as that taken at the time of SALT—focusing on limiting the numbers and size of Soviet systems—has not worked "because you cannot really constrain accuracy and yield effectively.'' Hence the basic requirement for deterrence, assuming the survivability of strategic forces, is a task that, first and foremost, must be accomplished not by arms control but instead as a result of unilateral action.

Both in Western Europe and the United States, arms control has been viewed as a key ingredient in the formation of consensus for defense modernization. The commitment to arms control negotiations for the removal of intermediate-range nuclear forces was a prerequisite for the deployment of new-generation INF forces in NATO-European countries in the early 1980s. Similarly, in the United States there was a protracted debate about the deployment of a new land-based intercontinental ballistic missile system, the MX, which the Reagan administration sought to deploy as part of its strategic modernization program. In an effort to build bipartisan support, the administration in 1982 appointed a commission headed by Brent Scowcroft. The President's Commission on Strategic Forces contained expertise drawn from a broad range of perspectives, including persons who had served in recent administrations of both parties. According to Scowcroft, "What we tried to do was to put together a solution to the problem of strategic modernization which was militarily and politically satisfactory, and which politically held out the promise of being able to provide a rallying point for a sufficiently broad consensus.'' It was Scowcroft's assessment that "it takes unusual circumstances for a commission like this to be effective. It takes an important problem, a consensus that the problem has to be solved, and some pressure or acknowledgment that it has to be solved in a short period of time.'' The Scowcroft Commission furnished a forum for reviewing past efforts to find a survivable basing mode for the land-based strategic force. It brought together key members of Congress for discussions and consultations. Scowcroft recalled, "We never broke down into subgroups, so that everybody had the same kind of information on which to come to a conclusion. The upshot was that . . . we had a very strong consensus toward a solution.'' As a result of the work of the Scowcroft Commission, the administration developed with the Congress a bipartisan approach to strategic force modernization and arms control sufficient to permit the initiation of MX deployment.

Decision Making and Crisis Management

Much of the focus of decision making has been upon crises and their management. Such an emphasis is understandable, for crises represent threats to vital national interests. By their very nature, crises hold the potential for escalation to the threatened or actual use of military power by one or more of the protagonists. Because the only basis for nuclear weapons is the preservation in extremis of crucially important interests that are threatened, there is an inextricable relationship between strategic nuclear forces, together with the doctrines on which they are based, and crisis management. It follows that, in crises, decisions are likely to be made with the participation of the highest authorities, namely the president, in the case of the United States. Recounting his experience with President Ford at the time of the *Mayaguez* crisis in 1975, Brent Scowcroft asserted that in crises "the president's political neck is on the line. As a matter of course, he is going to be very reluctant to leave in the hands of some unknown military commander decisions which could have a great impact on his political well-being. Therefore, the military has to expect that it is going to be subject to intensive scrutiny in carrying out crisis interventions." In keeping with the idea that crisis decision making is highly centralized in the hands of the president and his closest advisers, Tapley Bennett noted the propensity in Washington to send special missions in a crisis out to the field of action. Such groups are likely to consist of persons in whom the president feels especially confident. In Ambassador Bennett's view, such an approach is useful, for it enables "key players from the other parts of the decision-making structure" to see the crisis at firsthand. Last but not least, each president deals with crises in a way that is compatible with his decision-making style. Hence, existing organizational structures may or may not be used. From Admiral Moorer's perspective, "It is not the structure that determines the outcome of crises but rather it is the people." Formal structures exist to be used as deemed appropriate by the president. Although his constituted advisers, including the secretaries of state and defense, as well as his assistant for national security, are likely to play roles of central importance, the question is likely to be which one is most heavily relied upon and who are the other players in the process that leads to the resolution of the crisis on more or less satisfactory terms.

In the large number of international crises discussed in previous chapters, numerous insights, for comparative purposes, emerge. For example, there are several cases of "out-of-area" crises that provoked discord between the United States and its allies. The Eisenhower administration, as General Goodpaster points out, was not informed of British, French, and Israeli plans at the time of the Suez crisis of 1956. He maintained that the United States "heard nothing from the British, French, or the Israelis, and then they went ahead with the attack." The British embassy in Washington "was, to some extent, in the dark also" regarding the planned military strike into the Suez Canal Zone. By the same token, the French government was not informed in advance of the U.S. decision to deploy from NATO bases in France military capabilities needed for the intervention in Lebanon mounted by the United States in July 1958. As Edmund A. Gullion suggested, the Congo crisis produced a situation in which the United States was in disagreement with some of its NATO-European allies, and especially with France. During this crisis, President Kennedy's sympathy for the concerns of NATO allies (as recent colonial powers) was in conflict with his support for the anticolonial aspirations of developing nations. At the same time, President de Gaulle seemed to believe that it was necessary to avoid an increase in the U.S. presence in newly independent states at the expense of French influence. At the time of the October 1973 War, once again, NATO allies found themselves in disagreement. In order to mount a rapid U.S. re-supply to Israel, the United States, as Brent Scowcroft recalled, found it neces-sary "to use some equipment from our NATO forces stockpiled in Europe. We went ahead to do that and the Germans found out about it, and voiced strong opposition." Subsequently, the decision of the United States, according to Robert McFarlane, to back out of a proposed joint raid with France against terrorist strongholds after the attack on the U.S. and French contingents in Lebanon in 1983 led France to refuse overflight rights for U.S. aircraft en route from bases in Britain against Libya in 1986.

Another theme that recurs in the discussion of crises relates to surprise and the role of intelligence. Crises generally have surprise as a defining character-istic. As a result, the need for adequate intelligence is enhanced if those against whom the crisis is directed are to avoid being surprised. Yet precisely because crises usually erupt as events that are unanticipated and therefore marked by the element of surprise, intelligence is likely to be either inadequate in its availability or utilization, or on both counts. Intelligence may be insufficient before the crisis actually unfolds, as well as during the crisis itself. Not only did the United States not anticipate the *Mayaguez* crisis, but, as Brent Scow-croft pointed out, as the crisis proceeded, "it was very hard to know what was going on. We had very inadequate intelligence . . . We had not the foggiest notion that Koh Tang Island was so heavily garrisoned." At the time of the October 1973 War, as General von Kielmansegg pointed out, the Egyptians surprised Israel in a tactical sense. Although the Egyptian maneuver to cross the canal into the Sinai had been practiced by Egypt's forces and "shown to the Israelis six or seven times before," the Egyptians surprised Israel by the timing of their attack. In contrast, in the early 1960s, in the case of the nfolding Dominican Republic crisis, the Kennedy and Johnson administra-tions, according to Dean Rusk, had undertaken military planning to safeguard U.S. and foreign nationals in the Dominican Republic. Only later, however, did the United States, as events unfolded, conclude that a key purpose of the military action would be to preempt a possible drift toward a Castro-type Communist government in Santo Domingo. From his vantage point, Ambas-sador Bennett noted the inadequacy of timely intelligence during the Domin-ican Republic crisis: "It was terribly hard for people to communicate. It was very hard to find out what was going on." In the case of the Soviet inva-sion of Czechoslovakia in 1968, General von Kielmansegg maintained that "in the middle of April 1968 we had the first signs that something abnormal was going on." He continued, "There was no surprise at all, except for the date. . . . The Russians even deliberately leaked information in the weeks pre-ceding the invasion in order to test Western reaction—not only to test, but to try to get their result without invading." If NATO members had adequate intelligence, they failed to draw the conclusion that Soviet military action was imminent, for surprise was a principal feature of their reaction when the Soviet forces actually entered Czechoslovakia. At the time of the Polish crisis of 1981 leading to the imposition of martial law in December, there were numerous intelligence indicators of increases in Soviet military strength around Poland and expressions of concern, according to David Newsom, "that the Soviets were thinking of going into Poland." In Tapley Bennett's view, "The great concern shown by NATO was one of the factors that may have kept the Soviets from acting militarily because they knew . . . that there was great Western concern over how they were handling the Solidarity issue." While NATO planning, as well as discussion within the U.S. intelligence community, focused on the prospects for Soviet military intervention, the actual crackdown, when it came, with the use of Polish forces, appeared to catch Western governments by surprise.

Another crisis in which participants experienced surprise about the unfolding of events was that which erupted in Cyprus in 1974 when Turkish forces occupied those portions of the island inhabited by the Turkish population. According to Brent Scowcroft, the Ford administration was "certainly surprised by the Cyprus invasions." At the same time, in Scowcroft's view, "it was a crisis in which we were severely limited in our ability to affect a positive outcome either way." Conceivably, one of the problems confronting crisis managers is that of system overload. It should be recalled that the Cyprus crisis coincided with the final stages of Watergate, leading to President Nixon's resignation in August 1974. At the end of the 1970s, the Carter administration itself was burdened with several parallel policy problems and initiatives. As the administration pressed toward the completion of negotiations for diplomatic normalization with China, the SALT II Treaty, and the Camp David Accords, it confronted a rapidly deteriorating situation in Iran. Although there were inadequacies in U.S. intelligence concerning the gravity of events unfolding in Iran, the fact was, in Ambassador Newsom's estimation, that "people under pressure from all kinds of responsibilities are not prepared to focus on unthinkable possibilities [that is, the fall of the shah] until they are forced to." He suggested that "the greatest [intelligence] failure is the unwillingness of people in high places either to accept the full implications of intelligence or to know what to do about it if they do accept it." Furthermore, in the unfolding crisis with Iran after the fall of the shah, the United States confronted the situation in which its embassy in Teheran was occupied and American diplomatic personnel taken hostage. As Ambassador Newsom commented, "The pressure on a president in a moment like that to do something is very heavy, and particularly a president who feels the heat of a political campaign. [As a result] you cannot just stand there, you do something; [the United States] does not have the capacity for subtlety in [its] diplomacy in situations like that."

Those crises are managed successfully that bring about a resolution acceptable to as many of the participants as possible and, from the perspective of any one protagonist, on as favorable terms as obtainable. Judged by such criteria, there are of course mixed results in the case of crises examined by the various persons who took part. President Johnson was said by Tapley Bennett to have considered the Dominican Republic crisis successfully managed. As a result, according to Ambassador Bennett, Lyndon Johnson "hit his highest point of approval in the polls just after he took the Dominican action." Clearly, by all accounts, the Suez crisis was a failure, especially for Britain and France, with important implications for the Atlantic Alliance and for relations with the United States. If the problems of crisis management in general for the United States have been formidable, they have been especially difficult in the case of crises in Eastern Europe. The options available in Hungary in 1956, Czechoslovakia in 1968, and Poland in 1981 were seen to be severely limited. The United States could use little or no leverage either in shaping the escalatory phase or in determining the crisis outcome. In the October 1973 crisis the United States intervened in such a fashion as first to preclude the defeat of Israel and then to prevent the Egyptian military forces from being destroyed by Israeli action. With the cease-fire and force disengagement began a process leading to the Camp David Accords and peace between Egypt and Israel. In the Congo crisis the United States achieved its basic objective, the preservation, or restoration, of a politically intact Congo, faced as it was just after independence in 1960 with the challenge of a strong secessionist movement. In Lebanon in 1958, the Eisenhower administration used military power to thwart political forces that would probably have led at that time to disintegration. This U.S. action could be contrasted sharply with the far from favorable circumstances of the 1980s, in which the Reagan administration put a small marine corps contingent into Lebanon as part of a multinational force, only to confront the tragedy of a truck-bombing attack against the marine corps barracks near Beirut airport in 1983.

Numerous "lessons" in the form of insights can be drawn from an examination of crises as well as the other phenomena that shape the policy process. At the most basic level they include the need to develop, to the greatest extent possible, an anticipatory capability based on the availability of timely information, together with a willingness to take necessary action in timely fashion either to preclude a crisis or to resolve it on acceptable or favorable terms. Although crises, by their nature, are likely to encompass a relatively small decisional unit, they unfold between or among particpants, in the case of the United States and West European nations, characterized by broadly based political systems. In such a context the salient features of the period since the 1950s—the effective time span of these oral history interviews—has been the entry of new factors and participants into the decision-making process. Alliance politics, discussed from various transatlantic perspectives, is a case in point. From the

1950s to the 1980s, the Atlantic Alliance evolved from an organization in which American leadership was paramount to an association in which various NATO-European allies achieved roles of major political importance. Such changes are mirrored in the problems that confronted the alliance and its members in the numerous decisions that have been taken, usually marked by sharp debate and controversy, in the more than two generations since its founding. Whether in the discussion of executive-congressional relations, the role of the president and the Congress, respectively, in the national security process, or in the examination of the U.S. Foreign Service, or in the complex choices on defense modernization, the United States is in the midst of a growing number of members and of heterogeneity with respect to participants. As the world and the respective policy communities represented in the interviews set forth in the preceding pages move toward the twenty-first century, problems such as those that preoccupied policymakers in the recent and more distant past will remain, although perhaps in a different guise. There remain enduring problems of developing appropriate levels of political-military deterrence; reconciling defense modernization needs with arms control; maintaining necessary alliance relationships; building essential public support for national security policy choices; providing timely intelligence under conditions of crisis; managing crises so as to achieve resolution or satisfactory terms with minimum resort to force; and the development of integrative frameworks for the formulation of policy—to mention only the most obvious of the themes that have emerged here. Such issues will continue to provide challenges for the policy community in the years leading toward and beyond the threshold of a new millennium.

Glossary

ABM	Anti-Ballistic Missile
ACDA	Arms Control and Disarmament Agency
AFCENT	Allied Forces, Central Europe
AIRCENT	Air Forces, Central Europe
ALCM	Air-Launched Cruise Missiles
ANZUS	Australia–New Zealand–United States (Treaty Organization)
ASEAN	Association of Southeast Asian Nations
ATB	Advanced Tactical Bomber
AWACS	Airborne Warning and Control System
BAOR	British Army on the Rhine
CDU	Christian–Democratic Union (Federal Republic of Germany)
CEA	Commissariat à l'Energie Atomique (France)
CENTAG	Central Army Group
CENTO	Central Treaty Organization
CERN	European Nuclear Research Organization
CIA	Central Intelligence Agency (U.S.)
CINC	Commander-in-Chief
CINCEUR	Commander-in-Chief, Europe
CJCS	Chairman, Joint Chiefs of Staff
CRAF	Civilian Reserve Air Fleet (Israel)
CSB	Closely-Spaced Basing
CSCE	Conference on Security and Cooperation in Europe
CSU	Christian Social Union (Federal Republic of Germany)
DCI	Director of Central Intelligence
DCM	Deputy Chief of Mission
DIA	Defense Intelligence Agency

DPC	Defense Planning Committee
EDC	European Defense Community
EDI	European Defense Initiative
ERW	Enhanced Radiation Weapon
FDP	Free Democratic Party (Federal Republic of Germany)
FoFA	Follow on Forces Attack
FRG	Federal Republic of Germany
GDR	German Democratic Republic
GLCM	Ground-Launched Cruise Missile
GNP	Gross National Product
IBERLANT	Iberian–Atlantic Forces
ICBM	Intercontinental Ballistic Missile
INF	Intermediate-Range Nuclear Forces
JCS	Joint Chiefs of Staff
JSTPS	Joint Strategic Target Planning System
KGB	Committee on State Security (USSR)
LANCENT	Land Forces, Central Europe
LRINF	Longer Range Intermediate-Range Nuclear Forces
MBFR	Mutual and Balanced Force Reductions
MiG	Mikoyan-Gurevich (Soviet aircraft)
MIRV	Multiple Independently-Targetable Reentry Vehicle
MLF	Multilateral Force
MPS	Multiple Protective Shelters
NADGE	NATO Air Defense Ground Environment
NATO	North Atlantic Treaty Organization
NCC	National Command Center
NPG	Nuclear Planning Group
NSA	National Security Agency
NSC	National Security Council
NSDD	National Security Decision Directive
OAPEC	Organization of Arab Petroleum Exporting Countries
OAS	Organization of American States
OPEC	Organization of Petroleum Exporting Countries
OSD	Office of the Secretary of Defense
PDM	Presidential Decision Memorandum
PLO	Palestine Liberation Organization

PRC	People's Republic of China
PRC	Policy Review Committee
SACEUR	Supreme Allied Commander—Europe
SALT	Strategic Arms Limitation Talks
SCC	Special Coordinating Committee
SDI	Strategic Defense Initiative
SEATO	Southeast Asian Treaty Organization
SHAPE	Supreme Headquarters Allied Powers—Europe
SIGINT	Signal Intelligence
SLBM	Submarine-Launched Ballistic Missile
SLOC	Sea Lines of Communications
SPD	Social Democratic Party (Federal Republic of Germany)
SSBN	Ballistic Missile Submarine, Nuclear-Powered
START	Strategic Arms Reduction Talks
UN	United Nations
UNITA	National Union for the Total Liberation of Angola
USCENTCOM	United States Central Command
USCINCPAC	United States Commander in Chief—Pacific Region
USIA	United States Information Agency
USSR	Union of Soviet Socialist Republic
WASAG	Washington Special Action Group
WEU	Western European Union

Index

ABM Treaty (1972), 168–170
Adenauer, Konrad, 91, 92, 93; in China, 253; and nuclear force strategy, 192–193; and *Ostpolitik*, 122–126
Afghanistan: and Soviet invasion, 342
Air travel: and foreign policy decisions, 28–29
Algeria: and hostage negotiations, 301–302
Algerian War, 178, 179
Allen, Richard: and administration transition, 69; on Congress and foreign affairs, 59; on invasion of Czechoslovakia, 339–341; on NSC operation, 8–9; on NSDD-1, 71–72; on *Ostpolitik*, 128–129; on policy implementation, 72–75; on Soviet decision-making, 222; on strategic force modernization, 158–159; on Taiwan issue, 257–258
Alliance for Progress, 261
Ambassador, role of, 31–32
Anderson, Martin, 8, 73
Arms control, 229–251, 366–368; and Backfire bomber issue, 240–241; and cruise missile issue, 240, 241–242; and Eisenhower initiatives, 229–231; and Nixon administration, 231–232; and presidential campaigns, 81, 82; and verification, 242–243, 250
Atlantic Alliance: and bipartisanship, 57; and Federal Republic of Germany, 91–94; France's role in, 95–96, 101–104; and French nuclear force, 178–179; and Vietnam War, 264–265

Backfire bomber issue, 240–241
Baghdad Pact, 284
Baker, Howard, 55, 56
Baker, James: and NSC policy, 72–73, 75; and NSDD-1, 71–72
Ball, George, 193, 296
Basing systems: for nuclear weapons, 243–245, 247
Belgium: and Congo crisis, 45, 48, 78–79, 345, 346–347
Benitez, Jaime, 329–330
Bennett, W. Tapley, Jr.: on Congress and foreign policy, 57–58; on Congress and NATO, 61–62; on crisis decision making, 277; on Dominican Republic crisis, 316–334; on double-track decision, 112–113, 204–205; on France and Atlantic Alliance, 101–102; on Greco-Turkish relations, 105–106; on Johnson decision-making style, 27–28; on NATO structural dynamics, 35–36, 37–38, 41–43; on neutron bomb controversy, 109–111; on Polish crisis, 342–344; on Soviet European policy, 208–210; on Soviet strategy, 211–212; on Spanish membership in NATO, 104–105; on State Department and Foreign Service changes, 29, 30, 32, 33–34; on zero-zero option, 207–208
Betancourt, Romulo, 311, 314, 329
Bipartisanship: and foreign policy, 56–57; and military budgets, 244–245; and Scowcroft Commission, 248
Bosch, Juan, 311, 312, 313–314, 317–318, 320, 322
Bourges, Yves, 180, 190
Brandt, Willy, 116, 126, 127
Brezhnev, Leonid, 241; and October War, 291, 292; and Sino-Soviet relations, 254; at Vladivostok, 232, 233
Brosio, Manlio, 102, 103
Brown, Harold, 69, 109, 158, 164, 263
Brussels Treaty, 96, 133
Brzezinski, Zbigniew, 7, 69–70, 75, 263; and Iran crisis, 297, 300
Bunker, Ellsworth, 319, 328, 331
Burt, Richard, 205, 206
Bush, George, 18, 70, 232, 257
Byrd, Robert, 55, 56

Cabral, Donald Reid, 311, 317, 319, 320, 321, 322
Callaghan, James, 112, 116–117
Camp David Accords, 279, 305
Campbell, Ross, 200
Carlucci, Frank, 69, 70, 297
Carter, Hodding, 295–296
Carter, Jimmy: and Helmut Schmidt, 116–117; and Korean withdrawal, 82–83; and neutron bomb controversy, 110–112; and NSC decisions, 7–8
Carter administration: arms control policy of, 164; and China relations, 255, 256; human rights policy of, 59–60; and Iran crisis, 295–302; and Korean troop withdrawal, 82–83, 263; and neutron bomb controversy, 109–112; and Polish crisis, 341–342; and Siberian pipeline, 113; and State Department organization, 262–263

127-128; on tactical nuclear weapons, 148-149, 150-152; on Vietnam War and NATO, 265; on zero-zero option, 212-213

Scowcroft, Brent: on A/B team concept, 18; on arms control policy, 239-243; on Brezhnev-Ford relations, 233; on Greek-Turkish crisis, 272-273; on *Mayaguez* crisis, 273-276; on NSC operation, 6-7; on October War, 286, 287-292; on personality and NATO relationships, 116-117; on presidential decision making, 66-67; on SALT II, 81, 204; as Scowcroft Commission chairman, 245-249; on Sino-American relations, 255-256

Scowcroft Commission (Presidential Commission on Strategic Forces), 161, 245; and executive-congressional relations, 62-63, 167; and nuclear force modernization, 165-167, 246-249; political impact of, 167-168

SDI (Strategic Defense Initiative), 85, 86, 140, 163, 168; from NATO perspective, 171-174

Shultz, George, 116, 303, 305

Siberian gas pipeline: decision-making on, 113-116

Singlaub, Jack, 82-83

Six-Day War (1967): and Libya, 270-271

Solarium Project, 217-218

Solidarity movement, 341-342

Soviet Union: arms control negotiations with, 208-209, 233-235; and Berlin access, 336-337; and China relationship, 253-254; and Congo crisis, 345-346; and Czechoslovakia, 221, 337-341; and FRG relations, 121-129; and Hungarian crisis, 335-336; nuclear doctrine of, 235-237; and October War, 286, 289-293; and Poland, 341-344; policy formation about, 365-366; and Suez crisis, 281; as U.N. member, 42; U.S. policy toward, 217-228; and Watergate crisis, 80

Spain: as NATO member, 104-105

START (Strategic Arms Reduction Talks), 210, 237-239

State Department, 25-34, 354-355; and arms control, 205-206, 250; and Foreign Service changes, 29-32; Human Rights Bureau in, 59-60; in Nixon administration, 4-5; and NSC relationship, 11, 70-72; organizations of, 262, 282; and public diplomacy, 226; and U.N. relationship, 41-42

Stoczke, Andre de, 102, 103

Strategic nuclear weapons; basing systems for, 243-245; modernization of, 165-167, 246-249. *See also* Scowcroft Commission

Strauss, Franz-Josef, 93, 193, 196

Suez Canal crisis, 178, 179, 180, 280-284

Television: and public opinion, 84-86, 87; Reagan response to, 303

Test Ban Treaty (1963), 255, 340

Townes Committee, 159, 160, 164, 242, 245

Transition periods: between administrations, 67-69, 232

Tshombe, Moise, 45, 46, 79, 345, 347, 348

Turkey: and crisis with Greece, 272-273; as NATO member, 105-107

United Kingdom: and Congo Crisis, 349; nuclear arms development in, 185-186; and Suez crisis, 280, 281, 282, 283-284

United Nations, 41-49; and Congo crisis, 45-49, 346, 347; and Korean Command, 43-45; and Security Council decision making, 41, 42-43

United States: and British relationship, 185, 283; and French nuclear program, 182-185; global role of, 259-266, 347-348; and MBFR, 199-200; and NATO, 145-146, 359-361; and nuclear superiority, 213; and policy toward Soviet Union, 217-228, 339; and relations with Greece and Turkey, 272-273; and support for Israel, 279, 285, 287

Vance, Cyrus, 69, 262, 263, 330

Vessey, John: on defense intelligence, 17-18; on defense-policy decision making, 60-61; as JCS chairman, 20; on JCS reform, 21-24; on Korean troop withdrawal, 82-83, 263-264; on Korean U.N. command, 43-45; on Lebanon (1982), 302-305, 307-308; on MX basing mode, 159-163

Vietnam War: and Atlantic Alliance, 264-265; and Johnson decision making, 27-28; management of, 65-66

Vladivostok Summit Conference (1974), 232, 233, 240

War Powers Act, 58, 276, 355, 356

Warsaw Pact, 36, 143, 151, 213

Watergate crisis, 6; and public opinion, 79-81

Weapons. *See* Arms control; Conventional weapons; Nuclear weapons; Strategic nuclear weapons

Weinberger, Caspar W.: abilities of, 244; and JCS reform, 22; and Lebanon crisis, 305; and MX basing modes, 164; and Scowcroft Commission, 247; and zero-zero option, 207

Wilson, Harold, 116-117; and British nuclear force, 185

Woolsey, R. James: on ABM Treaty, 170-171; on defensive systems, 168-169; on MIRV deployment, 157-158; on MX basing modes, 163-166; on NATO maritime strategy, 145-146; on special commissions, 62-64; on strategic arms control, 237-239; on strategic defense planning, 169-170; on U.S. and Soviet negotiating styles, 234-235

Wright, James, 55-56

Zero-zero option, 205-208, 212

About the Contributors

Richard V. Allen is an international business consultant and President of Richard V. Allen Company, Washington, D.C. He was Assistant to the President for National Security Affairs for Ronald Reagan from 1981 to 1982. After leaving Stanford University's Hoover Institution on War, Revolution, and Peace in 1969, he served on the National Security Council for one year before becoming a Deputy Assistant to President Richard Nixon from 1971 to 1972. He was Ronald Reagan's Senior Foreign Policy and National Security Adviser from 1978 to 1980.

W. Tapley Bennett, Jr., is Adjunct Professor of International Relations at the University of Georgia and a consultant. His career as an American diplomat spanned the period 1941-1985, culminating in his becoming Assistant Secretary of State for Congressional Relations from 1983 to 1985. His State Department duties over the years included Central American and Panama Affairs, Caribbean Affairs, and South American Affairs. He was posted in Vienna, Rome, and Athens before becoming an Ambassador to the Dominican Republic (1964–66) and to Portugal (1966–69). From 1971 to 1977 he was Deputy U.S. Representative and Ambassador to the United Nations Security Council, and then served as Permanent Representative to the North Atlantic Treaty Organization (NATO) in Brussels from 1977 to 1983.

François de Rose, Comte de Tricornot, is the Vice President of the Council of the International Institute for Strategic Studies in London and a member of the European division of the Trilateral Commission. He ultimately achieved the rank of Ambassador of France, serving as Ambassador and Permanent Representative to the North Atlantic Council from 1970 to 1974. Before this he was posted to London, Rome, New York (with the French delegation to the United Nations), and Madrid. From 1956 to 1961 he was Chief of Atomic and Space Affairs at the Ministry of Foreign Affairs in Paris, and Assistant to the Chief of Staff for National Defense from 1961 to 1962. He served as a member of the

French Atomic Energy Commission (CEA; 1951–54 and 1956–64) and was President of the European Nuclear Research Organization (CERN; 1958–60). He was also French Ambassador to Portugal from 1964 to 1969.

Lawrence S. Eagleburger is Deputy Secretary of State. He retired from the Department of State in 1984 after serving twenty-seven years as a career Foreign Service Officer; from 1984 until early 1989 he was President of Kissinger Associates, Inc., an international business consulting firm. Early in his career, Mr. Eagleburger served in Tegucigalpa, Honduras, Washington, and Belgrade. From 1967 to 1972 his posts included Executive Assistant to the President for National Security Affairs, working for Henry Kissinger; Political Adviser and Chief of the Political Section of the U.S Mission to NATO; and Deputy Assistant to the Secretary of Defense. From 1973 to 1977 he worked as both Executive Assistant to Secretary of State Henry Kissinger and as Deputy Under Secretary of State for Management. He was Ambassador to Yugoslavia (1977–81), then Assistant Secretary of State for European Affairs (1981–82), and subsequently Under Secretary of State for Political Affairs (1982–84), the third-ranking position at the department.

Pierre M. Gallois is Professor of Strategic Studies at the French War College and the Sorbonne. He is a retired French Air Force General, a strategic nuclear strategist, and an author. He served General Charles de Gaulle during the 1960s, becoming a principal strategist in developing the independent French nuclear *force de frappe*. Previously, he served under General Dwight Eisenhower at Supreme Headquarters Allied Powers, Europe (SHAPE), and subsequently as Assistant to General Lauris Norstad (Supreme Allied Commander, Europe) from 1954 to 1957, where he was in charge of long-term strategic nuclear planning studies.

Andrew J. Goodpaster is a retired U.S. Army General and the Chairman of the American Battle Monuments Commission. He served as Defense Liaison Officer and Staff Secretary to President Dwight Eisenhower from 1954 to 1961, and as Commander-in-Chief U.S. Forces, Supreme Allied Commander in Europe from 1969 to 1974. In between these duties, he was among other things Assistant to the Chairman of the Joint Chiefs of Staff (1962–66), Director of the Joint Staff (1966–67), Commandant of the National War College (1967–68), and Deputy Commander of U.S. Forces in Vietnam (1968-69). He retired in 1974 only to be recalled to active duty as Superintendent of his alma mater, the U.S. Military Academy. He retired for the second time in 1981.

Edmund A. Gullion is a Career Minister (Retired) of the U.S. Foreign Service and former Dean of the Fletcher School of Law and Diplomacy. Tufts University. He was Ambassador to the Republic of the Congo (Leopoldville)—now the

Republic of Zaire—from 1961 to 1964. His Foreign Service career from 1937 until 1961 included posting in Marseilles, Salonika, London, Algiers, Helsinki, Stockholm, and Washington. Other positions included Consul General and then Counselor of the American embassy in Saigon, Indochina (1949–52); member of the Policy Planning Staff of the Department of State (1952–57); Foreign Service Inspector (1957–60); and Acting Director and Deputy Director of the U.S. Disarmament Administration (1960–61), until completion of legislation for creation of the U.S. Arms Control and Disarmament Agency.

Kai-Uwe von Hassell was Minister of Defense of the Federal Republic of Germany from 1963 to 1966. He was born in German East Africa (now Tanzania), served in World War II, and shortly after the war entered politics as a member of the Christian Democratic Union party. He was a member of the Landtag, Bundestag, and Bundesrat alternately from 1950 to 1980, and was President of the Bundesrat from 1955 to 1956, and of the Bundestag from 1969 to 1972. Following his term in the Bundestag, he served as a member of the European Parliament from 1979 to 1984.

Johann Adolf Graf von Kielmansegg is a retired four-star General of the Armed Forces (Bundeswehr) of the Federal Republic of Germany. From 1963 to 1968 he served in NATO's integrated military command structure as Commander-in-Chief of Allied Forces, Central Europe (AFCENT). Before this, he served from 1926 to 1946 in the Reichswehr (Imperial Armed Forces) and in the Wehrmacht (Armed Forces of the Third Reich), experiencing combat on the eastern front. After World War II, he worked in publishing firms and in the Federal Chancellery before becoming a general in the newly formed Bundeswehr in 1955. He then held positions as West German Military Representative to SHAPE in Paris (1955–58), and Deputy Commander and then Commander of two different Bundeswehr Panzer divisions (1959–63).

Joseph M.A.H. Luns is a former Minister of Foreign Affairs of the Netherlands (1956–71) and former Secretary-General of NATO (1971–83). He began his career in the Foreign Service of the Netherlands, with postings in Bern, Lisbon, London, and New York (as Permanent Delegate to the United Nations, 1949–52). He served as Co-Minister for Dutch Foreign Affairs from 1952 to 1956, and also as President of the NATO Council from 1958 to 1959.

Edwin M. Martin is a retired Career Ambassador of the United States. He served as Assistant Secretary of State for Inter-American Affairs for the Department of State (1962–64) and as Ambassador to Argentina (1964–68). Early in his career he worked as a government economist and later in the Office of Strategic Services during World War II before beginning his State Department career. After various positions, President Eisenhower appointed him Assistant

Secretary of State for Economic Affairs (1960–62). He resigned from the department in 1967 and subsequently chaired the Development Assistance Committee of the Organization for Economic Cooperation and Development; he later worked for the International Bank for Reconstruction and Development.

Robert C. McFarlane is a consultant and author on national security issues. He was Assistant to the President for National Security Affairs from 1983 to 1985 for President Ronald Reagan. Before this he served as a U.S. Marine Corps officer from 1959 to 1979, during which time he was a White House Fellow in the Nixon administration and a Military Assistant and Special Assistant for Henry Kissinger and later for Brent Scowcroft. He resigned from the marines in 1979 and worked on the staff of the Senate Armed Services Committee until 1981 when he became a Counselor to Secretary of State Alexander Haig. From 1982 until 1983 he served as Deputy Assistant to the President for National Security Affairs; from July to October 1983 he was President Reagan's Special Envoy to the Middle East.

Thomas H. Moorer is a retired U.S. Navy Admiral and Vice Chairman of the Board for Blount, Inc., of Montgomery, Alabama. He was Chairman of the Joint Chiefs of Staff from 1970 to 1974. He became an officer in the Navy in 1933 and advanced through the grades to the level of admiral by 1957; he held several fleet commands at sea and was Chief of Naval Operations from 1967 to 1970.

Lord Fredrick W. Mulley, Life Peer, is a British barrister-at-law, economist, and Deputy Chairman of Sheffield Development Corporation. He was Secretary of State for Defence from 1976 to 1979 and held other important Ministry of Defence positions. He was a Labour party Member of Parliament from 1950 to 1983, and served in many government posts over the last two decades, including Deputy Defence Secretary and Minister for the Army (1964–65), Minister of Aviation (1965–67), and Minister for Disarmament (1967–69). He was Chairman of the Labour party from 1974 to 1975.

David W. Newsom is Director of the Institute for the Study of Diplomacy and Associate Dean of the School of Foreign Service, Georgetown University. As a career Foreign Service officer, he was Under Secretary of State for Political Affairs—the third-ranking position at the Department of State—from 1978 to 1981. His early diplomatic postings including Karachi, Oslo, Baghdad, Washington, and London. He was U.S. Ambassador to Libya (1965–69), Indonesia (1974–77), and the Philippines (1977–78). He also served as Director of the Office of North African Affairs at the State Department (1963–65), and as Assistant Secretary of State for African Affairs (1969–74).

Rolf F. Pauls is a retired diplomat for the Federal Republic of Germany. He was the West German Permanent Representative and Ambassador to NATO from 1976 to 1980. Before this, he had postings in Luxembourg, Washington, Athens, and Brussels. Later he was the Federal Republic's Ambassador to Israel (1965–68), to the United States (1969–73), and to the People's Republic of China (1973–76).

John P. Roche is John M. Olin Distinguished Professor of American Civilization and Foreign Affairs at the Fletcher School of Law and Diplomacy, Tufts University. He was a consultant for Vice President Hubert Humphrey and the Department of State (1964–66), and was Special Consultant to President Lyndon Johnson (1966–68). He taught at Haverford College and Brandeis University, in addition to holding numerous visiting teaching appointments before coming to Tufts University. He served on the Presidential Study Commission on International Radio Broadcasting (1972–73) and on the U.S. Board for International Broadcasting (1974–77). He is a member of the U.S. General Advisory Committee on Arms Control and Disarmament and the Subcommission on Prevention of Discrimination and Protection of Minorities of the United Nations Human Rights Commission.

Donald H. Rumsfeld is the senior adviser for William Blair and Company in Chicago. He was the Secretary of Defense from 1975 to 1977. He was a Republican member of the House of Representatives from Illinois in the 1960s. He next served in President Nixon's cabinet from 1969 to 1973, before becoming the U.S. Permanent Representative and Ambassador to NATO (1973–74). From 1974 through 1975 he was Assistant to President Ford and White House Staff Coordinator.

Dean Rusk is Professor of International Law at the University of Georgia School of Law. He was Secretary of State under both Presidents Kennedy and Johnson from 1961 to 1969. He was a Rhodes scholar and Associate Professor before serving in the U.S. Army during World War II. He entered the State Department in 1946 and served as Special Assistant to the Secretary of War and as Director of the Office of UN Affairs. His other positions included Deputy Under Secretary of State (1949–50) and Assistant to the Secretary of State for Far Eastern Affairs (1950–51). He was President of the Rockefeller Foundation from 1952 to 1960.

Franz-Josef Schulze is a retired four-star General of the German Armed Forces (Bundeswehr) and was Commander-in-Chief of Allied Forces, Central Europe (AFCENT) from 1977 to 1979. After World War II, in which he served, he became an accountant and entered the Bundeswehr in 1956. He attended the Führungsacademie and served in the General Staff of the Defense Ministry

(1958–62). Subsequently, he attended the NATO Defense College and served at NATO Headquarters AFCENT (1965–66), commanded an armored division (1966–73), and became Deputy Chief of Staff SHAPE (1973–77).

Brent Scowcroft is National Security Adviser to President George Bush. He is a retired U.S. Air Force General and has served five U.S. presidents in the past two decades. He was Military Assistant to President Nixon (1972–73), Deputy Assistant for National Security Affairs under Presidents Nixon and Ford (1973–75), and later became President Ford's Assistant for National Security Affairs (1975–77). He served President Carter on the President's General Advisory Commission on Arms Control (1977–80). In 1983 he chaired President Reagan's Commission on Strategic Forces while working as Director of the National Bank of Washington and as Vice Chairman of Kissinger Associates between 1980 and 1989.

John W. Vessey, Jr., was Chairman of the Joint Chiefs of Staff from 1982 to 1985. He enlisted in the U.S. Army in 1939, fought in World War II, and advanced through the grades to general in 1976. His positions included Commander of U.S. Army Support Command in Thailand (1970–71), Chief of the Military Assistance Advisory Group in Laos (1972–73), Commander-in-Chief of the United Nations Command/U.S. Forces in Korea (1976–79), and Commander-in-Chief Republic of Korea/U.S. Combined Forces Command (1978–79). Before becoming Chairman of the JCS, he served as Vice Chief of Staff for the United States Army (1979–82).

R. James Woolsey, Jr., is a partner in the Washington, D.C., firm of Shea and Gardner. He served as Under Secretary of the Navy during the Carter administration (1977–79). He is a Rhodes scholar and Yale Law School graduate. He served on the National Security Council Staff in 1970 and was General Counsel for the Senate Armed Services Committee (1970–73). Under President Reagan he served consecutively on the Office of the Secretary of Defense (OSD) Panel, which studied alternate MX basing modes; the President's Commission on Strategic Forces; the Commission on Defense Management; and the U.S. Nuclear and Space Weapons delegation to Geneva.

About the Editors

Robert L. Pfaltzgraff, Jr. is Shelby Cullom Davis Professor of International Security Studies at the Fletcher School of Law and Diplomacy, Tufts University, and President of the Institute for Foreign Policy Analysis, Cambridge, Massachusetts, and Washington, D.C. Dr. Pfaltzgraff has written and lectured extensively on East-West relations, U.S. foreign policy, alliance policies and strategy, the interrelationships of political, economic, and security policies, technology transfer, arms control, emerging trends in both global and regional security environments, and international relations theory.

Jacquelyn K. Davis is Executive Vice President of the Institute for Foreign Policy Analysis, Inc., and President, National Security Planning Associates, a subsidiary of the Institute, where her work is focused on arms control, the Atlantic Alliance and NATO, the U.S.-Soviet strategic balance, and French defense policy. In addition, from 1984 to 1988 she served as a member of the Defense Advisory Committee on Women in the Services (DACOWITS), and was Chairperson of DACOWITS from 1986 to 1988. Dr. Davis has written and collaborated on numerous books and articles. She has lectured widely in the United States and abroad.